Leave the Gun, Take the Cannoli

Leave the Gun, Take the Cannoli

The Epic Story of the Making of *The Godfather*

Mark Seal

GALLERY BOOKS

NEW YORK   LONDON   TORONTO   SYDNEY   NEW DELHI

G

Gallery Books
An Imprint of Simon & Schuster, Inc.
1230 Avenue of the Americas
New York, NY 10020

Parts of this book were first published in the March 2009 issue of *Vanity Fair* magazine under the title "The Godfather Wars" by Mark Seal, and in a follow-up story on the *Vanity Fair* website on February 26, 2009.

First Gallery Books hardcover edition October 2021

GALLERY BOOKS and colophon are registered trademarks of Simon & Schuster, Inc.

For information about special discounts for bulk purchases, please contact Simon & Schuster Special Sales at 1-866-506-1949 or business@simonandschuster.com.

The Simon & Schuster Speakers Bureau can bring authors to your live event. For more information or to book an event, contact the Simon & Schuster Speakers Bureau at 1-866-248-3049 or visit our website at www.simonspeakers.com.

Interior design by Jaime Putorti

Manufactured in the United States of America

10 9 8 7 6 5 4 3 2 1

Library of Congress Cataloging-in-Publication Data has been applied for.

ISBN 978-1-9821-5859-0
ISBN 978-1-9821-5861-3 (ebook)

For my amazing Italian American wife, Laura

My mother, Evelyn,
for her endless devotion to her three sons

And for my father, Berney Seal,
who kept one book by his bedside: The Godfather

Contents

Preface

A STORY AS EXTRAORDINARY AS
THE ONE TOLD ONSCREEN

The early 2010s. A car pulls up to a Manhattan hotel. The door swings open and I'm on my way to a diner in New Jersey for a hush-hush meeting with Anthony Colombo. His father, Joseph Colombo Sr., was said to have been the powerful head of one of the organized-crime families in New York during the 1960s and into the 1970s. But Joe became publicly known for founding the Italian American Civil Rights League, through which he aggressively campaigned to stop the stereotyping of Italian Americans in the media and popular entertainment, agonies he felt would be epitomized in the movie he would initially try to stop, *The Godfather,* only to later facilitate the making of the film.

In 1971, Joe Colombo had been gunned down in an assassination attempt that paralyzed him before ending his life seven years later. I wanted to interview Anthony, who had played a central role in his father's campaign during the making of the movie, which I had written about in the 2009 Hollywood issue of *Vanity Fair,* a story I wanted to turn into a book.

I was a little apprehensive. Anthony had been indicted in 1986 on a variety of charges, pleading guilty to a federal racketeering conspiracy charge in a plea agreement that included a fourteen-year prison sentence. So I expected to encounter a tough guy. Instead, I found a gentleman in his sixties who walked into the diner with the help of a cane. Anthony was warm and welcoming, but only to a point. He had his own book to write, which he would publish in 2015 (*Colombo: The Unsolved Murder*, cowritten with Don Capria), and I had mine.

His book was about his father's murder.

Mine was about the making of the movie he and his father had initially tried to stop.

What I was doing in a New Jersey diner meeting with the son of Joe Colombo to discuss the role he and his father had played in one of the greatest movies of all time said everything about the making of *The Godfather.*

How these two titanic forces came together—the moviemakers and the Mob—is one of the most astounding stories in the annals of film. But telling the story of how that happened, along with the infinite other stories connected with the making of the movie, required a deep dive in an endless well. For *The Godfather* has spawned its own massive field of study, a trove of books, articles, documentaries, interviews, archives, reunions, commentaries, and more.

My own interviews for this book and the *Vanity Fair* story, which number almost one hundred, included everyone from the movie's executives and crew members to its stars and director, Francis Ford Coppola, who answered endless questions. Among the many books I relied upon were *The Godfather Legacy* by Harlan Lebo; *The Godfather Book* by Peter Cowie; *The Godfather Notebook* by Francis Ford Coppola; *The Kid Stays in the Picture* by Robert Evans; *Infamous Players* by Peter Bart; Mario Puzo's *The Godfather Papers and Other Confessions*; *Mario Puzo: A Writer's Quest* by M. J. Moore; *The Godfather Companion* and *Easy Riders, Raging Bulls*, both by Peter Biskind; *The Annotated Godfather* by Jenny M. Jones; *Hollywood Godfather* by Gianni Russo; *Me and Marlon* by Alice Marchak . . . The list goes on and on and can be found in the select bibliography at the back of this book.

Indispensable to any scholar of *Godfather* lore is *The Godfather Journal*, by Ira Zuckerman, who served as Francis Ford Coppola's assistant on the film and produced an extraordinary day-by-day account of the filming. A 143-page paperback published in early 1972, it places the reader squarely in the middle of the movie's production mayhem. I was also given access to voluminous notes taken by a stenographer Coppola hired to record a daylong meeting with his production team, which provides a fly-on-the-wall perspective of how the masterpiece was born. Added to this were the copious newspaper and magazine articles—from before, during, and after filming—as well as the mountains of writing, research, and interviews by by the admirable people who walked this road before me, many of whom were kind enough to speak with me about our shared fascination with *The Godfather*.

My hope is that I have added to their great work in further revealing the story of the making of a movie that is almost as extraordinary as the one told on screen, a movie that opened so many eyes and touched so many hearts, beginning with its premiere, fifty years ago, and continuing to this day.

I was a member of the enormous audience stunned by *The Godfather* in 1972—a college freshman sitting in a movie theater with no access to the proceedings detailed in this book as they occurred. Through the memories of those involved and the documents left behind, I have re-created some scenes to the best of my ability, research, and reporting.

"... Give me your tired, your poor,
Your huddled masses yearning to breathe free,
The wretched refuse of your teeming shore.
Send these, the homeless, tempest-tost to me,
I lift my lamp beside the golden door!"

—Emma Lazarus, "The New Colossus," 1883
Engraved in the pedestal of the Statue of Liberty

I believe in America.

—Amerigo Bonasera

Leave the Gun, Take the Cannoli

Prologue

TO THE MATTRESSES!

et's go to bed," Robert Evans said in his grand Beverly Hills home, which the movies built.

The house, known as Woodland, was a "hidden oasis"—a French Regency estate, a "miniature palace," Evans called it. It was walled off from the world on two private acres, shaded by hundred-foot-tall sycamores, redolent with the scent of thousands of roses. Once the residence of Greta Garbo, it had been, for forty years, the proud habitat of the mogul who turned Paramount Pictures, on the precipice of collapse, into the most dominant force in film.

Evans, the impresario who had risen from the womenswear business of New York City to international fame and fortune as an actor-turned-producer-turned-studio chief, was now seventy-eight, his voice strangled by strokes. But his mind was still sharp, and his home was lined with photographs should his memory ever lapse. He lived with those memories: the ghosts of the greats who gathered here, the deals that were consummated here, the movies that were screened here, and the loves that were kindled here.

It was 2008, and I had come to interview Evans for a *Vanity Fair* magazine story about the making of his most celebrated movie, *The Godfather*. He was prepared for me. His butler, Alan Selka, a very proper Englishman, opened the doors and escorted me to the dining room, where I waited for Evans at a table covered with clippings and mementoes from the production and its aftermath.

When the master made his entrance, it was impressive: his black hair slicked back, his face deeply tanned, his smile a dazzling white, his eyes staring out through rose-colored glasses. When he launched into his memories of the movie, his voice was as deep and melodic as a cello sonata.

"It's stranger than fiction," he told me.

Then Evans, a legendary lothario, suggested we go to bed together. *"What?"* I blurted out.

A fire had consumed his famous screening room in 2003, Evans explained, and since then he and his friends had watched movies in his bed. I followed him to the master bedroom. In his heyday, Evans entertained so many starlets here that his housekeeper would place the name of the previous evening's date on a card beside his coffee cup the next morning, so he could address her properly at the breakfast table. He had become production chief of Paramount Pictures in 1966, at the tender age of thirty-six, resuscitating the moribund studio and guiding it from the grave to its former glory with hits like *Rosemary's Baby*, *Love Story*, and *The Godfather*. He helped propel the career of his close pal Jack Nicholson, who starred in his studio's 1974 production of *Chinatown*. His ex-wives numbered seven, including the actresses Ali MacGraw, Leslie Ann Woodward, Catherine Oxenberg, and Miss America Phyllis George.

Now, Robert Evans, a master of staging and seduction, was leveling his immense powers of persuasion on me. The butler arrived with food and drink, and a large television screen was readied to run parts of *The Godfather*.

"Take those shoes off," Evans commanded as I hovered next to the bed, which was very large and covered in fur. There was a story he wanted to tell, and it might take a while.

So I climbed into bed with Robert Evans to hear the story of the film that had both made him and destroyed him. Today the movie features prominently in virtually every list of the all-time greats, a masterpiece that, upon each viewing, reveals some new jewel or fresh truth. But the process of making it was unlike that of any film before or since. Hollywood's greatest movie about the Mafia seemed to have been produced in some ways in tandem with the Mafia, as the capos of the Mob went to war with the tough guys of the movie business, in some instances trading places, mobsters as actors, filmmakers as fixers. And no one knew the behind-the-scenes story better than Evans, who had financed its struggling author, green-lighted its development, hired its producer and director, and fostered its creation, some would say far too obsessively for a studio head, until the movie became a global hit, and, for Evans, a curse.

His mind slipped back across the decades, to the grandest night of his life: March 14, 1972, the world premiere of *The Godfather*. A freak snowstorm had paralyzed New York City, but the advance buzz on the movie was red hot, its star Marlon Brando featured on the covers of both *Life* and *Newsweek*. And there he was, Robert Evans, Paramount's head of production, entering the Loew's State Theatre with his third wife, the actress Ali MacGraw, on one arm, and Secretary of State Henry Kissinger on the other.

"When the lights went down and Nino Rota's music swelled, my whole life seemed to pass before me," he would write in his 1994 autobiography, *The Kid Stays in the Picture*. "Watching this epic unfold, I felt that everything my life was about had led up to this moment."

"Two hours and fifty-six minutes later, Diane Keaton asked Al Pacino if he was responsible for all the killings," Evans wrote.

"No," Pacino lied.

Then the credits rolled. Evans sat in the premiere audience, stunned in the darkness, along with everyone else. "No applause," he wrote. "Not a sound—just silence."

It's a bomb, he thought, then turned to MacGraw and Kissinger, their faces solemn.

But it wasn't a bomb—it was a cultural phenomenon. The audience was in tears. When the lights went up, Kissinger turned to Evans. "Bob," he said, "when you can sit and watch a gangster who's killed hundreds of people, and yet when he dies the audience is crying, you've made yourself a masterpiece."

After the screening, during an ecstatic party in the ballroom of the St. Regis hotel, Evans played master of ceremonies, "introducing anyone and everyone"—the writer, the director, the cast, all of whom were on their way to becoming legends. And Paramount was on its way to becoming one of the richest and most powerful studios in Hollywood. "*The Godfather* did more business in six months than *Gone with the Wind* did in thirty-six years," Evans said. "It was the first time a picture opened in four hundred theaters."

In the process, the film created something Hollywood had never before imagined possible: a work of art that is also a blockbuster.

"The screaming, the fights, the threats that never let up since day one of filming, were worth it," Evans concluded. He paused at the memory of the battles—over the script, the cast, the location, the budget—that had threatened to derail the movie before a single frame was shot.

"The fighting," he sighed. "Tremendous fights."

Fifty years after its premiere, so much has been written about *The Godfather*, yet some things remain overlooked, or misrepresented. Many accounts of the movie are more Hollywood legend than historical fact, as many of those involved in its making have sought to play up their role in its creation. Thus, some of what has been said and "written about *The Godfather* is wrong," said Peter Bart, who was present throughout the film's birth as Evans's second in command at Paramount.

I wanted to know how the film was created—"behind the screen and in front of the screen," as Evans put it. In the process, I hoped to learn not only the secrets of the movie itself but also what it revealed about creating great and enduring art. Through years of research, and interviews with everyone from studio executives to Mob affiliates, I have sought to untangle the competing narratives and self-aggrandizing contentions that continue to enshroud the film. The real story, I found, is like the man I climbed into bed with—an unlikely amalgamation of brute force, artistic choice, market necessity, genius, and dumb luck. Evans would be dead a dozen years after his bedroom confessions, but now, after half a century, the film he banked everything on has attained the status of myth, an integral part of America's collective consciousness. Based on one of the bestselling novels of all time, it revitalized Hollywood, saved Paramount Pictures, announced the arrival of Francis Ford Coppola as one of the great directors of the new era of film, minted a new generation of movie stars, made its writer, director, and producer rich, and sparked a war between two of America's mightiest powers: the sharks of Hollywood and the soldiers of the Mob.

"It's the best picture ever made," Evans told me in bed that day. "It broke a whole barrier of film. It was opera, it was new filmmakers, great ideas, and fighting the organization. And I loved fighting the organization."

"What organization were you fighting?" I asked.

"Paramount," he said—meaning not just the studio, but the way movies had always been made. "The Boys," he added, meaning the Mob. "But they're both the same. Everything is monetarily focused. And I was looking to touch magic. Magic, to me, lasts longer. Why is it that Mozart is remembered far longer than Napoleon? Because the world of art is remembered far longer than the world of greed."

Just then, as if on cue, the lights in the bedroom dimmed. The screen flickered to life, the soundtrack swelled, and the now-famous cast began to parade before us, like decorated soldiers who had triumphed in a long and bitter war. *The Godfather* once again wove its hypnotic spell. Yet the tale it told is eclipsed by the story of how it came to be. Years before its first words were committed to paper, it began with a body engulfed in flames, cities stricken with fear, and real-life criminals who survived to reveal a world of violence and betrayal beyond the imagination of any writer.

1

"I JUST GO OUT AND KILL FOR THEM"

It was difficult to tell if the body was even human.

Soaked in gasoline and set ablaze, it lay burned at the center of an eight-foot circle that had been scorched into the grass like some demented sign from hell. The hands had been bound behind the back and a plastic clothesline had been wrapped around the neck as a garrote. Jaw and ribs broken, skull fractured, teeth missing. Both eyes had been brutally burned out—probably with a blow torch—and lacerations covered the body where thirty pounds of flesh had been removed. Most viciously, the genitals had been chopped off and stuffed into the victim's mouth "because he was threatening to talk," an FBI agent would write—all while the individual was still alive, over several unthinkable days of intense torture.

When the body was found, on Thanksgiving Day in 1961, a critical clue remained: one fingerprint. The corpse belonged to Alberto Agueci, a baker from Toronto whose real profession was importing heroin from Italy—via fake-bottom suitcases carried by unknowing Italian immigrants sailing to America—a lucrative business, until he made the mistake of running afoul of Stefano Magaddino, the crime boss of Buffalo, New York. It was Agueci's gruesome murder—and his brother's vow to avenge it—that would ultimately become a part of providing the world with its most detailed and graphic glimpse into the shadowy crime syndicate known as La Cosa Nostra. The man who would reveal this secret world, a midlevel mobster named Joseph Valachi, was an associate of the bloody corpse with his dick in his mouth.

In 1959, Valachi was indicted on federal drug-trafficking charges and, after holing up in a trailer in Connecticut for three months, was arrested and returned to New York City. He had jumped bail and was desperate to avoid prison when Agueci offered him a way out. Valachi met Agueci at Maggie's bar, a few blocks from Grand Central Station. Agueci said he could sneak him over the border, into Canada, where Valachi would hide out for a time in Toronto.

A year later, both men were indicted—along with seventeen others—for their involvement in a $150 million heroin smuggling operation. While in jail together, Valachi listened as Agueci raged against Magaddino, who had been expected to bail Agueci out, but instead was letting him rot in jail. Valachi warned Agueci not to let his complaints get back to Magaddino, the man they called the Undertaker—whose family really did run a funeral home—or else he'd be looking at a fate far worse than prison.

Agueci didn't heed Valachi's warning. He threatened to rat out Magaddino for his role in narcotics trafficking if he didn't help him with his bail and defense. Big mistake. After his wife sold their house and bailed him out, he returned home to Toronto—only to travel to Buffalo to meet with Magaddino. His mutilated body was soon found in a cornfield on the outskirts of Rochester.

The bad news for Valachi was that Agueci's brother, Vito, was dead set on revenge. When Vito heard that Alberto had been murdered, he insisted that Valachi was a snitch. True or not, the intel reached Vito Genovese, capo of the New York–based Genovese crime family, who became convinced of the same. Genovese had once been close with Valachi, who was one of his soldiers, even serving in Valachi's wedding party. But now in 1962, they were in an Atlanta prison together, and the friendly ties evaporated. Vito Genovese wanted Valachi dead, Alberto Agueci style, before he could spill a word about anything.

In prison, Valachi saw danger everywhere, real and imagined. Especially after Genovese kissed him, which Valachi took to signify "the kiss of death." But Valachi was a hit man himself: When a prisoner he thought was a would-be assassin approached him, he beat the man's head in first. The problem was that the guy had nothing to do with him—he was an innocent victim with no ties to the Genoveses or any other Mob family. Valachi pleaded guilty to second-degree murder.

Desperate for protection, Valachi employed the one thing that could shield him from the grisly fate that had befallen Alberto Agueci: his mouth. He began to talk—first to the FBI, then to a Senate subcommittee, providing eyewitness testimony that would make him the most famous mobster-turned-informant in history.

Valachi was not the first mobster to come before Congress. In 1951, a freshman senator from Tennessee named Estes Kefauver had led televised Senate hearings on organized crime in fourteen cities across America that had gripped the entire nation. The hearings proved to be a ratings extravaganza for the TV industry, still in its infancy—an estimated 30 million Americans tuned in. "Never before had the attention of the nation been riveted so completely on a single matter," *Life* reported. "The Senate investigation into interstate crime was almost the sole subject of national conversation."

The highlight of the hearings was the testimony of the mobster considered the "boss of bosses," Frank Costello, the all-powerful leader of the Luciano crime family, whose appearance riveted television audiences even though they mostly saw only his hands. In a feeble attempt to shield his identity, the Mob boss would be filmed only from the neck down. Costello proved an uncooperative witness, evading questions in his gravelly voice before pleading laryngitis and walking out of the hearings. Still, his appearance was a hit. "Costello TV's First Headless Star," proclaimed a front-page headline in the *New York Times*. "Only His Hands Entertain Audience."

Kefauver ran into even more trouble when he tried to investigate Hollywood's ties to the Mob. His committee claimed to have pictures of Frank Sinatra—dogged for years by rumors of involvement with organized crime—talking with mobsters. And for a star witness, the committee hyped the upcoming testimony of Sidney Korshak, a Mob lawyer who had represented Al Capone's associates in Chicago before transforming himself into one of the top fixers in Hollywood, soon to become consigliere of Paramount's senior vice president in charge of production, Robert Evans. "It was a reflection of his power that when Mr. Korshak showed up unexpectedly at a Las Vegas hotel during a 1961 Teamsters meeting, he was immediately installed in the largest suite, even though the hotel had to dislodge the previous occupant: the union's president, Jimmy Hoffa," the *New York Times* would report.

But for all the revelations Kefauver was promising, his committee wouldn't get a single thing from Korshak, a man who made his living in the movie industry by staying out of the spotlight. Korshak "had no intention of blowing his cover," wrote Peter Bart, who served as a top executive at Paramount during the production of *The Godfather*, in his book *Infamous Players*. "Arranging a private meeting with Kefauver at a Chicago hotel before his scheduled appearance, Korshak produced photographs purportedly showing the senator in a hotel room in the company of two underage girls. Upon glancing at the photos, Kefauver canceled Korshak's appearance." (Some accounts reported that it was a young woman.)

It was a scene that would make its way, in somewhat altered form, into *The Godfather, Part II*—and one that foreshadowed the kind of backroom tactics Korshak would employ to ensure the success of the first *Godfather*.

In 1963, it was Valachi's turn to come before Congress. At the time, Robert Kennedy, who had been appointed US attorney general by his brother, the president, was pressuring the FBI to provide the sort of insight into the Mob that the Feds simply didn't have. "If we do not on a national scale attack organized criminals with weapons and techniques as effective as their own," Robert Kennedy had warned a few years earlier, "they will destroy us."

Enter Valachi, a "made" man desperately seeking a way out. What he told the FBI was borne out by the bureau's wiretaps of major

American Mafia figures. It was Valachi who revealed that the secret term, "Cosa Nostra," meaning "Our Thing," was used by organized-crime figures to identify their organization, soon to be known by the singular term "Mafia."

The Mob put out a hit on Valachi to prevent him from testifying before Congress, offering $100,000 to anyone who could take him out. But it was too late. In September 1963, millions of Americans tuned in to watch as Valachi testified before a televised congressional hearing on organized crime, spelling out in gripping detail how the Mafia was run: how different crime families owned each major American city; how resort towns like Las Vegas and Miami were "open" for any family to operate in; how each family employed the same rigid hierarchy, from the lowliest foot soldiers to the capos to—and he used the term—"the Godfather."

And Valachi, as a trusted soldier, had been one of the Mafia's enforcers, taking his orders from the men at the top. "I just go out and kill for them," he confessed in his deep, raspy voice, with the TV cameras rolling and mobsters across America aching to kill him. "You live by the gun and by the knife, and you die by the gun and by the knife."

It was incredible television, a historic moment. Valachi's testimony provided most Americans with their first detailed glimpse into the inner workings of the Mafia. The term was born in nineteenth-century Sicily—from the adjective *mafiusu*, meaning swagger, boldness, bravado—but its rise was an all-American crime story, one that began when impoverished Sicilians began immigrating to New Orleans in the nineteenth century. By 1869, the *New Orleans Times* noted that the city's Second District had been overrun by "well-known and notorious Sicilian murderers, counterfeiters and burglars, who, in the last month, have formed a sort of general co-partnership or stock company for the plunder and disturbance of the city."

Over the next one hundred years, fueled by successive waves of Italian immigrants, the Mafia steadily expanded its territory and economic influence, establishing its control over a host of illegal activities, from gambling and prostitution to Prohibition-era alcohol and drugs.

But the stark, factual account laid out by Valachi touched on something deeper and more emotional than any Senate hearing could capture. It wasn't about the gruesome hit jobs or secret lingo or vast criminal enterprises. It was mythic in proportion, a story that encompassed the intertwined elements of family and brutality, of loyalty and betrayal, of fathers and sons, of immigration and the American Dream. Capturing its essence, its raw and epic power, would seemingly require a storyteller of immense talents—a modern-day Shakespeare, a Homer, or a Virgil, capable of peering into the blackest depths of human nature and drawing forth something vital and real. Yet the man who would ultimately realize the dramatic possibilities inherent in the Senate hearings would turn out to be the unlikeliest of messengers, a dead-broke writer who was lying on his couch in his middle-class home in the suburbs of New York, glued to his television set like everyone else. A writer who would claim to have never even met a genuine gangster, but who would create a fictional story so authentic that it seemed real, a saga that would be adopted by the Mob as its own, emulating its language and titles and creed. An abject failure who once lay in a gutter, staring up at the night sky and vowing that he would rise above his debts and his disaster of a life and redeem himself as writer.

His name was Mario Gianluigi Puzo.

2

THE MAN IN THE GUTTER

Mario Puzo was, by his own admission, "going downhill fast."
The only thing that wasn't clear was which of his vices would kill him first.

Maybe it would be the food: pasta and other Italian fare he'd grown up with; Chinese takeout, always served with a side of spaghetti; late-night snacks that had him struggling with diabetes and fighting off heart disease. Maybe it would be the gambling: a lifelong addiction that began with pitching pennies as a kid, graduated to poker, and culminated with betting on the ponies and ballgames, far more than he could afford, bets that had him constantly in debt to loan sharks and borrowing money from friends and family. Or maybe it would be the writing: the endless drudgery and humiliatingly low wages for literary fiction, the kind that took forever to write well, to which the market responded with polite reviews and thin sales, nothing near enough to support his growing, hungry family and his even more insatiable gambling habit. By the time Valachi testified before Congress, Puzo was $20,000 in debt, soon to be rejected by his publisher, and under investigation by the FBI. None of the bookies he frequented would have given odds on him becoming one of the bestselling authors in America, setting a new record for paperback rights, and cowriting screenplays that would lead to eight Academy Awards.

Puzo grew up poor, in a tenement flat in Hell's Kitchen, then the roughest part of the city, its name a testament to its depravity. But his story, like those he spun, had its roots in the Italian countryside. His mother, Maria Le Conti, grew up in the hills outside Naples. Her family was so poor that Maria was not allowed to even sample the ham produced from the lone pig the family slaughtered each year—it was far too precious to eat themselves. Fleeing the poverty of her homeland, Maria moved to New York to marry another Italian immigrant as poor as herself, a dockworker she barely knew and would not know for long. He died in an accident on the docks, leaving her a widow with four small children.

Maria soon had another suitor, a railroad laborer named Antonio Puzo, who asked her to marry him. "Perhaps out of ignorance, perhaps out of compassion, perhaps out of love," Mario would write of his estranged father. "Nobody ever knew. He was a mystery, a Southern Italian with blue eyes."

Antonio and Maria had three children together. On October 15, 1920, their son Mario, the future writer whose parents were both "illiterate, as were their parents before them," was born.

Soon there were seven kids in the cramped apartment in Hell's Kitchen, overlooking the stockyards of the New York Central Railroad, which Puzo would remember as "absolutely blooming with stinking boxcars freshly unloaded of cattle and pigs for the city slaughterhouse."

During Prohibition, the neighborhood was overrun by illegal distilleries and ruled by gangs, which would evolve into organized-crime families. By the time the Great Depression arrived, Hell's Kitchen was known as the "most dangerous area on the American continent."

The Puzos were impoverished but occupied "the best apartment on Tenth Avenue," Mario would write in his 1971 essay "Choosing a Dream."

It was a top floor of six rooms with access to the roof and a fire escape off the kitchen where young Mario could slip out on warm summer nights. "I remember it as comfortable, slum or not." Here, in "the heart of New York's Neapolitan ghetto," life was not exactly *West Side Story*. "I never heard an Italian singing," he wrote. "None of the grown-ups I knew were charming or loving or understanding. Rather they seemed coarse, vulgar and insulting."

The family ate well: "My mother would never dream of using anything but the finest imported olive oil, the best Italian cheeses."

With his father's easy access to the goods coming off the railcars, fresh produce could be had without the markups that stores tended to charge. Food, glorious Italian food, became a lifelong passion for Mario.

Antonio didn't stay long. Diagnosed with schizophrenia, he deserted the family when Mario was twelve, leaving Maria now with seven children to feed. The Puzos were forced to go on welfare to survive. Mario's school asked each student to bring in a can of food to help feed the poor. "The teachers didn't seem to realize *we* were the poor," he recounted. "We didn't, either."

So each of the Hell's Kitchen kids "went out and stole a can of food from a local grocery store."

The kids stole ice from the refrigerator cars of the railroads and made "easy money" reselling the silk from trucks they hijacked from the garment factories of Thirty-First Street. Graft and petty theft were as much their education as phonics and algebra, and Puzo's mother was an encouraging tutor. When Mario was ten or eleven, he saw the cops chasing down a chicken thief into their apartment, where his mom screamed at the officers to stop. "She believed he was entitled to steal the chickens," Puzo said, "and she was entitled to buy them."

One of Puzo's uncles, an assistant chef at a famous Italian restaurant, tucked "six eggs, a stick of butter, and a small bag of flour" under his shirt each day, the sales of which would earn him enough money after thirty years to buy a house on Long Island for himself, and another for his son, and a third for his daughter. Another cousin, using his college degree and materials he "borrowed" from the manufacturing plant where he worked, created a floor wax that he sold door to door.

Crime paid. It was the route—for some, the only route—for the poor, stuck in dead-end jobs with lousy pay, to move up to the middle class. And yet, surrounded by opportunities to enrich himself through crime, Puzo remained on the straight and narrow. "I had every desire to go wrong, but I never had a chance," he wrote. "The Italian family structure was too formidable."

The toughest, most formidable person in his life was his mother. Maria was known to brandish a policeman's club with which she threatened to discipline her rowdy brood. No one seemed to know where she had gotten it, though few doubted she might have filched it from a sleeping cop. Once, when she saw Puzo's brother skipping work and driving around in his beat-up Ford with some neighborhood girls, Mama Puzo picked up a cobblestone from the street and "brought the boulder down on the nearest fender of the tin lizzie, demolishing it."

Puzo used Maria as the basis for the matriarch Lucia Santa in his 1965 autobiographical novel, *The Fortunate Pilgrim*. In one scene, Lucia rebukes her son for not doing his share of chores and disappearing from the house, the policeman's club that Maria wielded replaced by a rolling pin. "By Jesus Christ, I'll make you visible," Lucia Santa threatens. "I'll make you so black and blue that if you were the Holy Ghost you could not vanish. Now, eat. After, wash the dishes, clean the table, and sweep the floor."

Puzo said that without his mother, he never could have created Don Corleone, much of whose voice and language came straight from Maria. "Whenever the Godfather opened his mouth, in my own mind I heard the voice of my mother," Puzo wrote in the preface to the 1996 reissue of his novel. "I heard her wisdom, her ruthlessness, and her unconquerable love for her family and for life itself, qualities not valued in women at the time."

She even provided him with some of the tale's grislier material. "Many parts are true stories my mother told me," Puzo told *Life*. "The man holding his hat to catch the blood from his cut throat, for one."

The seeds of *The Godfather* were planted in an experience from Puzo's childhood. One night the family was startled by a loud noise. "A neighbor across the tenement air shaft threw a blanket full of guns into the apartment and asked my mother to hold them for him, police were knocking on his door," Puzo would write in a 1970 article entitled "How the Mafia Makes Friends." "My mother did so (though like most Italian mothers she went into hysterics when my older brother got so much as a speeding ticket. A *disgrazia* for the family she would say)."

The next day the neighbor knocked on the Puzos' door.

"You got my stuff for me?" he asked.

The neighbor who owned the guns became "protector" of the Puzo family. "He 'reasoned' with the landlord who tried to throw us out because we kept a dog," Puzo wrote.

"Then he said, 'You want a nice rug?' My mother says, 'Sure.' He says, 'Send your son with me.' My brother was like twelve or fourteen years old. The guy takes him to the house, they start rolling up this very expensive rug. All of a sudden there's a knock at the door. The guy peeks out the window and draws a gun. My brother realizes it's not the guy's house and it's not the guy's rug."

The connection continued to pay off. "This kindly neighbor saw to it that free coal was delivered to our house and that we received not one, but two free Thanksgiving baskets from the local political club," wrote Puzo. "So the children in my family called him 'Godfather' in the same sense American kids in country towns call an elderly neighbor 'uncle.'"

It was the first time Puzo heard the term that would shape his destiny. "He was of course a 'Mafia' man," he wrote. "Undoubtedly my mother knew that he broke the law, but since he broke the law for us too, how could we judge him? How could he be denied a cup of coffee, an invitation for dinner? The word 'Mafia' never entered our heads. Our neighbor was a kindly man, a generous man, and we never dreamed that he was a man who could commit murder for a price."

Puzo would realize that "it is in just this way that the Mafia Family gets the politicians, the police, the judges and lawyers working for them. Friendship and favors, nice guys, help you when you need it—all to be repaid one day."

And where else could a poor tenement family like the Puzos turn for help? Surely not the police or the courts, which Puzo's older brother discovered the hard way when, after making a $300 down payment for furniture, money he and his fiancée had spent more than a year saving, the furniture wholesaler went bankrupt a few days after collecting the cash. Puzo's brother went to the law and got satisfaction—"but only after a year of hard work, harassment, and nervous tension that injured his health," Puzo wrote. "If only our old Godfather with his blanket full of guns had still been in touch."

The man, unfortunately, had mysteriously disappeared from Hell's Kitchen, never to be heard from again.

Maria Puzo was intent on making sure young Mario never stepped out of line. Her chief concern wasn't guns but girls. When she caught him coming home late one night, she screamed at him that he would be forced to marry whatever girl he'd been out with if he got her into trouble. "I only wished she was right," Puzo wrote. "I was too shy with girls to have any luck or any dates. I was out until four a.m. still trying to make my fortune in poker."

Gambling—that was Puzo's addiction. He pitched pennies in Hell's Kitchen and played poker with his buddies on Christmas Eve. His appetite for cards was enormous; soon he was "playing poker with very tough workingmen beneath lampposts" or in the back of corner groceries. "I squeezed in a lot of card playing," he would write, "while becoming a sports hero on Tenth Avenue and reading Dostoyevsky."

At Commerce High School on West Sixtieth Street, his teachers told him he had potential as a writer. And when he discovered Dostoyevsky, he found the theme that would dominate his work: the forces of evil. In Dostoyevsky, Puzo also discovered a kindred spirit who understood the powerful attraction of both writing and gambling: "Even as I approach the gambling hall, as soon as I hear . . . the jingle of money poured out on the table, I almost go into convulsions," Dostoyevsky wrote in *The Gambler*. Which surely spoke to Puzo, who knew the thrill of a perfect hand as well as a perfect sentence—neither of which seemed likely to make for a good career.

Puzo was only willing to admit one of his vices to his mother.

So at sixteen, he told her he was going to become a great writer. His mother, he wrote, "simply assumed I had gone off my nut."

For Maria—who had "never heard of Michelangelo" and "could not sign her name"—it was impossible to believe that her son could become an artist, wrote Puzo in "Choosing a Dream." "After all, her one dream in coming to America had been to earn her daily bread."

College "wasn't an option," he added. "There were two high schools in our neighborhood, and my mother and sister decided I should go to the one that didn't prepare you for college."

Later, the boy who would subsequently write, "My direct ancestors for a thousand years have most probably been illiterate," asked his sister why she didn't urge him to attend college. "Because you were stupid," she told him.

Maria wanted her son to become a railroad clerk—"that was her *highest* ambition."

With the country still in the grip of the Great Depression, a job that offered steady pay and hours was a lot to hope for. The other men in Puzo's family all worked for the railroad, in one capacity or another. But Mario didn't have the temperament for that; his part-time job as a messenger boy, which he despised, turned out to be a dead end. Nevertheless, high school was coming to a close, and despite his terrible experience as a messenger boy, it looked like he was going to get stuck on the railroad, in a job he dreaded.

In 1939, he tried making his escape: He signed on with the Civilian Conservation Corps, a New Deal program that sent him out west, all the way to Nevada, to improve and expand the state's waterways and irrigation systems. Bugsy Siegel and his backers in organized crime had yet to conjure Las Vegas out of the desert, but Puzo was stationed in Lovelock, a couple of hours from Reno, the center of legalized gambling in the state. There, his lifelong love affair with casinos was born.

But the New Deal work was designed to be temporary, a stopgap measure for the unemployed. Puzo soon found himself back in Hell's

Kitchen, slogging away at a low-level railroad job, stuck in the same tenement apartment with his family and their low expectations for him. He was headed into what he called a trap: "the steady job, the nice girl who would eventually get knocked up, and then the marriage and fighting."

Then came the bombing of Pearl Harbor. Puzo, like his fictional creation Michael Corleone, seized the moment to escape the iron grip of his family's business by donning a uniform.

"I hated my life....When World War II broke out, I was delighted," he wrote. "I was delivered from my mother, my family, the girl I was loving passionately but did not love....I drove a jeep, toured Europe, had love affairs, found a wife, and lived the material for my first novel."

Assigned to the 4th Armored Division, Private Puzo was deployed to Europe, where, in General George S. Patton's army, he drove the jeep and performed administrative duties, close to the front lines and under fire three times. "As a soldier, I was so inept that it's a good thing I never had to handle a rifle!" he told writer Camille Paglia in 1997. He spent three years traveling around the war-torn continent, mostly in the captured towns of France, dealing "a million hands of poker" and getting into scrapes over cards with his fellow soldiers. A hot streak on a troop ship to Europe got him threatened with a pistol by a paratrooper and taught Puzo a valuable lesson: "You have to be more careful when you are innocent than when you are guilty."

When the war ended, Puzo stayed on in West Germany, working a lowly job as a civilian clerk for the Department of Defense. In 1946, he met the German woman who would become his wife. "I think they met on a blind date," said Puzo's oldest son, Anthony. But Puzo, according to his future colleague John Bowers, related the meeting in the epic terms of a writer. "He said she was about to be assaulted, and he protected her," said Bowers. "He protected her so well that they fell in love and he brought her to the United States."

Her name was Erika Lina Broske, and she was twenty-five, with blue eyes, red hair, and a pale complexion. She spoke very little English and had the simplest tastes, but Mario Puzo had at long last fallen in love. They were married in 1947, in Bremen, Germany, and soon had their first child, Anthony.

Family life proved difficult for the gambling, food, and action addict who aspired to write. The couple returned with Anthony to New York, where Puzo's choice of wife—not an Italian—was difficult for his family. "The Puzos were very strong Italians, especially his mother, who Mario always said *was* the Godfather," said Puzo's longtime assistant, Lanetta Wahlgren. "And Erika was put in her place and she sort of stayed there. But Mario loved her and protected her."

Soon after Puzo took a job as a civil service clerk at a Manhattan armory, Erika had a second child, Dorothy. On the side, Puzo pursued his dream of writing: He took university classes in literature and creative writing on the GI Bill, and spent nights and weekends trying to turn all the observations and notes he had gathered during his time in Europe into a novel. His progress, however, was torturously slow. "This is the end of a bad year," Puzo wrote in his diary at the end of 1950. "Two short stories and hardly anything on the novel. If I keep this up, I might as well forget about writing or becoming a writer. And I keep wondering why I turned out so little."

What small change he managed to make, he gambled away. "He liked to do things first-class, even though we only had fifth-class money," his son Anthony told the *New York Post*. "He ran up a lot of debt."

Puzo was even harder on himself. "Every Italian family has a 'chooch,' a donkey. That is, a family idiot everybody agrees will never be able to make a living," he wrote in his 1972 book, *The Godfather Papers and Other Confessions*. And debt had made him the *chooch* in the Puzo family. "There is no question that I am incompetent," Puzo lamented in his diary in late 1951. "Monetarily insane. . . . But money is really killing everything."

One week later, he wrote, "It's funny to watch yourself disintegrating."

It was a vicious cycle: His gambling, and the debts he accrued, forced him to work longer hours at his clerk job, which in turn robbed him of the time he might otherwise have spent writing. In November 1951, with a third child, daughter Virginia, only two months old, Puzo was working an average of twenty hours a week of overtime, but still couldn't dig himself out from under his debts. "I'm too tired to do any writing . . . kids running around . . . no place to work," he wrote. "Time, money, emotional stability. . . . Right now it seems to be all gone."

There were fleeting glimpses of hope. His first short story, "Last Christmas," was published in *American Vanguard*, the literary magazine of The New School, where he was taking creative writing classes. And in 1952, thanks to a hot streak on his sports betting, he was able to quit his job to focus on writing full-time. He rented a room for eleven dollars a week and sat down to write the novel he'd been dreaming about since he left Europe. But even without the distraction of a full-time job, the writing was slow, and his gambling winnings were soon gone. "Paralyzed by this being in debt," Puzo wrote in his diary in December 1952. "Letter from bank about loan. It looks as if I have to go back to work in January."

A month later, in despair over what he considered a "hopeless" first draft, he wrote, "I can say . . . the whole business of quitting my job to become a full-time writer is a failure but still enjoyed it. Glad I tried."

Puzo bounced around for months, trying out different jobs; some he quit after a few hours. Unable to earn a steady income, he gorged himself on the Italian and Chinese foods he loved, along with late-night snacks of buttered noodles that left him with a waistline nearly as large as as his gambling debts, and seemingly just as inescapable. Although he stood barely five feet six inches tall, his weight ballooned to 250 pounds. He wore his hair slicked back, his face was obscured by thick glasses with big, dark frames and, more often than not, a massive cigar. He never wore socks, preferring instead to go barefoot in his loafers, Bally soon becoming his favorite brand. The things that people noticed most about Puzo, though, were his big belly, which protruded through his shirts, and his broad smile, which he always seemed to be wearing, even when things were tough. Everyone who met him fell in love with him. "He was the most beautiful man," said Wahlgren.

And the most tormented. His diary of Saturday, April 9, 1953, marked yet another low point: "Today got a letter from H turning down the book. Expressing sincere sympathy, he just couldn't take it . . . humiliating . . . the knowledge that people pity you."

In another entry, he lamented, "T[ony] is signing a note for me tomorrow so I can buy a bedroom set. This humiliates me but it humiliates him even more."

Still, he wrote. In the small windows of time between working overtime at his clerk job, to which he'd grudgingly returned, and his duties as a father, he kept toiling away on his novel. Finally, in 1954, he sold the book to Random House.

The Dark Arena was a distillation of his experiences as a vet navigating the world of postwar Germany. "Mario Puzo has written the ruthless, savage story of the postwar American occupation of Germany, written it in terms of men and women who are good and evil, greedy and generous, corrupt and pure," noted the publisher. Puzo hoped it would catapult him into the same conversation as authors like Norman Mailer. Instead, it only added to his humiliation. A few critics saw promise—*The Nation* called it "one of the finest works of fiction to come out of this country's occupation of Germany"—but some were blistering. "A book that shocks one to the fiber of one's being," *Kirkus Reviews* declared. "Did it have to be written? Or if written, published?" Next to no copies sold, and Puzo walked away with nothing but his advance of $3,500.

"My vision of Mario then?" his friend the writer George Mandel would tell *Time* magazine in 1978. "He used to go to his brother's in a taxi to borrow money for his kids' shoes."

On Christmas Eve 1955, Puzo suffered what he would call a "severe gallbladder attack," which drove him into the cold New York night alone in a taxi in excruciating pain. He directed the cab to the

Veterans Administration hospital on East Twenty-Third Street. Upon arriving, he opened the taxi door and stepped onto the street.

Just then, the pain struck. "I got out and fell into the gutter," he remembered.

Writhing in agony, his mind turned to his failed ambitions. *Here I am, a published writer,* he thought, *and I am dying like a dog.*

Faceup in the gutter, he made a vow.

"That's when I decided I would be rich and famous."

RICHES AND FAME, however, continued to elude him. By 1960, his family had grown to five children with the birth of his youngest son, Joseph. Adding to the financial pressure, his seemingly secure job as an army clerk was suddenly in jeopardy: the FBI was investigating allegations of bribery in his unit. Young men were apparently evading the draft by paying clerks bribes for coveted spots in the Army Reserve, and someone told the Feds that Puzo was part of the scheme.

On December 22, 1961, an FBI agent filed a report on the investigation. A young man, "knowing he would otherwise be drafted and required to serve two years active duty," had sought the advice of someone whose name is redacted in the report. The man "contacted MARIO PUZO at the suggestion of [name blacked out] and paid Puzo $225 to get into the Reserves as Puzo was employed with the Reserve Center at 529 West 42nd Street, New York City."

Someone, it appeared, had ratted him out.

The following month, Puzo was questioned by the FBI. He maintained his innocence, but the investigation dragged on for months, an experience that Puzo would disguise as fiction in his novel *Fools Die*: "At the office the FBI agents dropped by a couple of times a week, usually with some guy that they were obviously identifying me to. I figured it was some reservist who had paid his way into the six months' program," Puzo wrote. "Every time the doorbell to my apartment rang at an unusual time, my heart really jumped. I thought it was the cops or the FBI."

Puzo was never charged in the bribery scheme. But the ongoing investigation turned his job at the clerk's office into a daily horror. In 1962, Puzo quit. His career as a civil servant was over. Once again he was dead broke, with no salary and seemingly no future.

Desperate for full-time employment, Puzo headed straight to what was considered the trashiest, least literary branch of the publishing world: pulp fiction. For the past two years, he had been freelancing stories for Magazine Management Company, which owned a host of titles—rags like *For Men Only*, *Male*, *Man's World*, *True Action*, and *Stag*—devoted to war stories, crime capers, and seedy tales of lustful damsels and the brave studs who swooped in to save them. It was a world of sex and sin, of bloodthirsty weasels and killer turtles and underwater call-girl brothels and nudist-cult blackmail rings, a place where Puzo could turn his real-life war experiences into sensationalized stories with headlines like "The Battle Angels: Broads-and-Booze GI Hell-Cyclists Who Smashed Hitler's Panzer Highway."

It was pure schlock, but for Puzo it was a golden opportunity: the chance to *write* for a living.

Almost everyone who worked at the company's smoke-filled offices on Madison Avenue was as hard up as Puzo. "Magazine Management people seemed not so much to have been hired as to have washed ashore at the company like driftwood," Bruce Jay Friedman, the editorial director, would write in *Lucky Bruce: A Literary Memoir*. "We were all slightly 'broken' people. A few had gifts, but we were 'rejects' all, having clearly been unable to cut the mustard at the Luce and Hearst empires."

When Puzo showed up, hat in hand, to apply for job as an "editorial assistant," as the company's full-time writers were called, Friedman was on the verge of hiring another candidate with far better credentials. But the editor sensed something in Puzo, and Friedman, with pages to fill, "needed a writer and not an executive," Friedman would later write. "I hired Puzo for the princely sum of $150 a week."

The money was nothing compared to the education Puzo received in the art of popular storytelling. Magazine Management was a pulp factory, and workers on the assembly line were expected to churn out stories *fast*, packed with blood and sex and gore and more sex. Beautiful prose and fidelity to the truth had nothing to do with it—what mattered was to grab readers' attention and keep them turning the pages. "All of this, believe me, all of it, was made up," John Bowers, who worked in the cubicle next to Puzo's, would say. "We made up every battle, every commander, every situation, so it was really novelistic. It had no bearing on seeking the truth."

And in his eight years at Magazine Management, Puzo would become one of the best and most prolific schlock writers of them all, "an ace pulp writer," he said. "I wiped out whole armies," he told *Time* in 1978. "I wrote a story about an invasion in which I killed 100,000 men and then later read the statistics. There were only 7,000 killed."

Under the pen name Mario Cleri—the surname borrowed from his older half brother Anthony Cleri, to whom he would dedicate *The Godfather*—Puzo crafted potboilers like "Girls of Pleasure Penthouse," the *Male* magazine story of a Hawaiian gangster's paradise, offering "the ultimate in hot-fleshed women and cool-chip gambling."

His fellow workers were impressed by both his speed and his style. "He wrote furiously and well," said Patricia Bosworth, a former actress who worked with Puzo at Magazine Management before going on to a celebrated career as a journalist and celebrity biographer. "That's how he mastered his craft."

"Mario worked harder than any writer I knew," wrote Jules Siegel, another colleague at Magazine Management. "He used to turn out a minimum of thirty thousand to forty thousand words a month under four or five names . . . then go home and work on a novel or major magazine assignment."

Now he had two passions: writing and gambling. "Gambling was a bigger part of my life than writing at one time," he would later admit in an interview with his friend George Mandel. "You know the story—in the morning you get up, you look in the papers, figure out your baseball games for the afternoon and make your bets. During lunch hour you've got to run up from work, make your bets, see your shylock for more money to bet with and run back to work. Then at night you've got the night games and the trotters. You've got to pick them out. You've got to run up to the bookmaker again. Then you've got to drive out to the track. Then you come home and you've got to bet on the West Coast games. You turn on the TV—the game comes on at eleven o'clock, so you've got to sweat it out until two in the morning to see if you've won your bet. Then you're up at seven, doping out your bets again. You're really exhausted. There were a couple of years I was making a hundred dollars a week and betting a hundred dollars a day."

To keep pace with his losses, Puzo was writing like a man whose life depended on it—which it did. He was determined to make good on his vow in the gutter that night, and he wasn't going to get either rich or famous churning out pulp for Magazine Management. But the salary provided him with a degree of financial stability he had seldom enjoyed, and the pace of production seemed to free up something in him. The result was his second novel, *The Fortunate Pilgrim*, based on the life of his mother.

It was his most autobiographical novel, and the testing ground for Lucia Santa, the character modeled on his mother, whose strong voice and potent language would become the inspiration for Don Corleone. A Mob boss even featured as a minor character in the book.

The Fortunate Pilgrim was published to strong reviews and weak sales. In the end, Puzo earned only $3,000—$500 less than his first novel a decade earlier. And thanks to the book's commercial failure, it looked like there might never be a third novel. When Puzo went to his publisher for an advance to begin his next book, he was flatly refused. "The editors were cool," he wrote in his book *The Godfather Papers and Other Confessions*.

"They were courteous. They were kind. They showed me the door."

After struggling for more than two decades to realize his dream, Puzo was once again in the gutter.

This time, though, he had an emotional epiphany. "I came to the point where I was terribly angry at my wife and my brothers and sisters, at my mother, because nobody was on my side in this struggle,"

Puzo said in a 1978 interview for *Time*. "Then I sat down one day and said, why should they care because of my eccentricity? What did it have to do with them? They were perfectly right in the way they felt, and I was perfectly right in the way I felt."

For the first time, he didn't need anyone's support. All that mattered was his desire to write.

He even drew inspiration from his rejection. "The editors didn't like the idea behind my new novel," he wrote. "It sounded like another loser. One editor wistfully remarked that if *Fortunate Pilgrim* had only a little more of that Mafia stuff in it, maybe the book would have made money."

Puzo had always assured his family—and anyone else who would listen—that he could write a bestseller anytime he wanted. Instead, he had devoted his life to a higher calling: He was a "true believer in art."

It was Dostoyevsky he was after, not dime novels. "I didn't believe in religion or love or women or men," he wrote. "I didn't believe in society or philosophy. But I believed in art."

And where had that gotten him? "I was forty-five years old and tired of being an artist. Besides, I owed $20,000 to relatives, finance companies, banks and assorted bookmakers and shylocks. It was really time to grow up and sell out, as Lenny Bruce once advised."

A little more of that Mafia stuff. The editor's words rang in his head. He knew these people, these criminals, these killers, at least from afar. He had been raised in their world, and he knew he could make their world his own. "So I told my editors OK, I'll write a book about the Mafia, just give me some money to get started," he wrote. "They said no money until we see a hundred pages. I compromised. I wrote a ten-page outline. They showed me the door again."

Once more, though, a spark rose from the ashes. "There is no way to explain the terrible feeling of rejection, the damage, the depression and weakening of will such manipulation does to a writer," Puzo continued. "But this incident also enlightened me. I had been naïve enough to believe that publishers cared about art. They didn't. They wanted to make money. (Please don't say, 'No kidding.') They were in business. They had a capital investment and payrolls to meet. If some lunatic wanted to create a work of art, let him do it on his own time."

It was time, Puzo concluded, to give up on art. It was time to write for money. "My writing friends, my family, my children and my creditors all assured me now was the time to put up or shut up," he wrote. If he was going to spend his life in the gutter, he might as well make use of the trash.

PUZO THREW HIMSELF into his "Mafia Novel," as he called it, with an intensity he had never demonstrated before. This was like a story for one of Magazine Management's rags, writ large. "My father knew he could write a bestseller," said his eldest son, Anthony. "He was an avid reader [who] learned there was a formula for writing a bestselling book."

All he had to do was look to the stars: "Harold Robbins and Jackie Susann were known for their bestseller formula," added Anthony. "That is: over-the-top memorable characters; multiple plot lines; and some sex."

In addition to this, Puzo would, as he had done in his magazine stories, research the facts, then embellish them with his own overheated imagination. "Essentially my process is thinking out the story and research," he said. "Research is tremendously important."

Soon, his office and home were awash in research material: transcripts of congressional testimony, newspaper clippings, magazine articles, and books about the Mob. "I have a picture of him sitting in a chair with not one but six volumes in his lap, wetting his finger and taking 'tastes' of each one," Bruce Jay Friedman would say. Puzo gained access to *The Real Thing*, Valachi's personal account of his time in the Mafia, which was later turned into *The Valachi Papers*, written by Puzo's friend Peter Maas and published by Puzo's future publisher, G.P. Putnam's Sons. He also pored over the ten-volume transcripts of the Kefauver hearings, the "parade of over 600 gangsters, pimps, bookies, politicians and shady lawyers" that had so captivated the nation a decade earlier, which Puzo ordered for ten dollars. He quickly zeroed in on the hearing's most belligerent witness, Frank Costello, the crime boss who refused to answer questions or even show his face on television. With his raspy voice, his easy access to politicians, and his disdain for drug dealing, Costello was the clay from which Puzo would fashion his protagonist, the all-powerful leader of the top New York Mob family.

Writing fast and furiously, he cobbled together a ten-page outline. It would be a story of the Mob, yes, but told through the prism of a Mob family, whose name he took from one of the most notorious Mafia-infested towns in Sicily—Corleone—which he came to know through *The Honoured Society*, a 1964 nonfiction book about the Sicilian Mafia. It would have all the ingredients of a can't-stop-reading Magazine Management story. "It drew the reader in," says John Bowers, who saw in Puzo's novel the hallmarks of the tawdriest pulp magazine stories. "The reader read that first paragraph and was introduced to viable characters that were interesting and you wanted to turn the page. *Immediately*, you wanted to turn the page."

There were tough-talking gangsters, guns, and gambling. And, at every turn, sex. Because, as Puzo had learned during his time at Magazine Management, sex sells. In his handwritten notes for his future screenplay, scrawled in red marker, Puzo meticulously noted all of the sex he was incorporating. He wanted to make sure the people got what they wanted, and he spelled it out in the very first line of his notes. "Sex Scenes," it reads, followed by a list of seven couples who would engage in intercourse. "Too long a stretch without sex," he scrawled at one point. "Enlarge sex scene," he noted in another. And since the singer Johnny Fontane was at the center of so much sex and sin, Puzo tried his best to keep him disguised. "Change *any* resemblance to Sinatra of Fontane character," he would later write. "Don't make Frankie whine at the beginning," he added in his notes.

Sometimes the sex was too over-the-top even for Puzo. "She was wearing white silk panties embroidered with a little blue flower," he wrote, depicting a scene between a past-his-prime singer modeled on Frank Sinatra and presumably his movie star wife, Ava Gardner.

"Her thighs were flushing a pale pink and her eyes were shining as she watched him. Johnny slammed down on her body, one hand holding her head steady so that his mouth imprisoned hers in a brutally punishing kiss. His other hand savagely ripped the silk panties to shreds so that he had access to the warm moist velvety mound of flesh. He made love to her more punishingly than he had tried to beat her. When they were finished he was no longer drunk and no longer angry. He merely felt a self-disgust so overwhelming that it made him physically weak."

Across the top of the torn yellow file folder containing the passage, Puzo scrawled a single word with his thick red marker: "NO."

The scene never made it into *The Godfather*.

When the outline was done, Puzo began shopping it around to publishers. But the result was the same as before. "Nobody would take me," he complained. "I was ready to forget novels except maybe as a puttering hobby for my old age."

Then he met Saul Braun, a young editor just out of Yale, who was working for G.P. Putnam's Sons publishers. Braun was running a contest to crown the best unpublished novel in the English language. The prize was worth $210,000, which included hardcover and paperback rights and $100,000 from Embassy Pictures to turn the winning novel into a movie, television show, or radio program.

Three thousand manuscripts flooded into Putnam's offices.

Not one was deemed worthy of being the winner.

Then, Braun met the author he believed could win the contest: Mario Puzo.

Braun visited Puzo at his Magazine Management office.

"As a natural courtesy I gave him a copy of *The Fortunate Pilgrim*," Puzo wrote. "A week later he came back. He thought I was a great writer. I bought him a magnificent lunch. During the lunch I told him some Mafia stories and [showed him] my ten-page outline."

Saul Braun was so impressed with Puzo that he "invited him to submit whatever he was writing to the contest so I could win it for him, say this is the winner, and give him the money and the movie deal," Braun said. He also arranged a meeting for Puzo at Putnam, where the author met with the editors. For an hour, Puzo regaled them with tales of the Mob. To his surprise, they gave him the go-ahead.

"They also gave me a $5,000 advance, and I was on my way, just like that. Almost-almost, I believed that publishers were human."

The first novel contest ended without a winner. Puzo's book contract, however, came with a catch: it would be paid in installments, to make sure he wrote the book in a timely manner.

But that was not Puzo's way. "As soon as I got my hands on the Putnam money, I naturally didn't work on the book."

The reason was simple. "The thing is, I didn't really want to write *The Godfather*," Puzo would confess. "There was another novel I wanted to write."

His friends and coworkers were aghast. "All my fellow editors on the adventure magazine told me to get cracking on the book," he wrote in *The Godfather Papers and Other Confessions*. "They all were sure it would make my fortune. I had all the good stories, it was writing to my strength."

What drove him back to his outline was what had always compelled him over the years: debt. In September 1966, Puzo wrote to the IRS, requesting a three-month extension on paying taxes he owed. "I am now a freelance writer and expect advance on book which has been contracted for," Puzo assured the government. "Will use that money to pay tax."

Now he *had* to work on the book. He sat down at his cherished 1965 Olympia manual typewriter in the basement of his home in Merrick, New York, and began to dream. He had been around mobsters all his life, but he'd always observed them from afar. He had "never met a real honest-to-God gangster," he would say, but his fertile imagination, fueled by his research, was more than able to conjure up their world, maybe even a world bigger and more grandiose than the one they actually inhabited. He wouldn't so much write chapters as "accumulate notes. Then I come back and try to fix it up, put hooks in it so you can go from one place to another."

His gangster tale would be filled with hooks, snagging the reader from the first sentence and keeping them hooked until the final word. It would be the story of a Mafia don, Vito Corleone, "a man to whom everybody came for help," and his three sons. There was the eldest and heir apparent, Santino, known as Sonny—"built as powerfully as a bull" and "so generously endowed by nature that his martyred wife feared the marriage bed as unbelievers once feared the rack."

There was the middle son, the weak and subservient Fredo— "dutiful, loyal, always at the service of his father, living with his parents at age thirty."

And there was the youngest and estranged son, Michael, who chose to enlist in the military instead of the Mafia—"the only child who had refused the great man's direction," with "skin a clear olive-brown that would have been called beautiful in a girl."

As for plot lines, all Puzo had to do was draw from his extensive research on the Mob. The wedding of Don Corleone's daughter was said to resemble Joseph Valachi's in 1932, complete with live entertainment and envelopes stuffed with "gifts" for the bride, noted film historian Peter Cowie. The scene where the Godfather is gunned down while buying fruit from a grocery in the Bronx parallels the hit on Mob boss Frank Scalice in 1957, and the assassination of Moe Greene in the movie would mirror that of the crime boss Albert Anastasia, who was shot while sitting in a barber's chair in the Park-Sheraton Hotel that same year.

The manual typewriter clattered with authentic characters and irresistible themes: the Corleone compound ("modeled on the legend of the Kennedy compound at Hyannis Port," wrote M. J. Moore in his 2019 biography, *Mario Puzo: An American Writer's Quest*); the subplot of Johnny Fontane ("a variation on the legendary rise, fall and renaissance in the career of Frank Sinatra in the early 1950s"); the dramatic turning point in which Michael Corleone blows away the drug-dealing Sollozzo and the crooked police captain Mark McCluskey in an Italian restaurant and becomes the heir apparent to his father's throne ("as well as the subplot detailing Michael's exile in Sicily," Moore added).

With his structure set, the writing raced and rolled, fiction that the world would accept as fact. It was "infused with the elements of the 'postwar pulps' that Mario had written for throughout the 1960s," wrote Moore, adding that while the writing wasn't "tawdry or dirty simply for the sake of shock value," Puzo relied on his mainstays: "scenes of violence or sex that Puzo knew would keep any reader turning pages."

PUZO LOOKED FOR inspiration anywhere he could find it. One evening in 1966, the author Gay Talese, then a reporter for the *New York Times*, and his wife, Nan, soon to be a celebrated publisher of some of the greatest authors of her time, went to dinner at the Long Island home of Talese's aunt, Susan Pileggi. That night, assembled at the table, sat the future of Mob literature: Talese, who would write the organized-crime classic *Honor Thy Father*; his first cousin Nick Pileggi, who would write *Wiseguy* (the basis for the film *Goodfellas*); and Puzo, who was in the process of writing *The Godfather*.

Talese had met Puzo after reading *The Fortunate Pilgrim*. The *Times* reporter had been conducting research in Hell's Kitchen when he had "come across Mario's wonderful descriptions of that neighborhood in his book," he said. The two Italian American writers met for drinks and dinner and became fast friends.

Now, sitting down to dinner on Long Island, Puzo's eyes fell on Talese's wife. Dark-haired and attractive, Nan Irene Ahearn Talese possessed the kind of Upper East Side sophistication that would have struck an immigrant's kid raised in Hell's Kitchen as the epitome of class. The daughter of a banker, she attended Rye Country Day School, in New York, and became a Westchester Cotillion debutante who bucked her family's expectations when she married Talese, the son of an Italian-immigrant tailor from Ocean City, New Jersey. ("Nan," her mother pleaded with her, "you don't know what it's like to live with a *writer*.") At dinner, Puzo listened with rapt attention to her cultured speech, observed her refined mannerisms, and reveled in her understated beauty. He had found his Kay, the embodiment of culture and class who marries Michael over the objections of his family:

> *They were not impressed with her. She was too thin, she was too fair, her face was too sharply intelligent for a woman, her manner too free for a maiden. Her name, too, was outlandish to their ears: she called herself Kay Adams. If she had told them that her family had settled in America two hundred years ago and her name was a common one, they would have shrugged.*

It would be years before Puzo confessed the source of his inspiration to Talese. "He later told me—after *The Godfather* was published—that his character Kay is based on my wife, Nan," Talese said, recounting the story for the first time. "She went to convent schools, is of Irish Protestant background, and in marrying me—a kind of Pacino-looking guy—she definitely was descending in a social-status sense."

Week after week, month after month, Puzo banged away at his typewriter in his basement, haunted by the Corleones and surrounded by packing boxes and a pool table and the deafening sounds of his five screaming kids. "Keep it down," he would yell at them, "I'm writing a bestseller!" He quit his salaried job at Magazine Management to focus on the novel, though financial pressures would require him to continue churning out three freelance stories a month for the pulp magazines, as well as book reviews and occasional features for the Sunday *New York Times Magazine*. He thought the book was good, but he had been mistaken before. If it was a smash success, he figured it might bring him as much as $100,000.

When at long last he had a hundred very rough pages of his "Mafia Novel," a messenger arrived from the movies.

His name was George Wieser, and he was an advertising salesman straight out of the retro TV series *Mad Men*: a smart, suave, tall, handsome hustler, then in his midthirties. With ten years as the ad manager for *Library Journal,* Wieser had the inside track on books before their publication. Traveling from publishing house to publishing house, selling ads, Wieser had become a magnet for "what was going on in publishing-industry gossip and what the publishers were excited about," said his sister, Sally Wieser.

One evening in the clouds above Manhattan, Wieser was ushered into his future via a dinner at the iconic restaurant Top of the Sixes, at 666 Fifth Avenue. His host was Robert Evans, then trying to break into the movie business. Knowing that hot books made hot movies, Evans offered Wieser twenty-five to fifty dollars a week to bring him potential material before anyone else.

Wieser paid off. He pitched Evans a first novel by a writer named Jacqueline Susann titled *Valley of the Dolls* (which Evans tried to purchase but "naively" did not), then a potboiler entitled *The Detective* (which Evans helped turn into a film starring Frank Sinatra) and, finally, something called "Mafia Novel," which the editors at Putnam seemed excited about.

"I wanted the first taste of the first thing he tasted," Evans later said of Wieser. "He got me *The Detective*. For $5,000, I ended up a producer. He broke my virginity. It was a novel by Roderick Faulk, and I got Frank Sinatra to play the lead in it. Twentieth [Century Fox, which produced the film] didn't want me as producer. But I owned the property. That's when I learned, 'Property is king.'

"So when Wieser called me about Mario, the door was automatically opened."

By now, Evans was the newly installed head of production at Paramount Pictures. "He's a helluva writer, hungry, and writes your kind of shit, Evans," Weiser told him.

With Paramount sinking, the production head was desperate for good material, but he had never heard of Puzo, and he had no reason to think that some little-known author from New York had anything of value to offer.

With nothing but this one thin connection, Puzo arrived in Hollywood, his hundred pages tucked under his arm.

3

HURRICANE CHARLIE AND THE KID

By the time Mario Puzo arrived at the iron-and-stone gates of Paramount Pictures, in March 1967, the studio was on the brink of collapse. Commanding more than forty acres in the heart of Hollywood, Paramount was one of the oldest movie studios in the world; acquired by Adolph Zukor, a Hungarian immigrant, toward the end of the nickelodeon era, it had helped bring the movies to an America starving for entertainment. The talent pool at Paramount was legendary, from Gloria Swanson and Rudolph Valentino to the Marx Brothers, Bob Hope, Marlene Dietrich, Mae West, Gary Cooper, and Audrey Hepburn. Even better, the studios in those days owned every step of production, from the long-term, exclusive contracts they cut with talent to the theater chains that showed their movies.

The studio began its descent in 1948, when the Supreme Court ruled that Paramount and the other studios' lucrative hold on talent and distribution violated antitrust provisions against concentrated corporate power. As television began to compete with movies for American audiences, the studio proved unable to adapt to a changing Hollywood. When Puzo showed up with his pages, Paramount was perceived as old, tired, and dusty—symbolized by its chairman emeritus, the ninety-four-year-old Adolph Zukor. The studio had been in the red for years, reduced to little more than a Hollywood laughingstock. "There were eight major studios at the time," Robert Evans would famously say, "and Paramount was ninth."

Now the guards at the front gate were waving in Puzo, a man as down and out as the studio itself. What happened next is a matter of contention, one of the many competing claims that surrounds the origins of *The Godfather*. Evans, in a last-ditch effort to save Paramount, insisted that the struggling writer was escorted into his office for a personal meeting. In his telling, Evans sat behind a massive desk surrounded by framed photos of his overnight fame. A clothing merchant turned actor, he had never produced a movie when he was snapped up by Paramount, and he was still looking for a hit, a blockbuster that could restore the studio's reputation, shore up its bottom line, and save his job.

The writer standing in front of him extended his hand and introduced himself: Mario Puzo.

The name meant nothing to Evans—he had forgotten all about George Wieser's introduction. He would insist he didn't know who the hell this nobody was, with the cigar jutting from his jaw and the pages tucked under his arm. But Evans knew the look of being broke, which was written all over Puzo's face. "In trouble?" he asked.

And how. Puzo said he was into the bookies for ten grand. His only hope for not getting his legs broken was under his arm, his pages for a novel he was calling *Mafia*.

"I need a gig, Bob," Evans would remember Puzo telling him.

Evans asked the writer what the book was going to be about.

When Puzo told him he was writing about organized crime, the studio chief cringed. Paramount had just made a Mob flick, *The Brotherhood*, that had "flopped on its ass."

But listening to Puzo, Evans decided to do him a favor. "I'll give you ten Gs for it," he said, more out of pity than excitement, adding that the up-front money would be an option against $50,000 more if the studio made the movie. Puzo looked at him. "Could you make it fifteen?"

"How about twelve-five?" Evans countered.

Desperate for cash, Puzo agreed—forgoing any royalties that

might be earned on a future movie. Without even glancing at the pages, Evans sent them to Paramount's business department, along with a pay order. He never expected to see Mario Puzo again.

Five months later, Puzo called Evans with a question.

"Would I be in breach of contract if I change the title of the book?"

Evans almost laughed out loud—"I had forgotten he was even writing one."

Puzo said, "I want to call it *The Godfather*."

"The publisher *hated* the title," Puzo's son Anthony would later say.

As is often the case with Hollywood legends, almost everything about Evans's account of meeting Puzo wound up being disputed as either inaccurate or self-serving or both. Puzo insisted that the tale was pure fiction: He said he never met with Evans until he had been hired to work on the script. "I never saw or heard of Evans or [Peter] Bart until I got to Hollywood," he would say. "I dealt with Barry Beckerman [who supervised the studio's literary acquisitions]."

Puzo's editor, William Targ, wrote that he sent the pages "to a friend of mine at Paramount, Marvin Birdt," who "offered a $50,000 deal, $12,500 on signing."

Peter Bart, then the studio's vice president of production, contended that Puzo's pages came to him, not Evans. "I've never said this to anyone," Bart would say, "but I was solely responsible for buying Mario Puzo's sixty or seventy pages. No one else had read it. I made the decision. I ordered it to be bought. . . . Like so many things, it's part of the mythology. Most of the stuff I've read is simply just not true."

But Bart doesn't take credit for the success of the film. "*The Godfather* was created by Francis Ford Coppola and Mario Puzo," he said. "Under the direction of Bob Evans's supervision."

However, when multitudes work on a movie, some will try to stake a claim. "Because they don't understand what I did, what Bob Evans did, what [producer] Al Ruddy did, all kinds of people have taken credit for the movie. People I've never met."

Success, it would seem, has even more godfathers than fathers.

What no one disputes is that Puzo got the $12,500 and returned

home to Long Island, to work on the novel that few suspected he
would ever finish. As Puzo pounded away on his Olympia manual,
hour after hour, Evans struggled to keep Paramount afloat. He was
in a race against time, and against his boss, the man who had brought
him on board at the studio: Charlie Bluhdorn, Paramount's new
owner, who was looking toward cutting his losses and selling the ail-
ing studio. A takeover artist skilled at snapping up companies in a fantastic range of industries, from sugar and cigars to rocket jets and zinc
mining, Bluhdorn was the man without whom *The Godfather* would
never have been made—and whose involvement almost torpedoed the
project before it even had a chance.

THE BOY ON the boat was all alone, a refugee fleeing one life for
another.

He was barely sixteen, knowing no one, and he mangled his
English with his thick Austrian accent. It was 1942, and Hitler was
conquering Europe. The son of a Jewish mother, the boy was following
a directive from his parents, Rose and Paul, who had left Vienna for
New York two years before him: *Leave . . . immediately.* So he finished
his studies at Carlton Grammar School, a boys' school in Yorkshire,
England, and boarded a ship to America. Sailing from England to
New York on the HMS *Hilary*, a passenger liner requisitioned by the
Royal Navy and trailed by Nazi submarines intent on sinking it, the
boy's pockets were empty. But he was heading toward a future neither
he nor anyone who knew him could have imagined. His life would be
a saga, the stuff of legend, straight out of the movies he came to love
to the point of obsession: *Lawrence of Arabia, Dr. Zhivago, The Sound of
Music*—anything with what he called "the schmaltz factor."

And his was a story with plenty of schmaltz, a story that would
deliver him to fame, fortune, and, inconceivably, a movie studio of his
very own, one of the fantasy factories that, for the sixteen-year-old boy
on the boat, must have seemed as distant as America itself. Once he
arrived in New York, though, he embarked upon a circuitous route to

owning and resuscitating not just any studio but one whose films were deeply ingrained in the fabric of America, the movie studio appropriately called Paramount.

But before he could become a mogul—before he could become a macher—he would have to toil in the businesses of mundane things, which he would acquire company by company, until he turned the takeover into an art form.

His name was Karl Georg Blühdorn.

He landed in New York on October 29, 1942, on immigrant visa No. 275. Soon after his arrival, he went to work. Because there "wasn't a day in his life when he wasn't in business, or thinking about business," his daughter, Dominique, would say. His first real job in the New World was as a lowly clerk at a cotton broker's office. The pay was fifteen dollars a week. He attended night classes at City College of New York and, later, Columbia. Before long he had figured out how to trade commodities. Soon after that, he joined the army—stationed in Golden, Colorado, and Biloxi, Mississippi. By then he had ditched the old-world Karl for Charles. As a US citizen, he would adopt the all-American name of Charlie. And he would marry another immigrant, Yvette M. LeMarrec, who sailed to New York from France with fifty dollars to her name, like Charlie, all alone and knowing no one.

Charlie took a job at a shabby one-room import-export office. After his boss left for a trip, Charlie took control, firing up the phones and telegraph lines. He sold malt and spaghetti to Italy—as if Italy didn't already have enough spaghetti—and within a year had brought $1 million in business to the tiny firm. He bought up so much malt that the US Commerce Department threatened to slap a quota on him, prompting Charlie to fly to Washington and storm into the office of the assistant director of commerce, without an appointment.

"Sit down and listen," Charlie demanded, according to a 1967 *Life* profile.

He left with a higher quota. He was twenty-one.

Two years later, Bluhdorn went into business for himself, importing and exporting coffee, becoming such an expert he would regularly visit the coffee fields of Brazil, where he learned to speak Portuguese. Commodities trading was a gambler's game, with price swings as volatile as Bluhdorn's temperament. Standing in the commodity pit, he would issue thunderous tirades inflected with Yiddish—*Schmuck! Nebbish! Putz!* "That'll show those goddamn bluebloods!" he liked to bellow when he put one over on the more experienced speculators. "To Charlie, the only thing that was worth anything was doing the impossible," said Barry Diller, whom Bluhdorn would eventually enlist to run Paramount.

Bluhdorn usually won his bets. In 1958, he bought a failing auto-parts company called Michigan Bumper. The company, which had lost money three years in a row, owned a single run-down factory in Grand Rapids and a contract to make rear bumpers for Studebakers. Where others saw a dog, though, Bluhdorn saw opportunity. He merged the bumper company with a Houston auto-parts firm, which soon grew into a national auto-parts franchise with eight hundred stores. "He believed in buying incredibly cheap," said Dominique. "Everything was about the American Dream."

And the American Dream was there for the taking: its companies, its geniuses, its food (his favorite meal being hot dogs at Papaya King, on the Upper East Side, where he downed at least four hot dogs per visit). Soon he was gobbling up other auto-parts suppliers, which he bundled into a conglomerate he christened Gulf+Western, a conglomerate being Charlie's style of combining "a hodgepodge of different enterprises all roped together under one name," according to the *Life* profile. His company's new name signaled his ambition to stretch from the Gulf of Mexico to the western Canadian border. But "Hurricane Charlie," as he was dubbed in Robert Sam Anson's piece on him for *Vanity Fair*, wasn't content with peddling mufflers and spark plugs to Studebaker in South Bend, Indiana. He bought whatever seemed like a bargain—because he was "fascinated with taking something that was falling apart, a wreck job, and turning it around," said his daughter—and the wreck jobs he acquired included companies that produced rocket jets and musical instruments and baking supplies. "Aren't you tired of being a little $10 million company, just doing business day to day, when you could be a big $50 million company?" Bluhdorn pitched the owner of one business he desired. "We can give you everything you need so you can run it a bit harder, a bit faster, and make it a bit bigger."

By 1964, Gulf+Western was one of the fastest-growing companies on the New York Stock Exchange. The next year, with only $5 million in cash on hand, Bluhdorn borrowed $85 million from Chase Manhattan. It was one of the largest unsecured loans in history, three times as much as the combined annual worth of the companies comprising Gulf+Western. It landed Bluhdorn on the cover of *Time,* as one of its "Millionaires Under 40."

It also landed him in front of a House antitrust subcommittee, which was investigating whether Bluhdorn had secured the deal in return for funneling insider stock tips to Chase traders ahead of major Gulf+Western acquisitions.

Hurricane Charlie was a force of nature, determined to reshape everything in his path. "The more you're around Bluhdorn, the closer the moon is," said Lindsay Johnson, then the president of New Jersey Zinc, a mining company acquired by Gulf+Western in 1966. That year, Bluhdorn set his sights on Hollywood, an industry run by business titans as ruthless and ambitious as he was. "It's more than a place where streets are named after Sam Goldwyn and buildings after Bing Crosby," the director John Huston told the *New Yorker*'s Lillian Ross. "It's the jungle . . . a closed-in, tight, frantically inbred, and frantically competitive jungle. And the rulers of the jungle are predatory and fascinating and tough. . . . God, they are tough!"

Charlie Bluhdorn was determined to prove himself the toughest of them all. And true to his business model, the studio he set out to purchase was the biggest loser of them all.

BY THE TIME Bluhdorn showed up, Paramount Pictures needed a savior. The studio's Adolph Zukor was so old that he reportedly called

Barney Balaban, Paramount's chairman who was born in 1887, "the boy."

Stripped of its theater chain and sapped by a misguided investment in pay TV, the studio had been forced to sell off its stunning 3,664-seat palace of a movie theater in Times Square for cash. For more than a year, the studio had been fending off a hostile takeover spearheaded by Ernest Martin, the Broadway producer responsible for *Guys and Dolls* and *How to Succeed in Business Without Really Trying*, and Herbert Siegel, the president of General Artists eager to expand his media holdings.

But Bluhdorn had made his fortune by being able to see a company's underlying value, no matter how great its losses. "In Paramount, he saw this extraordinary jewel of an asset that could become something great if he got the right people," Dominique Bluhdorn explained. "He was obsessed with it from the beginning."

The studio had half a century of films, from *Double Indemnity* to *Duck Soup* to *Psycho* to *Breakfast at Tiffany's*, which it wasn't fully exploiting. Licensed to television, they'd be worth an estimated $200 million. Sensing an opportunity, Bluhdorn swooped in. He approached Siegel, whose takeover bid had grown increasingly nasty, and offered to buy out his interest in the deal. "Charlie flattered the hell out of him," a participant in the negotiations told *Life* in 1967. "He told Siegel his ideas for Paramount were marvelous, but there was so much bitterness he could never get them across. But he, Bluhdorn, could carry Siegel's banner, vindicate his ideas—and also Siegel would be a big hero with his backers for selling out at a big profit."

Siegel surrendered. Armed with the leverage—and the shares—he needed, Bluhdorn snapped up Paramount for $165 million, buying his way into yet another industry he knew nothing about. Just like that, Charlie Bluhdorn was a movie mogul. And unlike his far less glamorous investments in auto parts and supermarkets, which he left for others to run, Bluhdorn decided he would personally oversee Paramount. "I'm gonna rebuild this whole goddamned town!" he roared, throwing down the gauntlet to those who had spent their lives in the movie business.

Hollywood, not surprisingly, shunned him. "How many people want to invite the owner of New Jersey Zinc to dinner parties?" asked Michael Korda, who later worked for Bluhdorn as editor in chief of Simon & Schuster. Insiders sneered that Bluhdorn had bought Paramount so he could have his pick of young actresses ("the biggest purchase for pussy in the history of America," one insider called it, according to writer Kim Masters in her book *The Keys to the Kingdom*). They mocked his lack of experience ("a cliché of the showbiz novice"), his terrible taste ("the man simply has no sense for the artistic"), and his bad judgment ("the worst ideas known to man in the movie business"). Beneath the scorn, however, lay both envy and fear. Mel Brooks captured the prevailing sentiment in his 1976 film, *Silent Movie*, lampooning Gulf+Western as "Engulf & Devour."

Bluhdorn didn't care. Engulfing and devouring was his entire business model, and it had made him a multimillionaire. As he saw it, Hollywood was full of hacks and has-beens. "Half the people here are the accumulation of twenty years of errors!" he bellowed on the studio's backlot, striding through the set of *Bonanza*, NBC's popular TV Western, which was shot on the Paramount lot. At his very first board meeting, when the studio's top executives tried to explain why it was struggling so badly, he made no effort to contain himself. "Doubletalk!" he ranted. The executives were soon ex-executives, as Bluhdorn cleaned house, seeking to replace the putzes who surrounded him.

For a time he ran his studio himself, overseeing the process of making movies from top to bottom. "He was a monumental pain in the ass, a full-time kibitzer, and a tyrant," Korda wrote in his memoir *Another Life*, "but these are just the qualities that are lacking in most studios."

Bluhdorn was like the studio heads of old—"tempestuous, argumentative, emotional, shrewd," said Barry Diller, "[a] personality who would use any tactic, fair or unfair, to get his point across."

Bluhdorn's take-charge management style was on full display with *Is Paris Burning?* The war epic had a huge budget, a screenplay by Gore Vidal and Francis Ford Coppola, and a cast that included Kirk

Douglas and Orson Welles. But the movie was shaping up to be a box-office disaster, so Bluhdorn leapt into the editing room to try to salvage the film himself.

When Herbert Siegel heard that Bluhdorn was personally overseeing the editing, he was flabbergasted. "What the hell do you know about cutting a picture, for Christ's sake?" he asked his friend.

To which Bluhdorn replied, "I couldn't do any worse than they're doing!"

But Bluhdorn was no fool—he knew he needed help. Someone he could trust, both in taste and temperament. Someone to talk him down when he got carried away in his zeal for making deals. Someone who wouldn't hesitate, as one insider put it, to "tell Charlie Bluhdorn to go to hell."

What he needed, in Bluhdorn's view, was a "genius."

Then, on August 7, 1966, he found him in the *New York Times*.

"I LIKE IT, I Want It, Let's Sew It Up," read the *New York Times* headline of August 7, 1966. The article depicted the new breed of producer, spotlighting Robert Evans, then a thirty-six-year-old New York City dentist's son who had become a radio announcer, actor, and clothing-company executive (Evan-Picone, Inc., of which he was part owner, along with his brother, Charles, and Joe Picone). Evans had just been given a three-picture contract at 20th Century–Fox. Born Robert J. Shapera, he had embarked upon an almost magical life, thanks to his astonishing good looks and even more astonishing good luck. According to Evans in *The Kid Stays in the Picture*, it was a sunny day in 1956, as he tanned himself poolside at the Beverly Hills Hotel, where he was staying on Evan-Picone clothing business, when the husband of the movie star Norma Shearer told him his wife would like to meet him. Joining the conversation, Shearer asked if he was an actor. "No," replied Evans. "I'm in ladies' pants."

"He's perfect. He's Irving," she said, meaning Robert Evans was a dead ringer for her late husband, Irving Thalberg, the boy wonder who became head of production at MGM in 1925 at the age of twenty-six. To Evans's astonishment, Norma Shearer demanded that *he* play Irving Thalberg in *Man of a Thousand Faces*, a film about the horror star Lon Chaney, in which Shearer had approval over who would play her late husband.

An acting career commenced, after which Evans left ladies' pants to become an independent producer. Now, according to the story by *New York Times* reporter Peter Bart, he had become an up-and-comer with talent and taste. Whether it was Bart's description of Evans's relentless pursuit of books for movies, having "constructed the nucleus of a spy system in the New York publishing world," or the former actor's handsome headshot at the bottom of page D11, something about the piece captured Bluhdorn's attention. He threw down the paper and picked up the phone to inquire about this young Hollywood dynamo, Robert Evans.

Never mind that Evans had yet to actually produce a movie. Or that he was under contract at Fox. Somehow, some way, Bluhdorn knew this was just the genius he needed to revive Paramount. And when Bluhdorn wanted something, he got it. Or maybe Evans's ascension was merely the result of the same thing that got him noticed by Norma Shearer at the Beverly Hills Hotel pool. "He's gorgeous," Bluhdorn's wife, Yvette LeMarrec, told her husband when trying to persuade him to hire Evans as the head of the studio, according to the author Peter Biskind. "We've got to get a good-looking guy, really sexy, to run the company."

Either way, a few days later, Evans would write, he got a call from his lawyer Greg Bautzer. "Pack your bags, Bob," Bautzer told him. "We're going to New York."

"I've got plans, Greg," Evans replied.

"Break 'em," Bautzer said. "Charlie Bluhdorn, who just bought Paramount, wants to meet you. He read that article about you in Sunday's *New York Times*."

"What does he want to meet me for?"

"He's as tough and bright a guy as I've ever known, Bob. He's a doer, not a talker. He wouldn't ask me to waste my time if he didn't have something specific in mind."

Bluhdorn had something very specific in mind. "I want twenty pictures a year from you," he commanded Evans during their first meeting. "The Paramount *caca* in charge there now is ninety years old."

When Evans noted that he was still under contract to Fox, Bluhdorn's chief lieutenant, Marty Davis, told him that contracts were made to be broken. "If you're gonna run Paramount," Davis said, "you better be tougher than you are now."

IN 2011, AL Ruddy, the producer of *The Godfather*, would tell B. James Gladstone, author of the Bautzer biography, *The Man Who Seduced Hollywood*, that Bluhdorn wasn't attracted to Evans by that newspaper article alone, but more so by the urgings of Evans's attorney. "Greg Bautzer's the guy that set Bobby Evans up with Charlie Bluhdorn," Ruddy said.

Evans was soon living in London, in charge of European production for Paramount.

Bluhdorn kept trying to run the studio on his own. Looking to dominate television, he would snap up Desilu Productions—Lucille Ball's production company—for $17 million and ramp up film production to heights unseen since the Second World War. But the studio continued to stumble. Paramount lost *Funny Girl*, which Evans called "our ticket out of the basement," to Columbia, and instead produced a dog called *Darling Lili*, starring Julie Andrews, to indulge Bluhdorn's love of musicals. "The film's losses were so exorbitant," Evans wrote, "that, were it not for Charlie's brilliant manipulation of the numbers, Paramount Pictures would have been changed to Paramount Cemetery."

The final straw came at the world premiere of *Is Paris Burning?*, one of whose screenwriters—a young Francis Ford Coppola—would loom large in Charlie Bluhdorn's future. "We're going the wrong way," Evans told Bluhdorn, who had flown to Paris for the event. "If the product stinks, you can't sell it."

On this evening, as a galaxy of Paramount stars filed into the Paris Opera House, the product was personal: Bluhdorn had put his own stamp on the film in the editing room, and how it fared would reflect on his taste and judgment.

The lights went down. The curtain went up. After three torturous hours, when the lights went on again, it was Bluhdorn who was burning. His war epic was a bust, the latest in a string of Paramount flops. The *New York Times* savaged it as conveying "such a mishmash of melodrama and such a dumbfounding lack of suspense in the floodlike flow of action that it leaves one exhausted and irked."

Mad magazine, in its spoof, was even more direct, retitling the film *Is Paris Boring?*

Faced with another expensive loss, Bluhdorn considered selling the studio. Instead, he summoned Evans to New York, where he put him in charge of production. "Make pictures people want to see, not fancy-schmancy stuff people don't understand," Bluhdorn told Evans before dispatching him to LA. "I want to see tears, laughs, beautiful girls—pictures people in Kansas City want to see."

Evans returned to Hollywood to the same kind of mockery that had greeted Bluhdorn just a few years earlier. "Bluhdorn's Folly," one newspaper called him. "Bluhdorn's Blowjob," added a Hollywood scandal sheet. "Robert Evans is an outrage," *Life* sneered. "He has no more right to be where he is than a burglar. He has no credentials, none of the requirements for membership. Robert Evans has never even produced a film, doesn't know *that* about movies, so why should he be a boss of Paramount, with control of over 25 pictures a year, costing $100 million?" Evans, the magazine added for good measure, "is entirely too good-looking, too rich, too young, too lucky and too damned charming. The playboy peacock of Paramount."

*   *   *

HIS FIRST HIRE only fueled the skepticism: Evans brought on Peter Bart, the *Times* reporter whose profile had brought him to Bluhdorn's attention in the first place, to serve as his right-hand man. A journalist helping to run a movie studio? Even Bluhdorn paused when he heard the news.

"It's my ass on the line, Charlie," Evans told him. "If you're giving me the store, let me run it."

Bart, Evans knew, was a voracious reader, and the two men believed that books were the fuel that would power Paramount's resurgence.

"I told you the kid's got balls!" Bluhdorn beamed.

Evans threw himself into the job. "All he does is work," one of his girlfriends complained to a friend. "Even when he makes love, it's like—you know those wooden things they clap together when they start to film a scene? I keep having the feeling that someone's going to run in the room and bang one of them over the bed."

Evans heard the mockery, and he moved to silence the skeptics with the two things that count most in Hollywood: critical acclaim and financial success. He and Bluhdorn proved to be a good team. Paramount owned the option for Neil Simon's play *The Odd Couple*, and Evans lined up Billy Wilder to direct and Jack Lemmon and Walter Matthau to star in the film version. Bluhdorn was a fan of the project—until he saw the price tag. Wilder and Lemmon would come at a premium. "Evans," he raged, "I'll go back to coffee futures before I accept this blackmail!" From his suite at the Beverly Hills Hotel, Bluhdorn spent seventy-two hours working around the clock to hammer out a better deal, ultimately ditching Wilder for the more affordable Gene Saks. *The Odd Couple* became not only a comedy classic but Paramount's biggest hit since *The Ten Commandments* more than a decade earlier.

Evans proved to be as ruthless as Bluhdorn at deal making. Always on the lookout for bestsellers that could be turned into blockbusters, he heard from a B-movie director and producer named William Castle, who had optioned the rights to *Rosemary's Baby*, Ira Levin's horror novel about a young woman who is impregnated by Satan. Evans smelled money—but when Castle demanded that he be allowed to direct the movie, the studio chief "played hardball," as he wrote in his memoir. Evans threatened to sit on the project for three years, until Castle's contract with Paramount was up. "Or you can start tomorrow as producer," he told Castle, "and I'll double your deal."

Castle took the offer, and Evans handed *Rosemary's Baby* to Roman Polanski, an up-and-coming European director who had just made his first Hollywood film, *The Fearless Vampire Killers*. The result was "the smash hit of the summer," Evans wrote, but it "hadn't been enough to turn Paramount around."

The Gulf+Western board was pressuring Bluhdorn to sell off Paramount, and with it his dreams of being a Hollywood mogul. "Some Glitter Is Gone at Gulf+Western" read the headline in *BusinessWeek*.

On August 9, 1969, Bluhdorn flew to LA. "This time the threats sounded real: the studio would have to be closed down," Evans recalled. He picked Bluhdorn up from the Beverly Hills Hotel, and they returned to Woodland to decide what to do. Before they could start, however, Evans received an urgent phone call: Polanski's wife, Sharon Tate, who was due to give birth to their first child, had been brutally murdered by the followers of Charles Manson, along with four others.

Shaken by the news, Evans went back into the living room, where Bluhdorn was pacing impatiently. "Come on, Evans!" he barked. "Let's go outside and get started."

"I can't, I can't, Charlie," Evans sobbed, starting to cry.

Bluhdorn came over and put his arm around Evans. "What is it, Bob? What happened?"

Evans told him the news, and the two men went outside, where they sat beneath one of Woodland's towering trees. There, they mourned the passing both of Evans's friends, and the end of an era in Hollywood.

BLUHDORN WAS OUT of time. His board wanted blood. Despite the box-office uptick under Evans, Paramount continued to struggle.

Bluhdorn needed cash, and he needed it fast. So he supposedly turned to someone he knew could help: a Sicilian financier who ran money for the Mafia.

Michele Sindona, a hustler with an insatiable appetite for the kind of business deals that sometimes ran afoul of the law, had put together a sprawling empire of banking and real estate interests that reached from the Mob to the Vatican. He also owed Bluhdorn a favor. A few years earlier, Sindona had run into trouble when he tried to take over a paper company, drawing unwanted attention from antitrust regulators. Bluhdorn reportedly swooped to the rescue. On the phone from New York, he told Sindona to meet him at the Grand Hotel in Rome the next morning. The meeting was over in an hour. Bluhdorn agreed to buy the paper company for $15.5 million, and a beautiful friendship was formed. "Of all the men he came to do business with in America," Sindona's biographer Nick Tosches wrote in his book *Power on Earth*, "Sindona admired none more than he did Charles Bluhdorn."

Now, with Paramount on the line, Bluhdorn made a move that Vito Corleone himself would have admired: He called upon Sindona to do a service for him. First, Bluhdorn traded shares in one of his company's subsidiaries (whose primary asset was the rights to profits to the upcoming box office bomb *Darling Lili*) for a stake in Italy's largest construction and real estate firm, Società Generale Immobiliare (SGI), of which Sindona was the major shareholder (along with the Vatican). Then, SGI purchased half interest in Paramount's sprawling backlot—acres of prime Hollywood real estate that the studio used to construct and house sets for outdoor scenes. It wasn't clear what possible value the property could have to SGI, given that zoning laws severely restricted what could be built on the space. But such details were beside the point—this was about Sindona repaying a debt of gratitude to Bluhdorn. "I always sell a company for less than it is worth to someone I want to please," Sindona once said.

The deal, according to Peter Bart, sent "a shock wave through Hollywood."

The town was no stranger to mobsters: Bugsy Siegel had helped oversee the Mafia's enforcement arm, known as Murder, Incorporated, during the 1930s. But Bluhdorn had effectively turned the Paramount backlot into what Bart would call "a secret beachhead for the Mob."

Before long, the place looked like a scene straight out of a gangster film. "Deputations of Italians were soon wandering the lot arguing about the disposition of the property," Bart wrote. "Many of the soundstages were not in use—a problem Sindona resolved by leasing stages to a producer of porn movies."

Sindona himself met with an unhappy ending. After his banking empire collapsed, he faked his own kidnapping to gather blackmail material in Italy so that he could "persuade authorities in Italy and the United States to modify some of the charges pending against him," according to *Mother Jones* magazine—only to be found guilty on sixty-five counts of fraud and perjury. Extradited to Italy in 1980, he died in jail, poisoned by cyanide—"a favorite Mob medicine," as Bart noted. To the end, however, he maintained that Bluhdorn was innocent of any involvement in his fraudulent schemes. "His only crime," Sindona told Nick Tosches, "was to be my friend." ("As far as I know, my father did not have a close relationship with Michele Sindona," said Paul Bluhdorn. "Knowing my father, the chances of him having Mafia contacts are zero.")

The SGI deal bought Bluhdorn some time. He was soon boasting that he now had "virtually limitless funding for expansion, even to the point of allowing him to launch hostile takeovers of A&P and Pan American Airlines," Bart wrote in *GQ* magazine in 1997. "In retrospect, it's easy to see that Bluhdorn was over the edge—a maverick bent on self-destruction."

Until then, he would put everything on the line, at least when it came to being affiliated with a recognizable name. "At one point he wanted to buy the Simmons Mattress Company," said his son, Paul. "And people said, 'Why would you want to buy a mattress company?' And he said, 'Everybody's heard of Simmons! It's a famous name!'"

Paramount was the biggest name of all. But if the studio were going to survive, it still needed a hit, something to prove to Hollywood (and the board) that Bluhdorn and Evans could overcome years of financial losses and produce movies that people would actually pay to see—at a time when attendance was sinking to new lows. "The movie industry is collapsing. *Everybody* knows that," wrote Vincent Canby in the *New York Times*. "All you have to do is read the financial pages ('Proxy War Threatened at 20th Century-Fox') or look at a marquee "My Secret Life" at Loew's State 2), or listen to your friends ('I read all of your reviews even though I never go')."

"We need a miracle, not a movie," Bluhdorn lamented.

It arrived on Christmas Eve 1970, in the form of a tearjerker based on a slim script and an even slimmer novel by a Yale professor named Erich Segal, who spun a slim story about a college girl dying from a terminal illness. From these slim beginnings grew a giant of a movie that would cause audiences and readers worldwide to fall apart. "Love Means Never Having to Say You're Sorry," read the posters.

In theater after theater, the audience "turned into one big Kleenex," Evans would write. Yes, the girl dies, but Charlie Bluhdorn—and Paramount—were reborn.

"America!" Bluhdorn bellowed when Evans took him outside that Christmas into the snowy New York night where, with a flick of a switch, the dark Gulf+Western Building blazed with twelve-story letters spelling out *LOVE STORY*. "That's my building," cried Bluhdorn. "It's the first real Christmas I've ever had."

Lines would soon stretch around blocks outside theaters in every city in America, and soon the world.

For Charlie Bluhdorn and his boy wonder Robert Evans, the miracle was a reprieve, not a rescue—enough to keep the studio afloat, but not for long. They needed an even bigger blockbuster, a phenomenon that could take Paramount out of the basement and put it back on the path toward its former glory.

They needed yet another miracle.

A miracle that, as it happened, had already taken place.

4

THE BESTSELLING WRITER IN THE WORLD

In July 1968, five months after Bluhdorn was supposedly cutting a deal with the Mafia's moneyman, Mario Puzo turned in his rough draft of *The Godfather* to his publisher—not because he was proud of the work, but because, as always, he was broke. "I needed the final $1,200 advance payment from Putnam to take my wife and kids to Europe," he wrote. His wife, Erika, hadn't been back to her native Germany since coming to New York in 1949, and Puzo had promised he would take her and the children on a vacation to Europe.

"Suddenly, one day he brought in the whole manuscript," his Putnam editor Bill Targ recounted for *True* magazine in 1971, "a rough draft but complete."

"Goodbye," said the author. "I'm taking my family to Europe tomorrow."

Targ felt sure that was a veiled request for cash.

"But Mario, we can't give you that much money," he said.

Puzo assured him he had "plenty of credit cards."

"Mario, the day of reckoning must come," said Targ.

"*The Godfather* will take care of it. Or I'll sell my house," said Puzo.

Credit cards in hand, Puzo and his family went straight to the airport. "I need six first-class seats to Rome," he told the attendant at the Alitalia ticket counter, according to *Life* photographer Robert

Peterson. Informed that there were only two first-class seats left, Puzo slid $200 across the counter. "I found four more seats for you," the attendant informed him.

Puzo and his family flew off to Europe—London, Cannes, Monte Carlo, Wiesbaden—where Puzo financed the trip (and the gambling) by cashing $500 checks against his American Express card. "I had no money," he wrote, "but I had a great collection of credit cards."

As he usually did when he had access to cash, Puzo headed straight for the casinos. He proceeded to gamble away his advance at the best resorts on the French Riviera. "Things did not look good," said his son Anthony.

"I had failed as a father," Puzo later wrote. "I wasn't worried. If worse came to worse we could always sell our house. Or I could go to jail. Hell, better writers had gone to jail. No sweat."

When the family got home, Puzo owed the credit card companies more than $8,000. "I was in debt up to my ass and I had no job," he admitted.

HIS GAMBLING, IN fact, had been the biggest obstacle to completing the book, while simultaneously providing him with the primary motivation to keep going. Day after day, he had continued to pound away at his manual Olympia typewriter, taking breaks only to conduct research—a pursuit that sometimes doubled as a cover for Puzo's other, less lofty impulses. Sometime, most likely in 1967, not long after he had received his $12,500 from Paramount, he is said to have made one of his regular trips to Las Vegas. He rationalized that it would provide material for his writing. "I even had a rationalization for losing all that money," he told the *New York Times* in 1979. "I told myself I was really researching."

The trip provided Puzo with a wealth of material, even as it consumed his cash. Landing in Vegas, he headed straight to the casino where Frank Sinatra had once been a part owner: the Sands. In those days, the place was at its swinging, ring-a-ding-ding peak, the legendary desert palace where the original *Ocean's Eleven* had been filmed, where Sinatra and members of his Rat Pack (Dean Martin, Joey Bishop, and Sammy Davis Jr.) performed in the Copa Room. As in much of Vegas in those days, the casino's Mob ties ran deep—all the way back to its founders, Meyer Lansky, known as "the financial genius of the underworld," and Joseph "Doc" Stacher, who put up the money to open the town as a future gambling mecca in 1952, when top underworld figures, including New York boss Carlo Gambino, would fly out to meet with their West Coast counterparts.

At the Sands, Puzo looked like any other schlub from the suburbs: casually dressed to the point of disarray, a cigar jutting from his jaw, placing his bets at the roulette wheel. It was the day shift, and he wouldn't have stood out in any way, except for two things. First, roulette in those days was mostly a lady's game. And second, Puzo seemed more interested in quizzing the croupier about the Sands and how it operated than in following his bets.

"And that made me walk over to the table to find out what the fuck he was doing," said Ed Walters, the pit boss on duty that day.

Walters was a card hustler from New York whose talents at the poker and pool tables, along with a sixth sense for cheaters, had earned him the respect of a lieutenant for Carlo Gambino. Walters was offered a one-way ticket to Vegas, where he was installed at the Sands "on a very special assignment."

A dealer was cheating, and Walters was assigned to catch him in the act. And what happened to the dealer when Walters busted him? "All I'll say is, I promise you he never stole from us or anyone else again," Walters said.

For his services, Walters was rewarded with a plum job at the Sands. Now, as he walked over to the roulette table where Puzo was questioning the croupier, he decided to listen in before introducing himself.

Puzo asked about the casino's operations. *Was he a reporter?* Walters wondered.

He asked about the shadowy forces behind the casino. *Was he FBI?*

He asked about Frank Sinatra. *Was this fucking guy nuts?*

Whoever the guy was, Walters couldn't figure out his angle. "He had done a lot of background work," he said. "He brought up names and brought up people. He had some reason to being doing this, but I didn't know what his reason was."

Suspicious, Walters alerted the casino's manager, Carl Cohen, who became famous that same year for punching out a drunken and aggressive Frank Sinatra one night as the entertainer demanded more credit. Cohen, who knew people in New York publishing, made a few calls.

"He's a writer," Cohen told Walters. "He's writing a book on the Mob and the families of New York. Keep an eye on him."

The next day Walters introduced himself.

Puzo must have been excited to meet Walters. He wanted his Mafia novel to feel authentic, and Walters knew plenty. This—plus the gambling—was why Puzo had come to Vegas, the spot he loved, next to home, more than any place on Earth. "Should I go to heaven, give me no haloed angels riding snow-white clouds, no, not even the sultry houris of the Moslems," he once wrote. "Give me rather a vaulting, red-walled casino with bright lights, bring on horned devils as dealer. Let there be a Pit Boss in the Sky who will give me unlimited credit. And if there is a merciful God in our Universe he will decree that the Player have for *all* eternity, an Edge against the House."

Now, at least, Puzo had the pit boss. And while Walters wasn't offering unlimited credit, he was dispensing something almost as good: *material.* All it would cost Puzo was whatever he was willing to wager. So long as Puzo kept betting, Walters kept talking. The roulette wheel turned and the writer's chips diminished and Walters answered his questions to the degree he felt "proper."

"I was impressed by how much he already knew about the families of New York," Walters said. "He had done all kinds of research. His big interest was the Five Families. He knew who they were and he knew their names. He referred to them as the Mob. But it was also evident to me that he had never met any of the family members, in New York or anywhere else."

As one day stretched to two, and then three, Puzo's questions grew deeper. *Did Carlo Gambino really come to the Sands to play?*

"No comment," Walters said.

If they had to contact Meyer Lansky, how did they do it?

"No comment."

Out came the notebook, which Walters told Puzo to put away.

"People would write down numbers on the roulette wheel," Walters explained. "That's what I thought he was doing, originally. When I found out he wanted to take notes on what I said, I said, 'No, don't take any notes.'"

What is Carlo Gambino really like, as a person?

"He's actually a very mild-mannered guy, very smart," Walters replied of the all-powerful head of New York's most powerful crime family. "Very soft, doesn't brag, but his word is law. He comes from the old Sicilian school of less-said-the-better. Never gives instructions more than one sentence long. Among the Italian Americans who acted and reacted crazy, Carlo is the quietest and the most thoughtful. Of all the guys in New York, he is the sanest. He thinks everything out."

Is Gambino ruthless?

"What do you mean by ruthless?" Walters replied.

Well, he kills . . .

"Hold it, no, no, you don't understand," Walters told Puzo. "Mario, if Carlo Gambino was sitting right next to you, you would feel totally at peace. Now, one of his men may throw you out the window, but he's a very peaceful guy, very methodical."

Such details, straight from someone who knew Gambino, were invaluable to Puzo, who incorporated them into the character of his novel's protagonist:

> *Don Vito Corleone was a man to whom everybody came for help, and never were they disappointed. He made no empty promises, nor*

the craven excuse that his hands were tied by more powerful forces than himself. It was not necessary that he be your friend, it was not even important that you had no means with which to repay him. Only one thing was required. That you, you yourself, proclaim your friendship. And then, no matter how poor or powerless the suppli-cant, Don Corleone would take that man's troubles to his heart.

Puzo wasn't content with gathering details on New York's most powerful Mob boss. His novel's cast of characters included Johnny Fontane, a Mob-connected crooner based on Frank Sinatra. "How often does Sinatra perform here?" Puzo asked Walters.

"He's our top entertainer," Walters replied. "We respect him, but he's not a boss." The answer didn't seem to satisfy Puzo. "He kept try-ing to see if Sinatra was connected or in the Mob," said Walters.

"Sinatra is not liked by everybody in the Mob," Walters told Puzo. "They respect Sinatra, but they love Dean."

All of which went into the book, helping Puzo paint a portrait of a tempestuous, hard-drinking, sex-obsessed, almost over-the-hill crooner "who would grow up to hold the hearts of fifty million women in his hands," a character that so infuriated Sinatra that he would threaten Mario Puzo with physical violence.

The days and nights stretched on, Puzo at the roulette wheel, Wal-ters in the pit, the author and his source, until Puzo finally popped the most important question of all:

Could the Sands extend me some credit?

Puzo was out of cash, but not out of questions, and he needed money to continue playing and researching.

Walters almost laughed out loud. Puzo surely didn't have enough cash in the bank to be worthy of any credit. But the pit boss once again referred the question to Carl Cohen, who once again called his publishing contacts in New York. From across the floor, Walters saw Cohen hold up two fingers: Puzo had been approved for two grand.

*   *   *

ONE EVENING, AS the roulette wheel spun, a shadowy figure appeared at the table. A gray-haired, distinguished-looking gentleman: Hy Bedol, "one of the wise old guys," as Walters described him. Bedol, an associate of Meyer Lansky, had worked for Lansky's casino operations in Cuba before the revolution.

Walters pointed the man out to Puzo. "Would you like to speak with Hy Bedol?"

"Does he know anybody in the Mob?" Puzo asked.

Walters nearly laughed out loud again. "I'm thinking: *This is fucking funny. This writer is asking, 'Does he know anybody in the Mob?'* And he's talking to one of the most powerful guys, Hy Bedol, who reported directly to Lansky, who ran the major gambling operations of Vegas, Chicago, Detroit, everywhere."

For the next night or two, Puzo and Bedol spoke at the roulette table, Bedol talking as long as Puzo kept betting. Hy Bedol was not impressed. "He's got so many things mixed up," he told Walters. "He thinks we're all killers and that people who don't pay their bets in Vegas get shot or killed in the desert. So I'm trying to help him understand that we're not all killers. We don't beat up people. We're businessmen, running a legitimate casino licensed by the state of Nevada."

In the casino, Puzo learned about the hierarchy of the Mob, the invisible walls that kept the low-level soldiers from knowing anything about the workings of the broader organization. "Eddie, this guy thinks the Mob eats at the best restaurants," Bedol told Walters. "He doesn't know that most of the guys in New York couldn't order off the menu, had never been in any restaurant."

Once again, it all made its way into Puzo's novel, this time in the form of Moe Greene, "a handsome hood who had made his rep as a Murder Incorporated executioner in Brooklyn" who went on to become "the first person to see the possibilities of Las Vegas and built one of the first casinos on the Strip."

As Walters told it, the Sands rewarded Puzo with what would become perhaps the most famous line in *The Godfather*. One night, the actor David Janssen was causing a ruckus on the casino floor, apparently after having too much to drink. At that moment, Janssen was starring in the hit TV series *The Fugitive*, and none of the players or dealers or pit bosses wanted to approach him, much less attempt to subdue him. So Walters called Carl Cohen, who brought the actor to heel simply by speaking a few words to him.

"What'd you do?" Walters asked after Janssen was subdued.

"I made him an offer he couldn't refuse," Cohen replied.

"That buzzed around the pit," Walters said. "Then a wheel dealer . . . told that to Mario Puzo."

In *The Godfather*, Don Corleone would use the line to explain how he planned to convince a movie producer to give Johnny Fontane a part in his movie: *I'm gonna make him an offer he can't refuse.*

Was one of the most famous lines in cinema history first uttered by a suave casino manager subduing a famous actor in the Sands? Or did it come, as Francis Ford Coppola wrote in his introduction to the fiftieth-anniversary edition of Puzo's novel, from Maria La Conti Puzo, an Italian American mother raising seven kids alone in Hell's Kitchen? "Mario told me that all of the great dialogue, those quotable lines he put into the mouth of Don Corleone, were actually spoken by Mario's mother," Coppola wrote. "Yes, 'an offer he can't refuse,' 'revenge is a dish that tastes best when it is cold,' and 'a man who doesn't spend time with his family can never be a real man,' among many others, were sayings he heard from his own mother's lips."

Whatever the source of the line, Puzo's "research" in Las Vegas proved costly. When he ran out of credit at the Sands, he moved on to the Tropicana, where he lost so much money that the bosses there advised him not to leave town until he paid up.

Worried, Puzo called up Walters at the Sands: *Were their threats real?*

Walters told Puzo he was safe, as long as he stayed in Vegas. "In those days we had a rule—that there would be no contracts played out in Las Vegas," Walters said. "That was the rule. No one was ever, let's just say, hurt or damaged in Las Vegas. Out in Lake Mead, or in the desert, that's something different. But in town, you never hurt or did anything you shouldn't do to anybody in the sheriff's domain, you know? That was our agreement with the sheriff."

Still, Walters knew the guys at the Tropicana—"a rough fuckin' crew"—and he advised Puzo to take them seriously. Besides, the Sands wasn't going to let Puzo leave Vegas, either. "He couldn't get out of the Sands," said Walters. "He owed us thirteen thousand. We weren't gonna let Puzo out of the place just 'cause he wanted to go back to New York. In those days, we could control getting airline tickets."

Then, according to Walters, a savior appeared beside Puzo at the roulette wheel. The slicked-back hair. The silken voice. The thousand-dollar suit and the killer smile. The lifelong knack for negotiation.

Robert Evans.

"Bob Evans was smooth," Walters said. Evans had somehow heard about Puzo's gambling debts. "How? I still don't know. He wouldn't tell me."

Paramount's chief of production knew a bit about gambling—and about losing—having once blown half his annual salary at the Riviera before Sidney Korshak, said to be the casino's silent owner, forced him to close out his markers and walk away from the tables. "He came up to Puzo right at the table, and they started talking," said Walters, who never learned the details of what was said—only that Evans worked out Puzo's Sands debts with Carl Cohen, and presumably the Tropicana. Puzo was allowed to return home to finish his book, armed with the research that had almost cost him his life. "Evans convinced the Sands to let this guy go back to New York, and everyone would end up getting paid," said Walters. "And it turns out everybody did."

As with many tales involving *The Godfather*, it is difficult to confirm whether Puzo actually hobnobbed with a mobster in Vegas. Walters told parts of the story in a British documentary, *The Godfather and the Mob*, and in an oral history for the University of Nevada, Las Vegas. Puzo never corroborated or commented on it directly, but did say of his inspiration, "Let's say I parlayed what I knew about people in gambling with people in the business world . . . and I put two and two together and constructed Mafia types," he told writer George Mandel for *True*. "Of course, I read everything I could on the underworld. But mainly it's from my experience in the gambling world."

Puzo insisted he never met Evans until after the book was published. As for Evans, he didn't discuss rescuing Puzo from his debts in Vegas, but he did confirm that the studio fronted several cash advances to the "destitute" Puzo while he was working on the book. "We kept Mario alive with $5,000 here and $7,500 there," he told *Variety*.

WHILE PUZO WAS on his fun-filled vacation with his family in Europe, the real world was descending into chaos. College students being drafted to fight in Vietnam. The recent assassinations of Robert Kennedy and Martin Luther King Jr. The full-scale police riot at the Democratic National Convention in Chicago. It was a tumultuous moment in the country's history, full of dread and explosive violence, and the somber and uncertain mood worked its way into Puzo's novel. To a nation in flames, the Corleones, with their deep-rooted sense of honor, their devotion to family, their feelings of woundedness and betrayal, and their willingness to resort to violence to defend their hard-won empire, would seem less like fiction and more like a dark and mythic reflection of the American Dream.

Meanwhile, as Puzo gambled the last of his advance away in Europe, the draft of his novel he had turned in to his publisher didn't even seem to be on his mind. He would deal with that when he returned. After all, he had issued strict orders not to show the rough draft to anyone. "It had to be polished," he said. But while he was away, Putnam disregarded his instructions. A copy was sent to Ralph Daigh, the vice president of Fawcett paperbacks, who was vacationing on Nantucket. Daigh devoured *The Godfather* in one sitting, then called Putnam to ask if there had been any paperback offers for the book.

"Yes, one for $35,000," he was told.

"I'll give you $350,000 for it right now," Daigh said.

"I'll have to ask his agent," replied the Putnam rep.

Puzo's agent at the time was the fierce Candida Donadio. Then among the top New York literary agents, if not the very top, Donadio represented some of the most acclaimed writers in the business, from Philip Roth to Joseph Heller to John Cheever. A small woman with large black eyes, she always seemed to be in her Midtown Manhattan office, "hiding behind her desk and melting away with shyness," said Puzo's friend and colleague Bruce Jay Friedman, who most likely introduced Puzo and Donadio. Of Sicilian ancestry, she was tougher than she looked. "I've read it and liked it, but I'm not in love, which I can do in my personal life, but not in my professional, so I must pass," was Donadio's famous missive when rejecting an author's submission.

With Mario Puzo's latest, she was obviously in love. Deeply, madly. Not only with the book, but also with the money.

When Puzo got home from Europe, another $8,000 in debt, he went straight to Donadio's office. He was hoping, he wrote, that she would "pull a slick magazine assignment out of her sleeve and bail me out, as she had so often done in the past."

As for the novel, he felt it was yet another failure. If he had ever thought he was writing a masterpiece, he said, he would have written it better. He felt *The Godfather* was just another example of what he had always done: dreaming up worlds for a paycheck.

Instead, Donadio informed Puzo that Putnam had just gotten an offer of $375,000 for the paperback rights to *The Godfather*.

Puzo was dumbfounded: *$375,000!* The amount was unthinkable. At the time, the record for a paperback sale was $400,000. Puzo told Donadio he didn't believe a word of it. So she picked up the phone and called his editor at Putnam, Bill Targ.

Targ, to Donadio's surprise, informed Puzo that the amount was incorrect. It wasn't $375,000—the offer had already gone up to $400,000. Targ was holding out for even more, hoping to break the previous record for a sale of paperback rights.

Puzo still didn't believe it. He had every reason for doubt. Eight publishers had rejected his outline for *The Godfather*. His last novel had netted him only $3,000. How could this be?

Targ asked Puzo if he would like to speak with Clyde Taylor, the subsidiary rights director at Putnam who was handling the negotiations.

"No," Puzo said. "I have absolute confidence in any man who would turn down $375,000."

Targ invited his disbelieving author for a late-afternoon lunch at the Algonquin Hotel. When Puzo arrived, he looked despondent.

"What's wrong, Mario?" Targ asked.

"I'm broke," Puzo replied. "I just had to borrow $800 from a loan shark."

That was when Targ gave him the news: Taylor had closed the deal that morning. Fawcett had bought the paperback rights to *The Godfather* for a record-breaking $410,000. In today's money, it was more than $3 million.

"I don't believe a fucking word you've told me," Puzo told his editor. "This must be some kind of Madison Avenue put-on."

When the reality finally sunk in, Puzo went straight to the Magazine Management offices where he had been freelancing and quit, celebrating the news of his book sale with colleagues over drinks. Then he went to the garage to retrieve his car, so he could go home and share the news with his family.

While he was waiting for his car, Puzo called his brother Anthony Cleri from a phone booth. Cleri had supported him with loans for most of their lives: whenever Puzo would call him, "frantic for a few hundred bucks to pay the mortgage or buy the kids shoes," Cleri "always came through." For his patience and generosity, Puzo had promised him 10 percent of whatever he earned on *The Godfather*. With an even split of the paperback rights between Puzo and Putnam, his brother stood to see a little over $20,000.

Cleri had always been home when Puzo *needed* money, but now that Puzo was calling with news that he was finally able to pay him back, he wasn't home. So Puzo called his mother, the fiery, endlessly quotable Maria Le Conti Puzo, whose spirit and speech had fueled her son's depiction of Don Corleone. He told her his book had sold for $410,000.

"Forty thousand dollars?" she blurted.

"No, Mom," Puzo told her. "Four hundred and ten thousand dollars."

After two more attempts, the number finally sank in. "Don't tell nobody!" his mother told him, advising him to say he received $40,000 "to avoid relatives asking for money," said Puzo's son Anthony.

It took Puzo two hours to drive home to Long Island in the summer traffic. When he arrived, his wife, Erika, was asleep in front of the TV. Puzo kissed her on the cheek.

"Honey, we don't have to worry about money anymore," he told her. "I just sold my book for $410,000."

She smiled and closed her eyes again.

"I started getting annoyed," Puzo would write of this pivotal passage in his life. "Nobody seemed to think this was a big deal. My whole life was going to change. I didn't have to worry about money. It was almost like not having to worry about dying."

"Did you hear?" he asked his older sister over the phone.

"You got forty thousand dollars for the book," she said flatly. "Mama called me."

"No!" Puzo said, exasperated. "It was four hundred ten thousand dollars."

"Now I got the reaction I wanted," Puzo wrote. "There was a little scream over the phone and an excited minute of conversation."

When he called his mother back to ask how she could have made such a mistake after so many explanations, she scoffed. "I no maka a mistake," she explained. "I don't wanta tell her."

Puzo fell into bed, exhausted but exhilarated. The next morning, he awoke to find the bed surrounded by his wife and five kids.

"What was that you said last night?" his wife asked. Perhaps she had just realized that she was married to one of the world's most financially successful authors.

Later that morning, Puzo called Putnam and asked Targ for a $100,000 advance. Driving back to the city, he picked up the check from the publisher and took it to the bank where he had so often bounced checks on his overdrawn account. "I brought the check to the guy who used to sneer at my overdrafts and reluctantly cash my paychecks and remind me about my late payment," Puzo told his colleague Jules Siegel. "It was so satisfying to watch him grovel."

He paid off his debts, his agent's commission, and the 10 percent cut to his brother.

After only three months, Puzo was back at Putnam asking for another $100,000.

Bill Targ was stunned. *What had happened to the $100,000 he had just given Puzo?*

"A hundred grand doesn't last forever," Puzo said.

ON MARCH 10, 1969, *The Godfather*—with its stark black-and-white cover of strings hanging down from a puppeteer's cross designed by S. Neil Fujita, the modernist graphic designer who had also created the pinprick cover for Truman Capote's *In Cold Blood* and the logo for NBC's *Today* show—was published in hardback.

The critical acclaim was immediate. The *Saturday Review* hailed the novel as "a staggering triumph."

It was a "big, blunt, battering ram of a book, one intended to shock and to stun," the magazine gushed, praising Puzo for crafting his prose "so skillfully that the most outrageous episodes seem totally natural. All the blood, all the slaughter, all the raw sex are in consonance with the people about whom he is writing."

In the *Washington Post*, novelist Geoffrey Wolff called it "an epic of crime, sung in the plain idiom of the streets" and hailed its author for managing "to suspend moral judgment of the killing and torture he describes."

Most reviews marveled at the novel's compulsive narrative. "You can't stop reading it," reported *New York* magazine, "and you'll find it hard to stop dreaming about it because it transports you to a world of experience where some of the values are strikingly familiar and some are like nothing you've ever encountered but have a logic all their own."

The Godfather was "bound to be hugely successful," the *New York Times* predicted, "and not simply because the Mafia is in the news. Mr. Puzo's novel is a voyeur's dream, a skillful fantasy of violent personal power without consequences."

The *Times* was right. Readers had been eager for a glimpse into the world of organized crime ever since the Kefauver hearings in the 1950s. *The Godfather* crept up the *New York Times* bestseller list throughout the spring, and by April 27, it was at No. 2, closing in on Philip Roth's *Portnoy's Complaint* for the top spot. "If Philip Roth has created a Jewish mother who can actually give you heartburn, Mario Puzo has created a Sicilian father who will make you shiver every time you stroll on Mulberry Street," the legendary sports journalist Dick Schaap raved in the *Times*. "What Roth has done for masturbation, Puzo has done for murder."

In a sense, Puzo had tapped into something even deeper than the age-old thrill of violence. As the author Stefan Kanfer put it in his biography of Marlon Brando, *Somebody*, Puzo fed "the public's desperate appetite for rationality and control—even at the hands of criminals. Readers, battered by too much news, too much information about strife at home and abroad, made *The Godfather* a phenomenal bestseller. It was as if they needed to believe a Vito Corleone existed, that . . . a Mafia don could exact revenge against wrongdoers, seeking his own kind of justice, controlling vast swatches of modern life from his living room."

The most important critic, though, wasn't a book reviewer.

Sometime between rough draft and publication, Puzo's pages had fallen into the hungry hands of the takeover titan Charlie Bluhdorn. On a rare getaway with his family at their residence in the South of France, he emerged one morning from his bedroom, still in his pajamas, clutching the pages like a prized contract.

"This is *terrific!*" he roared in his Viennese accent, thrusting the massive stack toward his teenaged son, Paul.

"I want you to read it and tell me what you think of it," he told Paul.

"It was *huge,*" said Paul. "Pages and pages, the typed manuscript, probably weighed five pounds, with a rubber band around it, and it was *The Godfather.*"

Paul retired to his bedroom, began reading and could not stop until he was done.

"Do you think it would make a good movie?" asked Charlie.

Not only would it make a good movie; it would make a great one, said Paul.

On September 21, 1969, after twenty-six weeks on the bestseller list, *The Godfather* reached No. 1, where it would remain until it was dethroned by *The French Lieutenant's Woman* on February 8, 1970.

The novel went through reprint after reprint, as bookstores rushed to keep up with the demand. In modern-day parlance, Puzo had discovered a way to make mobsters *relatable.* "It was Puzo's genius to turn them into family men," observed author Maria Laurino in the *Wall Street Journal.* "All those elaborate passages in *The Godfather* which describe the family patriarch presiding over weddings and baptisms and then ordering murders gave a new dimension to the image of the Italian father. Movies had always shown the murders but never told us that these men had daughters and godchildren."

Breaking with tradition, Fawcett rushed *The Godfather* into paperback while its hardcover edition was still on the *Times* bestseller list. It instantly set a record for the largest first printing for a paperback—3.1 million copies—and soon became the fastest-selling and bestselling fiction paperback of all time. Eventually translated into more than seventeen languages, the novel reached No. 1 on bestseller lists across Europe and, soon, the world.

At age forty-eight, Puzo found himself flush with the literary and financial success he had hungered for all his life. With each new copy of *The Godfather* that sold, he pocketed a percentage. He wasn't being hailed as the next Dostoyevsky, but he had climbed higher up the literary ladder than any pulp-fiction writer before him. Above all, he was no longer the family *chooch*—he had far surpassed the immigrant dreams of his parents. He moved his family to a larger, fancier house on Long Island's South Shore, and he enjoyed having plenty of cash to blow at the casinos, though he found that being flush took away some of the thrill. "When I used to really need that $5,000, I was trying to win at craps," he said. "There was a special excitement. Now that I'm a success, some of the fun is gone. Still, all things considered, I'll keep the success."

What he could do without, he discovered, was all the unwanted attention. "I loved the money," he wrote. "But I didn't really like being 'famous.' I found it quite simply distressing. I never much liked parties, never liked talking to more than two or three people at one time. I dislike interviews and having my picture taken."

Puzo had to be talked into appearing on NBC's *Today* show. "It's just damn uncomfortable," he confessed. "It's not a writer's medium. Interviews come out sounding like someone I didn't even know; and I couldn't even blame the interviewers. I did make those dumb statements, but I didn't say them like *that*. So I quit on TV and all publicity, including interviews."

With success also came suspicion. To some readers—including many in the Mob circles that Puzo had brought to life—the book seemed *too* good. Rumors began to swirl. The Mafia, according to one account, had paid Puzo a million dollars to write *The Godfather* as a public relations con. Or perhaps the author had an undisclosed connection with the Mafia, given how vividly he had portrayed the Five Families. Or maybe he was even a Mafia man himself.

Puzo laughed at the thought of it. Him? A wiseguy? "I treasure the compliment," he wrote, adding, "*The Godfather* was a romanticized version of what the Mafia is like. They're really not that nice."

The novel's authenticity, he explained, came from a combination of his mother's gift of language, his gambling habit, and a life spent listening to Mafia stories in New York City. "I'm ashamed to admit that I wrote *The Godfather* entirely from research," he said. "I never met a real honest-to-god gangster. I knew the gambling world pretty good, but that's all. After the book became famous, I was introduced to a few gentlemen related to the material. They were flattering. They refused to believe that I had never been in the rackets. They refused to believe that I had never had the confidence of a Don. But all of them loved the book."

By then, *The Godfather* had become something of a bible to the real-life gangsters who saw themselves in its pages. Somehow, the man who spent so much time on his living room couch had conjured up a world so real it made those who lived in it feel like it was a "home movie," wrote Nicholas Pileggi in the *New York Times*. "When it was published in 1969 word quickly spread across the country's most regularly tapped telephone wires about this different book on the 'honored society.' . . . It was filled with bits of underworld gossip and its characters could be compared to live dons, singers, movie moguls and hit men. It depicted not only their lives, but the lives of their children, wives, enemies and friends. It emphasized their peculiar code of honor rather than their seedy, greedy little maneuverings. It dealt with their strong sense of family and their passionate loyalties . . .

"But most important, it humanized rather than condemned them."

Mobsters told reporters that they had taken to using lines like "I'm gonna make him an offer you can't refuse" and "If you have an enemy, that enemy becomes my enemy."

Puzo "influenced the life, absolutely," said Salvatore "Sammy the Bull" Gravano, a former underboss in the Gambino crime family who had turned stool pigeon against John Gotti.

Gravano, for one, didn't believe that Puzo could have written *The Godfather* without assistance from the Mafia. "No way," he told a writer for the *New York Times*. "Somebody had to be helping him . . . because he knew about our life cold. He had the whole atmosphere, the way we talked. That wedding scene—I mean, that was so real."

The writer, Jeffrey Goldberg, told Gravano that the author was a homebody with no Mob connections. "If you say so," the mobster replied, unconvinced. "Remember that scene where Michael goes to whack that drug dealer and the police captain? Remember how Michael couldn't hear anything as he's walking up on them? Remember how his eyes went glassy, and there was just the noise of the train in the background, and how he couldn't hear them talk? That's just like I felt when I killed Joe Colucci."

It was the first man he killed, Gravano said, adding that he killed nineteen more after seeing the movie. "Somebody who wrote that scene had to have a feeling for that. I mean, I felt like I was pulling the trigger myself."

Real-life mobsters were eager to meet the author of what had become their Bible. "In Las Vegas he found that a gambling debt he had run up was somehow marked paid," reported the *New York Times*. "When Puzo protested, he was told, 'It's a certain party's pleasure.' On other occasions, bottles of champagne would arrive at his table unordered. Multisyllablic names were whispered in his ear by reverential headwaiters, and men with sunglasses and diamond rings waved at him across darkened restaurants."

It was the highest praise a writer could hope for—a seal of approval from the very people he had brought to life on the page. But to many readers and reviewers the page was starting to seem insufficient. People wanted to see *The Godfather* brought to life on the big screen. The novel "has instant celluloid currency," observed the *Times*. "There are set scenes crying for the cameras (they have rarely failed before): a rigged trial, beatings, gang slayings (always ambushes, never firefights), a national Cosa Nostra summit meeting, a wedding, a gangland funeral."

Having scaled the heights of New York publishing, Puzo had only one place to go next: Hollywood. There the Mob would not only go to war over the making of the movie but would also demand its share of the action.

5

THE PRODUCER: THE MAN
WHO GETS THINGS DONE

The critical and financial success of the publication of the novel *The Godfather* seemed like nothing short of a godsend for Paramount. The studio was desperate to overcome its status as the laughingstock of Hollywood, and Puzo's novel was clearly, as Robert Evans called it, "the Hope Diamond of literature."

Plus Paramount had already snapped up the film rights for a measly $12,500.

There was only one problem: Paramount's distribution department didn't want to make the movie.

"Sicilian mobster films don't play," Evans explained. A year after he arrived at Paramount, the studio released *The Brotherhood*. It was a gangster flick, and despite an all-star cast and some terrific reviews, it had bombed at the box office. To Evans, the lesson was clear: "When you bat zero, don't make another sucker bet."

So the project sat on the shelf, until Paramount was propelled by the one thing guaranteed to motivate a Hollywood studio: competition. Burt Lancaster's production company was offering $1 million for the film rights, plus the $12,500 that Paramount had paid Puzo, with Lancaster to star in the title role. "Paramount was determined to sell it to them," Evans insisted.

To keep someone else from getting their hands on the book, Evans began to turn it into a movie. Accounts vary on how much Paramount was prepared to invest in the film. Peter Bart said the preliminary budget was somewhere in the range of $5 million to $6 million. But Francis Ford Coppola remembered the film having a "very limited" initial budget of $2.5 million. Whatever the actual figure was, Paramount needed a producer who knew how to keep costs down. "Period pictures" cost extra, so *The Godfather* would be set in contemporary times, not in the 1940s. It would be filmed on the studio's backlot, or in a city like St. Louis or Kansas City, because the novel's setting—New York City—was one of the most expensive places in the world to film. Which the Paramount brass would not tolerate.

As for a producer, who could bring the movie in on the cheap?

And who would be even willing to take on the assignment?

THE THIN MAN standing before Charlie Bluhdorn in the Gulf+Western Building in New York City was much like him: smart and tough, a fighter who rose up from the streets to become somebody. Albert Stotland Ruddy, forever known as "Al," just as Bluhdorn was known as "Charlie," was a producer with an office on the legendary lot at Paramount. He had a reputation for getting things done—on time and on budget—which he had been doing pretty much all his life. Like Charlie, he was an immigrant, snuck across the border at age seven in the dark of night from Canada into America by his mother, who was fleeing her husband in Montreal. "If they ask you where you were born, say you don't know," she instructed Al and his two siblings. They settled in New York City, where Al began his journey to becoming a producer, that nebulous title given to the dynamic men and women able to *get things done*—and movies made—in the dream factories out west.

Ruddy found a roundabout route into filmmaking. He put himself through the University of Southern California, where he earned a degree in architectural design in 1956, working nights at a gas station for $90 a week. Then he got a hardscrabble job that would pay off in unexpected ways when he became a movie producer: supervisor on a construction site in New Jersey. He learned how to lead and coordinate large groups of people, and how to work with the Teamsters and other unions. Most importantly, though, the job showed Al Ruddy what he *didn't* want to do. "I don't want to grow up to be you one day in mud boots twenty years from now walking up and down the streets of New Jersey," he told his boss. And with that, he returned to California.

He went to work for the RAND Corporation, a think tank created in 1948 to supply the US military with research and analysis. Starting as a programmer trainee, he quickly rose to head of the Design Change Acceptance Committee. Eager to get away from the office, he turned over some of his workload to his assistant, which gave him time to "roam around Hollywood," looking for a way into the movies. As he was driving around in his new Jaguar XK120, which was heavily financed, he passed a shoe store on Pico Boulevard with a HELP WANTED sign in the window. *Hell,* he thought, *I could get a part-time job there and pay my car off faster.*

"I don't want any part-time guys!" the manager told him. "I need a full-time guy."

"I could sell more shoes for you part-time than any guy you got selling full-time," Ruddy replied.

Just then a woman walked into the empty store. Ruddy sold her fourteen pairs of shoes. The part-time job was his.

While working at the store, Ruddy got the break he'd been looking for. An agent friend stopped by one day. His name was Elliott Kastner, and he was accompanied by Brian Hutton, an actor who had secured the rights to *The Connection*, a hit off-Broadway play that he wanted to stage in California. Kastner was impressed by Ruddy, the part-time shoe salesman with the full-time job at the RAND Corporation, and thought he'd be perfect to produce the play. The catch was, neither Kastner nor Hutton had the money to finance the production.

But Ruddy knew someone who did: a rich girl he'd gone to school with "who always kind of had the hots for me."

He convinced her to invest $15,000 in the production—and just like that, he was a producer. He even took a role in the play as "The Producer," introducing the show to audiences each evening for the last seven months of its run.

Soon, Ruddy and Brian Hutton found a dusty script that had long ago been sold to Marlon Brando's production company: *Daffy*, a romance about a runaway girl hitching a ride with a guy from New York to LA. It had once seemed to be a suitable vehicle for Marlon Brando, but this was 1964, and the forty-year-old Brando was too old to play the young stud. (He was thirty-three when he bought the rights.) Kastner, who would go on to produce movies like *The Long Goodbye* and *Angel Heart*, connected Ruddy with Brando's production company, which offered him a deal: If he could make *Daffy* on a shoe-string budget, Universal would release it.

"The atmosphere on the set of *Daffy* has been marked by an almost fanatical intensity that some veteran technicians find slightly amus-ing," the *New York Times* reported in March 1964. "But the ability to adhere to a fast-moving shooting schedule that will bring in the pic-ture for less than $300,000 has won grudging admiration."

Daffy was released as *The Wild Seed*, and Ruddy had established himself as a producer who could get a movie made quick and cheap.

Ruddy's next move was even more audacious: He teamed up with Bernie Fein, a comic actor on the 1950s *The Phil Silvers Show*—who once worked as a professional "laugher" embedded in audiences at comedy shows to encourage the crowd with his riotous laughs—to write a pilot for a half-hour sitcom. Ruddy nor Fein had barely any screenwriting experience.

"Bernie, you don't have to know how to be a writer to do a half-hour script," Ruddy advised his new writing partner.

They leased a fifty-dollar-a-month office in Beverly Hills, and, sitting across from each other at a rickety table over a manual typewriter, began mining ideas for a television show. Day after day, they stared at a blank page, struggling to come up with something, *anything*.

Al and Bernie.

Staring at the blank page.

Coffee. Days. Drinks. Nights. The clock ticking. The future on hold. *What about this? What about that?*

At long last, they hit on something. What about . . . *a comedy set in an American prison?* They wrote the pilot, which was greeted with a yawn. "We couldn't give that thing away!" Ruddy exclaimed. Back at the typewriter, they "did about twenty permutations."

Finally, as the crumpled pages rose in the wastebasket along with their despair, Bernie Fein took a flight to New York and sat next to a man reading the Nazi prison camp escape novel *Von Ryan's Express*. Back in LA, he and Ruddy felt they had struck upon an idea they felt was sitcom gold: *Change the setting from an American prison to a Nazi prisoner-of-war camp during WWII.* The lead would be a handsome, gregarious leader of the valiant American prisoners, who are actually running a special-ops effort from inside the camp. His foil would be a gullible, monocle-wearing Nazi commandant, oblivious to everything but his own authority, appropriately named Colonel Klink.

And for a title: *Hogan's Heroes*.

The sleepy typewriter jolted awake.

Words flowed. Laughs, tears, drama, comedy. Dumb Nazi devils outfoxed by smart American heroes.

When the pilot script was finished, they gave it to the only agent they knew: a friend of a friend of a friend.

Two weeks later, the agent called back. "Meet me at CBS on Fairfax," he said.

The next day, Ruddy and Fein arrived at the network's Los Angeles office for a meeting with God: William S. Paley, the legendary chief executive and chairman of CBS.

When they showed up at Paley's office, though, Paley wasn't smiling.

A prominent Jewish American, he had worked as the Chief of Radio Broadcasting for the Allied forces' Psychological Warfare Division during World War II. Paley immediately made one thing clear: He wasn't meeting with Ruddy and Fein to buy their script. He was meeting to scold them for committing such blasphemy on paper. "I find the idea of Nazis as comic characters to be reprehensible," he told them.

Al Ruddy hadn't gotten this far to be turned away. So he acted out the pilot. He played the hero, Colonel Hogan. He played the villain, Colonel Klink. He pantomimed firing a submachine gun, romped his way through the POWs' resistance operation, lampooned the hapless Nazis. And in that room, a miracle happened. William S. Paley started to laugh. And when Paley laughed, the whole room started laughing.

And then another miracle: Paley reached across the table and shook Al Ruddy's hand.

He couldn't buy the show, he said. "But that's the funniest thing I've heard this year."

Two weeks passed and Ruddy's phone rang again: William S. Paley had changed his mind. Ruddy and Fein had a deal with CBS for *Hogan's Heroes.* The hit comedy would run from September 1965 to April 1971, at the time the longest run ever for an American TV show about war. Overnight, Ruddy was considered a genius. "I got a call from an agent who said, 'Can I agent you around town?'"

Before long, Ruddy found himself being ushered through the fabled black gates of Paramount to sit before Robert Evans and Peter Bart. Did Ruddy have anything in mind for them? He named a few projects he'd be interested in developing, and Evans smiled. "Everyone laughed at me when I got this job," said Evans, who had jumped from the dress business to movies, just as Ruddy had jumped from construction, the RAND corporation, and selling shoes. "I want to give you a shot."

Just like that, Al Ruddy was a producer on the Paramount lot. When a reporter from *Variety* demanded to know how he had gone from creating a half-hour TV series to having his own office and a secretary at the studio, Ruddy didn't puff himself up. "Don't tell anyone

I don't know what I'm doing," he told the reporter. "They'll find out soon enough."

The reporter shook his head. "You're the first honest producer I've ever met," he told Ruddy.

The first project Ruddy produced was *Little Fauss and Big Halsy*, a motorcycle racing movie. Drawing on his talent for salesmanship, he convinced none other than Robert Redford to star as Big Halsy, and Michael J. Pollard, fresh off his Oscar nomination for *Bonnie and Clyde*, as Little Fauss. Redford loved the script but reportedly disliked his costar, and the critics panned the end result. But the film stayed under budget and grossed nearly $2 million, enough to earn Ruddy a reputation as a producer who could get movies made on the cheap. Add to that what Peter Bart called his "mobster-like voice" and his "willingness to laugh off setbacks," and Ruddy seemed like the perfect producer for *The Godfather*. According to Bart, he had to talk Evans into the idea. "I was totally responsible for hiring Al Ruddy, who Bob didn't know," Bart said.

Ruddy got the call on a Sunday. "Do you want to do *The Godfather*?" he was asked. Ruddy initially thought the call was a joke. "Yes, of course, I *love* that book," he replied, even though he had never read the novel.

He was summoned to the palatial office where Evans held court. There, the former garment industry executive Evans and the former newspaper reporter Bart offered the former shoe salesman Ruddy what would turn out to be the opportunity of a lifetime. Ruddy asked Bart for a copy of the novel. "I instructed him to set a precedent and buy his own," Bart said. The penny pinching had begun.

Ruddy rushed to a Beverly Hills bookstore and bought a copy of the book, which he read from start to finish in one sitting. Now all he needed was the blessing of Charlie Bluhdorn. So he boarded a plane for New York, his copy of *The Godfather* under his arm.

Arriving at the Gulf+Western Building, Ruddy lugged his suitcase into the towering skyscraper on Columbus Circle, where he was ushered into the office of Stanley Jaffe, Paramount's president. As the two men prepared to talk strategy, the door burst open, and in blew Hurricane Charlie.

"What do you wanna do with this movie?" he demanded of Ruddy.

Ruddy knew it was his move. Should he mention the novel, which he had spent the plane trip so carefully marking up? Should he try to play up some experience from his thin résumé? Should he talk about his vision or the budget or how to appeal to American audiences?

Instead, he appealed directly to Bluhdorn's inner hustler. "Charlie," he snapped, "I want to make an ice-blue, terrifying movie about the people you love."

Bluhdorn's face went momentarily blank, before breaking into a delighted grin. "That's brilliant!" the takeover titan erupted. Then he bolted from the office, vanishing as quickly as he had appeared.

Ruddy turned to Jaffe. "What the fuck was that?" he asked. Jaffe left the room to find out.

"You got the job," Ruddy said he was told upon his return.

"I'm now the producer of *The Godfather*?" Ruddy asked, dumbfounded.

"He thinks you're great," said Jaffe.

"Stanley, can you do me a favor?" Ruddy asked. "Can you get me a night flight back to Los Angeles? I just want to be the producer of *The Godfather* for a week before they find out I don't know what the hell I'm talking about."

A flight was booked for 6:00 p.m., and Ruddy headed for the elevator, hoping to make a fast exit. Just then, another door burst open, and Bluhdorn came barreling down the hallway. He gestured to a movie poster on the wall for an upcoming Paramount film, *The Adventurers*, a steamy thriller starring Candice Bergen. "How do you like that poster?" Bluhdorn demanded.

Ruddy had suffered through a screening of *The Adventurers* in Los Angeles. Most of the audience had left during the movie's intermission.

"Charlie," he told his new boss, "I think the last thing you have to worry about is the poster."

"Yeah, you saw the movie?"

"I did, Charlie. And to be very candid, I was about the only guy left in the theater after the intermission."

Ruddy began frantically pressing the elevator button, hoping to get inside before Bluhdorn could ask him anything more.

"I want you to know I personally cut twenty minutes out of that movie!" Bluhdorn said.

The elevator arrived, and Ruddy darted in. As the doors closed, he said, "Charlie, cutting twenty minutes out of that movie is like dying of cancer and trimming your toenails."

Ruddy assumed that was the end of his tenure as producer of *The Godfather*. But when he landed in LA, he discovered he still had the job. So he turned to the first order of business: the screenplay. Which would take him back to New York City, to meet the now-famous nobody who had turned a fictional Mob family into a masterpiece.

LUNCHTIME AT THE Plaza: The hotel's famous fountain flowed, the pianist played, the lobby was filled with ladies who lunch and tourists who gape. And there in the middle of this rich Manhattan tapestry was the newly anointed producer of *The Godfather*, sitting with his first wife, Francoise, when the man he was waiting for sauntered in.

Ruddy did a double take.

The big cigar. The greased-back black hair. The enormous body sweating in an overcoat.

No, it couldn't be. But tucked beneath the man's arm was a black-brick copy of *The Godfather*, and he was ambling toward the table, where he extended his fleshy hand in greeting.

"Mario Puzo," said the author.

On the spot, Ruddy gave him a nickname: the Little King.

Puzo had been surprised by the invitation to meet with Ruddy. His novel had been published more than a year earlier, and he believed Paramount had lost interest in *The Godfather*. "They didn't want to make the movie," he assumed.

Now, his agent, Candida Donadio, had gotten a call from Paramount, asking if Puzo would adapt his novel into a screenplay. Puzo, flush with cash for the first time in his life, turned down their original offer—too low. But when they came back with more, and a percentage of the net, Puzo agreed to have lunch with Ruddy and hear him out. Even though Puzo had never written a screenplay before, and novelists were famously sensitive about cutting down their masterpieces for the screen—a serious consideration when the masterpiece in question is 448 pages long.

And Mario Puzo still had no intention of writing the screenplay.

"Mario, just to save a lot of time, let's get to the end of the conversation first," Ruddy said.

"Okay," said Puzo.

"Nothing against you, but there is great reluctance in Hollywood to hire the novelist to adapt their novel, especially someone who has never done it before and especially when the novel is excessively large."

"My father was prepared to say no again," said Anthony Puzo.

Just then, Ruddy's wife opened her purse and a miniature poodle emerged to "let out a yip," Puzo wrote. "It seemed Al and his wife took the poodle everywhere . . . At the end of the lunch, I was enchanted by them and the poodle and I agreed to write the script."

As for any sensitivity about cutting down his novel, Puzo grabbed his copy of *The Godfather* and threw it on the carpeted floor.

"You have my word of honor that I will never look at the book again," he told Ruddy.

"Mario, you just got the job," Ruddy said, extending his hand.

Puzo would, of course, have to write the script in Los Angeles, in an office on the Paramount lot, and he would, of course, be well compensated. There would be money up front, plus $500 a week for expenses and 2.5 percent of the movie's net profits. (A sucker bet, as he learned the hard way, given how studios routinely used accounting tricks to claim a film had netted them nothing.) But to seal the deal, Ruddy needed the approval of the one person who had veto power over Puzo's affairs: his wife.

Erika Puzo had long kept watch over her diabetic husband's appetite, worried he would eat himself to death without her constant supervision. So Ruddy drove out to their home on Long Island to assure Erika that Mario would be safe in his care.

"Mrs. Puzo, I will pick him up in the morning, will have dinner with him at night," Ruddy said amid the cacophony of the kids—the soundtrack of the world in the home that Puzo's opus had paid for. "I will be with him every day, and I will make sure he stays on his diet."

"Fine, Mr. Ruddy," she replied. "I trust you."

In April 1970, Puzo headed to Hollywood, the family *chooch* flying first class. For the past twenty years he had led what he called "the life of a hermit."

Drinks with writer friends. Movies with family. Gambling and more gambling. "But mostly I had been living in my own head, with all my dreams, all my fantasies. The world had passed me by."

He saw himself, according to his friend Seymour Krim, as "a fat funny little guy . . . who thought he was an ugly man," who refused to take publicity photos or appear on TV, even to promote his own struggling books. "I knew the blood dues Mario had paid, and I wanted him to have every reward there was," Krim wrote. Now Puzo was on his way to becoming a literary sensation, the bestselling writer in the world, and Hollywood was calling. On the flight, Puzo tried to bring himself back to Earth. He knew well how writers were lured to Hollywood by money and fame, only to wash up on the shores of drugs and debt and divorce. That wouldn't happen to him, he vowed. He was a writer for hire, just as he had always been. "*The Godfather* was their picture, not mine," he wrote. "I would be cool. I would never let my feelings get hurt. I would never get proprietary or paranoid. I was an employee."

Then he landed, and Al Ruddy was waiting for him at the airport to whisk him into another world, one where people were eager to meet him, and to listen to him, and to spend time with him. "They were charming to me, and I loved it," Puzo would write. He was delivered to the door of the Pink Palace—the renowned Beverly Hills Hotel, with its endlessly long red carpet and its white-and-green-striped awning—where the author was immediately surrounded by a battalion of attendants, leading him not to a mere room, but to his $500-a-week suite, all arranged by Paramount.

MARIO PUZO ARRIVED at Paramount not merely as a bestselling author but as something of an emerging American hero. After so many years of failure and near-destitution, he was riding what could only be viewed as an absolutely unbelievable hot streak. He was rolling nothing but sevens, in a once-in-a-lifetime moment. He had based much of *The Godfather* on a 1910 Western classic, "a book I read when I was a kid, Zane Grey's *Heritage of the Desert*," he said. His novel would represent a new form of Western with a new style of outlaw justice and at the perfect time. "The Western has been replaced by the mob story as the central epic of America," wrote the media scholar Robert J. Thompson in the 2002 reissue of *The Godfather*. He noted that the year of the novel's publication, 1969, was a time when "the whole myth of America was up for grabs." Traditional TV Westerns like *Gunsmoke* and *Bonanza* were still popular but fading, and that year's crop of movies included *Easy Rider* ("counterculture cowboys who rode hogs instead of horses and did drugs instead of driving dogies"), *True Grit* ("featuring John Wayne as an over-the-hill marshal"), and *The Wild Bunch* (which "essentially pronounced dead the myth of the West").

"It was into this contested cultural environment that *The Godfather* introduced another myth," wrote Thompson.

Mario Puzo's new American Western had "an unbreakable code, a solid sense of family, and an ability to bypass bureaucratic loopholes and inefficiencies," Thompson wrote, and it "presented a seductive alternative world. These people could get things done, and while some of those things were horrible, most of their victims deserved what they got and were usually outlaws themselves."

The literary gunslinger who created this brave new world—and this new outlaw reality—was now in Hollywood to create the same frenzy on the screen as he had done in his pages. And like every Hollywood hero, he required a suitable assistant, which Paramount found for Puzo in an almost celestial occurrence.

An exclusive Academy Awards party in a private home in Los Angeles. Janet Snow, then twenty-three, had the good luck to be standing beside a stranger, an older man. He introduced himself as Gray Frederickson.

"What do you do?" he asked.

"Nothing," she said.

She was an innocent, naïve young woman just going out into the world, a single parent with two children at home.

"Well, I've just been hired to be the associate producer on *The Godfather*," said Frederickson.

"Oh, my gosh, I'm reading that book, and I love it," Snow replied.

Frederickson was a "people person," she would soon learn, "a very smart, very savvy individual gifted at putting people together." He had only just met Mario Puzo, who had recently arrived in Los Angeles, and he knew a perfect match when he saw one.

"Do you play tennis?" asked Frederickson.

"Yes, I play tennis," replied Snow.

"Mario Puzo, the author of *The Godfather*, will be at Paramount tomorrow morning," said Frederickson. "He's a tennis buff. He needs an assistant, and it would be great if the assistant were able to play tennis."

Paramount wanted Puzo to be happy and at peace while he worked on his screenplay. He needed guidance; he needed someone with energy, personality, and knowledge of the city and its citizens. Because Mario Puzo knew absolutely *nothing* about Los Angeles, who was who or how to get anywhere. He worked at home for so much of his life. Everything was brand new to him.

Tennis was the way in, and in the kismet that would follow the making of *The Godfather* from this day forward, Frederickson asked Snow, a native Angeleno he had only just met, a question that would change her life.

"Would you be interested in coming to Paramount tomorrow

morning at nine thirty to meet the producers and Mario Puzo and interview for the job as his assistant?" he asked her.

"Sure!" she replied.

She didn't take him seriously. She knew that people in Hollywood make promises that vanish by morning. Especially at parties. So the next morning, waking up late (it was a very late party), the incredible offer from the stranger rolled through her mind. It had been, she remembered, "Huge! One second I'm a single parent, twenty-three, and wondering how I'm going to survive and educate my children, and the next someone is telling me, 'Come to Paramount Pictures and work with the author of the biggest, hottest book ever written to date.'"

Had it all been a dream? She dialed the number Gray Frederickson had given her, but before she could ask, "Did you mean what you said last night?" he spoke first:

"Janet, where are you!? The heads of the studio, Mario Puzo, and Al Ruddy, we're all here in Al's office waiting for you!"

She had to get over to Paramount *fast*, but she didn't have a car. *Where to turn for help?* She knocked on her apartment building owner's penthouse door and told him her dilemma: the incredible job interview at Paramount *immediately* and no way to get there . . .

"How exciting! How wonderful!" the building's owner exclaimed. "I have a spare car in the garage," he added, and he led her into his building's subterranean garage. And there sat one of his cars, a most gorgeous new white Lincoln Continental convertible, with a red leather interior. "This car just sits down here," he told her. "And I'm thrilled for you to drive it to your interview."

And just like that, Janet Snow was driving down Melrose Avenue in a brand-new white Lincoln Continental for a meeting at Paramount Pictures. *What could be better than this?* Just then, she noticed that the car was equipped with something very few cars had back then—a phone, on which she immediately called a friend.

"I'm on my way to Paramount Pictures for an interview with the author of *The Godfather* and I'm scared to death," she said.

"Janet, don't worry! You'll *never* get that job," the friend replied.

"You have no experience, and you can't type. How are you going to work for a writer if you can't type? I'm sure they'll be enchanted by you, but you don't have the qualifications."

"Oh, that takes the pressure off, thank you," she said.

Then she was pulling up to the glorious gates of Paramount, where she was issued a pass and welcomed royally. *Right this way, Ms. Janet Snow! Mr. Ruddy is expecting you!* She parked in the lane reserved for the guests and walked into the Directors' Building. She was soon entering what she said was "the most gorgeous office I had ever seen in my entire life," the office of Albert S. Ruddy. The shutters were closed. But she could see inside from the waiting room. Huge. Dark. Softly lit. Al Ruddy sat behind his enormous desk, surrounded by other men on leather chairs and sofas. There were big bookcases everywhere and the musky scent of cigar smoke.

A receptionist ushered her inside. The door closed behind her. And there she stood before six men, all staring and shooting questions: *Where are you from? What do you do?*

She felt she would be in and out in seconds.

Instead, she began hearing reverberations, whispers, one or more of the men saying, "Oh, my God, she's perfect, she's perfect."

"The realization hit me, and I looked around the room for a safe place to sit down," she said. "It was incredibly overwhelming. The job was becoming a reality. I saw a heavyset man with a sweet face and his feet on the coffee table, holding a big cigar. I sat down next to him."

The others kept asking questions, but the big man nudged her arm with his elbow, and once he got her attention, whispered, "The money. Ask them about the money."

It was Mario Puzo.

Al Ruddy, the producer of the film, asked what the whispering was about.

Janet pointed at Mario. "He said, 'Ask about the money.'"

Ruddy asked everyone to leave so he could work out some "details" with the young woman. The money, he insisted, was secondary to the experience. The film was on a very tight budget. "But I do know if you decide to take this position, this will change your life in a wonderful and dramatic way," said the producer.

Janet Snow took the job.

Ruddy's receptionist escorted Snow and Puzo up to their new offices on the third floor. "This is your office," she told Snow of the outer office. "And Mr. Puzo this is your office," she said of the inner.

"He went to his office, and I sat at an empty desk trying to understand what to do next," Snow said. Time passed. Puzo sat quietly, until finally, he emerged, "with his cigar and looking as bewildered as I felt."

"Enough of this," he said. "I have no idea what I'm doing here."

"Neither do I," said Snow.

"Okay, I'll give you your first assignment. Please call me a cab to take me to the Beverly Hills Hotel, and after the cab comes, take the rest of the day off. There's nothing for you to do."

She told him she lived near his hotel and would happily give him a ride. So they went downstairs and to the private lane on the lot, which was lined with the Ferraris, Mercedes, and Rolls-Royces owned by the directors and producers. Puzo saw an old beat-up Volkswagen, which he assumed belonged to Janet Snow.

"What are you doing?" she asked as he began to climb in.

"I thought this was your car," he said.

She turned to the brand-new Lincoln Continental and said, "No, *this* is my car."

Puzo's eyes grew wide as he climbed inside. Janet Snow put the top down and drove Mario Puzo into a dream world, which left him "bewildered" and amazed. Even more so when he saw that the car had a telephone.

"What's that?" he asked of the device that sat between them.

"It's a telephone," she replied.

"Who can you call on that phone?"

"Anybody in the world," she said.

"Oh, my God, can you call Al Ruddy for me?"

Snow called Al Ruddy and handed the phone to Puzo, who felt

sure that Paramount had arranged everything: this magical moment, in this magical car, this magical world in which the wizards of the movies can do *anything*. "He's got the phone to his ear and his arm with his cigar out the window, and he just yelled, 'WOW!!!!!'"

Wow was the world that he now inhabited, and Wow was the life he was embarking upon, but Wow wasn't some of the miseries that he would soon encounter. He had been able to write a masterpiece about the Mob, but now he was a naïve innocent among the wolves of Los Angeles. "He was wise and kind, but I didn't realize how vulnerable he was," said Snow, who drove him through Bel Air before taking him to the hotel. He gaped at the big homes and the manicured lawns, and exclaimed, "Oh, my God! Look at this. But something's missing. *Children.* There are no children."

"He was used to Bay Shore, Long Island, with big families and kids playing in the front lawns," said Snow.

Now, he was in a world where family life was hidden behind big doors and tall hedges.

"The only place he was really comfortable was on the tennis court," said Snow.

Soon he was playing tennis every day, determined to get fit and slim like all the actors and models and producers in Beverly Hills. "He also traveled to Las Vegas most weekends," said his son Anthony.

Puzo loved his office on the Paramount lot, "with a refrigerator and an unlimited supply of soda pop free," he marveled. "And I had an adjoining office for my secretary and a telephone with a buzzer and four lines. This was living."

The phone would buzz, summoning him to the executive suite, where he would sit down with Ruddy and Robert Evans and Peter Bart to discuss the movie. In the very first meeting, he abandoned his plan to play it cool and act like an employee. Venturing far beyond the purview of a screenwriter, Puzo suggested Marlon Brando for the role of the Godfather.

The name was met with silence. Brando, at that point, was considered unbankable in Hollywood, a washed-up actor with a string of box-office flops and a reputation as a temperamental terror. "They were kind to me," Puzo wrote, "but I got the impression my stock had dropped 50 points." Then Ruddy suggested Robert Redford for the role of Michael Corleone. "I didn't care how nice a guy he was," Puzo continued, "his stock dropped 50 points. I spoke out and was pleasantly surprised when Evans and Bart agreed with me. It was going to be a fair fight, I thought."

"I HAD TO write the script before they got a director," wrote Puzo. "Directors like to read scripts before they sign." But he wasn't making much progress. "I'm a fast writer, and I expected the job to take four weeks," he told a Hollywood columnist that summer. "Now I've been working for two and a half months, and I'm just finishing the first draft."

Puzo, like all true gamblers, believed in magic. "As a child, I used books as magic," mused the semiautobiographical protagonist of his 1978 novel, *Fools Die*. "I could spirit myself away and escape by reading and then weave my own fantasies." The books he loved best were about King Arthur and the brave knights of his Round Table. "But most of all, I loved Merlin because I thought myself like him. . . . I fantasized myself as cunning and far-seeing and was firmly convinced that I would rule my own life by some sort of magic. And so I came to love King Arthur's magician, Merlin, who had lived through the past, could foresee the future, who was immortal and all-wise."

Puzo's literary surrogate in *Fools Die* developed what he called "the trick," in which he could transfer himself from whatever grim present he found himself trapped in, to a glorious future in which he became, among other fantasies, "a young man with clever bookish friends," an intellectual living "in a luxurious apartment," a Romeo who would "on the sofa of that apartment make love to a passionate, beautiful woman."

"It worked, it really worked," he wrote. "I magically disappeared."

Now, through the magic of a book, Puzo had transported himself from Hell's Kitchen to Hollywood, into a fantasy greater than anything he could have imagined. Still, he couldn't magically write the script. As he had done while writing his novel, Puzo had been "goofing off for some four months." Now he was past his deadline for the first draft of the screenplay.

He and Janet Snow worked side by side at the studio and on the tennis court, Puzo becoming a "father figure" to his young assistant. "I got him. I understood him. He felt like he could rely on me, and it meant a great deal to him. He was out of his environment, away from home, and while he handled himself beautifully, he was socially very shy."

She still didn't type. But she helped him write his screenplay by putting the plot points of his novel on three-by-five-inch cards, which they taped to the walls of his office. Soon, the phone began ringing, with invitations to, well, everything. "Everybody started calling, everybody wanted to meet him," said Snow. "Everybody wanted to play tennis with him, be in business with him. He was really uncomfortable with all of that. That's why he included me. Mario and I became very protective of each other."

She accompanied him to lunches, dinners, meetings, and met his friends: the authors Gay Talese, Bruce Jay Friedman, and the actor-writer-comedian Mel Brooks . . . as well as his best friend, George Mandel, whom Puzo considered the best writer of all of them. And she helped him deal with the deluge of wannabe actors vying for parts in the movie, believing that *The Godfather*'s author-screenwriter had some sway. They overwhelmed Puzo's office, in person, by telephone, and through the mail. Suddenly, *The Godfather* had gone from something that the studio had been hesitant about, to becoming a hot property. "Everybody in Hollywood wanted to be a part of this project," said Snow.

And the big-hearted Puzo, the man Snow described as a "very shy, very sensitive, vulnerable person who cared deeply about everything," couldn't bear to turn anyone down. "One poor guy kept sending his picture—every day! And you could just see by his correspondence that he was getting more and more depressed. He sent a postcard with two boxes—yes or no—and wrote, 'Just give me a yes or no . . .' so he could go on with his life."

One early evening, as the two were planning to go to a movie after a match of late-afternoon tennis, the phone rang in Puzo's suite.

"I answered the phone and this amazing voice said, 'Is Mario Puzo there?' "

"Who's calling?" asked Snow.

"Orson Welles," said the voice.

"It's a man named Orson Welles," said Snow, who didn't know the name.

"Janet, Orson Welles!" exclaimed Puzo. He took the call and was told by Welles that he had taken a bungalow for the express purpose of inviting the acclaimed author of *The Godfather* for dinner.

The bungalow door swung open, "and here was another very large man with a big cigar in his hand," said Snow of the acclaimed director and leading man of so many iconic films, including *Citizen Kane*, rumored to be interested in playing the godfather. There in the suite, Orson Welles was surrounded by the passion that he and Puzo shared: food, a dizzying array of food, piled high on room-service tables, everything from mounds of seafood on ice to every other conceivable delicacy and drink. "They hit it off the moment they met," said Snow. "It was a feast and the most brilliant conversation possible, truly a once-in-a-lifetime amazing experience."

Once, for her birthday, Puzo offered to take Snow anywhere she wanted for dinner, and she chose her parents' favorite: Perino's, the old-school Italian restaurant frequented by the likes of Frank Sinatra, Bette Davis, and the mobster Bugsy Siegel. And when she couldn't decide between the rack of lamb and the filet mignon, he would tell the waiter, "Bring both."

When she objected, Puzo said, "Take a bite and take the rest. You've got two kids at home!"

Al Ruddy tried his best to honor his promise to Erika Puzo and keep her husband on a strict diet. He picked the writer up every morning and drove him to the studio, where the two shared their meals: egg whites and raw tomatoes for breakfast, a hamburger patty and a broiled pear for lunch. Sometimes they would even meet for a low-calorie dinner.

But something curious happened: Ruddy lost weight, while Puzo continued to pack on the pounds. The mystery deepened until one night when Ruddy walked into a local pizza parlor with his family.

"Mario Puzo is a great guy," the proprietor told Ruddy.

"How do you know Mario?" Ruddy asked.

"I take a pizza to him every night at the Beverly Hills Hotel."

PUZO WAS TYPING out the script on his portable manual typewriter. The work was excruciatingly slow. His typed pages were marked up with his notes, which he scrawled with a thick felt-tip pen in his illegible handwriting.

A final deadline was set. Puzo promised Peter Bart he would be finished by the end of the week. "There was a final section that I wanted to rewrite and give it that extra polish and editing a solid piece of work needs," he said.

Then, as he had done when he shipped his novel to his agent and took his family to Europe, he decided that enough was enough. Plus, he surely needed the money a script completion would bring; he had moved into an expensive rental in Malibu for a month. *What the hell do I care?* he thought. *It's not my movie.* "I told my secretary to just type out what I had already written," Puzo wrote. "I then put on my bathing suit, and for the first time since I moved into the house on the beautiful beach in Malibu, I took a dip in the ocean."

Now that he had sent the script off to the studio, Puzo was free to embark upon what he called "adventures."

The most memorable was a face-to-face meeting with the entertainer whom Puzo considered his "idol from afar," Frank Sinatra.

Ruddy had invited Puzo to dinner at Chasen's, the legendary show-business restaurant where movie stars and presidents mingled. There,

while having a drink at the bar, Puzo saw Sinatra stride through the restaurant. Not the Sinatra Puzo had thinly disguised as Johnny Fontane,
the hard-drinking, womanizing, past-his-prime crooner who turns to
the godfather to revive his career. This was an immaculately dressed and
superbly tanned superstar Sinatra. As he was escorted to Booth #1, the
best in the house, Sinatra stopped to chat with John Wayne. "They both
looked absolutely great, better than on the screen, twenty years younger
than they really were," Puzo observed. "And both beautifully dressed,
Sinatra especially. It was really great to see. They were beribboned kings
meeting on the Field of the Cloth of Gold; Chasen's is regally formal."

Puzo might have been starstruck, but Ruddy knew trouble when
he saw it. "Oh, God, it's Frank Sinatra—let's take a wide turn," he told
Puzo, dragging the writer to a table on the far side of the restaurant.
Before *The Godfather* was even published, Sinatra's lawyers had made
a demand to Puzo's publisher to see his manuscript. Now, furious over
the character of Johnny Fontane, Sinatra was supposedly considering
suing to stop the movie. Ruddy told Puzo to keep his distance, then
left the table momentarily to greet a friend.

What happened next could have come straight from the horror
films of another luminary who often dined at Chasen's: the director
Alfred Hitchcock.

While Ruddy was away, someone hurried up to Puzo. He would
write that it was "a famous millionaire," but Ruddy would later say he
was the show-business impresario Marshall Edson. "You gotta meet
Frank!" Edson exclaimed, grabbing the author by the arm and leading
him to Booth #1. Unaware of Sinatra's raging hatred of *The Godfather*,
Edson hoped to impress the star by introducing him to the novel's
famous author.

"I'd like you to meet my good friend Mario Puzo," Edson said.

"I don't think so," Sinatra replied.

Puzo tried to "get the hell out of there," but Edson urged him to
say hello.

"I don't want to meet him," Sinatra said, this time a little louder
and angrier.

Edson, realizing his mistake, was practically in tears. "Frank, I'm sorry," he stuttered. "God, Frank, I didn't know. Frank, I'm sorry."

Sinatra was suddenly all benevolence. "His voice was now the voice I had heard while making love as a kid, soft and velvety," Puzo recalled.

"It's not your fault," Sinatra consoled Edson.

Then Puzo spoke up.

"Listen, it wasn't my idea," he said.

Sinatra misunderstood. He thought Puzo was "apologizing" for the character of Johnny Fontane. "Who told you to put that in the book, your publisher?" the singer said, his voice softening.

Nobody told Mario Puzo what to put in his books. He set Sinatra straight: "I mean about being introduced to you."

Ol' Blue Eyes saw red. He began to scream at Puzo, calling him a pimp and threatening him. In recounting the story afterward, Puzo wrote, "But what hurt was here he was, a Northern Italian, threatening a Southern Italian, with physical violence. That was roughly the equivalent of Einstein pulling a knife on Al Capone."

Puzo insisted that he walked away peacefully and left the restaurant. "Choke!" Sinatra yelled after him in a frenzied, high-pitched snarl. "Go ahead and choke!" But Ruddy insisted that Puzo gave as good as he got. "I mean *screaming*!" he said. "There's two waiters holding Mario back. They dragged Puzo out, put him in my car."

As Ruddy drove Puzo home, he said, the writer began to cry. "Al, you don't understand what Italians are," he said. "In the house where I grew up, my mother had two pictures in the kitchen: one of the Pope and one of Sinatra. And the fact that Frank Sinatra doesn't like me or would think I would do anything to hurt him, breaks my heart."

"Mario, there's nothing I can do about that," said Ruddy. "Frank has it in for all of us."

Puzo would concede that the incident was partly his fault. "I could have pulled away and I wonder to this day why I did not," he wrote. "But the humiliation did me a lot of good. I was really beginning to think I was important."

6

COPPOLA: A CELESTIAL OCCURRENCE

Ali MacGraw met Robert Evans while still modeling in college. Evans, on a constant quest for a beauty, spotted her wearing a fake fur in an advertisement, and invited her to lunch in New York through her agent Eileen Ford. "He was considered one of the great ladies' men of his time," wrote MacGraw in her autobiography, *Moving Pictures*. She accepted his invitation to lunch, at the star-studded Harwyn Club, on East Fifty-Second Street. Evans ordered her food, without consulting her, then spent the entire time on not one but two telephones. They shared a cab afterward, which Evans exited first, leaving her with the cab fare and a parting line while staring at her Capezios: "Those are the ugliest shoes I've ever seen."

Later, MacGraw would say that her first meeting with Evans was the opposite of the giving, loving, and kind man with whom she would fall in love.

Years passed before they met again: Evans, now head of production at Paramount, and MacGraw, an aspiring actress. She was one of the many who tested for the role of the beautiful Radcliffe student Brenda Patimkin in the 1969 Paramount production of *Goodbye, Columbus*, based on the Philip Roth novella. Casting of the role came to a head one day in Robert Evans's screening room in Woodland. When MacGraw's face came on the screen, an executive said, "Thank

God we found a real nineteen-year-old reading for the part," to which Evans exclaimed, "Nineteen my ass. She's been around for at least ten years."

"Because it had been about that length of time since I'd seen him," said MacGraw. "Anyway, oddly enough, I got the part."

After that, Evans sent her agent the script for *Love Story*, which made MacGraw cry, and which was followed by an invitation to Woodland under the guise of vetting the potential *Love Story* director Arthur Hiller, who had already been hired. It "was probably little more than a high-powered seduction scene," wrote MacGraw. "It sure worked."

"Speechless at the opulence" of Woodland, where she was served a glass of Champagne upon arrival, she proceeded to descend into "one of the great drunks of my life," sleeping through dinner and the movie and, upon awakening, throwing herself into the cobalt-tiled swimming pool, "fully clothed, high heels and all," after which she spent the night in Evans's bed. "I never left," she wrote.

They were married on October 24, 1969, which afforded Mac-Graw a front-row seat to the making of *The Godfather*.

The work at Paramount consumed Evans. MacGraw estimates he had thirty-two telephones in the house—two in every room—and he would work them around the clock. "He was married to his work, and I do not mean it negatively," she said. "I mean, there was nothing sloppy or cynical about his connection with this job. He *loved* it. Every day, twenty-four hours a day. He cared about every single detail. He worked it, dreamed it, fought it, slept it."

Every morning at 6:00 a.m. Los Angeles time, the phone would ring: Charlie Bluhdorn, calling from New York. "They would talk and talk and talk and talk about every single possible thing that could have been happening, on any aspect of Paramount, which was of course just about ready to fold up and be turned into a mortuary," MacGraw said. Then every night, "as soon as we sat down for supper," the phone would ring again: Bluhdorn calling. "I finally said 'Could we just please have supper without you being on the phone?' I loved Charlie Bluhdorn.

He was blustery, no filter, powerful, really successful, exhausting, and I loved him. But the phone thing just got a little bit intense at mealtime. The morning one I understood. We would stall the evening one for an hour."

In the mornings, after the 6:00 a.m. call from Bluhdorn, Peter Bart would swing by Woodland to pick up Evans, who did not drive, and the two young studio executives would drive to Paramount together, talking projects on the way. On one of these drives to work, Evans brought up *The Godfather*.

"It's not just a Mafia novel," he said.

"It's a novel about the building of a dynasty," Bart agreed. "But what the hell do we do with it?"

They already had their producer and their screenwriter. Now they needed to find a director. The problem was, everyone they'd approached—Arthur Penn (*Bonnie and Clyde*), Richard Brooks (*In Cold Blood*), Costa-Gavras (*Z*), Otto Preminger (*Advise & Consent*), and Peter Yates (*Bullitt*)—was either occupied on other films or didn't want to do it. More than one was put off by the novel's approach to its subject matter. "You can't romanticize the Mafia," they told Evans. "It's immoral."

"What about your agents?" Evans shot back. "You deal with them every day."

The directors who did express interest didn't seem right. They included Sidney J. Furie, who directed *Little Fauss and Big Halsy* (too expensive), and "Bloody" Sam Peckinpah, who directed *The Wild Bunch* (too gory).

Peckinpah, in particular, lobbied hard for the film. "He was screaming about what a great movie it would make," said Bart. "He talked about several scenes—he'd really thought it through."

What Peckinpah saw was bodies—lots and lots of bloody bodies. "Sam could always tell you the body count—'Seventy-five of these bums mowed down in the second act,'" Bart told Peter Biskind for a 1997 *Premiere* magazine article.

Another Paramount executive had also been casting for directors.

"Bluhdorn, impressed by the book sales, had sent the script of *The Godfather* to other directors," said Peter Bart, including Warren Beatty, fresh off his Oscar nomination for Best Actor in *Bonnie and Clyde*. "I was offered *The Godfather* to produce and direct," Beatty remembered. "Charlie Bluhdorn was a fan of *Bonnie and Clyde* and sent me the book. I read it. Sort of. And I said, 'Charlie, not another gangster movie!'"

Evans was getting frustrated. "We can't get one director, not even a half-assed one, to commit!" he roared one night.

"They're scared of it," Bart replied.

They stayed up late trying to figure it out. Why didn't gangster films work? Finally, at 2:00 a.m., Evans thought he had the answer. "Outside of red ink, every one of the films shared another thing in common—they were written, directed, and produced by—and usually starred—Jews, not Sicilians."

As Evans recounted the tale, he and Bart called Stanley Jaffe, Paramount's president, at 6:00 a.m. and told him they had cracked the code: *The Godfather*, to be a success, had to be directed by and star Italian Americans.

"It must be ethnic to the core," Evans said. "You must smell the spaghetti."

There was one snag. "In 1969," Evans would write, "there wasn't a single Italian American director with any credibility to be found."

Bart had a solution—albeit a controversial one. "I want to give it to Francis Coppola," he announced at a Paramount production meeting.

At thirty, Francis Ford Coppola was the youngest director on Paramount's list: a big, burly, bearded, long-haired intellectual. By now, he had traded his neat college attire—jacket, sweater, and tie—for what his assistant would call his "Castro outfit": green shirt, green pants, military boots, befitting a director for whom filmmaking had become war. He had recently cowritten the screenplay for the World War II movie *Patton*, for which he would win an Academy Award, and he had defiantly left Hollywood to start his own film production company in

San Francisco. "He's a brilliant writer," Bart argued, "and he loves telling stories about his Italian family. I think he'll fight it, but I also think he may bring something to it."

"Are you nuts, Peter?" Evans replied. "He's crazy."

"Brilliant, though," said Bart.

Bart was pushing Coppola's Italian heritage, but that wasn't why he wanted him to direct *The Godfather*. "One of the myths of this goddamn thing is that the only reason Francis got the job is because he's Italian, which is ridiculous," said Bart. "But being opportunistic myself, I felt that in persuading Bob how brilliant Francis was, I would emphasize how Italian he was. He wasn't another Jewish guy who made *The Brotherhood*."

Bart even gave Coppola instructions for what to say when he first met with Evans. "Talk about some Italian recipes, talk about pasta," he told Coppola. "Don't be so goddamn cerebral. Talk about Italian shit."

Bart laughed at the memory. "The fact that Francis was Italian helped me in making his case, though you wouldn't exactly call him a prototypical Italian," he said. "His father was a brilliant musician, and he comes from a very creative family, and they may have had pasta now and then, but I don't think their family is any more Italian than my family."

THE OFFER TO direct *The Godfather* came to Francis Ford Coppola at an opportune time:

The director was dead broke.

Yes, he had his own film production company, American Zoetrope, he called it, named for an early animation device he had received as a gift, and, yes, it was filled with bright young talent, including future *Star Wars* director George Lucas. But at this moment in early 1970, they were all still struggling and unknown and broke.

And Coppola, who aspired to create film as art, wasn't interested in directing some cockamamie gangster picture.

Yet, it seemed, he had been heading toward *The Godfather* for all his life.

He was born far from Italy, in the suburbs of Detroit, though Queens, New York, is perhaps the closest thing he had to a hometown. His father, Carmine Coppola, was a flautist, teacher, songwriter, composer, and conductor, who performed on *The Ford Sunday Evening Hour*. The show's sponsor—Ford—was the middle name Carmine and his wife, Italia, bestowed on the second of their three children. As his father moved between jobs and orchestras, Francis shuffled from school to school, rarely enrolled anywhere for longer than two months, until his family landed on 212th Street in Queens. He soon launched his film career, editing himself out of his family's 8mm home movies and using the footage to create a short film about himself, to which he charged neighborhood kids an admission fee.

In 1949, his education would be even more dramatically disrupted. At nine years old, Francis was stricken with polio. The doctor said he would never walk again, and Francis was exiled to nine solitary months in bed. It was there, with a television, a tape recorder, and an 8mm projector, that he became a director. As other kids played outside, he staged puppet shows for himself, invented soundtracks "imitating Mickey Mouse," and devoured comic books. "They're so much like screenplays," he said. His mother, Italia, would say that every time she came into his room, he would "hold out his little hands, like he was lining up a shot."

"Dear Mommy, I want to be rich and famous," Francis wrote in a note he left for her. "I'm so discouraged. I don't think it will come true."

But when he emerged from bed—and his illness—he had found his calling. When he needed a few dollars to make a film, his baby sister, Talia, volunteered to help him out. "I was very shy, but I went around to take a collection, twenty-five cents here and there," she said. "I would say, 'You don't understand. My brother's a great director.' I just knew! He was different, unique, inventive. There was *nobody* like him."

Early on, he learned how to make dreams come true. "My father's proficiency on the flute acted, he felt, as a barrier to the career he wished for: as composer, conductor, etc.," said Coppola. "So our lives were always lived in the shadow of his 'getting his break.'"

As his father moved through musical positions—the first principal flautist for the Detroit Symphony and the NBC Symphony Orchestra, staff arranger for Radio City Music Hall—the Coppola family incessantly moved from town to town, job after job. Finally, young Francis took matters into his own hands. "I did something terrible to my father," he would tell *Esquire*. "When I was twelve or thirteen, I had a job at Western Union. And when the telegram came over on a long strip, you would cut it and glue it on the paper and deliver it on a bicycle.

"And I knew the name of the head of Paramount Pictures' music department—Louis Lipstone. So I wrote, 'Dear Mr. Coppola: We have selected you to write a score. Please return to L.A. immediately to begin the assignment. Sincerely, Louis Lipstone.' And I glued it and I delivered it. And my father was so happy."

Overjoyed. Ecstatic. Carmine Coppola was surely preparing his family to pack up and move yet again. Until his son had to break the news that the magical telegram was a fake.

"He was totally furious," said Coppola. "In those days, kids got hit. With the belt. I know why I did it: I wanted him to get that telegram. We do things for good reasons that are bad."

In 1955, Coppola enrolled in the theater arts department at Hofstra University. He wanted to make movies, and, after graduating, he enrolled in UCLA's graduate film program, where he quickly became a top screenwriter in his class.

Peter Bart met Coppola near the inception of his career as a filmmaker, which had started with a scene like this: The location: an abandoned department store in Venice, California. The date: April 9, 1966. The directors: Coppola and his UCLA classmate, Jack Hill. The cast: a man and woman, lying naked on a bed.

Bart, who in those days was still a reporter, wrote of when Coppola and Hill directed the actors on a makeshift set. They were making a sex film, "a nudie," in the parlance of 1960s Hollywood—at the time the primary path open to aspiring filmmakers, no matter how prestigious their education. "The studios weren't interested in turning over million-dollar projects to inexperienced young directors," Bart explained to readers of the *New York Times*. "And the tightly knit unions weren't interested in admitting college-educated newcomers to train in subordinate positions."

Up-and-comers like Coppola were reduced to making skin flicks "not because they are sex-crazed but simply because they love filmmaking and nudies are the only route into the Hollywood studios."

The results, with titles like *The Bellboy and the Playgirls* and *Tonight for Sure*, "played out in grubby little emporiums that line Manhattan's West 42nd Street."

Coppola's entry into "nudies" came after he filmed an "art picture," Bart wrote. He hadn't been able to find anyone to distribute it until a "nudie" company agreed to take it on—"provided the boys wove in some sexy footage."

Coppola reluctantly agreed. "I had so little money in those days that I had nowhere to sleep except on our own sets," he told Bart. "It was rather depressing to shoot these wild bedroom scenes and then have to sleep in the same bed at night."

He was determined to break into the business, by any means necessary. "I was prepared to do anything to make films," he said.

"I called UCLA and I said, 'Who is your best graduating senior in editing?'" said the prolific B-movie director Roger Corman. It was the early 1960s and Corman needed "some reediting done on some Russian science fiction films. They sent over several people and I felt Francis was the brightest and most creative, and he had tremendous knowledge of films. He told me his theory about going to film school," which was essentially getting a liberal arts degree to provide him with a general understanding of the world, and then attending film school as a graduate student "so that he wasn't trapped, as many film students were, with a knowledge of film and not of the world around him."

This is the guy who really figured it out when he was in high school, thought Corman, who hired Coppola as his assistant.

His first assignment: "cutting the anti-American propaganda out of Russian science fiction films and also shooting a little monster to cut into one of the films," said Corman. "And he did a great job."

"We set to work in the bathtub and with lots of latex, trying to make these monsters out of rubber and film them—and we did!" Coppola would tell the author Peter Cowie. To gain experience, he did whatever Corman required: position the camera, hold the boom mike, bang out script revisions. Corman, even more impressed, told Coppola, "I can give you the thirty thousand dollars if you can write a little horror script and shoot it in Ireland with a skeleton crew." The film would be called *Dementia 13*.

In Ireland, Coppola assembled everyone—cast, crew, hangers-on—on the top floor of an old house outside Dublin, where they worked on the movie around the clock. Shirt off, his hair and beard wild, Coppola sat in the midst of the chaos, reworking the script on a manual typewriter. One bleary day or night, he was reintroduced to a fellow UCLA graduate who had been dispatched to Ireland by Corman to serve as assistant art director. Her name was Eleanor Jessie Neil, and she was there to do what she called the "grunt work" on the film. She and Coppola had met once before, when a friend took her to Key Largo, a club on Sunset Boulevard. "I met him when he was shooting a nudie film in a nightclub," she said with a laugh. Now, in Ireland, they became lovers, and she soon became pregnant. She told Coppola in a "calming voice," she wrote, "so he would not feel pressured." Instead, he surprised her. "I've always wanted a family," he said. On February 2, 1963, they were married in a quickie ceremony in a Las Vegas chapel. Soon after that, the baby on the way, they moved into their own home, an A-frame in Mandeville Canyon in the hills above Los Angeles.

Coppola had some initial success, thanks in part to the Samuel Goldwyn Screenwriting Award he won at UCLA. He was hired by Seven Arts to write the script for *Reflections in a Golden Eye*, and soon landed a $500 a week screenwriter's job at the studio. He worked on eleven scripts, only to agonize over how little of his work actually wound up in the finished films. His family was growing—Gian-Carlo was born in 1963, followed by Roman in 1965—and there were worse things than being young in LA in the 1960s. ("Warren Beatty and Joan Collins at two in the morning, and jumping in the swimming pool," Eleanor said of the parties, "and I was a mom with two kids at home.")

But Coppola, like Mario Puzo in New York, was beginning to despair about his prospects as an artist. And like Puzo, he turned to gambling as a solution.

"I decided I was going to risk it all on the stock market," Coppola told film critic Joseph Gelmis in 1968. Taking his entire savings of $20,000, he invested it in what he called "the jukebox with the little films"—Scopitone, an early forerunner of music videos. "I would either have $100,000 to make a film, or have nothing," Coppola said. "I lost it, every penny of it. In one stock."

To make matters worse, he was $10,000 in debt. "I had nothing. Not even a friend," Coppola said.

The aspiring director was saved when 20th Century–Fox offered him $50,000 to write *Patton*, for which he shared the Academy Award for Best Original Screenplay. From there it was on to Paris, where he cowrote the screenplay for *Is Paris Burning?* with Gore Vidal and others. The film was one of Charlie Bluhdorn's early disasters at Paramount, and Coppola knew a bomb when he saw one. To "stay sane," he spent his nights working on another script, something he could call his own. It was an adaptation of the novel *You're a Big Boy Now*, about a young man coming of age in New York City. Coppola had used his own money to buy the rights, to ensure he could direct the movie himself.

The project earned him only $8,000, but it served as his MFA thesis at UCLA, where he was still technically enrolled. Screened at the 1967 Cannes Film Festival, the film brought him the kind of headlines that open doors in Hollywood. "Coppola Breaks the Age Barrier," the *Los Angeles Times* had reported by then, marveling over Coppola's success at twenty-six, while "the men in Hollywood's drivers' seats are grandfathers."

In a 1966 story entitled "Offering the Moon to a Guy in Jeans," *New York Times* film critic Rex Reed, noting that the scruffy, bearded

Coppola looked more like "an organ grinder or a hot dog vendor" than a Hollywood director, dubbed him "the Orson Welles of the hand-held camera."

Even Coppola was surprised by his success at such an early age. "I can't get used to coming to work every day and watching all these people making more money than my father made in his lifetime, and they're all waiting for me to tell them what to do," he told Reed, at age twenty-seven. In December 1966, no less a Hollywood kingmaker than Samuel Goldwyn hosted a screening of *Big Boy* in honor of Coppola.

The young filmmaker, observed Peter Bart, had become "one of the few nudie filmmakers to go legit."

Coppola was quickly signed by Warner Bros. to direct *Finian's Rainbow*, starring Fred Astaire. "Warners had this creaky old property lying around, and they wanted a young director to modernize it," Coppola later told the *Los Angeles Times*. But he was already growing disillusioned with Hollywood's emphasis on commerce over art. In 1968, in a deal with Warner Bros.-Seven Arts, he launched his own enterprise, Coppola Company, to sponsor other young talent.

Its first project was *THX 1138*, a sci-fi movie written and directed by George Lucas, who had served as Coppola's assistant on *Finian's Rainbow*. "Youth Leading Youth" read the headline in *Variety*.

"The whole trick, and the secret," he said in a short documentary called *The New Cinema*, "is of creating a film by literally saying you're doing it. It's not a matter of asking someone to let you make a movie, it's to announce that you're making it."

It was a philosophy he put into action on *The Rain People*, a movie he was directing that starred two young actors named James Caan and Robert Duvall. When Warner Bros. hesitated to approve the project, Coppola pushed forward with a bold bluff.

"It's Friday," he said he told the studio's executives. "On Tuesday we're flying to New York and we're going to shoot some film for my new movie."

"Well, what's it about? What's the story?" the executives demanded, according to Coppola. "We gotta approve it."

"If you don't want to make it, I'll pay for it myself," Coppola replied. And with that, he walked out.

On Tuesday, he was indeed shooting. "The idea is, you've gotta really want to do something," he said. "And then nothing can stop you, I believe."

And oh, did Coppola *believe*: in his films, in himself, and in his future. As the crew of *The Rain People* traveled across the country in search of filming locations, he even shaved his beard and reverted to his clean-cut college look, in hopes of winning the permits he needed. "I'm going to make the movie *now*," he told the powers that be, in a tirade that was recorded by George Lucas in the documentary *Filmmaker—A Diary*. "Unless you can get the police to come and stop me from shooting."

Before long, though, all the fighting started to take a toll. "I'm getting ulcers, and I'm only twenty-nine," he said at the beginning of filming, a few days before his birthday. So instead of angling for a bigger film, Coppola turned his back on the Hollywood studio system that tried to marginalize him. "Imagine if we went to a beautiful city like San Francisco and implanted ourselves as a filmmaking commu-nity," he told his friends. "We would have independence, and we'd still be close enough to LA to be able to draw on talent from there."

In 1969, Coppola packed his family into a VW bus and left Los Angeles, trailed by his sister, Talia, and his secretary, Mona Skager, in Skager's Mustang. Close behind them in the caravan was George Lucas. Arriving in San Francisco, Coppola set up his own studio, American Zoetrope. His dream, as the Sixties drew to a close, was to leave behind the rampaging egos and unbridled greed of Hollywood and to create art, not commerce.

The studio's first office was south of Market Street. Skager referred to the neighborhood as Wine Country, "because every wino in town was down there."

There, Coppola believed, he and his fellow filmmakers would be "like Robin Hood and his band."

They were young and energetic and talented, and they had the "filmmaking machine in our hands."

He and Eleanor bought what she called a "dollhouse," a small but charming Victorian rowhouse, and American Zoetrope moved into a cavernous former warehouse at 827 Folsom Street, complete with offices, espresso machine, pool table, and its own remote-controlled postproduction suite—"the only one in America," Coppola boasted. The "new, unique dream studio," as the *San Francisco Chronicle* dubbed it, opened to great fanfare on December 12, 1969. "The difference is that in LA you talk about deals," Coppola told the paper. "Here you talk about films."

The dream lasted about two years. By late 1971, Zoetrope had all but collapsed, "picked clean," Coppola said. "Everyone had used it, no one had contributed, and there was a time when I literally was staving off the sheriff from putting the chain across the door."

He was thirty-two, and once again nearly bankrupt. "Zoetrope was down to one mini-skirted secretary and instant coffee instead of espresso," the *Los Angeles Times* reported. But by then, Coppola was already hard at work on the project that would fulfill his San Francisco dream of artistic freedom—a project handed to him, ironically, by the Hollywood commercialism he had been trying so hard to escape.

IT HAD BEGUN on a storied day in 1969, like something out of a movie. He would remember it as a celestial alignment of forces—three seemingly unrelated events that occurred simultaneously, each pointing to his future, in which Coppola, an Italian American, would be offered the job to direct a movie about a group of Italian Americans that most every bankable director had turned down. "All the elements that ultimately found themselves as essential in *The Godfather* peaked in me that one Sunday in our home in San Francisco," Coppola said.

First, he noticed an advertisement in the Sunday *New York Times*. It was for a new novel entitled *The Godfather*. Coppola thought the author's name, Mario Puzo, sounded like an Italian writer of classic literature.

Next, a knock at the door. It was Albert Ruddy and Gray Frederickson, in town to film *Little Fauss and Big Halsy* for Paramount.

And third, with Ruddy and Frederickson still in the room, the phone rang. It was the actor Marlon Brando, turning down Coppola's offer to star in *The Conversation*, his long-germinating passion project based on a real-life surveillance-technology expert.

The book, the producers, the star. "All magically coinciding on that one day," Coppola said. "I've often pondered how those disconnected elements were destined to all come together and make such an impact upon me."

The man who eventually approached Coppola about *The Godfather* was someone he had known back when he was just starting out, shooting "nudie" films and sleeping on a dirty bed in a vacant department store. Peter Bart had become Paramount's "resident intellectual," advising Robert Evans on the latest hot book or manuscript or script. He had been pushing for Coppola from the start, recognizing the young director as the leader of a new vanguard.

"That's your esoteric bullshit coming out," Evans told Bart when he first suggested Coppola. "The guy's made three pictures: *You're a Big Boy Now*, artsy-fartsy, no business. *Finian's Rainbow*, a top Broadway musical he made into a disaster, and *The Rain People*, which everyone rained on," Evans wrote in *The Kid Stays in the Picture*.

But Bart had a trump card to play. At the time, Burt Lancaster was still trying to buy the rights to *The Godfather* from Paramount, and the studio was tempted to take him up on his million-dollar offer. "It's Coppola or Lancaster," Bart pointed out. So Evans sold Stanley Jaffe on the idea of doing the film with an Italian American director and Italian American actors, which offered a way to stave off the Lancaster deal.

When Bart approached Coppola, however, the director didn't want the job. "Why make another Mafia movie?" he said. "They don't work anymore. The audience has moved past all that."

Bart couldn't believe it. Coppola *needed* this, and he was turning it down. He "seemed almost offended that the studio had submitted the material to him," Bart said.

Bart sent him a copy of the book anyway. "I started to read the book, and I got only about fifty pages into it," he said. "I thought it was a popular, sensational novel, pretty cheap stuff. I got to the part about the singer supposedly modeled on Frank Sinatra and the girl Sonny Corleone liked so much because her vagina was enormous. I said, 'My God, what is this? *The Carpetbaggers?*' So I stopped reading and said, 'Forget it.'"

Evans, still trying to fend off the Lancaster deal, pleaded with Coppola to reconsider. "He couldn't get a cartoon made in town, yet he didn't want to make *The Godfather . . . ,*" Evans wrote. "Did he need a job? He owed more money around town than Nathan Detroit in *Guys and Dolls.*"

But time, Evans knew, was not on his side. Without an Italian American director, the Paramount brass was ready to sell to Lancaster. "Here I am, on my knees, begging this director who had made three features, all flops, to *please, please* put *The Godfather* on screen," Evans wrote.

Coppola continued to refuse. "Francis felt *The Godfather* was beneath his artistic temperament," said the film's sound effects supervisor, Walter Murch, recalling a barbecue with Coppola in Mill Valley in the summer of 1970. Then Coppola noticed that Murch's wife, Aggie, was engrossed in Mario Puzo's novel.

"Is it that good?" Coppola asked.

"I can't stop reading it," said Aggie Murch.

"She was so riveted, she sort of stayed off to herself reading. I remember Francis looking at that," said Murch. "Probably somewhere in the back of his mind he was thinking: *If it's that riveting, if it can grab somebody so much that they won't stop reading it, there must be something in it.*"

Coppola had an additional motivation to do the movie: At that point, the sheriff really was about to shut down American Zoetrope over unpaid taxes, and his studio owed $600,000 in overhead and development costs to Warner Bros. "A few weeks later, [Peter] Bart decided to phone Coppola again and tracked him down at George Lucas's home in Mill Valley," wrote Gene D. Phillips in *Godfather: The Intimate Francis Ford Coppola*. "Lucas remembers that Coppola covered the receiver with his hand and asked, 'George, should I make this gangster movie?'"

"Francis, don't turn it down. We are broke. We're out of business. We're closed," Lucas, then twenty-six, admonished Coppola. "You have to accept the job; we have no money, and the sheriff is coming to chain up the front door."

The Godfather, Lucas added, could be a "lifeboat," to save the company.

"But, gee, George, I wanna make *The Conversation*," Coppola replied. "And, you know, the book is so sleazy."

"Well," Lucas said, "find something in it that you like."

Coppola took his friend's advice. Setting the novel aside, he went to the Mill Valley Public Library, where he scanned the shelves for books on the Mob: "the old classic books," he called them, histories of the New York families. He read about the murder of Mafia boss Salvatore "Little Caesar" Maranzano by Lucky Luciano. He read about Vito Genovese and Joe Profaci and Joe Bonanno, all the old-world mobsters and their bloody reigns. Beneath all the blood and gore, he realized that these criminals weren't merely cold-blooded killers but family men with wives and children and grandchildren. They were also consummate American entrepreneurs. "I was fascinated by this whole idea that there were these various families that had divided up New York and they ran them like businesses," Coppola told *Cigar Aficionado*. "One would take drugs and one would take prostitution and they were all in the businesses that were made illegal by our laws. But people like to gamble and like to go to prostitutes and like to do drugs."

This Mafia stuff is really quite interesting, he thought.

Perusing the history books, he remembered a name from his own past: "Trigger Mike" Coppola, a famous Mafioso in New York, a capo of the Genovese family, was no relation to Coppola, but he was a running joke in the family when Francis was a kid. "Oh," his father and uncle would joke when they needed something taken care of, "we're gonna go see Trigger Mike."

His library research was a revelation. "Having finished the books, I had new reference points," he said. "So I went and I read *The Godfather* again."

This time Coppola envisioned the movie as he read. When he turned the last page, he knew *The Godfather* could be about more than guns and goons and sex and spaghetti. There was an epic saga to be unearthed in the Corleone crime family. "I realized that there was the core of a profound story," he said, "one of a classic succession concerning a great king with three sons, each of whom had a single element of what made the king great," he said, later adding, "The oldest was given his passion and aggressiveness, the second his sweet nature and childlike qualities, and the third his intelligence, cunning, and coldness."

He had found something in *The Godfather* he liked.

"Coppola will make the picture on one condition—that it's not a film about organized gangsters but a family chronicle," Bart told Evans. "A metaphor for capitalism in America."

"Fuck him and the horse he rode in on," Evans replied. "Is he nuts?"

Now that Coppola could see the movie in his head, he still had to convince Paramount to give it to him. He flew to Los Angeles and Al Ruddy picked him up at the airport, stressing the qualities that would get him the job. "Remember one thing Francis: this is a low-budget movie," Ruddy told him. "So when you meet the guys, start figuring out how to downgrade."

Based on Coppola's reputation, Ruddy thought the director was a creative but quiet *artiste*. All that changed when they arrived at the studio. "I was in for the shock of my life," said Ruddy. "Ten minutes into the meeting he was up on the table, giving one of the great sales jobs of all time. They couldn't believe what they were hearing—it was phenomenal."

To Ruddy, Coppola was suddenly transformed into Bill Starbuck, the charismatic con artist in N. Richard Nash's 1954 play, *The Rainmaker*. "Oh, God, he ranted on, but philosophically, about the value of film and the beauty of film and the messages of this book, the continuity and the characters. He's throwing up so many diamonds and so much flash. I remember the line about the domino theory of making movies: It only takes one piece to get the energy going—the attack, the assault, don't ever stop, just keep going. You know, they loved it; they loved *him*. Believe me when I tell you this guy can bullshit like no one you've ever met in your life."

Coppola apparently left it all on the table that day—literally. A half century later, asked about his performance at that supposedly magical meeting, the director drew a blank. "I have no idea of how Ruddy described what I may have said," he said. "Sorry, I can't remember that day at all."

There was one more person he needed to convince. "It's time to bite the bullet," Peter Bart told Robert Evans. "Let's send Coppola to talk to Bluhdorn."

"A Charlie meeting will be a massacre," Evans replied.

Coppola heard from his agent, Freddie Fields. "I want you to get on the red-eye tonight and go talk to Charles Bluhdorn," Fields told him.

The director flew to New York, where he gave another impassioned, bravura performance—first at Gulf+Western's headquarters, then over dinner, and, finally, on a late-night walk around Central Park. "Francis kept Bluhdorn up to three in the morning, pitching his idea on how he saw *The Godfather*," said Mona Skager, Coppola's assistant. "Because Francis is Italian. He understands plastic on the sofa. He grew up in that whole environment. He gave Bluhdorn his vision of how the movie should look—that it's not a gangster story, it's a story about a family."

Coppola was struck by Bluhdorn's power and eccentricity. "I was impressed by how all these others looked up to and feared him," he said. "I liked his enthusiasm and the way he talked with his strange accent."

Bluhdorn was equally impressed by the young director. "We hired Francis walking up and down Central Park South," said Stanley Jaffe. "Charlie Bluhdorn and myself. We agreed he was our director. During the walk, we shook hands and said, 'Francis, we have given this a lot of thought, and we would like you to direct the picture.'"

The next morning, Skager got an excited call from Coppola. "Call Ellie and tell her to pack up Gian and Roman and get the red-eye," he said. "We're sailing out of New York on the *Michelangelo* tomorrow."

He was referring to the SS *Michelangelo*, a luxurious Italian ocean liner once described as a "floating showcase for art, style and culture."

Like the dead-broke Mario Puzo, who had dashed off to Europe with his family the minute he had finished his novel, Coppola was celebrating his signing by taking everyone to Italy.

As they set sail for the Sorrento Film Festival, the Coppola party occupied a two-bedroom penthouse aboard the 1,775-passenger ship. During the eight-day voyage, when he wasn't joining his family for dinners of pasta and cherries jubilee, Coppola worked on *The Godfather*. He tore pages out of the book and taped them to the portholes of one of the ship's bars. "He was sitting there with his portable typewriter and just typing away like a mad dog," said Skager. Like Michael Corleone, Coppola was sailing off into the past, in search of his future.

ROBERT EVANS'S DATEBOOK for Tuesday, September 29, 1970, contained an entry scrawled in green ink: "10:00 Press Conference Ruddy, Puzo and Coppola."

That morning at the appointed hour, the four men sat elbow to elbow at Evans's expansive desk at Paramount's new office in Beverly Hills. For the moment they were all smiles, as they introduced Coppola to the press as the director of *The Godfather*.

"Three of the four men seated at the table would become multimillionaires as a result of that announcement," the film historian Peter Cowie would observe. "The fourth, Robert Evans, seemed to dominate them by virtue not just of a superior sun-tan, but also of well-dressed charisma and enthusiasm."

Shooting, Evans announced, would begin in early January. "*The Godfather* will be our big picture of 1971," he proclaimed. It was, *Variety* reported, "that old *Gone with the Wind* buildup."

Behind the bluster, Evans and his studio were betting everything on one roll of the dice. "The studios are dying," someone involved in the movie was quoted as saying at the time. "Paramount is depending on *The Godfather* to save its life—just like some racket guys in the book do."

Now at the helm of a major studio picture, Coppola was about to usher in a new era in American film. Along with Roman Polanski, who had directed *Rosemary's Baby* for Paramount in 1968, the new guard would change the rules—and the movies. "The two filmmakers who marched into combat with the greatest swagger," Bart wrote. "Both were brought to the studio under the rules of the old regime, but with promises of change. They were hired guns who nonetheless exuded confidence in their ability to expand the boundaries of cinema . . . They came to think of themselves not merely as rebels but as outlaws. They viewed the studios not as wellsprings of support but as targets to be plundered."

It would be one of the great wars in American cinema: Robert Evans, head of production at Paramount, versus Francis Ford Coppola, the headstrong director. "Francis and I had a perfect record," Evans would write. "We didn't agree on anything."

From the beginning, it was a "very big fight," according to Coppola. "The studio had this young director who was hired mainly because he was Italian American, and that would possibly be good in terms of saying, 'Well, an Italian made the film.' I had some acclaim as a screenwriter and they knew the script needed to be worked on, so they figured they'd get a free rewrite out of it, which they did. And also I was young and had no power, so they figured they could just boss me around, which they proceeded to begin to do."

Coppola lost the first skirmish. The studio had offered him his choice of deals: $125,000 and 10 percent of the film's net profits, or $175,000 and 6 percent of the net profits. "I had no money," he said. "I had kids. So I had to take the $175,000."

But he had asked for more of the box office. "I'll do it for seven percent of the picture, because seven is my lucky number," he told the studio. "I was born April seventh, I have to have seven percent."

Paramount agreed—then turned around and stuck him with 6 percent. "The studio even lied [about] what my fee was," Coppola said.

At the press conference announcing his hire, Coppola smiled for the cameras. But the pose masked his true emotions. "I was getting into a type of production which was the opposite of what I craved," he remembered. "I wanted to make personal art films, and here was a studio production with a lot of bosses, a very limited budget, and opinions different from my own on every aspect. I had two kids, a pregnant wife, and no money.

"I was terrified," he admitted.

7

THE MIRACLE ON MULHOLLAND

"I believe in America."

The first four words of *The Godfather* are among the greatest opening lines in cinema history. They are spoken by an immigrant, Amerigo Bonasera, an undertaker whose first name is Italian for the country he has come to call home, a country that has both enriched him and betrayed him. The words speak not only to the bittersweet experience of Italian Americans but to all those whose faith in the nation's ideals have been driven to the breaking point.

"I believe in America," Bonasera says, his brooding, moonlike face peering out from the shadows after the title has rolled. "America has made my fortune. And I raised my daughter in the American fashion. I gave her freedom, but—I taught her never to dishonor her family. She found a boyfriend, not an Italian. She went to the movies with him; she stayed out late. I didn't protest. Two months ago, he took her for a drive, with another boyfriend. They made her drink whiskey. And then they tried to take advantage of her. She resisted. She kept her honor. So they beat her, like an animal. When I went to the hospital, her nose was broken. Her jaw was shattered, held together by wire. She couldn't even weep because of the pain. But I wept. Why did I weep? She was the light of my life—beautiful girl. Now she will never be beautiful again."

He breaks down in sobs. The camera pulls back, and the audience sees the hand of a man behind a desk, gesturing to his son to bring the sobbing undertaker a drink.

"I—I went to the police, like a good American," Bonasera continues after regaining his composure. "These two boys were brought to trial. The judge sentenced them to three years in prison, and suspended the sentence. *Suspended sentence!* They went free that very day! I stood in the courtroom like a fool. And those two bastards, they *smiled* at me. Then I said to my wife, 'For justice, we must go to Don Corleone.'"

The man behind the desk speaks for the first time, his voice a raspy murmur. "Why did you go to the police?" he asks. "Why didn't you come to me first?"

"What do you want from me?" says Bonasera. "Tell me anything. But do what I beg you to do."

"What is that?"

The undertaker rises and whispers in Don Corleone's ear. The camera pulls back, and the old man's face is seen for the first time: the greatest actor in the world, Marlon Brando. Not the youthful Brando of *A Streetcar Named Desire* or *On the Waterfront*, nor the aging Brando of his recent string of box-office bombs. This is a Brando reborn. The jowly, jaw-jutting face of a bulldog. The tuxedo. The vagabond cat that had wandered onto the set on his lap. A Mafia don who can deliver what the state has failed to provide: justice. As he rises to console the undertaker, his unmistakable power establishes the tone and trajectory of everything to follow, a dark and brutal descent into the American Dream.

It was not an obvious place to begin. In Mario Puzo's book, the scene doesn't appear until well into the first chapter: after the novel's opening, with Bonasera awaiting justice in New York Criminal Court Number 3; after Johnny Fontane beats his beautiful, cheating wife and Nazorine the baker confronts his homely, lovestruck daughter; after the long scene of Connie Corleone's wedding; after the torrid stairwell sex between Connie's maid of honor, Lucy Mancini, with her oversized vagina, and Sonny Corleone, with his oversized sexual equipment. Others might have overlooked the short, solitary sentence buried deep in the middle of an overstuffed paragraph on page twenty-nine. But Francis Ford Coppola saw its potential. The line, he realized, represented "the real appeal of *The Godfather*, that you could go to someone if you weren't being treated fairly, and the Godfather would make it right."

"I thought, *This is what made the movie!*" Al Pacino said, recalling his reaction to the hypnotic opening. "Everyone can relate to that. The universe can relate to that. . . . His daughter's been raped and beaten. He goes to the Godfather because no one else will help him."

Coppola had always been able to see things others couldn't, conjuring up entire worlds from thin air. He laid out his vision for *The Godfather*, from the opening scene to the final credits, at a corner table in the back of Caffe Trieste, a legendary Italian institution in San Francisco's North Beach neighborhood. Coppola would arrive each day, usually wearing a safari jacket covered in pockets and epaulets, a big brown satchel slung over his shoulder, carrying his yellow Olivetti Lettera 32 manual typewriter. There, amid the smoke and clatter and the music, he would work away on the script, fueled by two of the most primal elements in all of nature: strong coffee and "profound fear."

"It's important to understand that at the root of it all, I was terrified," Coppola said. If he could only create a plan for the movie, something to guide him on the long journey ahead, "I would then be able to sleep at night. I would feel that at least I would be taking a step forward, that doing it this way would help me get a handle on how to do the script. I was sort of blindly looking for a structure to organize myself in order to get the most out of the subject matter."

Searching for that way forward, Coppola remembered something from his theater arts background: a prompt book, created by pasting a script or book's pages into a three-ring binder and writing notes and stage directions in the margins. Creating such a book would enable Coppola to deconstruct Puzo's massive novel page by page and create what he called "a multilayered road map for me to direct the film."

He set to work on the novel, ripping it out of its binding and trimming each of its 448 pages with a razor blade. Then he pasted them on oversized paper, which he fortified with "really good grommets" and placed into the rings of an oversized notebook. Sitting at his typewriter in Caffe Trieste, pens and pencils next to the sugar shaker, he would pull out the prompt book and pore through the pages, giving free rein to his imagination.

"I went there every day for many weeks," he said. "I sat at a corner table next to the phone booth, which was sort of private, and I would just sit there, looking at the people coming and going, and go through these pages. I loved it; I was living a dream. I was in a café where there was lots of noise and Italian being spoken, and cute girls walking through, and that was my dream. It was *La Bohème* for me."

"Francis was this young buck, with talent just oozing out of him," remembered Lanetta Wahlgren, Puzo's longtime assistant. And that deep well of talent spilled out straight into the prompt book. Soon the extrawide margins were blackened by his overactive pen and his sharp-ruled lines. "As I was reading the book and making these notes, and then putting them on the margins, obviously the more pens I was using and the more rulers, lines, the more squiggly lines, sort of implied the excitement of the book was higher and higher," he said. "So that the sheer amount of ink on the page would tell me later on— this is one of the most important scenes. . . . Whenever I felt there was a really important part of the book that was going to be in the movie, I would sit there with my ruler and really underline."

He underlined sections he imagined as scenes and scribbled frantically in the margins, blackening the pages with notes. "Go really big in this scene," he wrote beside the wedding scene. "It immediately says that this Big Book has been made into a Big Movie."

And at the slaughter of the mountainous henchman Luca Brasi: "I Want His Face to Change Color Right Before Our Eyes!" "His Eyes Bulging!" And when he's dead: "The Luca Brasi Payoff. 'With the Fishes.'"

On the page of his prompt book where Bonasera tells his agonizing tale, Coppola wrote, "Bonasera's story. *Rigoletto*," a reference to the classic Verdi opera that depicts a court jester's failed attempt to protect his daughter. And when the undertaker asks Don Corleone to "do what I beg you to do," whispering his desire for revenge in the don's ear, Coppola wrote in the margin, "Bonasera knows that the Don has the power to bring about *death*." "POWER, POWER, POWER— never forget that it is from a fascination of the limits and manipulations of Power that keep people interested in this book," he wrote.

Now, as director, Coppola possessed the power to bring *The Godfather* to life. By that point, he was also serving as the film's primary screenwriter. Puzo had already completed his second draft of the script. But while the author had crafted his novel in solitude, screenwriting is an industrial assembly line, driven by the bottom line. As Puzo wrote, Paramount pressured him to save money by setting the movie in the present day, rather than the postwar years. They also pushed him to emphasize whatever was fastest and cheapest to film—especially the sex. "Start off with a love scene between Michael and Kay," Al Ruddy instructed Puzo in an early draft.

"Al," Puzo protested, "you can't start *The Godfather* off with a love scene."

But Ruddy insisted, and Puzo felt as though he had no choice. "I went back upstairs and read the contract," he wrote, "and, sure enough, it said the producer can tell the writer how to write the script. I had to start off the movie with a youthful love scene. So I wrote it and it was lousy."

Then he took it to Ruddy. "I showed it to Al and he loved it."

Peter Bart also approved of Puzo's draft. "I think you have done an excellent job in developing the construction and the characters, and I think we are well on our way to an enormously successful motion picture," Bart wrote the author on July 13, 1970. He provided a dozen notes: "I do not believe that the courtroom setting represents the best way to open this picture. . . . I wonder if it's entirely clear why the Godfather is so ardently opposed to narcotics. . . . I hope we can find a way to keep Luca Brasi alive. . . . The restaurant scene in which Michael murders Sollozzo lacks suspense.... Kay again is too naive here. She must know about the Mafia and about Michael by this time."

Puzo had worked on the screenplay alone before the arrival of Francis Coppola in late September 1970. The director met the novelist for the first time in Al Ruddy's Paramount office, said Janet Snow, "two Italian Americans, both incredibly creative, with great and immediate respect for the other's talent."

Coppola's arrival was "a huge relief for Mario," said Snow. Because Puzo quickly realized that Coppola had the perfect vision for transforming his novel into a movie. But first, food. "On his first day at Paramount, Francis invited Mario and me to dinner, and he took us to a great Chinese restaurant in Hollywood," said Snow. "He had obviously combed every single page of the book. He was incredibly prepared."

From that very first night, over a dinner of every conceivable Chinese dish, they fell in love with each other as collaborators, friends, and fellow food lovers, the first of many dinners to come. "When Mario heard Francis's vision for the movie, he knew he really got it. And Mario was able to relax."

Over the dinner, Puzo told Coppola that his assistant, Janet, was "half Italian."

"And Francis said 'Ah, *paisano* [fellow countryman],' and Mario just loved that," said Snow.

"I immediately liked Mario; found him funny, wise, and lovable," said Coppola. "He spoke in clear, short, wise statements. I must say, certainly after the entire term of my work with him, that I admired and respected him. And I loved him."

Coppola's sister, Talia Shire, joined the two men for dinner when Francis would come to Los Angeles from San Francisco. "They had something wonderful!" she said. "I saw it. Those two loved each other, and it was quite remarkable what they had. I saw collaboration and friendship, a great writer, Mario, and this young director, Francis, who had this great respect for Mario and his years of writing dramatic literature."

Puzo's script was a different matter. The suits at Paramount might have been happy with Puzo's work, but Coppola had a decidedly different reaction. "I liked Mario much more than his script," he said of the author's early draft. "Judging from the opinions of all around him, he pretty much did what he was told to do. They wanted contemporary because that is much cheaper, and I felt the setting during the war years was essential to the story and characters."

The director also recognized that Puzo had a few blind spots of his own. "He couldn't speak Italian," Coppola said. "He had taken most of what he knew about the Mafia from *The Valachi Papers*. He didn't know that calling the character Don Corleone was incorrect—it would have been Don Vito."

Puzo, accustomed to working with other writers since his Magazine Management days, suggested that he and Coppola work on the script together. "Francis looked me right in the eye and said no," Puzo wrote. "That's when I knew he was really a director."

They would correspond long distance—Puzo in Los Angeles or back home in New York (returning when he got homesick), Coppola in San Francisco.

"Now that he was successful, watch out," said Puzo's son Anthony. "He purchased books instead of borrowing them from the library; ate at expensive restaurants; flew to Las Vegas on a whim. And he spent an obscene amount of money renting a house in Malibu. He loaned money to all that asked. By the time the movie was released he was broke again!"

Until then, he would live very large. During one of his first summers in Los Angeles, Puzo rented an obscenely expensive house on the beach in Malibu Colony for a month and invited his family to visit, which was an impressive gesture, although not so much to his wife, Erika, who preferred home and family to Malibu and movie stars. "When they moved to Bay Shore, New York, Mario bought a spec house," said Lanetta Wahlgren. "It was a big square box, but it was a palace to Erika. All she wanted to do is stay there and be queen of her castle. She loved to knit, to make German food. She loved being a mother, and she was a very typical suburban housewife. She didn't drive. She didn't really even understand Mario's writing."

Wahlgren had come into Puzo's orbit on February 4, 1971, and began working with him later that year. A twenty-five-year-old model, she had grown up in Brentwood and attended Bel Air Town and Country School alongside the children of movie stars. She knew everybody and, most importantly, she knew how the town worked, who Puzo should meet and who he should steer clear of.

Wahlgren arrived for an interview at Puzo's suite in the Beverly Hills Hotel, where she found the author lounging on the couch in a surfer shirt.

The first thing she noticed was his big belly, then his long slicked-back hair and, finally, his cigar, the biggest Cuban Montecristo she had ever seen. "He was extremely fat then," she said. "And very intimidating, because of the way he looked and because he was a man of very few words."

As Puzo stared at her through his thick black glasses, Wahlgren tried to list out her qualifications. Puzo interrupted her.

"Kid," he said, "you've got the job."

Wahlgren soon saw what the public didn't see: "the frog prince," she called him, a writer whose gruff and off-putting, frequently slovenly appearance belied a kind and loving man. "He was self-effacing and shy, and he soon depended on me for everything," she said. "I was his Girl Friday."

And like the frog prince, Puzo soon underwent a startling metamorphosis. The first thing to go were his clothes, the ragged tracksuits and New York City leisurewear he wore on his arrival. Wahlgren took him to the store of his dreams: Gucci on Rodeo Drive.

Once they arrived, however, Puzo was met with a frosty reception. "The first time we walked into Gucci—this was before the movie came out—we were almost asked to leave," said Wahlgren. "Mario was unkempt, greasy haired, in tracksuits zipped up the front. His pants would work their way down until they were below his bare belly, and the cuffs were worn out because they dragged on the ground over his old loafers, which he always wore without socks."

Puzo pointed out clothes he wanted—"I like this and that"—but the salesman ignored him and focused on Wahlgren, who was stylishly dressed. "They thought he was a slob," she said.

Puzo was used to it. He turned to Wahlgren. "Hon, let's leave," he said.

They went back another time or two, but it was always the same. Finally, Wahlgren turned to the salesman. "Do you know who this man is?" she asked. "He wrote *The Godfather*!"

They locked the doors and Puzo spent $50,000.

Gone were the vagabond clothes of the struggling writer, replaced with a rich wardrobe of Gucci tracksuits and cashmere sweaters in a rainbow of bright hues, most prominently Puzo's favorite color, pink. All of which he slipped into as easily as he had slipped from one life into another. His new clothes gave him an outward splendor that in no way reflected his innermost feelings. "Mario lived two different lives," said Wahlgren. "When he first came to Hollywood, he had been deprived for so long of so much. He really thought himself to be the geek, the nice but dumb Fredo, and that he didn't have the talent to write something great. He felt *The Godfather* was not good. It was a sell-out, and he wanted to be taken seriously. His humble background and hardships overshadowed anything he accomplished with his beautiful mind. He looked at the success of *The Godfather* as something of a joke."

It didn't help that diversions beckoned him from all sides. Most mornings, it would take Wahlgren forever to convince Puzo to climb into her Corvette so she could drive him to the studio, where he would continue his work, now remotely with Francis Coppola, on the screenplay. "Writing was painful for Mario," said Wahlgren. "He would lay down on the sofa and read three books a day. Or he'd put the ballgame on. Or go shopping. Eating. Playing tennis and playing pinochle. Everything but working on the script."

One day, Puzo invited the author Gay Talese to play tennis. Talese drove to Puzo's Malibu rental, where he parked his car and stepped out into a sea of yellow tennis balls, so many balls, he could hardly walk. "Because of all the balls blocking my path."

He followed the balls to the tennis court, where he found Puzo practicing his serve.

"What amazed me was that the entire court was filled with hundreds and hundreds of yellow tennis balls," said Talese. "He would open a tin of balls, take three balls, swat his serve across the net to the opposite end of the court. Then he would open another tin, swat three more balls across the court . . . and then open another tin . . . and another . . . and another . . . And finally there were about seven or eight hundred tennis balls literally covering the entire green concrete court. He never stooped down to pick up a ball. Why should he? Paramount was paying for everything."

Often when Puzo and Wahlgren were driving toward work at Paramount, Puzo would speak up. "Get on the freeway," he would say.

"I knew what that meant," Wahlgren said. "We were going to the airport, and we were going to Las Vegas."

Wahlgren would park her Corvette at the airport, and they would take the next flight to Vegas. There, they would head straight to the casinos, either the Sands or the Tropicana. "He would gamble all day, starting with roulette and then high-stakes baccarat," she remembered. "We would end up in Vegas for fourteen hours, from eight thirty in the morning until deep into the night. It would make me sick the amount of money he would lose. Like over $100,000, which was a lot then. The rent on my apartment, a really nice apartment, was $187 a month."

Puzo couldn't get enough of his new life. Wherever he went—craps table or dinner table—he was in demand, even desired. He whisked a photographer doing a spread on him for *Life* magazine off to Vegas, where he stayed in Bugsy Siegel's presidential suite at the Flamingo and ordered Dom Pérignon for the *Life* crew, all compliments of the house. ("Author Mario Puzo Can Afford to Live It Up at Last," the headline read.)

He played pinochle with the chocolatier Marvin Winkler and was regularly invited to dinner at the home of William Wyler, the director of *Ben-Hur* and other classics. On the way, he would direct Wahlgren to stop off at Maria's Italian Kitchen for the biggest possible pizza, loaded with the works, which he would polish off quickly with a Diet Coke—for insurance, in case the Wylers were serving fish, which, no matter how "Hollywood" he had become, he would never eat.

Other temptations beckoned: long drives to the beach, fabulous food, and eager women. "Women threw themselves at him!" Wahlgren said. Puzo would be working in his suite at the Pink Palace when the phone would ring. "Mr. Evans is sending someone over," a voice on the phone would tell her. Then he would go down to the Polo Lounge, the hotel's famous restaurant, and eat everything in sight while he waited for the woman that Evans was sending him. "As far as the studio goes, he wasn't taken seriously unless they wanted something," Wahlgren said. Evans thought it might help him work if he sent over a woman for sex—"usually very beautiful."

Invariably, though, the woman would arrive at the restaurant and plead hardship. "She would start telling Mario she needed money for her child," said Wahlgren. "And instead of taking advantage of her, he would give her money but he wouldn't ask for anything in return."

Puzo never said no to someone who needed money.

IN THE FIRST of his many moves to gain artistic control over the film, Coppola had taken over the screenplay. Sitting in Caffe Trieste day after day, he had drawn from his prompt book and Puzo's draft.

Then he would send what he had written to Puzo, who would make corrections and offer notes. "Frankly," Coppola said, "I felt he had done the hard heavy lifting by writing the novel, which yielded tons of great stuff, as evidenced by the notebook I prepared. So I did the heavy lifting of the screenplay, and he commented and revised by adding comments and crossing out things. This work was nonetheless crucial and greatly improved the script."

In the scene where Clemenza tells Michael how to make spaghetti sauce, Coppola had written, "First, you brown some sausage, and then you throw in the tomatoes."

In his notes on the line, Puzo scribbled, "Gangsters don't brown. Gangsters fry!" Coppola's draft, which eventually expanded to encompass five acts and fifty scenes, was soon sprinkled with Puzo's terse, precise observations. "It was like that throughout my draft of the script—just handwritten notes here and there, but they made a powerful difference."

"Mario loved to gamble, so I suggested that we go and stay at a gambling casino in Reno to work on the emerging script," said Coppola. It was a process they would repeat for both *Godfather* sequels. "A casino is the perfect place for writers to collaborate," Coppola wrote in his introduction to the fiftieth-anniversary edition of the novel. "There are no clocks, so you can order up bacon and eggs (or anything) at any hour. When you reach a snag, you can always go downstairs to play roulette, which Mario loved to do. And then if you hit big losses—which Mario hated to do; he was a truly terrible gambler, despite knowing tons about it—you could escape back upstairs to continue working."

Like all gamblers, Puzo trusted that the math would work itself out. "I'm losing thousands down here," he told Coppola, "but making millions upstairs."

AS COPPOLA MINED Puzo's novel for themes and characters, he found himself particularly drawn to Amerigo Bonasera. Here was an Italian immigrant who tended to the dead, begging Don Corleone for more death. "Good scene," he wrote in the margin of his prompt book.

Followed by "We need a terrific actor for Bonasera."

Casting, Coppola knew, was the key to everything. Just as he had unearthed that jewel of an opening line buried in Puzo's novel, he now had to find the perfect actors to breathe life into his characters and make them worthy of the magnified dimensions of the screen. The choices Coppola made for each role would determine, in large part, whether *The Godfather* succeeded at breaking the seemingly endless chain of box-office disasters involving movies about organized crime.

To find his Bonasera, the director searched beyond the bounds of Hollywood. "It is always my tradition to have an open casting call where anyone can meet me and be considered for a role," Coppola would say. "Even without an agent."

At one open call, an Italian barber and character actor named Salvatore Corsitto read for Bonasera. He was, as Hiro Narita, the cameraman who recorded his audition remembered, "a regular person, not an actor, nervous, if not petrified, stumbling on some lines during the test."

But Coppola knew he had found his undertaker.

By the time Coppola signed on as director, casting had already been unofficially underway for months. The novel's runaway popularity had turned the process into something bordering on a nationwide frenzy, the likes of which Hollywood hadn't seen since the movie mogul David O. Selznick had launched a nationwide search for Scarlett O'Hara in *Gone with the Wind*. Some of Hollywood's brightest stars, along with many of its biggest has-beens, were pulling every string they could to land a part in the film, and the studio was drafting its own wish lists. Al Ruddy found himself besieged by phone calls from actors and agents, begging for roles. Anthony Quinn and Ernest Borgnine were rumored to be vying for the part of Don Corleone. "Everyone had an opinion on who should play what," Ruddy said of the first frantic months.

Hollywood actors weren't the only ones pressing Ruddy for a part. The producer had inadvertently fueled the casting frenzy by publicly announcing that there would be no major stars in *The Godfather*. "No part will be played by any actor who has an instantly recognizable face," Ruddy told the *Hollywood Reporter*. "The book is the star, not the actors, I want the audience to see real people, almost as if they are looking through a window. I just don't feel I can achieve this if I hire well-known actors."

What he didn't add was that big stars cost big money, and Charlie Bluhdorn hadn't made him producer to blow through Paramount's cash.

The announcement that the producer of *The Godfather* planned to cast unknowns in the film inspired every shop clerk and extra who dreamed of Hollywood stardom. "Every 'unknown' would-be actor and actress has been after one part or another ever since," reported the *Los Angeles Times*. Robert Evans poured even more gasoline on the casting blaze. "We're going to cast real faces, people who are not names," the studio chief announced at the September press conference. Fans of the book were soon bombarding the studio with letters and telegrams, proposing themselves for various parts. A reader from Gary, Indiana, who felt destined to play the title role, called Ruddy's office and told his secretary he was hopping on a plane that afternoon to come out and talk with the producer. A wannabe Michael Corleone spent $2,000 on his own screen test. "He had his wife play Kay, and then friends play other parts," Ruddy told the *Hollywood Reporter*. Another man finagled his way onto the Paramount lot by having the guard at the gate call Ruddy's office and announce, "Michael Corleone is out here to see you."

Ushered up, he presented Ruddy's curious associates with business cards he had printed up bearing Michael's name. Someone else sent the producer a photograph of himself holding a pizza, as evidence that he would be perfect for a part in the movie.

"In a way it's sad," Ruddy lamented. "We are not going to use amateurs, just unknown faces. There's a big difference."

But the damage was done. The excitement grew to such a fever pitch that "talent schools" began approaching people on the street with portable videotape cameras, handing them a card, and charging them $100 to record a screen test for *The Godfather*. Paramount's legal department issued restraining orders against schools in both New York and Los Angeles. "They are not affiliated with us in any way, and I'm not looking at any of the 'tests,'" Ruddy told the *Hollywood Reporter.* "It's all a fraud and I want to warn everyone."

Italian Americans, who saw themselves reflected in Puzo's book, felt emboldened to lobby for parts, especially after Evans announced that there was a "good chance" the film would feature Italian performers. "At one point the head of HR in our company came to me and Bob," said Stanley Jaffe, the studio's president. "He was Italian. He said, 'Stanley and Bob, can I test?' I said, 'Here's what I'm gonna tell you: If you're not back in your office in five minutes you can forget testing and also forget your job.' That's how lunatic it got! People out of the blue were showing up."

Melvin Belli, the famed personal-injury attorney, repeatedly called Ruddy to demand he be cast as Don Corleone. When Belli said he was coming to see the producer, Ruddy's secretary said she would leave a drive-in pass at the studio gate. "I drive a pink Rolls-Royce," Belli scoffed. "I don't even need a drive-in pass at Fort Knox."

EVEN REAL-LIFE MOBSTERS were clamoring to get in. Someone sent Louis DiGiaimo, one of the film's casting directors, a message lifted straight from the book. "I remember getting a dead fish delivered to me, wrapped," DiGiaimo said. Another time, after a young woman auditioned for a part, DiGiaimo got a visit from one of her admirers. "I know some of the guys downtown," the man said, explaining what would happen if the woman wasn't cast in the film. "These guys are going to come looking for you. They're going to break your legs."

At Paramount's office in New York, mysterious men arrived with mysterious offers. One showed up in Jaffe's office not long after the movie was announced. "The first thing he did was sit down and run his fingers under my desk to make sure there was no wire," Jaffe said. "Then he said 'they'—whoever 'they' were—would like to cofinance the picture."

Jaffe diplomatically turned them down.

Paramount's New York–based casting director, Andrea Eastman, then twenty-eight, also felt the pressure of shadowy forces, via creepy calls to her office regarding a certain "Mr. Dante."

"Then one day on a Saturday morning the same guy calls me at home, and he goes, 'Girlie, you listen and you listen carefully,'" she remembered the chilling voice insisting over the phone. "If you ever want to shoot *The Godfather* in New York, you have to use Mr. Dante.'"

Soon after that, she accompanied Al Ruddy to lunch at an Italian restaurant in New York. Joining them was associate producer Gray Frederickson and several others. Eastman was seated, she said, "next to a man in a brown suit who looked like an accountant." He gave his name as Mr. Butter.

Presumably, it was the infamous George "Butterass" DeCicco, a trusted lieutenant of the Gambino crime family, described as a "bloodthirsty" capo by the *New York Post*. "So I'm telling Mr. Butter about this conversation about Mr. Dante," she recalled.

A flash of recognition from Butter.

"You want me to drop him out a window?" he asked.

"No, no, don't do that!" Eastman insisted.

She never heard from the man pressuring her about Mr. Dante again.

Back in LA, Mario Puzo was also besieged with actors and wannabes lobbying him for roles. A fury arose before the gates of Paramount: Italian Americans picketing a film that was supposed to have been cast with authentic Italian Americans and unknowns. "Godfather Casting, An Italian Uprising" read the *Los Angeles Times* headline.

"More Advantages for Italian Americans," read one of the picket signs.

"Italian Actors for Italian Roles," demanded another.

Would-be actors and actresses of Italian descent felt they were *owed* a part in the film merely due to their blood. Calls and letters poured into Paramount from all over the country: "I'm an unknown . . . I've read *The Godfather* . . . I've always wanted to come to Hollywood . . . My father was slightly connected to the Mafia . . ."

In Mario Puzo's office at Paramount, "all hell has broken loose," reported the *Times*. The author had become a magnet for would-be Michaels, Sonnys, and Fredos, letters and telegrams flooding his office, along with tough-guy threats for parts—or else. "You want any heads cracked?" one actor seeking a part asked Puzo. "I've read that you may be filming the picture in Cleveland. My father is the Godfather in Cleveland, and he can make things easy for you," wrote another.

"Michael Corleone arriving 10 a.m.," telegrammed another, who actually made his way into Puzo's office "and bird-dogged the writer around town for a few days," reported the *Times*. Another tracked down Puzo in the Polo Lounge of the Beverly Hills Hotel. "Call for Michael Corleone!" announced the hotel's uniformed phone messenger upon which an individual identifying himself as "Michael Corleone" appeared at Puzo's table, gave him his card (which bore the name Michael Corleone), and disappeared without a word.

Another unknown spent $2,000 on a ten-minute film, in which he played both Michael Corleone and Tom Hagen, while a wannabe Sonny Corleone showed up at the office claiming to have a meeting with Puzo, and "slammed" his secretary on the shoulder, according to the *Times*, "knocking her across the room."

(She called security.)

"One day three huge, sinister-looking men suddenly appeared in the office," dressed in 1940s Mafia attire, the *Times* reported.

"Puzo here?" one of them asked, which brought forth Al Ruddy's assistant with a prop gun to scare them off.

"The casting began," wrote Puzo. "Actors would come in and talk to Coppola and exert all their art and skills to make him remember them. I sat in on some interviews. Coppola was cool and courteous to these people, but for me it was simply too painful. I quit. I couldn't watch them anymore. They were so vulnerable, so open, so naked in their hope for lightning to strike."

One day in his office, Puzo's phone rang: Sue Mengers. "Who I didn't know was a famous agent," he confessed. "She wanted to have lunch. I asked why. She said she represented Rod Steiger and he wanted a part in *The Godfather*. I told her as the writer I had no power, she should talk to the producer and director. No, she wanted to talk to me."

Puzo said he couldn't make lunch, and suggested they speak by phone.

"Okay, she said, Rod Steiger wanted to play Michael. I started to laugh. She got mad and said she was just stating her client's wish. I apologized. Steiger is a fine actor, but, Jesus Christ, there is no way he can look under forty. And the part of Michael has to look no more than twenty-five."

JUST AS COPPOLA had taken control of the screenplay, he moved quickly to assert control over the chaotic casting process. Coppola began assembling his own team, and among his first hires was the producer and casting director Fred Roos, who had worked with Jack Nicholson on his recent films and had cast *Five Easy Pieces*. Coppola had never met Roos, but he used to call him out of the blue to kick around names. "He just wanted to schmooze about actors," Roos remembered. "What do I think of so and so? Who have you seen lately that is interesting or new or good? They were long phone conversations that didn't have any point to them, other than two guys schmoozing."

After Coppola was hired to direct *The Godfather*, he called Roos to offer him a job. "He didn't talk like he had been hired to do a great piece of literature," Roos said. "But he said, 'I think we can do something with it. Would you like to cast it with me?' And I said, yeah, great! He said, 'Get over here and make your deal and let's go to work.' So I was hired before even having a face-to-face with him."

"Casting formally began in New York, at 'THE GODFATHER' Production Offices on 28th floor of #1 Gulf and Western Plaza, on November 20, 1970," Coppola wrote in a January 29, 1971, letter. "I saw approximately 600 New York actors; then, I moved our offices in

Los Angeles, where, working with Mr. Fred Roos, I saw another 500 actors; then to San Francisco where I saw a smaller number and tested some of the New York and Los Angeles callbacks."

Authenticity rose up from the streets. "Made men," or those close to them, felt they had a right to be in the picture. Out of this netherworld stepped Gianni Russo, the unknown who would land the role of Carlo Rizzi, Connie Corleone's abusive husband, who sells out Sonny. The role would make Russo an actor and media personality—but it was something of a miracle that he could test for it, much less land it.

A child of Little Italy, he had been left with what he called "a gimp arm" after a childhood bout with polio, which led him to selling ballpoint pens outside the Sherry-Netherland hotel, on Fifth Avenue. Every morning, Mob boss Frank Costello came out of the hotel, and soon, Russo wrote in his autobiography, *Hollywood Godfather,* Costello was giving him a five-dollar bill every day. One day, Costello gave him one hundred dollars and told him to meet him in the lobby of the Waldorf-Astoria Hotel the next morning.

"From that day on I was with him every day," Russo said.

From his start as a messenger, he rose up in the ranks, and claimed close connections to such Mob bosses as Carlo Gambino and John Gotti, and even closer bedroom connections with too many famous women to count, from Marilyn Monroe to 1980s New York hotel queen Leona Helmsley. After appearing in *The Godfather,* he would go on to kill three men in self-defense, he said, including a member of the Medellín coke cartel, who had stabbed him in the belly with a broken Cristal champagne bottle at his nightclub Gianni Russo's State Street casino, in Vegas. He claimed to have beaten twenty-three federal indictments, and, he added, "never slept in a jail."

Russo was starring in his own Las Vegas television series, *Welcome to My Lifestyle,* when he read the news that Paramount, and Al Ruddy, were seeking unknowns to cast in *The Godfather.* "In the acting trade, I was so unknown, I was damn near invisible," he wrote. "I had a new goal in life: I was going to make it my mission to get a part in that movie—no matter what it took."

Russo called a cocktail waitress to come up to his apartment and help him read the book. Determined to become part of *The Godfather* phenomenon, he made up his own lines and commissioned a crew to film and edit a thirty-seven-minute screen test of him auditioning for three roles: Michael, Sonny, and Carlo. Hearing that Ruddy loved "flashy cars and Asian women," he enlisted an Asian showgirl from the chorus line of the Tropicana, dressed her in a shiny vinyl chauffeur's costume ("skimpy enough to have gotten her arrested in a Las Vegas whorehouse," Russo wrote), put her behind the wheel of his Bentley, and dispatched her to LA, with instructions to personally place the screen test in Ruddy's hands. As Russo told the story, Brando eventually ended up with the showgirl, and all he got for his trouble was a rejection from Ruddy, who told him that "the budget for this movie necessitates we get proven talent for the major roles as a draw."

"Now my balls are in an uproar, because I spent thousands on this shoot," said Russo.

He wouldn't take no for an answer. "I really kept on their ass and made a real pest of myself," he said. "I shouldn't say this on tape, but Charlie Bluhdorn had a lot of good friends," he added, presumably referring to Bluhdorn's alleged underworld connections. "So I had some people call him and say, 'You know, this guy Gianni Russo is a very close friend of ours.'" He was eventually able to "read" for the role of Carlo.

Russo flew to New York and reported to the Gulf+Western Building to perform before Ruddy, Evans, Jaffe, and Bluhdorn. It would be an enactment of the scene where Carlo viciously belt-whips his pregnant wife, Connie. Paramount president Stanley Jaffe's secretary stood in for Connie, but Russo couldn't get into the scene. "It just wasn't working," he acknowledged.

When everyone broke for lunch, Russo drank steadily from a gallon jug of Almaden Chablis, as he had done every day to lose eighty-seven pounds for the role on a wine and popcorn diet. When filming resumed, he was ready to rage. "I'm sorry, but I gotta get this part, so get ready," he warned the secretary. Then he "went crazy," screaming and cursing and "throwing her all over the place, finally across a desk, where she landed on Bob Evans's lap. They thought I was going to kill her."

"Stop, stop! You've got the part!" Russo remembered one executive yelling.

The next day, by way of apology, Russo sent the secretary a huge arrangement of flowers. He also introduced the executives to some real-life mobsters, to provide them with what Jaffe called "a flavor" of that world.

Al Lettieri as Virgil "the Turk" Sollozzo, the drug-dealing, double-crossing gangster who sets up the hit on Don Corleone, reeked of authenticity from a lifetime of preparation. Lettieri didn't have to study the Mob for his role; his brother-in-law, Pasquale "Patsy Ryan" Eboli, was "a reputed capo in the Genovese crime family," according to the *New York Times*. "Al was the real deal," said Jan Lettieri, the actor's ex-wife. "When he went out, Al always had bodyguards with him, because his brother-in-law was terrified he would spill the beans on certain things."

Lettieri was also said to have served as an inspiration for Marlon Brando's Oscar-winning performance in *On the Waterfront*. "It was through Al that he got a lot of the 'I could have been a contender' scene," Peter Manso wrote in his 1994 biography, *Brando*, quoting a woman who knew Lettieri, who knew Brando: "It was sort of based on Al's brother-in-law, a Mafioso who once put a gun to his [Al's] head, saying 'You gotta get off smack. When you're on dope, you talk too much, and we're going to have to kill you.' For Marlon, the story was like street literature, something to absorb."

"When Al walked into the room, most people disappeared," Jan Lettieri observed of his enormous presence.

Then there was the singer who felt he had been destined to play the Godfather's godson, Johnny Fontane: Al Martino, born Jasper Cini, who had worked in gangland nightclubs from Atlantic City to

Las Vegas. His fight to win his role in *The Godfather* began when he got a call from Phyllis McGuire, one of a famous singing-sisters trio and the girlfriend of mobster Sam Giancana. "I just read a book, *The Godfather*," Martino remembered McGuire telling him. "Al, Johnny Fontane is you, and I know you can play it in the movie."

She was referring to the drunken crooner who yearns to be an actor and enters Puzo's novel on the second page, sloppy drunk and fantasizing about "murdering his trampy wife when she got home"— from a night "out fucking," as she told Johnny—modeled on Frank Sinatra. In his desire to rise from singer to actor, Johnny Fontane also seemed to resemble Al Martino.

The singer Vic Damone had already been cast as Johnny Fontane, but would soon bow out. "As an American of Italian desccent I could not in good conscience continue in the role," he would say. Martino, sensing an opportunity, said he contacted Al Ruddy in 1970, and— amazingly, given that Martino had never acted—that Ruddy gave him the part.

Some insisted that the real reason Damone dropped out was that he discovered that he'd have to film one scene and then wait five weeks to film another—which would cause him to miss lucrative Las Vegas appearances. ("The suspicion was that Damone had gotten the word from the Mafia to bow out because they had officially sanctioned Martino previously," wrote the syndicated columnist Dick Kleiner.)

Nonetheless, Martino had the part—or at least thought he did. Martino arranged to be released from his contract at the Desert Inn in Vegas, forfeiting what he estimated was $250,000 in appearance fees while he waited for production on the film to begin. Then Coppola signed on as director, and Martino said he was dropped from the cast. If they thought that would stop him, they were mistaken.

In 1952, when his recording of "Here in My Heart" was the No. 1 single in America, two thugs showed up at the door of his manager's house, asking to buy his contract. Informed that it was not for sale, the men threatened the manager's life. "And he just gave them my contract for free," said Martino.

After Martino fired the mobsters as his managers, he received a warning never to go back East, which he ignored. He showed up to appear with Dean Martin and Jerry Lewis at the 500 Club, the legendary Mob-frequented nightclub in Atlantic City, where two more thugs beat him bloody. Then they held a promissory note for $80,000 in front of him, which they explained was "future earnings, the money we could've made off of you," forcing him to sign. He then fled to England, where he stayed for six years. In 1958, he called Angelo Bruno, "the Gentle Don," to broker his return.

Once he'd been through all that, Martino said, who could stand in his way? To convince Coppola he was the right choice for Johnny Fontane, Martino spent $20,000 on a party for Coppola, Ruddy, and Puzo in Vegas, complete with "booze, showgirls, the works," said Martino. When that didn't work, he took a page from Puzo's novel. "I had to step on some toes to get people to realize that I was in the effin' movie. I was going to get in this movie, whether they liked it or not."

"I'm trying to make you understand: *no one could have gotten that part but me!* I was *locked in!*" he said. "If I'm told I'm not in the movie, and Bob Evans calls me and said I'm in the movie, what do you think happened?"

"Somebody got to somebody," he continued, and not even Frank Sinatra could stop Al Martino from playing Johnny Fontane.

"If you take the role, Sinatra will bar you from Las Vegas," Martino said he was told.

"Did he play Las Vegas afterwards?" he was asked.

"Of course I did!" he said. "I'm the last guy you could threaten. I got hardnosed about it. I took the bull by the horns!"

Again, it was like a scene straight out of the movie.

"Didn't the Don send Tom Hagen to convince Jack Woltz that Johnny Fontane must be in the movie?" he asked. "Well, I had to convince Coppola that I would be in this movie! Woltz didn't want Johnny, and Coppola didn't want me. There was no horse's head in the bed, but I had ammunition."

Martino said he went to the crime boss Russ Bufalino and asked him to intervene. When the official cast list was announced, the role of Johnny Fontane was his. The answer to how he got the role, Martino said, was simple: *"I went to my godfather!"*

Coppola smoothed things over with Sinatra, who had almost come to blows with Mario Puzo over the character. "I met Sinatra several times before filming started," the director remembered in a 1975 *Playboy* interview. They were friendly meetings, as Coppola "never liked the idea of exploiting a fictionalization of a man, any man—and I told him so."

He added that he would minimize the role Johnny Fontane played in the film, which Coppola would indeed do. "Sinatra was very appreciative," he said.

Then Sinatra turned to Coppola and said something that shouldn't have surprised the director, given the nationwide frenzy over casting.

"I'd like to play the Godfather," Sinatra announced.

The singer assured Coppola that he was serious. "Let's you and me buy this goddamned book and make it ourselves," Sinatra suggested. Coppola demurred and the matter seemed to be forgotten.

FROM THE START, Coppola knew exactly who he wanted for all the major roles. He wrote out his wish list on lined yellow paper, with asterisks next to his top choices: Al Pacino as Michael, James Caan as Sonny, and Robert Duvall as Tom Hagen. Thus began the major battle of *The Godfather*, one that would far eclipse the heated skirmishes over where the movie would be shot and its increasingly escalating budget. On one side was Coppola, a young director determined to cast the actors he saw so vividly in his imagination. On the other side was Robert Evans, a studio chief determined to avoid the miscasting that had plagued Mob films like *The Brotherhood*. "Bob Evans was very handsome, tall, and impressive," Coppola remembered. "I wanted him to accept and have confidence in me but wasn't at all convinced that he did."

And if Evans continued to harbor doubts about the young, untested director, they were confirmed by Coppola's choice to play Don Corleone.

At forty-seven, Marlon Brando was viewed in the industry as a washed-up, temperamental has-been. For the past decade, almost all of his movies had bombed at the box office amid reports of the actor's tardiness and tyrannical behavior. "His antics in *Mutiny on the Bounty* were legendary," noted the film historian Peter Biskind. "He was reputed to have given the clap to half the women on Tahiti, where the film was shot. He was hugely overweight, and worse, his most recent picture, Gillo Pontecorvo's *Burn!*, had flopped."

Added the syndicated columnist James Bacon, "The last decade has been a been a disaster for him. Even his agent fired him."

"Eight Bombs in a Row; Brando Won't Change," blared the headline over a story by syndicated columnist Bob Ellison. "There was a time, a very long time ago when Marlon's fellow actors defended him and some of the bad movies he made," wrote Ellison. "But that time, like the dime box of popcorn, seems to be gone forever."

Brando held his Hollywood peers in equal contempt, deriding the directors he worked with as "no-talent assholes . . . who all think they're young Eisenstein Misunderstood, or Orson Welles."

He tried his own hand at directing: *One-Eyed Jacks*, the Western he directed and starred in, which cost Brando two years of his life and the studio $1.1 million. Brando knew his star had fallen. "You couldn't even get $50,000 for me now, Tony," he bemoaned to actor Anthony Quinn.

Mixing Brando and Coppola in a film about the Mob seemed certain to produce the kind of pyrotechnics that could cause a film to crash and burn. Charlie Bluhdorn greeted the idea with his usual hot-tempered, spittle-spewing aplomb. "At the first mention of Brando's name, Bluhdorn launched into a tirade that he was 'box-office poison,'" Peter Bart wrote. Hurricane Charlie had his own ideas of who should play Don Corleone. "Bluhdorn proposed Charlie Bronson for the God-father, and, again, chaos prevailed," Bart added. Stanley Jaffe suggested casting an unknown. Evans pushed for Carlo Ponti, an Italian producer who was married to Sophia Loren, or Ernest Borgnine, who had won an Oscar for his lead role in *Marty*—anyone but Brando. "Marlon was as dead as could be," Evans said in a 1993 interview with *Movieline* magazine. Burt Lancaster was still after the role, as was Danny Thomas, who had starred in the popular and long-running TV sitcom that bore his name. (The show's original title—*Make Room for Daddy*—would have been perfect for a laugh-track version of *The Godfather.*)

IT WAS THOMAS, oddly, who had inadvertently sparked the movement to cast Brando as Don Corleone. Back in January 1970, Mario Puzo had checked into a weight-loss clinic in North Carolina. There, he read a story in the morning paper that caused him even more distress than his bathroom scale: Danny Thomas was thinking about acquiring a controlling interest in Paramount Pictures with the sole purpose of casting himself as Vito Corleone. Thomas was certainly wealthy enough to buy a stake in the still struggling studio: in addition to starring in *The Danny Thomas Show*, he had produced a string of television hits that were generating a gusher of syndication rights, including *The Dick Van Dyke Show*, *The Andy Griffith Show*, and *The Mod Squad*. "My father was terrified by that prospect," said Anthony Puzo. "He said, 'No way.'"

In what he would call "a panic," Puzo dashed off a letter in longhand to Brando, the actor he had imagined in the title role while he was writing *The Godfather*. Across the top of the letter Puzo scrawled his current address: "North Carolina Fat Farm."

Dear Mr. Brando,

I wrote a book called THE GODFATHER which has had some success and I think you're the only actor who can play the Godfather with that quiet force and irony (the book is an ironical comment on American society) the part requires. I hope you'll read the book and like it well enough to use whatever power you can to get the role.

*I'm writing Paramount to the same effect for whatever good
that will do. I know this was presumptuous of me, but the least
I can do for the book is try. I really think you'd be tremendous.
Needless to say, I've been an admirer of your art.
　A mutual friend, Jeff Brown, gave me your address.
　Mario Puzo*

The letter arrived in Brando's life at a moment when he desperately needed a role, even if he refused to admit it. By that point, the actor widely regarded as the greatest of his generation was deep in debt, dependent on Valium, headed toward his third divorce, and determined never to work as an actor again. He lived alone in a rambling house at 12900 Mulholland Drive, high above Los Angeles, where he was tended to by his secretary and all-purpose assistant, Alice Marchak. It was Marchak who had discovered that Brando, who struggled with reading, was actually dyslexic. "Oh, what a happy day it was for him when I told him he wasn't dumb because he didn't have a high school diploma," she said.

Marchak took over the task of reading all the scripts and books that were sent to Brando. "I was inundated," she said. She turned down offers for *Dirty Harry* and for *Butch Cassidy and the Sundance Kid*, after Paul Newman offered Brando his choice of the lead roles. The problem, as Marchak recently emphasized, was simple: "*Marlon decided he would not work*—and he didn't."

He was, as she put it, "ready for a breakdown."

Marchak forced him to face reality. "Something had to be done," she said. Brando needed millions to climb his way out of debt, and he needed to kick his drug habit to maintain visitation rights with his children. He promised Marchak he would limit himself to one Valium a day, and he agreed to make three pictures—but only if the parts required no more than three weeks of shooting.

"He was adamant," Marchak remembered. "But at last we were talking acting."

To keep track of potential roles, she subscribed to the *Hollywood Reporter*. "It became my early-morning read to know what was going on in the industry," she said. Brando found the magazine in her office and went ballistic. "This is my house," he roared, "and I will not have anyone bringing movie magazines into it!"

Marchak left the house and stayed away for days, waiting for Brando to cool down. One morning, while she was reading the magazine that had driven her boss into a frenzy, she saw that Paramount was still looking for an actor to play the godfather. When Brando finally called her and asked her to return, she went straight to the mail that had piled up in her absence. There, atop the stack, was *The Godfather*, along with Puzo's note.

Marchak took the book to Brando. "Puzo, the author, sent this to you," she remembered telling him in her 2008 memoir, *Me and Marlon*. "It's a book about a Mafia don."

He tossed it back to her. "I'm not a Mafia godfather," he said. "I'm not going to glorify the Mafia."

Marchak took the book home and read it over the weekend. "I just knew that this was for Marlon," she said, "and I was determined to change his mind."

Her best chance was to appeal to the weak spot he shared with virtually every Hollywood actor: professional jealousy. Every time she heard of another actor being mentioned for the part of Vito Corleone, no matter how implausible, she would nonchalantly mention it to Brando. He listened in annoyance to the growing list of rivals being considered by Paramount, but ultimately ignored her.

Switching tactics, Marchak dug up Puzo's note and placed it on his bedside table. Brando never mentioned it to her, but she knew he had read the letter because she noticed it had been moved. He surprised her by bringing it up, unprompted.

"Maybe I should call and thank Puzo for thinking of me for the part—and for sending me the book," Brando said.

Marchak immediately set up the call.

"We had a talk on the phone," Puzo wrote. "He had not read the book, but he told me that the studio would never hire him unless a strong director insisted on it. He was nice over the phone but didn't sound too interested."

Brando's read on the situation was exactly right: no one at Paramount was going to ask him to play the part. "If Brando plays the Don, forget about opening the film in Italy," producer Dino De Laurentiis told Charlie Bluhdorn. "They'll laugh him off the screen."

On March 7, 1970, Puzo sent a second letter to Brando, all but admitting defeat.

> *Dear Marlon,*
>
> *Talked to Paramount and the producer, Al Ruddy. They are very cool, seem to have other ideas. So unless you have read the book and want to use your muscle, I guess that's it.*
>
> *I'm sorry I wasted your time. I still think it was a good idea. And thanks for taking the trouble to call and talk to me.*

Still, there were the debts and the drugs and the greatest actor of his generation lying fallow. Marchak had one more card to play. She had heard that Paramount's other idea for the role of Don Corleone was Laurence Olivier. She casually informed Brando of the news.

"Laurence Olivier! He *can't* play a Mafia don!" he exclaimed.

"They are going to test him, I read," Marchak said.

Brando, suddenly, was interested.

FROM THE MOMENT he was hired as director, Coppola had two actors in mind for the leading role. "For me it came down to Marlon Brando or Laurence Olivier," he said. Playing the Godfather, he knew, required star power of the highest order—"an actor of such magnetism, such charisma, just walking into a room had to be an event."

On his yellow legal pad, he toyed with a few other names, including character actors John Marley and Frank DeKova. But he quickly realized he had to think bigger. "We finally figured that what we had to do was lure the best actor in the world," Coppola said.

Which narrowed the field down to two contenders: Laurence Olivier and Marlon Brando.

At forty-seven, Brando might have seemed too young to play an aging Mafia don. Olivier, at sixty-four, was old enough, but his proper British persona might make him a tough sell as an Italian American crime boss. Olivier also had health issues that would make it difficult for him to travel from England to America for an extended time.

Dean Tavoularis, who signed on early to serve as Coppola's production designer, recalled flying back to Los Angeles with the director from a scouting trip to New York. On the five-hour flight, they discussed what Tavoularis called the endless national "guessing game" over casting.

"Guess who I want to play the Godfather?" Coppola asked.

Tavoularis was stumped. "Who?"

"Marlon Brando," said Coppola.

"It was a big shock to me, but it should not have been," Tavoularis said. "He's the best actor in the world."

Tavoularis knew Brando "quite well," having worked with him in Rome on the 1968 film *Candy*, a satirical comedy about pornography that turned out to be a mediocre movie. "I'd like to have dinner with him," Coppola told Tavoularis.

When they got home, Tavoularis called Christian Marquand, the director of *Candy*, who had grown so close to Brando that the actor named his firstborn son after him. The dinner was set for Chianti Ristorante, a famed restaurant on Melrose that had served Hollywood royalty from W. C. Fields to Liz Taylor. Brando arrived with Marquand, sliding into the booth with Coppola and Tavoularis.

"It was there that Francis popped the question," Tavoularis said. "He asked Brando if he had read the book. Brando laughed and said no. Francis painted a picture of the book sweeping the country, and Paramount wanting to make the film, and the character having a lot to offer Brando as an actor. I think Marlon was an easy sell. He was ready to go that night. Marlon was like a cupcake to creative people. He would say yes to the craziest things and no to the stupid, arrogant things."

Against all odds, it looked as though Coppola might actually be on the verge of coaxing Brando out of seclusion to play the most sought-after role in Hollywood. "The only thing in the country against it," Tavoularis said, "was the group that mattered the most: Paramount."

"ONE OF THE Paramount Pictures execs in those days was a guy named Frank Yablans," Coppola explained to *Cigar Aficionado* in a 2003 interview. "He was already working on Charlie to take over and be the big shot.... He said, 'Charlie, this Brando idea is ridiculous. First of all, he's not Italian and he doesn't look Italian. Second of all, if he comes on the production, you're gonna end up just having cost overruns because he's such a pain in the neck. You get no value at all because people will stay away. He's washed up, he's finished.'"

Coppola was called into a meeting with "all the big shots" at Paramount. "You know how they are sometimes," he said. "They gang up."

Stanley Jaffe sat the young director down and gave him a direct order: "As long as I'm president of the studio, Marlon Brando will not be in this picture, and I will no longer allow you to discuss it."

Coppola, who had suffered from epilepsy as a teenager, resorted to cheap theatrics: He fell to the floor in convulsions and pretended to have a fit. "I did it as a gag," he said. "I knew the floor was carpeted, so it wouldn't hurt."

But his response was dead serious.

"I give up," Coppola told Jaffe. "You hired me; I'm supposed to be the director. Every idea I have you don't want me to talk about. Now you're instructing me that I can't even pursue the idea. At least let me pursue it."

After a brief discussion, Jaffe agreed to consider Brando—on three conditions. First, the actor had to put up a bond of $1 million, to ensure that his temperament and tardiness wouldn't delay the production. Second, he had to forgo his usual salary and do the film for next to nothing. Third—and most unusual for a star of Brando's magnitude—he had to do a screen test for the role.

"Coppola had employed this gambit of faking a seizure years before, in his student days, to compel a backer to cough up the additional funds he needed to finish *Tonight for Sure,* and the ploy worked equally well with Jaffe and the other executives," wrote Gene D. Phillips in his Coppola biography, referring to one of Coppola's early "nudie" films. Yet the demand for a screen test was "the joker in the deck, as far as Jaffe was concerned, since it was common knowledge that Brando refused to be tested for any role. So Jaffe assumed that he would turn down the part."

Coppola, who was, he confessed, "scared shitless" of Brando, knew better than to call it a screen test. "I was thinking, *How am I gonna handle this?* . . . I call up Brando. I say, 'Mr. Brando, don't you think it would be a good idea if we fooled around a little bit, and do a little improvisation for this role, and see what it would be like.' I didn't say it was a screen test. I said it was like a little experiment with a video camera."

He called it a "makeup test"—a way to explore what it would look like for Brando, whose ancestry was Dutch, Irish, English, and German, to play an Italian. "The word *screen test* was never mentioned to Marlon Brando," said Fred Roos.

Brando readily agreed. By now, he had read *The Godfather,* or had Alice Marchak read it to him. "He thought it was a delicious part," Coppola remembered. "He used that word, *delicious.*"

He took the task seriously. And as usual, he turned to Marchak for help. "One day he said he wanted me to look at some photographs with him," Marchak wrote in her memoir. "We sat in the living room and he began to pass me photos of different men. I asked who they were. He said he had asked Francis to get him some photos of the Mafia. I knew who Francis was as I had been following all the news about *The Godfather* and updating Marlon. This was the first time he mentioned he had spoken to Francis Coppola, who was to direct. Surprise! Surprise! Marlon had been busy, too."

Brando and Marchak looked through the photos, which had been taken in everyday locations: "on the street, in cars, in restaurants," Marchak wrote. They were struck by how unremarkable the Mob bosses looked. "After we had gone through the stack a few times, we concluded the Don should be an ordinary-looking man you passed on the street," Marchak continued. That's when Brando stumbled on "the germ of the idea."

He would start with how he himself might look when he aged and build the character from there. And with that, according to Marchak, "Marlon morphed into the Don."

The process wasn't without its bumps. First, Brando walked into Marchak's office "and asked if there was any black shoe polish in the house," she wrote. Marchak found it and gave it to him. Brando asked her to come into his room. "I walked in, and there was Marlon's version of a Mafia Don sitting in a chair. I burst out laughing. He had darkened his eyebrows and lined his eyes, and the black shoe polish glistened on his hair that was slicked back. He asked me what I thought. I laughed and said I expected him to jump up and tango me around the room. I didn't know if he was Rudolph Valentino or a gigolo. He laughed, too."

Marchak put her foot down. "My only advice was, *No black shoe polish! No Edward G. Robinson! Make him Brando.*"

"I had done my part," she said. "Now he had to convince them he was the Don."

BRANDO ALWAYS SLEPT late.

Up most nights until 3:00 a.m., he rarely rose before noon. But on that morning in January 1971—the exact date is lost to time—he was ready. His longtime makeup wizard, Philip Rhodes, was ready to prep him, and Coppola had arrived at 7 a.m.

"Francis told me about filming Brando at his house. It was a clandestine mission and we were to keep it absolutely secret," said Hiro Narita, the young cameraman Coppola selected for the screen test. "He said he needed to convince the studio executives of his choice of Brando."

Coppola and Narita arrived at Bob Hope Airport, in Burbank, on the early-morning flight from San Francisco and climbed into a white van with their equipment and aspirations. They were accompanied by the Italian American barber-turned-actor Salvatore Corsitto, who had won the role of the undertaker Bonasera despite his shaky audition, and an assistant or two. Together they drove skyward, toward Brando's home on Mulholland Drive.

Arriving at the back door, everyone removed their shoes and entered. Alice Marchak made a cup of coffee and took it down the hall to Brando's bedroom, where she woke him.

"Is Philip here?" he asked, referring to his makeup maestro.

"No," she said. "You didn't tell me he was coming, too."

"When he gets here, send him down."

When she returned to the kitchen, Rhodes had arrived. She sent him to the bedroom and served Coppola and his crew some coffee. "They were in the living room standing around and talking in whispers," she said. "I left them, as I thought they were checking the light, and where to shoot, and I didn't want to disturb them."

Coppola had brought along some props: Italian prosciutto, cheese, and cigars, which he thought might help Brando get into character. He instructed Corsitto to wait outside, until it was time to deliver his lines.

Then, into the all-white living room—white carpet, white walls, white drapes—walked the man of the house: dressed in a Japanese kimono, his hair long and blond. He was "soft-spoken and reticent, very different from his screen persona," said Narita. "I could have mistaken him for another person if I was not there to film Brando."

Narita set up a single soft light and his 16mm camera and waited.

Brando nibbled on the prosciutto and cheese. Then, to the astonishment of everyone in the room, he began the transformation into Don Vito Corleone. He tied back his ponytail, darkened his blond hair with shoe polish, jutted out his jaw, and wrinkled the tips of his shirt collar.

"You t'ink I need a mustache?" Brando asked, slipping into a subtle accent.

"Oh, yeah," Coppola said. "My uncle Louis has a mustache."

Brando dabbed some shoe polish on his upper lip.

Then he reached for the Kleenex, stuffing it into his cheeks to give himself jowls. "I want to be like a bulldog," he said, his voice suddenly full of gravel.

Brando moved to the living room couch. "I just wanna improvise," he said. Coppola called for silence. "I told my guys to keep quiet," he said. "I'd heard that noise bothers him. He always wears earplugs when he's working."

Brando began moving this way and that, experimenting with his posture and mumbling to himself.

Finally, after fifteen or twenty minutes, he looked up. "Okay, I'm ready," he said.

Brando told Coppola not to record his voice, because he hadn't settled on the don's speech pattern. The director nodded to Narita to begin rolling, and Marlon Brando, supposedly washed up and finished as an actor, began to turn forty-seven years of preparation, experience, and talent into art. "Slightly, from a low angle, I filmed him holding a glass of wine in one hand and a cigar in the other, going through animated gestures," said Narita. "Francis was videotaping at the same time. At one point Brando dipped the end of the cigar into the wine. The phone rang unexpectedly. Brando calmly picked it up, staying in character, and mumbled a few words as if talking to someone on the other end of the line. Then he hung up and continued his pantomime."

Coppola felt the moment was right to spring his surprise. "Without warning, I ushered in my barber friend, who went up to Brando and launched right into his speech," he said. "Brando didn't know what was going on for a moment, but he listened and then just started doing the scene. It was my shot. The thing worked. I had it down on tape. I'd watched forty-seven-year-old Marlon Brando turn into this aging Mafia chief. It was fantastic."

Everyone in the room was stunned. Brando had inhabited the essence of Don Corleone, creating the character for the screen as surely as Mario Puzo had created it on the page. "Brando's consummate transformation was stunning and complete," Narita said. "He was unrecognizable from the man who greeted us at the door."

The crew packed up and departed. Back in the van, no one could put into words what they had just witnessed. The performance had left Narita speechless.

Coppola, however, was already planning his next move. This time he wouldn't go to Evans and the other Paramount executives in Los Angeles. He would take the tape straight to the top, to the man who owned the studio: Charlie Bluhdorn. "I knew what Brando had done on that videotape was extraordinary," Coppola would say. "So I figured if I went right to New York and showed it directly to Charlie Bluhdorn, that would settle the matter. If he liked it, all the others would fall in line."

With the tape in his satchel, he took the next flight from LA to New York, where he went to the Gulf+Western Building. In the conference room, he set up his video equipment and prepared to play the tape.

"Could I just see Mr. Bluhdorn a minute?" he asked an assistant.

Soon Bluhdorn came rolling around the corner like an impending storm.

Coppola played the tape.

"Francis, what are you doing?" Bluhdorn asked, peering at the small video screen. Then the shock of recognition hit him: it was Marlon Brando. "No, no, absolutely not! I don't want a crazy guy!" he shouted, according to Peter Biskind. But before he could storm out, he found himself transfixed by what Al Ruddy called the Miracle on Mulholland. Before his eyes, Brando became Don Corleone.

"That's *terrific!*" Bluhdorn exclaimed.

Afterward, everyone else was as startled as their boss when they watched the screen test: Bob Evans, Peter Bart, even Stanley Jaffe. "I remember Al Pacino coming up to my office before we shot the movie and saying, 'Can I see that film?'" Jaffe said. "I mean, it was somebody looking at God. It was just an amazing transformation from Marlon Brando to the Godfather, right down to stuffing his cheeks. It was spectacular!"

Still, the studio held Brando to a relatively lowball deal: a $50,000 fee, $10,000 a week in expenses during his contracted six weeks on the shoot, and a percentage after the picture brought in $10 million. The film in which Brando became Don Corleone in his living room vanished, like a treasure lost in a shipwreck.

The Hollywood press greeted the announcement of Brando's casting with derision. "No Stars for 'Godfather' Cast—Just Someone Named Brando," read the headline in *Daily Variety*. Only months earlier, the trade paper noted, Evans had vowed to cast "real faces" in *The Godfather*, "people who are not names."

Now the title role was going to one of the biggest names in Hollywood.

Evans was ready with some fresh spin. "What makes this casting all the more gratifying and exciting," he declared in a statement, "is the fact that while writing the novel and first-draft screenplay, Mr. Puzo had always envisioned Mr. Brando as the Godfather."

"Fortunately, he won that battle," said Puzo's son Anthony.

8

THE WAR OVER CASTING THE FAMILY CORLEONE

In the all-out war over casting, Coppola had won the Battle of Brando. But the fight to cast the rest of the leading roles would prove even more tumultuous. Coppola was seeking what amounted to total control over the movie, and to get his way, he was willing to go behind the backs of those paying the bills. He would cast the film as he envisioned it, then convince Paramount to approve his choices.

From the start, Coppola had a firm idea about the kind of actor he preferred. "I want to cast every Italian character with a real Italian or an Italian American actor as far as we can," the director told Fred Roos. Coppola's theory, Roos said, was that those who grew up in Italian households had ingrained "behavioral characteristics" that would emerge naturally on screen. "He wouldn't even have to give specific directions," Roos said, "because it would be part of their heritage. In their genes, so to speak. You don't have time as a director to stop and direct every little minute detail."

Coppola wanted to "smell the garlic coming off the screen."

Authenticity was at the top of the casting director's list. The word went out to agents that any actor could get an interview with Roos. Then the frenzy continued, with Coppola sitting in on many of the auditions. "We saw everybody," said Roos. "A lot of actors lied to say they were Italian, but I didn't turn anybody away. Even if they didn't have agents. If they cold-called me, I said, 'Yeah, c'mon over.'"

The process went on for three months, on both coasts. In New York, the line of actors stretched out the door of the small studio where the auditions were held. "It wasn't a soundstage," said Roos. "It was a tight, crowded space. There was very little waiting space for the actors. So they would have to be out in this kind of crowded outer space. Eyeing each other, until someone said, 'Okay, you're on, you're next.'"

Then they would stand on a small, forty-foot-wide stage and pour their hearts out to Roos and the ultimate arbiter, Francis Coppola. "Francis was willing to go deep into the casting process," Roos said. "That's how you get quality. You leave no stone unturned."

Coppola was one of the first in the movie business to employ reel-to-reel videotape, a primitive new technology, which allowed him to keep the camera rolling during auditions. "The actor wouldn't know when it was rolling and when it was not," Roos said. "We had so much fun that invariably we would fall behind—if the actor was interesting, or if Francis would tell stories or sing a song. Sometimes we would be forty-five minutes behind, and the actors would be outside pissed off."

Robert Evans and the other executives at Paramount, however, had a very different idea of who should play the major roles. Early on, they met with Coppola to discuss casting. Their first idea confused the director, who recalled their discussions in the interview with *Cigar Aficionado*. "What about Robert Redford for Michael Corleone?" they suggested.

Coppola tried to remain calm. "Well, Redford's a very bright guy and wonderful," he responded. "But he doesn't look Italian."

"Well . . . there's a lot of Italian blonds," the executives pressed. "Sicilians are blond and have red hair and blue eyes."

"Yeah, but don't you think that Michael, the son that is not gonna go into the family business, ought to look Italian, so it's like he can't escape his destiny?" Coppola asked. "If he's blond, he'll become Robert Redford. He will be a WASP banker."

Evans had another idea. The studio had its first recent major hit with *Love Story*; the tearjerker would haul in $136 million at the box office and bring Paramount some much-needed time. The film starred Evans's wife, Ali MacGraw, and a young heartthrob named Ryan O'Neal. What about O'Neal for Michael, Evans suggested, and Ernest Borgnine as Vito?

"They really thought Ryan O'Neal was a good compromise because he was younger and had become a big star," said Coppola.

Evans, he realized, was trying to cast the film on his own. "One of the reasons I got the job is because they thought they could push me around," Coppola acknowledged.

The director dug in his heels. "There's a young actor that I know," he told Evans. "He has never been in a movie, but every time I read the scenes with Michael Corleone in the book, like him walking in Sicily with the two bodyguards and the girl, I kept seeing his face. And when I read it, that's the only one whose face I saw."

"What's his name?" Evans asked.

"Al Pacino," said Coppola.

Pacino was hardly an obvious choice. At five foot seven, he seemed too short to play the future head of the Corleone family, and at nearly thirty-one, he seemed too old to play a college boy who had enlisted in the marines. But when he took the stage on Broadway, where he had won a 1969 Tony Award for his role as a teenage drug addict in *Does a Tiger Wear a Necktie?*, his height and age became irrelevant. "He looked about seven feet tall," Al Ruddy would marvel after watching Pacino perform. His eyes, dark and brooding, seemed perfect to reflect the torment of a good man who sought to escape his father's dirty world, only to be tapped as its leader. "Cast Al," George Lucas's wife, Marcia, urged Coppola. "He undresses you with his eyes."

Like almost everyone else in Hollywood, though, Evans had never heard of Pacino. "Who is he?" he demanded.

"He's a theater actor, but he's never been in a movie," Coppola said.

Then Evans was told Pacino's height. "A runt will not play Michael!" he exploded.

"What d'ya mean, a runt?" Coppola said.

"He's a little short guy," Evans insisted.

"Well, yeah," Coppola conceded, "but he's a good actor, he looks Italian, and he has power and I think he should play that."

"Absolutely not," Evans replied. "Michael Corleone will not be played by Al Pacino."

Coppola was out of cards. "I was very disappointed, because I was sure that this young actor was really great," he remembered. "I couldn't convince them. I couldn't get any support."

So he decided to stall. Why not "go look at all the best young actors," he suggested. "Give me a little time and I'll do it."

He mentioned James Caan, Robert Duvall, and Diane Keaton, "all sort of old friends and all unknowns."

Then he set out to show the studio bosses what they were unable to see on their own.

IN THE FIRST few days of January 1971, Coppola summoned Pacino, Caan, Duvall, and Keaton to San Francisco. There, at his American Zoetrope studio and the nearby Palace Hotel, he would film screen tests of the four actors in absolute secrecy. Coppola felt sure the tests would convince the suits at Paramount that he had found his ideal cast. The tests would cost no more than $500—the price, as James Caan would joke, apparently referring to the lunch that Coppola bought them, "of four corned beef sandwiches."

Pacino was still a struggling actor, so broke he often had to borrow cab fare—a scruffy, unpredictable former messenger, theater usher, and building superintendent who fully came alive when he was on a stage. His father, Salvatore, had abandoned the family when little Alfredo was only two. He and his mother went to live with his grandparents in an apartment near the Bronx Zoo. As a boy, he would hide at the top of a billboard and tell fantasies—that "I was from Texas," he said—that took him far from his miseries. Pacino found his friends in the movies, through which he created an imaginary world. He began drinking at thirteen, and, after dropping out of the High School of Performing Arts at sixteen, took on a string of low-wage jobs to support himself. After ten years bouncing between boardinghouses and friends' couches, Pacino found work as an apartment building superintendent, and moved into the building's basement apartment. He wrote "super" on the bottom of one of his many leftover eight-by-ten glossies and taped it to his front door with Band-Aids. "That was down about as far as anyone can get," Pacino told *Time* in 1972.

"I got back into acting to save my life," he said of returning to his high school passion. Soon he was landing small parts in New York plays, then larger ones. Despite the accolades he earned onstage, he couldn't imagine himself carrying the weight of a major movie on his shoulders, let alone as the dramatic center of the film.

"He's seeing something I don't see," said Pacino, who had read Mario Puzo's novel. "It was a real page-turner, I must say," he would remember. But the call from Coppola came out of the blue. "Francis had only seen me onstage, so it was a bit ephemeral knowing that was all he had to go by. . . . However, I didn't see how the studio would ever want to take me, and not to my surprise I was sort of right. I was an unknown and the only film that I had made was *Panic in Needle Park*, and it hadn't even come out yet."

Coppola saw Sonny Corleone in Caan, a Queens-raised son of German Jewish immigrants. The two had known each other from their student days at Hofstra University, where they both studied theater arts. Caan wasn't Italian, but he was powerfully built—the captain of his high school baseball team and the star of its basketball team—and he could convey the hair-trigger temper that personified Puzo's original vision of Sonny as a physically imposing force. Plus, like Sonny, he was headstrong, bolting high school and driving from New York City to Michigan State to try out for the university's powerhouse football team. "In person, at 5 feet 11 inches, 162 pounds, he is shockingly small," a reporter for the *New York Times* wrote. "The celluloid aura of size and strength is a mirage formed out of personality and focused energy."

Coppola could see the perpetually calm German Irish Catholic Mob lawyer, Tom Hagen, in Duvall, who had played the mute and mysterious Boo Radley in *To Kill a Mockingbird* in 1962. Duvall envisioned Hagen just as Coppola and Puzo did. He "was like a Secret Service guy," Duvall would say. He drew inspiration from a story he heard from a friend about Carmine Tramunti, then boss of the Lucchese crime family, who had a "high-powered gofer" who waited on him hand and foot. The guy would "light his cigarette and hold his chair, do whatever he wanted," Duvall said. "You couldn't belittle that position. I took it from there."

He would be the Secret Service agent to protect and assist Don Corleone, respectful and subservient.

Perhaps strangest of all, Coppola could see Kay Adams in the young actress Diane Keaton, best known at the time as the housewife in a television commercial for Hour After Hour deodorant. ("Excuse me, ma'am, why the tracksuit?" the off-camera announcer asks, to which she replies in a rush, "Are you kidding? With housework, kids, and shopping, I put in five miles a day.") Keaton, who was invariably described in the press as "kooky," long before she had become a household name, had starred on Broadway in the hippie musical *Hair* and would soon be a frequent guest on *The Tonight Show*, where her giddiness provided a perfect foil to Johnny Carson's deadpan delivery. Coppola thought she could enliven the "straight, boring character" of Kay Adams "because she was so eccentric and kind of weird in a way."

Just as Pacino was puzzled by Coppola's faith in him, Keaton was surprised by his interest in her for the movie. "When I was first asked to come in and test for *The Godfather*, I just couldn't believe it," she said. "Me? Diane Keaton in *The Godfather*? Never! I wasn't even Italian."

Now, as the four actors assembled in San Francisco on January 7, 8, 9, and 10 to shoot their secret screen tests, Coppola went to work transforming them into Don Corleone's family. "My wife [Eleanor] cut their hair, and got some clothes," he said. "We shot on sixteen-millimeter a whole bunch of tests of scenes."

For the freshly shorn Pacino, who lost his shaggy locks for a screen test for a role he felt he had no chance of landing, the haircut seemed to be an exercise in futility. "Of course, when you are doing the actual film, yes, do whatever necessary, but not for an early screen test," he said. "To be honest, I kind of missed my hair, and if getting the role is because my hair is cut a certain way, then we have a problem, don't you think?"

But there they were, forever enshrined in their youth, excitement, and inexperience: Pacino, Caan, and Duvall sitting around a table filled with take-out Chinese food, acting out their parts. In another test, a uniformed Al Pacino sits with Diane Keaton over a bottle of wine, Keaton reacting to Pacino revealing how his father got Johnny Fontane out of his long-term contract with a stubborn bandleader. ("Luca Brasi held a gun to his head, and my father assured him that either his brains or his signature would be on the contract.") In each of these homemade tests the actors are giddy and exuberant, fumbling over their lines and frequently breaking into laughter but unmistakably all future movie stars.

Once the tests were finished, Coppola sent them to Los Angeles and New York so Bob Evans and Stanley Jaffe and Charlie Bluhdorn could take a look. The reaction was swift and unanimous. "They hated them," Coppola said. "That's when the Paramount guys really started thinking about firing me."

Not only did the studio executives hate the screen tests, but they were upset that Coppola had wasted so much money—$500!—on meals and other expenses.

"Terrible!" Bluhdorn said when he saw the homemade tests. Then, to Coppola's dismay, he added something even more chilling:

"But those actors can't all be terrible," Bluhdorn said. "It's the director who's terrible."

Paramount laid down the law. "Listen, Francis, we're taking over," they told him. "You have to really cast this movie. Don't give us this Al Pacino and all these people like Bobby Duvall. We don't want them."

Coppola was ordered to go into what he called "a very intensive screen test mode. We had to test every young actor for every part and shoot it on film, and so we tested everybody. We tested Martin Sheen as Michael. Dean Stockwell as Michael. Ryan O'Neal as Michael. There were hundreds of tests, and we spent hundreds of thousands of dollars on them."

Their casting lists included forty potential Michaels, one hundred Kays, forty Sonnys, twenty-five Fredos . . . many of the actors already established but happy to be tested for the various parts. "It was the best job in town, to get into *The Godfather*," said Roos.

Not long after the screen test disaster, Coppola moved his entire operation—and his family—to New York. Even with the $175,000 fee that Paramount had given him to direct, he was deep in debt. He owed money to Warner Bros. on his unfinished contract, and the unpaid bills for American Zoetrope were piling up. "I was so broke, I couldn't afford anything," he said. "They give you what's called per diem, about $1,000 a week to live on. I decided if I just banked the fee for all my debts, I could live really cheap."

Coppola's brother-in-law, the composer David Shire, let him use a vacant apartment he owned on the Upper West Side. "It was a little studio apartment on Sixtieth Street that was being painted," Coppola said. The place was nowhere near big enough for the director and his two young sons and his wife, Eleanor, who was pregnant with their daughter, Sofia. "The kids got chicken-pox, and the apartment needed repainting," Eleanor remembered in Peter Cowie's *The Godfather Book*. "It was living hell."

Making things even more cramped, the family was joined by Coppola's father, Carmine, who was composing music for the wedding and other scenes in *The Godfather*. "We lived like real paupers," Coppola said. "We're all like this impoverished Italian family. And it was just miserable."

Now settled in New York, Coppola and his casting team, which included Fred Roos, along with Paramount's casting director Andrea Eastman and Lou DiGiaimo, who cast the extras, launched into a frenzied round of screen tests. Filming was scheduled to start in under three months. "There was always a kind of tension between the creative side of *The Godfather* and the studio," said Eastman. "Casting went on for a really long time. We literally worked seven days a week. It was intense, believe me."

In a casting list dated January 19, 1971, Coppola scrawled the names of his dream lineup in red pen: Brando, Pacino, Caan, and Duvall. But the director clearly sensed it would be an uphill battle. On the second page, he listed a "#2 cast," imagining Dustin Hoffman or Warren Beatty for Michael if he couldn't push through his preferred choice of Al Pacino.

Back at the studio, the Paramount brass had a list of their own, neatly typed out beneath the studio's mountaintop letterhead. The "Overall Michael List," showed just how far the studio remained from Coppola's vision:

STARS: Dustin Hoffman, Robert Redford, Warren Beatty, Ryan O'Neal, Jack Nicholson, James Caan, Michael Sarrazin, Michael Parks, Christopher Jones, Robert Forester, James Farentino

KNOWN BUT NOT STARS: Tony Lo Bianco, Robert De Niro, Al Pacino, Frank Langella, Martin Sheen, Dean Stockwell, Robert Fields, Perry Lopez, Barry Newman, Michael Brandon, Adam Roarke, Mike Margotta

UNKNOWN: David Selby, Don Furcillo, Bob Capace, Geo. Welbes

The list for Kay included stars like Karen Black and Tuesday Weld, and known actresses like Blythe Danner and Michelle Phillips. Diane Keaton wasn't listed in any category. Other actresses who tested included Jill Clayburgh and Jennifer Salt; also considered were Jennifer O'Neill, and Geneviève Bujold.

"The casting of *The Godfather* was a battle between the Old

Hollywood approach of Evans and the New Hollywood ideas of Coppola," wrote Peter Biskind. "Everyone had a candidate for every part, and no one seemed to have the ultimate authority."

Then Robert Evans attempted to take control.

ON FEBRUARY 3, 1971, a banner headline in *Variety* signaled the coming war.

"Cut Directors Down to Size," it blared across the top of page one. Beneath the large type, a smaller headline made the source of the sentiment clear: "Bob Evans: We Keep Control."

It was something of a manifesto. Evans was announcing a top-down, hands-on approach to moviemaking at Paramount. He would be "involved" in every aspect of a film, he told *Variety,* instituting a policy of Hollywood-based "control" that would enable him to person-ally oversee every step in the making of his studio's movies. The move would set Paramount apart from the "partnership" model employed by other studios, who allowed producers greater latitude. "I want to be close to script development, the casting, and the final cuts," Evans declared.

And what about the producers and directors who were being denied creative autonomy? "They shouldn't be angry if they are rea-sonable, Evans reasons," according to *Variety*.

Francis Coppola was angry—very angry. According to someone present throughout the filming, he and Al Ruddy "took offense" at the broadside from Evans, which many correctly interpreted as a declara-tion of war. The power struggle soon focused on a single part: Al Pac-ino as Michael, which still seemed to be an impossibility—especially to Pacino. "I mean, he wanted me to play that part like nobody has ever wanted me to play a part, ever," Pacino would later say. "He wanted me to do it so much more than I ever wanted to."

Even before the informal casting sessions in San Francisco, Cop-pola had met Pacino in New York in late 1970 in a small studio for an initial audition that blew him away. "Through the course of the entire afternoon, he asked Al to do the role of Michael four different ways," remembered Pacino's agent at the time, Stevie Phillips. "It took all afternoon long and he kept asking Al, 'Try this, try that.' And Al would automatically do it. He was incredible! I came away from this believing that not only did he have the part but that he was a talent of infinite ability, almost incredibility.

"His acting was mind-blowing," said Phillips, but his persona was erratic, as Phillips and the agent Sue Mengers discovered when putting him up for various jobs.

Mario Puzo also loved the idea of casting Pacino. "I gave Francis a letter saying that above all Pacino had to be in the film," he wrote. ("I think that Al Pacino is the 'perfect Michael,'" Puzo wrote on January 21, 1971. "I've never been surer of anything in my life.")

The problem was that while Pacino dazzled Coppola in his initial interview, he flunked his screen test. "He didn't know his lines," said Puzo. "He threw in his own words. He didn't understand the character at all. He was terrible. Jimmy Caan had done it ten times better."

After the scene was over, Puzo went up to Coppola. "Give me my letter back," he said.

"What letter?" Coppola asked.

"The one I gave you saying I wanted Pacino."

Coppola shook his head. "Wait a while," he told Puzo. But to himself, he muttered, "The self-destructive bastard. He didn't even know his lines."

The action moved to the Paramount screening room in the Gulf+Western Building. The executives sat in the room day after day, watching test after test. "On screen, Pacino still didn't strike anybody—excepting Coppola—as right for the part of Michael," according to Puzo.

Evans moved to end the debate. "Francis," he said, "I must say you're alone in this."

Someone asked Jaffe what he thought. The studio president had spent days "patiently and quietly viewing stuff he hated without saying a word," Puzo would write in his memoir about the making of

The Godfather. Now he was "so pissed off" that he jumped out of his seat. "You guys really wanta know?" he said. "I think you got the worst bunch of lampshades I've ever seen."

Puzo couldn't bear to watch anymore. He left the studio and stayed away for a week.

By now, the production had switched into high gear.

"Albert S. Ruddy sits in his private office, feet up on his desk, smoking a cigar as he talks on the phone. The tall and lanky *Godfather* producer is wearing a gray turtleneck sweater, blue double-breasted sport jacket, gray flared trousers and slip-on shoes from Gucci, the bootery most favored at the moment by the Hollywood crowd. He hangs up and turns to one of the art directors.

"'Look, don't take Francis too literally. We don't have the time and the money to get all the things he says he needs to make this film look good. He wants us to spend $5,000 to reconstruct that famous Camel smoke-ring sign on Broadway, which would end up on the screen for just a few seconds. Just do the best you can.'"

Details like this would be lost to time, as most film sets are closed, forever sealed off from the outside world. But Coppola had an assistant on *The Godfather*, Ira Zuckerman, a thirty-four-year-old theater director and acting teacher. It was his first film, and he had been subsidized by a grant from the American Film Institute. He turned out to be a keen observer, taking meticulous notes, which he turned into a 142-page paperback entitled *The Godfather Journal.* Published in early 1972, it is an extraordinary day-by-day chronicle of the preproduction and filming of the movie, capturing what Zuckerman called "the behind-the-scenes atmosphere" of the making of the film.

Thanks to the late Zuckerman's book, scenes from the production unfurl almost as vividly as scenes in the resulting movie:

On Tuesday, February 11, 1971, during an arduous final casting session that would stretch past midnight, the war between Evans and Coppola spilled out into the streets of New York. That afternoon, Evans arrived with his entourage at the Producers Artists Studios on West Fifty-Ninth Street, on a soundstage Paramount had rented to film its endless battery of screen tests. "He looks younger than his forty years, small and slim in a handsomely tailored blue blazer, gray flannel flared trousers and wide silk tie," noted Zuckerman. He was smoking a cigar that "looks too large for his delicate hands and face," and his face was burnished in "that special dusky California tan."

Soon, they were discussing casting once again, and the conversation quickly erupted into a very public shouting match. "It's out of my hands!" Coppola exclaimed at last. "I have no more time to spend on this. I'm flying to London Saturday. Let me know your decisions as to who's playing what when I get back. I wash my hands of the whole thing."

With that, Coppola rushed out of the studio, trailed by his assistants, leaving Evans on the soundstage with his own entourage. "Al Ruddy hurries back and forth between the two camps, trying to smooth things out," wrote Zuckerman. A routine began to develop: every time Evans called Coppola, the conversation would end with the director slamming down the phone.

Later that day, Coppola had returned to the studio, still in the middle of the last excruciating round of screen tests to be done, the final round. The confident young director who founded his own studio was now reduced to testing actors he knew weren't right and having to fight for those he knew were perfect.

Every day at 8:00 a.m., the beauty pageant commenced again: one actor after another, running through lines and hopes and dreams before the cameras of cinematographer Gordon Willis and his two assistant cameramen. Makeup artist Dick Smith arrived to help with the paint and powder; wardrobe supervisor George Newman, for the clothes.

And the actors, scores of them, paraded before the camera, one after the other.

"Keaton sits hunched up, biting her nails and stares in rapt concentration at the director," Zuckerman observed.

The actors poured their hearts out for Coppola. He was running it all, they believed, but actually he wasn't: the tests would be shown the next day to Robert Evans, who was still in New York, in the screening room of the Gulf+Western Building a few blocks away.

The budget for tests had already gone haywire, soon totaling $420,000, as hour piled upon hour, and double time ran into triple time for the crew. At 7:00 p.m., twelve giant pizzas arrived; at 10:00, cauldrons of hot soup. "Twice, production assistants have to be sent out for additional film stock and sound tape," wrote Zuckerman.

Diane Keaton ran through her lines as Kay Adams for the cameras, once, twice, and then again and again, until she had done it more than one hundred times, obliterating the competition until no one could refuse her the role. Zuckerman noted: "Each time the camera rolled, incredibly, she performed it as if for the first time."

At 11:00 p.m., having already tested David Carradine and Al Pacino for Michael, Coppola called back James Caan to play the soldier who becomes the king. It was very late, but Caan ran through yet another screen test, this one in his own clothing, instead of the Marine uniform he wore that morning. It was all a massive waste of time and money, and everyone, including Caan, knew it: "That was the last thing Francis wanted, because he had it in his mind that Michael was the Sicilian-looking one and Sonny was the Americanized version," he would say. But here he was testing again for Michael before a cavalcade of others for whom this moment would be the closest they'd get to the movie.

That's when Caan got hot. "I go in and witness one of the great apparitions of all time," he said. "There's every friggin' actor you can imagine—with Irish accents, with Spanish accents, with Dutch accents. You name the actors, they were there. Eventually I tested for every part. I got disgusted. I said, 'I'll tell you what. Stick this picture up your ass. I'm outta here.' I was so angry that I got on a train and went to Chicago to that *T.R. Baskin* thing"—a Paramount movie in which he would be cast.

The tests continued past midnight, with two actors who had been waiting since 9:00 a.m. They got their tests, which were quickly discarded. "Coppola has already decided on the cast he will fight for tomorrow, during the screening of the tests and the long day has exhausted him," Zuckerman wrote.

It was 1:00 a.m. when Coppola finally left the set.

He was in London five days later, meeting with Marlon Brando, when the office memos went out: Diane Keaton cast as Kay Adams and Robert Duvall as Tom Hagen; and John Marley, the silver-haired, distinguished thespian, then sixty-four, as the hot-tempered studio head Jack Woltz.

The all-important roles of Michael and Sonny were yet to be finalized.

Word circulated that Dustin Hoffman was interested in playing Michael, "and negotiations are already underway to sign him," wrote Zuckerman, adding that intel usually came from the Teamsters. "The drivers always seem to be the first ones to get the news; they quickly pass on the information they gather from conversations heard in their cars."

"THE CASTING OF Michael Corleone became a cause célèbre between the two of us," Evans wrote, acknowledging the wide attention that his battle with Coppola was receiving. To Evans, Pacino was an unremarkable unknown, "diametric in every way" to his vision of Michael Corleone. And worst of all, he was short. In private, Evans referred to Pacino as "that little dwarf."

Evans kept searching for someone else to play Michael. He was especially drawn to the French actor Alain Delon, at the time one of Europe's biggest sex symbols. "Alain came to stay at our house when the casting was incomplete," said Ali MacGraw. "In his back pocket he always carried the paperback of *Le Parrain*, which is *The Godfather* in French. I think he wanted very much to be in it."

The choice of a smooth man-about-town like Delon, who bore no resemblance to the edgy and brooding Pacino, seemed telling. "I realized at one point, Bob Evans wanted a guy that sort of looked like him, and I wanted a guy that sort of looked like me," said Coppola.

At an impasse with Evans, Coppola remained intent the whole time, cobbling together enough footage of Pacino in an attempt to convince the studio brass that the actor was the right choice for Michael. The process was hell on Pacino. Whenever there was going to be another round of tests, Coppola would call him. "Please, come again," he would say.

Pacino's girlfriend at the time, the actress Jill Clayburgh, would rip the phone away from him. "What are you doing to him?" she scolded Coppola. "You're torturing him! Don't call him anymore! They're never gonna give him the part."

"One last time," Coppola would beg. "Please."

And Pacino, as loyal and relentless as Michael Corleone, would come.

DIANE KEATON JOINED the growing chorus of voices pushing for Pacino to play Michael. "In the auditions, she indicated he was her favorite," Coppola told the *New York Times*. Pacino was equally attracted to Keaton. "I knew Diane before the test," he said. "We had an immediate like for each other. And Francis, I think, recognized that and thought it might be useful in the picture."

To fuel their chemistry, the director booked a room at the St. Regis hotel and "set up an improv" with Keaton and Pacino. "I had them order room service," he said. "Then I left them alone and I went home, and I'm sure that was the incubation."

Keaton was smitten. "The greatest loves of my life were all the men in all the movies I had to kiss," she said.

What about Pacino? she was asked.

"I kissed him for sure," she said.

As the first day of shooting drew near, there was one other major role that was still uncast. "We hadn't found a Fredo we liked," said Fred Roos, referring to Don Corleone's weak and inept middle son.

One night, Roos got an invitation from an old friend, the actor Richard Dreyfuss, to come see him in an off-Broadway production he was doing, an Israel Horovitz play called *Line*. "Richard, of course, was good," said Roos. "But there was this guy in it, John Cazale, who I had never heard of before. He was wonderful. He had all the qualities of a Fredo. And he was Italian American."

Cazale, a stage actor, had never appeared in a feature film. Subsidizing his acting with part-time jobs as a messenger and cab driver, he was largely unknown. (Several years later, he would share a small apartment and a close relationship with an aspiring actress: Meryl Streep.)

That night, Roos went backstage to speak with Dreyfuss, and was introduced to Cazale, "known as a terrific actor in New York actors' circles, but he was a nobody in the industry, "said Roos. He didn't know if Cazale had read Puzo's novel, but every actor on both the West Coast and the East knew that casting had commenced for what was shaping up to be a very prestigious film.

"John, I'm casting *The Godfather*, and I think you're right for the part of Fredo, and I want you to come in and meet Francis," said Roos.

Cazale's jaw dropped to the floor.

"Really!?" he responded.

The next morning Roos called Coppola. "I found Fredo," he said. "John Cazale."

"Who?" asked Coppola.

Roos brought Cazale in for a meeting right away, and in the first five minutes, Coppola said, "Yeah, that's our Fredo."

"It was a slam dunk," said Roos.

Another easy call was Richard Castellano as Clemenza, the don's warm-hearted lieutenant who was in real life hard-nosed and "wanting things done his way," said Roos. As Clemenza, though, "He was right on the money."

Coppola had seen the actor in his Oscar-nominated role in *Lovers and Other Strangers*, a 1970 film in which Castellano played what the *Los Angeles Times* called a "soup-slurping, lower-middle-class Italian father who lived in a world of pasta and plastic furniture coverings."

An Italian American from the Bronx, Castellano was also, according to his widow, the nephew of a Gambino family crime boss. Authenticity was his birthright, so much so that in a March 3, 1971, letter to one of the film's crewmembers, Castellano, whom everyone called Richie, approved the recipe in which he would show Al Pacino as Michael how to prepare spaghetti sauce after the shooting of Don Corleone. "I went through the sauce a few times and think this will work . . . Hope all goes well . . . All love, etc. Richie."

The role of Clemenza's fellow capo, the tall and elegant Salvatore "Sal" Tessio, went to a stage actor named Abe Vigoda. Appearing at an open casting call, he was interviewed by Coppola "to see if there was anything in *The Godfather* for me."

One look at the regal, towering Shakespearean actor convinced Coppola he would be perfect for Tessio, even though Vigoda was of Russian Jewish descent and had never been credited in a feature film. "Francis said, 'I want to look at the Mafia not as thugs and gangsters, but like royalty in Rome,'" Vigoda remembered. "I think he was look-ing for the subtext of these people. And the subtext of Tessio is he'd go to church, was a good family man."

To research the role, Vigoda spent considerable time in Little Italy. "What Tessio did was because of business," Vigoda said of the char-acter, who eventually turns on the family and tries to have Michael Corleone assassinated. "Remember when Tessio says, 'Tell Michael it wasn't personal. I always liked him'? That's the character. Tessio's a gentleman."

The result was so convincing that Vigoda became a star, with many more Mafia roles in his future.

The casting decision that caused Coppola considerable consternation—as well as complaints about nepotism among the crew—was the choice of his sister, Talia Shire, to play Connie Cor-leone. "I wanted an audition, but I was avoiding acting because I had enormous fear," Shire would say. "I had been more in theater. But I just thought *Hey, can I have an audition?* I just wanted the experience of an audition."

She auditioned for Coppola and Roos, but felt it didn't go well. Then, to her surprise, she got a phone call a month later. "Could I go to New York to audition?" But when she got to the studio on West Fifty-Ninth Street, where she was scheduled to film the scene in which Connie is beaten by her husband, she saw how tough things had gotten for her brother. "After I got on set, I realized how awful it must have been for Francis, this young director, and what he was going through every day to hold on to his job," she said. "The last thing you need is your sister."

By that point, Coppola was certain he was about to be fired. His dogged insistence over casting Pacino and the rest of his choices had earned him the enmity of almost all the top executives at Paramount. "It got to be really hot and heavy," he said. "It reached the point where they were really gonna get rid of me."

He didn't even think his sister was right for Connie. "I thought she was too pretty for the role," he said. "I mean, this is the Mafia. She only gets married because she's the guy's daughter. Anybody would want to marry you if you're the big boss's daughter."

He told his mother that Connie should be "a fat little dumpy Italian girl with an ugly face."

But it turned out that Robert Evans liked Talia. "Evans saw something in Tallie," Coppola said. "So I said, 'Let Tallie have the part, because I'm gonna get fired anyway.'"

Shire was both surprised and terrified. And it didn't help to hear all the whispering: *She only got the part because she's the director's sister.* But she and her brother were used to it, given their father's success as a composer. "Nepotism is like a disease," she said. "It's a terrible word. Because everybody thinks it's a free ride. But in our case, it really is almost a hundred times more difficult. And maybe that's because we come from Carmine Coppola, who worked for Toscanini. We've got to be ten times as good."

*   *   *

WITH MOST OF the roles cast, and filming set to begin in less than a month, Evans and the studio were ready to officially cast Michael Corleone. In a surprise move, they chose one of Coppola's favorite actors—not Al Pacino, the grandson of Sicilian immigrants, but James Caan, the Jewish kid from Queens. It would prove to be the final battle in the casting war between Coppola and Evans.

Caan got the call from Coppola. He was still the frontrunner to play Michael. And he would have been great in the role. But not as perfect as Pacino.

Nevertheless, with Caan heading toward being cast as Michael, the role of Sonny went to an actor who seemed like a character straight out of Puzo's novel: Carmine Caridi, a six-foot-four, black-haired Italian American bull from a tough section of New York. When a producer asked him how he was able to play a mobster so well, Caridi replied, "Because I almost was one."

At his screen test, Puzo leapt out of his chair and declared, "That's Sonny!" The next day, after the news was announced and Caridi was measured for his wardrobe, he went for a walk around his old neighborhood. "Women were coming up to me with their babies to kiss for good luck," he said.

The contract wasn't signed yet, but Caridi was already partying. "He was running around with some friends of mine, celebrating," said Caan. "He was going to this club and that club" with the "boys" from Caan's old neighborhood. It was a tough crew. "They said, 'What do you want to hang around us for?' And he said, 'Well, I want to get the feeling.' They said, 'We'll give you the feeling. We'll throw you out of the fucking car at ninety.'"

Caan tried to warn Caridi to slow down. "Hey, don't do this," he said. The studio, he explained, was "very shaky" about the role, and Caridi was far from Coppola's first choice. "I know what Francis wants," Caan told him. "No disgrace to you."

Caan's warning proved prescient. Caridi was soon eliminated—but not by the Mob. Up in the Gulf+Western screening room, Paramount's top brass were watching Caridi's screen test for Sonny. He was paired with Al Pacino as Michael. One man a shrub, the other a towering oak. At six foot four, Caridi was "kind of like a Saint Bernard," said Andrea Eastman, the casting director. "I had negotiated the deals for *The Godfather*. So poor Carmine Caridi, there was no deal in place. He wasn't officially set to play Sonny, he was just *told* he had the job."

The combination of short and tall was a dealbreaker for Charlie Bluhdorn and Stanley Jaffe. Eastman saw an opportunity. "Why don't we go back the way Francis wanted it?" she suggested. "Al Pacino is Michael, Jimmy Caan is Sonny."

"No, Andrea," Jaffe said. "You just feel sorry for Jimmy Caan."

Then Robert Evans spoke up. "No, actually she's right," he said.

It was a shocking about-face. After months of battling Coppola over his casting choices, Evans was finally ceding to the director's wishes. Pacino and Caan, at 5'7" and 5'10", he had to admit, were more conceivable as brothers than Pacino and Caridi. Bluhdorn agreed, directing his ire at Eastman. "This little pipsqueak playing Michael and this big goombah playing Sonny?" he raged. "You're the head of casting, Andrea! This is our most important movie, and this is just awful."

Once again, Evans spoke up. "Let's go with Jimmy Caan," he said of the role of Sonny.

That was all Eastman needed to hear. "I was so excited I ran up the stairs because the screening room was one floor below my office, and I made the deal with Jimmy Caan's agent before anybody could change their mind. Poor Carmine Caridi, he was going, I imagine, to feel awful. But it would have ruined the movie."

Carmine Caridi got the news right after he had given his two weeks' notice in *The Man of La Mancha*, the Broadway musical he was acting in at the time. He walked offstage to find that Robert Duvall had called him four times. "I called him back and he said, 'Al Ruddy's talking to Jimmy [Caan] about Sonny. Did he say anything?" said Caridi.

"I don't think I've gotten over it, still," Caridi added decades afterward, ruminating on his life in his West Hollywood apartment. "Evans changed his mind about Pacino, and Jimmy moved over to my part, and I was out the door. I walked around in a daze. What the freak is this shit? My sister and my brother were crying, my friends were crying. People in this business, they make promises and they renege. I don't blame Jimmy. I blame Evans. When his book came out, I almost hit him over the head with a fucking chair at The Palm. It was heartbreaking. You're told you have one of the best parts in movie history and then, *ba boom!* They give it to you with a big bang, and then they take it away with a whisper."

Now, the only main role left to cast was Michael.

COPPOLA HAD WON, but he didn't know it yet. He was on his way back from England, where he had flown to meet with Brando and discuss his role as Don Corleone. As far as he knew, James Caan was being cast as Michael. Shortly after landing he called his assistant, Mona Skager, who had bad news: the next body to be disposed of in the bloody battle over *The Godfather* would be his.

"Don't quit," she said, relaying a message from his lawyers. "Let them fire you."

Coppola knew what that meant. If he quit, the studio would have grounds not to pay him the $175,000 fee he had been promised as director. "I started thinking, *So I'll get the $175,000 and I'll be done with this mess and I'll just go and make my own personal film,*" he said. "I was totally sure that I was gonna get fired. But I go to the meeting and they said, 'Everything's changed.'"

The executives, it seemed, had gotten their hands on some scenes from a new movie Pacino had done called *The Panic in Needle Park.* "Pacino was very good in that picture, and they could see that he had something," said Coppola. At the meeting he was told, "Pacino can play Michael if you'll have Jimmy Caan move over and play Sonny."

That was what Coppola had wanted all along. But there was a snag: Pacino had accepted a part in *The Gang That Couldn't Shoot Straight,* a Mafia comedy being produced by MGM. "Boy, I like Jimmy Caan, but Pacino's taken another job," Coppola told the executives. "How you gonna get him?"

Robert Evans was one step ahead of him. "They had gone with their gangster connections and had a guy call up to get Pacino out of the part he had taken," said Coppola.

Evans didn't deny the "gangster connection."

But as usual, he offered a more dramatic version of how Pacino and Caan ended up as Michael and Sonny—one in which he cast himself as the victor.

"The war over casting the family Corleone was more volatile than the war the Corleone family fought on screen," Evans wrote. In his account, which is difficult to believe, Coppola initially refused to cast Caan as Sonny, even if it meant getting Pacino as Michael.

"Carmine Caridi's signed," Coppola insisted, according to Evans. "He's right for the role. Anyway, Caan's a Jew—he's not Italian."

"Yeah," Evans replied, "but he's not six five, he's five ten. This ain't Mutt and Jeff. This kid Pacino's five five, and that's in heels."

"I'm not using Caan."

"I'm not using Pacino."

"Slam went the door," Evans wrote. "Ten minutes later, the door opened. 'You win.'"

Evans elaborated. "Francis was obsessed with Pacino. I didn't like his screen test. We were a month away from shooting, and we didn't have the lead in the picture. At 2:00 a.m., Francis said, 'Look, let me have Pacino and you can have Jimmy Caan to play Sonny.' We shook hands on it."

Then Evans called Pacino's agent, only to learn that the actor had just signed to do *The Gang That Couldn't Shoot Straight* for MGM.

Evans called Jim Aubrey, the head of MGM. "They used to call him the Cobra. He said, 'Forget it.' I said, 'Jim, this is *The Godfather*! Pacino is desperate to do it.' And Aubrey said, 'You have *The Godfather*? I have *The Gang That Couldn't Shoot Straight*, which is as important to me as *The Godfather* is to you.'"

Slam went the phone.

Evans had only one phone call to make. The Carlyle Hotel, where Sidney Korshak was staying.

The Chicago Mob lawyer, who had refused to name names during the congressional investigation into organized crime during the 1950s, was by now what the *New York Times* would call "one of Hollywood's most fabled and influential fixers," able to change the course of empires with a single phone call.

"I need your help," Evans told his consigliere.

"Yeah?" asked Korshak.

"There's an actor I want for the lead in *The Godfather*."

"Yeah?" said Korshak.

"I can't get him," said Evans.

"Yeah?"

"If I lose him, Coppola's gonna have my ass."

"The actor, what's his name?"

"Pacino . . . Al Pacino."

"Who?"

"Al Pacino."

"Hold it, will ya? Let me get a pencil. Spell it."

"Capital A, little L—that's his first name. Capital P, little a, c-i-n-o," said Evans.

"Who the fuck is he?"

"Don't rub it in, will ya, Sidney. That's who the motherfucker wants."

"Sit by the phone," said Korshak.

"And he hangs up the phone in my ear. Twenty minutes later, my secretary buzzes me. 'Mr. Aubrey on the phone, Mr. Evans.'

"You no good fucking cocksucker," Evans remembered Aubrey roaring. "He took out my eardrums for a week. 'You can have the runt. I'll get you, you prick.' He hung up the phone. I called Sidney.

"How did you do it?"

Korshak said he had called Kirk Kerkorian, the new owner of MGM, in Vegas. Unless MGM agreed to release Pacino, Korshak warned, Kerkorian might encounter some union problems. "You're building an awfully big hotel there, the MGM Grand," Evans would say Korshak told Kerkorian. "Would you like to finish it?" Just like that, the deal was done.

A spokesman for Kerkorian would deny that the conversation ever happened. The week's headlines, however, told a different story. "Injunction in Pacino Suit on 'The Godfather,'" the *Hollywood Reporter* trumpeted on March 11, 1971, reporting that MGM was suing to keep the star for itself. On March 17, apparently after the call from Korshak, *Variety* reported that it was all over: "Suit Settlement Clears 'Godfather' Role for Pacino."

The role cost Pacino more than the initial rejection. "MGM sued me for two million dollars because they said I was committed to *The Gang That Couldn't Shoot Straight*," he told the men's magazine *Saga* in 1975. "So I paid for lawyers. I paid for everything. I was broke after that. But I didn't care. I've been broke before."

In return for freeing Pacino from *The Gang That Couldn't Shoot Straight*, MGM poached another young unknown from *The Godfather*: Robert De Niro. The actor, who was set to play a small part as Don Corleone's turncoat driver Paulie Gatto, had actually auditioned for Sonny, playing him as a cold-blooded killer. But De Niro's screen test portrayal of Sonny was too brutal even for Coppola, who in two years would hire De Niro for a career-making role as the young Vito Corleone.

At long last, two weeks before shooting was set to begin, *The Godfather* had its cast. The main roles were set: Brando, Pacino, Caan, Duvall, and Keaton. It was the cast Coppola had envisioned from the moment he was hired, the very same actors he had auditioned for the cost of a few corned beef sandwiches. "We're all set to go, with the same cast we had done in San Francisco for the $500 eight months before," said Coppola. If Paramount had listened to him in the first place, he added, it could have saved the $420,000 it wound up spending on screen tests.

With the casting of Pacino as Michael, almost every Italian American character in the film was played by an Italian American, with the notable exceptions of Vito and Sonny Corleone.

Then, out of the shadows of New York City, a new foe arose, and this one would make the war over casting seem like a cakewalk.

9

THE GODFATHER VS. *THE GODFATHER*

The threats seemed to come out of nowhere. Congressmen were reaching out to express their displeasure, hundreds of letters of protest began arriving from some of the most powerful politicians in America, and the newspapers were suddenly filled with stories about a new organization called the Italian American Civil Rights League. The group, formed to stamp out the stereotyping of Italian Americans in motion pictures, television, and the government, was expressing its demands not merely in words but in actions. If Paramount didn't scrap its plan to turn *The Godfather* into a movie, it would be stopped by any means necessary.

To make matters worse, the production soon moved in on the Mob's home turf: New York City.

As the film grew from its original concept—"to do it like an *FBI* TV series, shoot it on the back lot in Los Angeles . . . for one million dollars," according to associate producer Gray Frederickson—so had its budget and its aspirations, especially concerning filming location. Because Francis Coppola was adamant that filming a movie about the New York Mob could *only* be filmed in New York—to which Al Ruddy initially disagreed. "Though *The Godfather* will be made on location, it won't be made in NY, site of most of the action," *Variety* had reported on September 2, 1970. "It costs more to film in New York for what you could easily spend and never see on the screen," Ruddy told the newspaper, citing the living expenses, higher than anywhere else, and the unions, and, most problematic, the then Mob-controlled Teamsters.

Potential alternate cities included Cleveland, Kansas City, and Cincinnati. "When you're shooting in tight, I defy you to tell the difference," said Ruddy.

Coppola fired back. "Major difference of opinion on filming Mario Puzo's novel, *The Godfather,* has sprung to the fore with revelation that recently signed director Francis Ford Coppola is unhappy with producer Al Ruddy's nixing New York as shooting site," read *Variety.* "The atmosphere is strictly New York," said Coppola, "and since I want to do the film as a period piece, if possible—say the 1940s—any other locale is going to make it more difficult to capture the special flavor of New York." He was flying to New York to scout locations the following week, he noted, even while his production designer Dean Tavoularis was dispatched to St. Louis as a possible backup. "I was trying to get out of it," said Tavoularis. "Seemed like a waste of time."

Tavoularis dutifully went to St. Louis, while Coppola kept pushing for New York.

"Finally, they gave in and said, 'Do it in New York,'" said Tavoularis.

And here *The Godfather* came head-to-head with the League.

The League pressured Italian American actors to drop out of the production, denied film crews access to homes and businesses in Little Italy and Long Island, where they were planning to shoot on location, and threatened to organize a union strike to "deprive the film crew of drivers and deliveries."

All of which would soon be traced back to one man, the founder of the League, a flamboyant real estate salesman from Long Island named Joe Colombo. He had cast himself as an outspoken watchdog on behalf of his fellow Italian Americans, denouncing anyone he perceived as defaming their noble heritage. "The League is under God's protection," he often declared, beginning with one of the organization's early rallies. "Those who go against the League will feel His sting."

Colombo mobilized tens of thousands of protestors to march through the streets of New York, organized a benefit concert headlined by Frank Sinatra, and amassed a war chest of roughly $600,000—which he used, according to Al Ruddy, for "the sole express purpose of stopping the filming of *The Godfather*."

By 1970, Colombo was seen by many as on his way to becoming one of the most powerful men in New York City, alongside Mayor John Lindsay and Governor Nelson Rockefeller. He campaigned with special zeal against any mention in the media of the Mafia, a word he felt summed up all the negative portrayals of his people.

Which was ironic. Because Colombo was said to be the boss of one of New York's most powerful Mafia families.

The Godfather, it turned out, was feeling the wrath of a real-life godfather.

"The threats against Paramount were coming from the League and the Mob," Joe Coffey, a legendary NYPD detective who specialized in taking down the Mafia, explained in the British documentary *The Godfather and the Mob*. "There was no distinguishing one from the other."

Lawmen like Coffey would contend that, like Colombo's real estate business, the League operated as a front. Initially called the American Italian Anti-Defamation League, the organization was composed of pillars of the community—wealthy doctors, lawyers, judges, and businessmen. But with the veneer of respectability came an element of timidity. "Behind closed doors, these men all agreed that Italian Americans were facing severe discrimination and infringements on their civil liberties, but they would only go so far in making their grievances public," wrote Colombo's son Anthony, who served as the League's vice president, alongside the president, Natale "Nat" Marcone, a retired union organizer who ran the day-to-day operations. "They were concerned that if they were too vocal, they might jeopardize their businesses or professional reputations."

A top priority was to eradicate *Mafia* from the English language, since Joe Colombo contended that the word had been turned into a one-word smear campaign. "Mafia? What is the Mafia?" he asked a *New York Times* reporter in 1971. "There is not a Mafia. Am I head of a family? Yes. My wife and four sons and a daughter. That's my family."

The League's first target had been *The Valachi Papers*, the explosive soon-to-be-published tell-all biography of Joseph Valachi, the former mobster, written by Peter Maas. Maas interviewed Valachi in his jail cell after he had testified before Congress about the Genovese crime family. The Justice Department had initially authorized publication of Valachi's own memoir, *The Real Thing*, hoping it would encourage other members of organized crime to come forward with information of their own. But the League, arguing that Valachi's memoir would sully the reputation of hardworking Italian Americans, put pressure on Attorney General Nicholas Katzenbach to do an about-face. In a stunning reversal, Katzenbach asked a district court to stop publication of *The Real Thing*. "It was the first time an Attorney General of the United States had initiated action to ban a book," wrote Maas.

Flush with success and eager to expand, the League recruited Frank Sinatra—arguably the country's most prominent Italian American—to serve as its national chairman and perform at a benefit concert in Madison Square Garden. But if the move was intended to distance the League from the perception that it was a front for organized crime, it backfired badly. In the New York *Daily News,* a former NYPD detective pointed to Sinatra's open association with mobsters from New Jersey to Nevada. The singer, he said, "hardly matches the image the league is seeking to project as representative of the twenty million Americans of Italian birth or ancestry."

Two years before the publication of *The Godfather*, on August 6, 1967, in the *New York Times Magazine*, a little-known writer joined the growing chorus of protest. In an essay entitled "The Italians, American Style," the writer scoffed at the League's insistence that Italian Americans weren't involved in organized crime. "Do Italians and American

Italians control organized crime in America?" he asked. "The answer must be a reluctant but firm yes."

The writer described the League's membership drive as "sheer madness," arguing that Italian Americans required no special favors or protection. "The culture of Italy is stamped across the broad face of America," he observed. "From the Yankee hills of Vermont to the cattle plains of Texas, from sooty New York to sunny San Francisco, the dripping tomato pizza pie has virtually supplanted the D.A.R. hot dog. The great Joe DiMaggio (his feat of hitting safely in 56 straight games is considered the one unbreakable baseball record) not only filled the gargantuan shoes of Babe Ruth but married the sex goddess of the civilized world—a parlay of fantasies not even Horatio Alger would have dared imagine."

But that, the writer added, didn't mean the Mafia wasn't just as Italian as pepperoni pizza or Joltin' Joe. "It must be said that most Italians—99.999999 per cent, at least—are honest and law-abiding," he wrote. "On the other hand, it must also be admitted that most of the operators in organized crime in this country will bleed Italian blood. That fact must be accepted, and such bodies as the American-Italian pressure groups that are reported to have suppressed the Valachi book and the American Italian Anti-Defamation League do everyone concerned a great disservice."

He also weighed in at length on the chairman of the new incarnation of the League, Frank Sinatra, an analysis that reflected the considerable time the writer had spent thinking about both Sinatra and the Mafia:

> *Sinatra is, in this country, the most powerful American of Italian descent. He is also, it would seem, a man of extraordinary force, having burst the shell of a callow crooner to become perhaps the shrewdest and richest executive in the movie world. Interestingly enough, he has very obviously modeled his personal behavior on that of the great Mafia chiefs who reigned in Sicily—let me add hastily, on their best behavior.*

These Mafia chiefs were men who inspired a fierce loyalty, respect, and an enormous amount of fear. They did so by giving unstinting aid to followers who were completely faithful to them, treating these followers with a hungered-for "respect" no matter how humble their station in life. Sinatra, too, has helped talented people up the ladder of success, and has befriended the famous who have fallen on hard times. He would also seem to have that special quality all great Mafia chiefs possessed: the ability to inspire respect and affection in men of equal power and rank.

It follows, then, that Sinatra would be a valuable asset to the league. He is loyal to his friends, generous to any cause he champions and, above all, he performed the astonishing hat trick of remaining a good husband and father after getting divorced. That alone endeared him to thousands of American-Italians, and if any one person can make them join the league, if anyone can cure them of the Red Cross syndrome and persuade them to send $10 through the mail to perfect strangers, that person is Mr. Sinatra.

Who was this writer who had the gall to throw down such a gauntlet to the League and Frank Fucking Sinatra? Who dared to begin his conclusion with "American-Italians do not need any help from the league; they do not need the championship of the redoubtable Frank Sinatra."

It was none other than Mario Puzo.

At the bottom of the first page of the story was an author's note— one that likely gave the League fresh cause for concern: "Mario Puzo," it read, "is working on a novel about a Mafia family."

IN THE EARLY days of the League, Joe Colombo was the man behind the curtain soon to emerge in an extremely public way. Mobsters, by necessity, learn to avoid the spotlight, and Colombo was trained in the old ways practically from birth. The son of a Brooklyn racketeer and bootlegger, he catapulted his career in what appeared to be a low-level job as a salesman at Pride Meat Company, "part of the expanding legitimate business interests of Paul Castellano, a brother-in-law of Gambino, and a *capo* in Gambino's Mafia family . . . ," according to *The Colombo Family* by Andy Petepiece, who cited an FBI informant who said Colombo ran craps games out of various ever-shifting locations "in hopes of avoiding raids." One of those locations, a "social club" on Thirteenth Avenue, was soon raided. "Colombo, by 1961, was a recognized Mafia member involved in gambling," wrote Petepiece. "No one in law enforcement was predicting that he was a future boss."

It was a fortunate time. The New York Mafia was in upheaval, as older bosses were falling ill, passing away, or going to prison. The same year Colombo's club was raided, he and five other members of the Profaci crime family were seized by the Gallo crew as part of a rebellion against Joe Profaci, the Sicilian-born boss known as the Olive Oil King. The men were released unharmed, but Profaci went back on his promise not to seek revenge. That August, Profaci's men lured Larry Gallo to a meeting at the Sahara Club in Brooklyn and garroted him with a rope tightened by a steel pipe. Gallo was near death when a police sergeant on a routine inspection walked into the club, interrupting the execution.

The next year, after Profaci died of cancer, his underboss Joseph Magliocco succeeded him as head of the family. However, the Commission, the governing council founded by Lucky Luciano in 1931 to iron out disputes among the Five Families, did not approve the appointment. When crime boss Joseph Bonanno sought his help in seizing control of the Five Families, Magliocco was all in. They put out a hit on Carlo Gambino and two other members of the Commission, and Magliocco handed the contract to a supposedly loyal soldier in his employ: Joe Colombo.

A dapper, highly intelligent man, Colombo was said to be little more than a "bust out guy," a second-tier man in charge of a few gambling operations. Now, sensing an opportunity, he turned on his boss.

Instead of carrying out the contract, Colombo told Gambino about the planned assassination, a move that earned him a significant promotion. (And for Magliocco, a speedy retirement.)

At forty-one, Joe Colombo became the alleged boss of the Profaci family, the youngest in Mob history.

But taking over one of the Five Families brought with it a new level of scrutiny from the Feds. Colombo found himself harassed at every turn. In 1966, he and Gambino were among thirteen gangland figures arrested while dining at La Stella, a restaurant in Queens. The following year, Colombo was denied a broker's license for his real estate business. In September 1967, he opened *Life* to find a feature about the Mafia, illustrated with *his* picture. In 1968, he and other bosses were busted during lunch at a Chinese restaurant in Midtown, and on March 6, 1970, he was charged with perjury stemming from falsehoods he made while applying for his broker's license. On March 24, he was indicted for tax evasion.

Then came the event that convinced Colombo to step out of the shadows. On April 30, 1970, the FBI arrested his twenty-three-year-old son, Joe Colombo Jr., and charged him with scheming to melt down coins and sell the silver. "I was willing to suffer through the attacks made by authorities," Colombo told the *New York Daily News*. "But when they framed my boy Joey, then I knew I had to do something."

Springing into action, Colombo mobilized a small group to picket his son's arrest, which included thirty angry protestors. Colombo's wife berated the agents, shouting "Give me my son back!" His eldest son, Anthony, challenged the agents to a fight one night. In a stroke of genius, Colombo armed the protestors with signs accusing the FBI of unfairly targeting *all* Italian Americans. TIME HAS COME FOR ITAL-IANS TO TAKE A STAND, one sign proclaimed. WHY ARE ONLY ITALIAN-AMERICANS INVOLVED IN ORGANIZED CRIME? asked another.

"Within a week of the first protest, Colombo formed the Italian-American Civil Rights League," according to *The Colombo Family*. Superseding the old American Italian Anti-Defamation League, the

new League would be bigger and brasher. Soon thousands of protestors were picketing outside the FBI's headquarters in Manhattan, denouncing the Feds for their "Gestapo" tactics. "We respect the
FBI—it's the greatest organization in the country," Colombo told the
New York Times. "But they're framing our children and harassing our
pregnant women, and we want them to stop."

It was unheard of for a Mob boss to thrust himself so prominently
into the public eye; even the Feds seemed caught off guard by the
move. "That's the new trend," one agent told a reporter. "Everybody,
even the Mafia, is demonstrating now."

On June 8, local residents went to court to try to shut down
the protests, arguing that they constituted a public nuisance. But
Colombo turned the hearing into a public spectacle. "Three busloads
arrived at the courthouse in Foley Square from Brooklyn yesterday,"
reported the *New York Times* of the protestors. Joining Colombo
and his sons, they filed into the courtroom in silence, holding tiny
American and Italian flags and wearing green-white-and-red badges
that declared ITALIANS ARE BEAUTIFUL and WE WANT EQUAL RIGHTS.
"The audience hardly made a sound," the *Times* reported, "but it was
raucous with color."

The protestors listened as Barry Ivan Slotnick, the same lawyer
who was representing Joe Jr. on his criminal charges, addressed Justice
George Starke. "The defendants in this courtroom have all taken a day
off to maintain the last semblance of dignity they have—their right
of free speech," Slotnick said. Justice Starke noted the orderliness of
the spectators, saying they had "impressed me with their reasonable
conduct here."

In unison, the crowd replied, "Thank you, Your Honor."

The court, rejecting the plaintiffs' arguments, upheld the League's
right to peaceful assembly.

Three weeks hence, Colombo arranged an even bigger show of
force. On June 29, the Italian American Civil Rights League organized a massive Unity Day rally at Columbus Circle. Shopkeepers and
restaurant owners were reportedly ordered to close in observance of

the rally—or face the League's wrath. "The terror among the merchants is unbelievable," one anonymous caller told the *New York Times*. The League denounced the rumors—"exactly the sort of thing we are fighting," one leader declared—but hundreds of businesses closed their doors on the day of the rally. Many of the city's unions, including the longshoremen's, also took the day off, effectively shutting down all shipping in and out of New York.

The rally took place beneath the statue of Christopher Columbus on Fifty-Ninth Street. A crowd of fifty thousand packed Broadway for blocks in both directions and stretched deep into Central Park. "The atmosphere was mostly celebratory and harmonious," wrote Don Capria and Anthony Colombo in their book, *Colombo: The Unsolved Murder*, "with children waving flags and eating ice cream."

American banners of red, white, and blue competed with Italian bunting of red, white, and green. Rallygoers sported buttons with a short but unmistakable message: ITALIAN POWER.

The rally included speeches and performances by a host of prominent Italian Americans and their political allies. "Anthony LaRosa, a 12-year-old from Brooklyn, his head barely peering above the massed microphones, stilled the crowd with his address," the *Times* reported. "I am a young Italian-American boy who doesn't want to grow up labeled," he said. "I want to grow up with my constitutional rights, not to be harassed and discriminated against."

But the highlight of the rally was as dramatic as it was unexpected. As chants of "We want Joe! We want Joe!" broke out, Colombo himself emerged to the tune of "For He's a Jolly Good Fellow" and proceeded to address the masses he had assembled.

"You are organized. You are one. Nobody can take you apart anymore," he declared. "This day belongs to you—you the people."

The crowd erupted in a roar of approval. As Colombo tried to continue, he was drowned out by a thundering, rhythmic chant: "ONE! . . . ONE! . . . ONE! . . . ONE! . . . ONE!"

After the speeches were over, the pent-up anger flared into violence. More than ten thousand rallygoers marched through Central

Park to the FBI's headquarters on Third Avenue. "The surging crowd of marchers forced the police to fall back twice around the FBI office as barriers were trampled underfoot and tempers flared," read the *Times* account. Two officers on crowd-control duty were stabbed in a scuffle. Anthony Colombo climbed on top of a police truck and implored the rioters to disperse. "We have achieved a greatness here today!" he shouted. "We are one now! We must keep this peaceful and nonviolent! As a favor to me, be a super-human being now—turn around and go home!" The protestors booed and grumbled but soon they "were straggling down the side streets toward home," reported the *Times*. "A rally marshal with a bullhorn urged them on gently with: 'Have a glass of wine now and a plate of spaghetti in your house.'"

"The first annual Unity Day rally surpassed everyone's expectations," wrote Capria and Colombo. "It had only been thirty days since Joe had introduced the idea at a meeting in the League's Park-Sheraton offices." Now, the entire city had been subjected to a demonstration of his strength. It was unprecedented, a Mafia boss doubling as a civil rights leader, and Colombo ingeniously insisted that his public prominence was proof he couldn't be a mobster. "If I'm a leader of the Cosa Nostra or Mafia or whatever they are calling it," he told the *Daily News*, "then maybe the rumor that I'll be killed is true. I've broken all the rules I've heard about—I'm talking to the press."

The headline over the article read, "Colombo: OK, I'll Be a Mafioso for Good."

Colombo and the League were now rich in cash, members, and influence. In November 1970, the organization raised nearly $500,000 at a sold-out benefit at Madison Square Garden headlined by Frank Sinatra. The following February, Colombo wept tears of joy when Joe Jr. was acquitted by a jury in Brooklyn after the chief witness for the prosecution suddenly recanted his testimony. And a month later, the Mafia boss was honored by the League with its Founders Award and named Man of the Year by the *Tri-Boro Post* at a $125-a-plate testimonial dinner.

By then, emboldened by his success, Colombo had set his sights on an ambitious and far-reaching mission: changing how Italian Americans were viewed and treated in popular culture. Under pressure from the League, the Justice Department and New York State Police had banned the word *Mafia* from press releases, and some newspapers followed suit. When other newspapers and television stations refused to fall in line, the League descended on them with picket lines. At the *Staten Island Advance*, not long after Colombo's protestors arrived, a delivery truck was attacked and two drivers were beaten. "They were forced to lie face down in the back of the truck," the paper's associate publisher told the *Wall Street Journal.* "The hoodlums set the papers in the truck aflame with lighter fluid, closed the back of the truck, and said if the two [drivers] tried to get out, they'd shoot them." ("Fortunately, the assailants left, and the drivers escaped," Harlan Lebo wrote of the incident in *The Godfather Legacy.* "Police escorted *Advance* trucks until picketing ended in March.")

Soon, no less than the *New York Times Magazine* noted Colombo's astonishing achievements, "In the year since he had founded his group, Colombo had drawn 50,000 people to a rally in Columbus Circle; had forced the Justice Department to order the FBI to stop using the terms 'Mafia' and 'Cosa Nostra' in its press releases (and had watched the Governors of New York, Connecticut, Alaska, Texas, and South Dakota follow suit); had persuaded Frank Sinatra to come to New York to help him raise money at a concert in the Felt Forum, and had been named Man of the Year by *The Tri-Boro Post*, a New York neighborhood weekly. After forty-eight years of hiding behind his lapels, Colombo had emerged as a formidable public figure. He posed for pictures, kissed children, signed autographs, talked to Dick Cavett and Walter Cronkite and generally comported himself more like a political candidate than a Mafia boss."

To Colombo, evidence of anti-Italian sentiment was everywhere, and he was determined to rise up against all those who disparaged his people. And the target soon at the very top of his hit list was *The Godfather.* Although the film was only in preproduction, it was already under intense scrutiny by Colombo and the League. If they could stop a major Hollywood movie that was based on a bestselling novel—a novel originally entitled *Mafia*, the word they hated above all others—they could, by extension, change the way America viewed Italian Americans and the Mob.

NO ONE WORKING on *The Godfather* had anticipated any public controversy over the film, much less one that erupted before the film had even been cast. It was initially a low-budget movie about a family of gangsters, being produced by a struggling studio and directed by a relative unknown. Who would care, much less object?

But then came the letters, delivered to Al Ruddy's office at Paramount. They were, he told the *Detroit Free Press*, from "prominent senators, congressmen, state senators, and others expressing their concern that *The Godfather*, if not treated properly, would defame the Italian American community."

Others threatened direct action against the film: "demonstrations, boycotts and wildcat strikes by everyone from maintenance men to electricians," reported the *New York Times Magazine*. P. Vincent Landi, who identified himself as the "Grand Venerable" of the "Grand Lodge of the State of New York, Order Sons of Italy in America," wrote to express dismay that Paramount was turning *The Godfather* into a movie. "In our opinion, the book is a cruel hoax," he wrote, "and unfairly stigmatizes all Americans of Italian descent."

He helpfully provided a list of exemplary Italians, including Enrico Fermi, Giuseppe Garibaldi, and Guglielmo Marconi, whose lives would make for "constructive and intelligent movies," and suggested there were "many books dealing with the constructive, wholesome and pleasant Italian family life" that "could be made into beautiful movies."

At a meeting of the organization's Grand Council, he warned, lodges throughout New York had voted unanimously to boycott *The Godfather*, distribute protest petitions against the film, and file a complaint with the Human Rights Commission. Furthermore, the lodges all agreed, "No cooperation should be granted the producers of this picture by any governmental authority."

Francis Ford Coppola received a handwritten letter expressing a similar sentiment:

> *Mr. Coppolla!* [sic]
> *So now you have succeeded in dragging all Italian-Americans into the mud.*
> *To make amends, I think you should do stories on the really great Italians. For starters—Pope John XXIII the ecumenical pope, the late, great Vince Lombardi, the great Federal Judge John J. Sirica, Pope Paul VI, war heroes Capt. Don Gentile, Sgt. Michael Smerillo, the great Rep. Peter Rodino, etc.*
> *John Smerillo*
> *Commander, American Legion*
> *Post 388*

The Godfather was feeling the League's sting. "There was pressure put on the company, on all of us," Al Ruddy would say. An early sign of trouble was a call from the most notorious mobster in Los Angeles, Mickey Cohen, the former henchman to Bugsy Siegel. Now in his sunset years, Cohen was calling to invite Ruddy to lunch.

Ruddy, eager to meet the legendary crime boss who had once ruled the city, readily accepted. After they were seated at a Beverly Hills restaurant, Cohen leaned over and said, "The guys are watching you. Nobody's looking for anything except for a certain amount of respect."

"He was never threatening and he was actually curious: Who was going to be playing the don, what problems we were having," said Ruddy.

"Mickey, you won't have any problem with me," Ruddy told him over lunch that day. "Call off your dogs."

The Mob didn't seem to get the message. A mysterious man showed up in the office of Paramount's vice president of finance with a check for $1 million. The money, he said, would be the studio's if it agreed to drop the picture. Death threats became routine: menacing calls from nameless men. He began keeping a .45 pistol in his desk, which he thought he might actually have to use. "I didn't know whether the calls were coming from the Mafia or not," said Ruddy. "But the calls threatened my life."

His assistant, Bettye McCartt, received threats as well: one caller vowed to kidnap her son from military school. Los Angeles police warned Ruddy that he was being followed, and McCartt remembered Paramount's head of security telling her boss that "he should be very careful, because they were really after him."

In hopes of throwing off his trackers, Ruddy and McCartt and others on Ruddy's team began switching cars before leaving the Paramount lot. McCartt lived off Mulholland Drive, high in the Santa Monica hills. Then one night, someone—she suspected the Mob or its emissaries—found her. She had driven home in Ruddy's car, an expensive French Facel Vega convertible. She saw a car following her all the way to her home, which was at the end of a winding, narrow street. She rushed inside and called the police. But by the time they arrived, her trackers were gone. Then, in the middle of the night, gunshots rang out in the neighborhood. The next morning, she discovered the convertible's windows had all been blasted out. "Somebody had left a note where the windshield had been saying they didn't want the picture made," McCartt said.

Ruddy was undeterred. Moving to New York, he had set up offices in the Gulf+Western headquarters on Columbus Circle. There, the production team went to work overseeing the process of re-creating the look and feel of New York in the 1940s and 1950s. "Scattered around in cardboard boxes and spilling over onto desks are piles of old copies of *Life* and photographs of New York streets and nightclubs, and even of furniture auctioned from the homes of famous racketeers," wrote production assistant Ira Zuckerman. "All this material has been studied by the set and costume designers, prop-master, hair and makeup artists, to help them to create the authentic look of the period on which Coppola insists. Prop men are on the phones trying to line up a fleet of period cars, around eighty in all, including trucks, taxis, police cars, and vans. Ads have been placed in the newspapers and the men are now following up on the replies."

Ruddy and Coppola were about to get a level of authenticity they hadn't counted on. In November 1970, the League had picketed a New York City television station that aired Paramount's feeble 1968 Mob movie, *The Brotherhood*, which dared to use the term *Mafia*.

The League felt the word "created the perception that the only organized crime in the United States was conducted by Italians; and further, that most Italian Americans were criminals," according to Colombo's son Anthony.

As the preproduction teams fanned out across the city, arranging for transportation and services, all manner of mayhem began to occur. Many of the movie's initial sixty-two shooting locations, which had been secured with their owners, suddenly became unavailable. "Sixty-two!" exclaimed Ruddy. Olive oil companies, hospitals, funeral parlors—the story was the same everywhere the location scouts went. They would show up at a home or an office or a factory that had already been arranged, only to find decals in the window, identifying the establishment as affiliated with the Italian American Civil Rights League. The owners, many who had paid the League for membership, now refused to allow Paramount to use their properties as locations. Construction on a Long Island estate that had been chosen to serve as Don Corleone's compound came to a halt when the homeowners suddenly withdrew their cooperation. "They just didn't want to get involved," said Ruddy. A similar fate befell Gray Frederickson when he tried to find filming locations in New York City. "They all turned us down, every one," Frederickson said. "They all had that little Italian-American Civil Rights League decal in their windows. They paid $100 a year and there were thousands of them. They said, 'Don't cooperate with the *Godfather* people. They put Italian Americans in a bad light. It's anti-Italian American.'"

What would be called a "campaign of intimidation" continued. Paramount's offices at the Gulf+Western Building were evacuated twice following bomb threats, and Ruddy took to wearing a disguise. "He had Groucho glasses and nose," McCartt said. Then, one day, the telephone rang at the Sherry-Netherland, the luxury hotel overlooking Central Park where Robert Evans was sharing a suite with his wife, Ali MacGraw, and their newborn son, Joshua. The switchboard had assigned an extra operator to screen the studio chief's calls, but Evans picked up anyway.

"Take some advice," a deep voice said, according to Evans's memoir. "We don't want to break your pretty face, hurt your newborn. Get the fuck outta town. Don't shoot no movie about the family here. Got it?"

"Fuck you, mister," Evans said. "If you got any problems, take it up with the producer, Al Ruddy."

There was a moment of silence before the voice began again, slowly.

"Listen carefully, motherfucker," the caller warned. "I ain't gonna say it again. When you wanna kill a snake, pretty boy, there's only one way to do it—you go for for its head."

Evans was rattled. So was MacGraw, even though she didn't hear the actual call. "I knew that happened," she said. "They were playing with fire with this back in the day. There were various Mob suggestions, let's put it that way."

It was one thing to make a movie about mobsters; it was another to be confronted by the real item.

Anthony Colombo insisted that his father never said or sanctioned such threats—especially by telephone, which Joe Colombo felt sure were tapped by the Feds. "The truth was we didn't need to make threats to stop the picture," Colombo was quoted as saying in the book *Colombo: The Unsolved Murder*. "If we didn't want it made in New York, it wouldn't have been made, period. At the time, the League had over 40,000 members, and the majority of them were blue-collar workers who believed in the power of protest. The entire Italian-American community was waiting to hear our next move with the picture."

When the next move came, it must have frightened Evans as much as the supposed threats on his life. The Teamsters threatened to freeze all transportation involving *The Godfather*. The movie would be literally stalled in its tracks.

Evans and Ruddy had to do something, *fast*. The only way forward, they realized, was to arrange a meeting with the real-life Mafia don who was preventing them from making a movie about a fictional Mafia don. But how? Who could dare to go face-to-face with Joe Colombo?

Being in Hollywood, Evans turned to the obvious source of assistance in times of crisis: he called an agent.

EDDIE GOLDSTONE WAS sitting in his new office in the Gulf+ Western Building when the phone rang. It was Bob Evans, summoning him to a meeting.

Goldstone, in his thirties, was an agent at Creative Management Associates, the preeminent Hollywood talent agency of its day. He had been dispatched to New York to watch over CMA's *Godfather* clients: Ruddy, Coppola, Caan, and Keaton. Goldstone wasn't surprised to get a call from the Paramount brass. "They knew I was a pretty good negotiator," he said. He arrived at the meeting to find Evans and Ruddy, looking glum.

"We're having a problem with Joe Colombo," they told Goldstone. "Would you mind going in to talk to him?"

Goldstone knew the havoc Colombo and his League were inflicting on *The Godfather,* but he wasn't sure what he could do to stop it. A meeting was arranged by Caan, who had grown up in New York City and "always knew the big boys downtown," said Goldstone. "The purpose of the meeting was to see if we could get Al Ruddy into a meeting with them to discuss the union problems, which had to do with the truck drivers. They didn't want to work for the wages, or work for the company; Colombo told them not to work for the company."

It was up to the agent to bring the League to the negotiating table.

The morning of the meeting, Goldstone took a taxi to an address on Mott Street, in Little Italy. Wearing his trim agency suit and his broad agency smile, with "a lump in my stomach," Goldstone knocked on the door of the building, trying not to think about what lay behind it. "If I had thought about it, I would have said no," he said. "Because this guy is a killer gangster."

The address turned out to be an Italian American social club. The door opened a crack, then wider, and Goldstone launched into his pitch. "Hello," he began. "My name is Eddie Goldstone and I'm an agent with CMA . . ."

He could see men, a dozen of them, some speaking Italian. The air was filled with smoke and conversation. And there in the middle of the room was the obvious leader, dressed in a suit and tie, "eyes close together," staring out from beneath his hat at Goldstone, sizing up the Hollywood agent, this alien from another world.

Goldstone walked inside and began all over. "I'm an agent with CMA," he explained, "and we represent a number of people on the film . . ."

· Joe Colombo extended his hand.

". . . including Al Ruddy, the producer, and Francis Ford Coppola, the director," Goldstone continued, accepting Colombo's grasp. Then, like a good agent, he cut to the chase. "Is there anything I can help you with?" he asked the mobster.

It seemed like a ridiculous place to start. Colombo didn't need Goldstone's help—it was the other way around. The agent trudged forward. "We think somebody's interfering with our business, with our drivers, the Teamsters on the set who drive the trucks and the cars," he said, his words pouring out in a torrent.

Somebody offered Goldstone coffee and a roll. "We can work something out, and it's going to be a hell of a movie," the agent continued, feeling a bit more confident. "This is a film you're going to be proud of. I can tell you it's certainly going to be there for the award season."

"What's the award season?" he was asked.

Goldstone explained the annual Hollywood ritual of self-congratulation to the men in the room. Some back-and-forth ensued. "They were aggravated with the way they were being treated in the business. They thought they were being stepped on," said Goldstone. "You know what they say about respect? I don't think they were getting the respect that they wanted."

Now, at last, they were. And what they wanted, it turned out, was simple:

"They wanted to know all about Brando."

Goldstone barely knew Brando—but the truth is no obstacle to a good agent. "I gave them a bit of bullshit," said Goldstone. "I said I knew Brando well, which I didn't. I had to dance."

Twenty minutes of dancing, and it was over. "He [Colombo] shook my hand twice and I was out of there," said Goldstone. He had achieved what he had come for. Joe Colombo, the Mafia godfather, would meet with Al Ruddy, the producer of *The Godfather*, to see if they could find common ground—or at least broker a truce between the parties. Ruddy was so pleased, Goldstone said he called him into his office and told him, "I want to thank you for everything you did."

BEFORE RUDDY WAS allowed to meet Colombo, an initial meeting was set up between the producer, Colombo's son Anthony, and League president Nat Marcone. Over dinner at La Scala, on West Fifty-Fourth Street, they outlined a tentative deal. "Ruddy had agreed to delete 'Mafia,' 'Cosa Nostra' and all other Italian words from the script. He had promised to allow the League to review the script and change anything it felt was damaging to the Italian-American image," wrote Nicholas Pileggi in the *New York Times*. "And finally he had agreed to turn over the proceeds of the film's New York premiere to the League's hospital fund."

It was an unprecedented set of concessions for a Hollywood producer to make. Ruddy seemed to be agreeing not only to censoring the movie's script but also to turning over a portion of its profits to a group founded by one of the country's most powerful mobsters. He had agreed to every one of Colombo's demands, and then some. With this broad outline in place, Anthony told Ruddy he could now meet his father—on the condition that Joe Colombo would be given an opportunity to read the script and point out any additional offenses he felt should be deleted.

On February 25, 1971, Ruddy arrived at the Park-Sheraton Hotel for the meeting. Colombo's choice of meeting place had dark undertones. The hotel was the site of one of the most infamous killings in Mob history—the assassination of the crime boss Albert Anastasia, who had been shot dead in a barber chair on the Park-Sheraton's ground floor on the orders of Carlo Gambino and Vito Genovese. But if Ruddy was worried, he didn't show it. "At only 36, after all, he had managed to parlay the dubious distinction of producing *Hogan's Heroes* for television and two money-losing films (*Little Fauss and Big Halsy, Making It*) into the job of producing Paramount's biggest potential money maker," wrote Pileggi. "Ruddy had always been able to talk his way through obstacles." Now, confident in the deal he had struck with Anthony, he considered the meeting with Joe Colombo to be a mere formality.

He was wrong. When he strode into the hotel's Grand Ballroom, he was confronted by more than six hundred members and supporters of the Italian American Civil Rights League.

Ruddy was greeted by a thunderous reception, with some jeers and boos. Some members of the audience "looked like they were out on parole," he said. For a man who had been receiving death threats for months, the scene must have been chilling. But Ruddy was as tough as anyone who might try to intimidate him.

Richard Capozzola, a League official, rose to speak, wrote the authors of *Colombo: The Unsolved Murder*. He was opposed to *The Godfather* being made at all, and Colombo knew he was prepared to denounce the film in no uncertain terms. So he decided to ease the tension. Before Capozzola reached the podium, Colombo jumped in.

"I want everyone to know who this fellow is that's coming up to the microphone," he told the audience. "This is Dickey, and he is my button man."

The ballroom fell silent. Colombo had just used the Mafia term for *hit man*.

"I said to myself, *holy shit*," Capozzola remembered. "I had the place looking at me sideways for a minute—until Joe explained to everyone that I had designed the League's logos and buttons, and was in charge of producing them. It was good for a laugh, even Joe smiled."

Anthony Colombo attempted to calm the crowd by telling them of the concessions Ruddy had already agreed to, including the money from the New York premiere. Once again, his father cut in.

"I couldn't care less if they gave us two million dollars," Joe Colombo said. "No one can buy the right to defame Italian Americans." Later, he told Ruddy, "This Hollywood, we've had it with the movies you people do about us and it's embarrassing. Hollywood has gotten to the point where my community is defamed. Every illegitimate thing that happens in the United States, it's always the Mafia. There's the Russian Mafia, the Irish Mafia, the Jewish Mafia. They're saying there's Italians mixed in there, and I find [it] very depressing. Why don't they call it organized crime? Why is it always *Mafia*?"

At the meeting, Ruddy didn't give an inch. "He argued that despite their occupations, the members of the Corleone family were the heroes of the story," according to *Colombo: The Unsolved Murder*.

"Look, Joe," he later told Colombo in his trademark, tough-guy growl. "This movie will not demean the Italian American community. It's an equal opportunity organization. We have a corrupt Irish cop, a corrupt Jewish producer. No one's singling the Italians out for anything. But I'll tell you what I'll do. You come to my office tomorrow. No one has seen the script. You come to my office tomorrow and I'll let you look at the script. You can see, Mafia, whatever's in. And you like it or don't, and you read it and we'll see if we can make a deal."

As he spoke to the crowd, the producer must have seemed like he fit right in. "If he wasn't Jewish, Al Ruddy would be a great godfather," the author Nicholas Pileggi later observed. Anthony Colombo was equally impressed. "His firm demeanor, raspy voice, and guileless answers were the elixir Paramount needed that night to assuage the League's fears," he wrote.

Joe Colombo, meanwhile, sat back and observed the confrontation he had orchestrated. "[He] didn't do much talking," according to the book *Colombo*. "Joe just listened and watched, carefully monitoring the emotions in the room and carefully studying Ruddy."

Finally, Colombo had heard enough. He had one more order of business he wanted Ruddy to address. Who would be playing the bit parts and the extras in the movie?

"Look at who's playing the roles," Ruddy said, ready to list various cast members who represented ethnic groups other than Italians.

"Who is playing?" Colombo suddenly asked, according to the *New York Times Magazine*.

"Lots of people," Ruddy said.

"How about a good kid from Bensonhurst?" Colombo suggested.

Of course, Ruddy thought. *These guys are just like everyone else— they want parts in the movie.* Colombo began proposing various delegates for potential roles. The crowd's jeers now turned to cheers, as Colombo reeled off a list of names, followed by Ruddy's nods of approval.

By the end of the meeting, Ruddy had won over the crowd. The pariah had become a prince—a transformation that Colombo made official by attaching a pin to Ruddy's lapel, knighting him as a capitan of the Italian American Civil Rights League.

THE NEXT DAY, the negotiations shifted to the Gulf+Western Building. It was a bitter-cold evening. So blustery the slender skyscraper swayed in the wind, as it usually did. Colombo arrived to read the script with two associates: George "Butterass" DeCicco and Caesar Vitale, the League's secretary-treasurer. The visitors in brown coats and felt hats; Ruddy, wearing Hollywood casual. The producer locked his office door the moment his guests stepped inside in case the Feds—or worse, any enemies—had tailed them there.

It had been a busy time for Colombo. On March 11, he would be sentenced to two and a half years in prison, following his conviction on perjury charges stemming from the falsehoods he made on his application for a real estate broker's license. Free on appeal, he sat down to read the 155-page script of *The Godfather*, an opportunity seldom afforded to industry outsiders. As Ruddy watched, Colombo put on "his little Ben Franklin glasses" and stared at the first page for a full minute.

"What does this mean—FADE IN?" he asked Ruddy.

Ruddy knew it was over before it had begun. "I realized there was no way Joe was going to turn to page two," he said.

"Oh, these fucking glasses. I can't read with them," Colombo said, tossing the script to Butter DeCicco. "Here, you read it."

"Why me?" exclaimed Butter, throwing the script to Vitale, who regarded it as he might a ticking time bomb.

Exasperated, Colombo grabbed the script and slammed it on the table. "Wait a minute!" he asked his men. "Do we trust this guy?"

Yeah, they replied in unison.

"So what the fuck do we have to read this script for?" said Colombo. He looked at Ruddy: "Let's make a deal."

Colombo reiterated his principal demand: he wanted any and all mentions of *Mafia* deleted from the script.

Ruddy knew the word was only used a single time in the entire screenplay: when Tom Hagen visits movie producer Jack Woltz at his studio in Hollywood to persuade him to give Johnny Fontane a part in his new film, and Woltz snaps, "Johnny Fontane will never get that movie! I don't care how many dago guinea wop greaseball Mafia goombahs come out of the woodwork!" It would be a simple excision for a world of cooperation.

"That's okay with me, guys," Ruddy said, and the producer and Joe Colombo shook hands.

There was one more thing: Colombo wanted Ruddy to honor his

agreement to donate the proceeds from the world premiere of the film to the League, as a goodwill gesture. The producer agreed to that as well. "I'd rather deal with a Mob guy shaking hands on a deal than a Hollywood lawyer, who, the minute you get the contract signed, is trying to figure out how to screw you," Ruddy would say, justifying his willingness to negotiate with Colombo. (In the end, the proceeds did not go to the League.)

Two days passed. Colombo called Ruddy and invited him to an impromptu press conference. "To get the word out to our people that we're now behind the movie," he explained.

Ruddy thought it was a great idea. To get the movie made, he needed the cooperation of the Italian community in New York, and he figured there might be "a couple of Italian newspapers" covering the press conference. Instead, he arrived at the League offices in the Park-Sheraton Hotel to discover that Colombo had invited reporters from every major newspaper and crews from all three television networks to chronicle Paramount's historic deal with the Mob. Colombo, it seemed, had staged an ambush.

The reaction was scathing. The *Times* called the deal a "hypocritical, craven act of 'voluntary' self-censorship." ("YES, MR. RUDDY, THERE IS A . . . ," read the headline.)

A state senator from Staten Island issued an open letter to Ruddy, accusing him of committing "a monstrous insult to millions upon millions of loyal Americans of Italian extraction who must deeply resent this assault on free expression at their expense."

"If you want to produce a film on the Mafia," the *Village Voice* instructed its readers, "please ask their permission first."

Paramount scrambled to distance itself from the controversy. The deal Ruddy made, a spokesman for the studio told *Variety,* was "completely unauthorized."

Nothing had been cleared with Robert Evans, who was away in Europe, or with Stanley Jaffe, who was vacationing in the Caribbean, or with Mario Puzo, who was attending a weight-loss clinic.

But the damage was done. Gulf+Western's stock dropped two and a half points on the news, according to Ruddy. And no one was angrier than Charlie Bluhdorn, the businessman trying to save Paramount from ruin.

Hurricane Charlie went into full hurricane mode. Bluhdorn had spent his career trying to distance himself from organized crime, only to have Ruddy tie his company directly to the Mafia on the front page of the *New York Times*. Not only had Ruddy held a major press conference without Bluhdorn's consent but he had cut a deal to turn over money to the League. The producer was summoned to meet his maker.

"I ran to the Gulf and Western Building, to Mr. Bluhdorn's floor, and there's a board-of-directors crisis meeting going on," Ruddy remembered. "I walk in, and it was the most solemn group I'd ever seen in my life. If Charlie had a gun, he would have killed me on the spot."

"You wrecked my company!" Bluhdorn roared at Ruddy. Thirty years in America and Charlie Bluhdorn, at this moment in 1971, stood atop a powerhouse that was the sixty-fifth largest industrial corporation in America, with $4 billion in assets and 85,000 employees. But his gamble on *The Godfather* was rising up to haunt him. "All these years, and look what's happening," he said. "The Mafia moves in!"

"You think I'm going to stand here and apologize for anything I did, you're mistaken," Ruddy replied. "Bob Evans was *threatened*. They [the League] told us this movie would never go. I did what I had to do. That's what a producer does."

Bluhdorn was "freaking out" in a screaming, cursing, spittle-flying rage, said Ruddy, leaving it to his lieutenant, Martin Davis, to offer a solution: "disavow" any deal with the League and "fire Al Ruddy publicly."

"So now I'm fired."

Before leaving, Ruddy addressed the board: "Guys, I don't own one share of your goddamn company. I'm not interested in what happens to Gulf and Western stock. I'm interested in getting my movie made."

With that, he grabbed a handful of expensive cigars from Bluhdorn's humidor and stormed out.

Bluhdorn's timing couldn't have been worse. Across town, Coppola had already embarked upon the first day of filming—the scene where Diane Keaton and Al Pacino come out of a Fifth Avenue department store in the snow. Bluhdorn shut down the set—which had paused production for a few days anyway—and advised Coppola and Evans to find another producer. There was only one problem: Thanks to Ruddy's deal, Paramount was now completely dependent on Colombo's goodwill to secure shooting locations and union cooperation. "Al Ruddy's the only guy who can keep this movie going!" Coppola protested.

Bluhdorn had no choice. Ruddy was back on the picture. "But one more line in the press," Bluhdorn warned him, "and I will personally choke you to death!"

With Ruddy back on the job, the League sprang to life on behalf of *The Godfather*. "The next day, everybody opened up their doors, and our office was filled with Italian Americans wanting parts in the movie," said Gray Frederickson. A funeral parlor in Brooklyn and other businesses were suddenly willing to be used as locations, and League captains visited local residents and urged them to be "hospitable" to the crew. When the producers had trouble gaining clearance for the Staten Island compound that was slated to serve as Don Corleone's home (chosen to replace the Long Island site that fell through), Gianni Russo, the former Mob messenger who had landed the part of Carlo, stepped in. "I grew up around Staten Island, and I knew that house well," he said. Russo visited the property and talked to the owner. The man had a simple request. "Can you fix the roof for me?" he asked. "It's got a leak."

Russo arranged for Paramount to pay for the repair. "I'm like, 'You could have had thousands of dollars a day.' But they made the deal."

Having the cooperation of what he diplomatically called "syndicate men," Ruddy told *Ladies Home Journal* in 1972, enabled the production to avoid a host of problems. "There would have been pickets, breakdowns, labor problems, cut cables, all kinds of things," he said. "I don't think anyone would have been physically hurt. But the picture simply could not have been made without their approval."

After being reinstated as producer, Ruddy attended a $125-a-plate testimonial dinner for Colombo, who was being honored by the League for his humanitarianism. And the League itself now had more money than ever, thanks to *The Godfather*. The filmmakers paid the owners of apartments and bars and restaurants to allow the movie to be shot on their premises—but the bulk of the proceeds were said to have been handed over by the property owners to the League. "They gave a pittance to the owner of the establishment," said Joe Coffey, the NYPD detective. "But the Mob got most of the money."

Francis Ford Coppola, right, directs Marlon Brando as Don Corleone in the *The Godfather*'s mammoth wedding scene, which Coppola designed to show Corleone's "enormous power." *Steve Schapiro*

Robert Evans in his bed at his storied Beverly Hills home, Woodland, from a 1969 *Life* magazine profile. *Alfred Eisenstaedt/ The Life Picture Collection/Getty Images*

Writing *The Godfather* transformed Mario Puzo—pictured here at the Beverly Hills Hotel in May 1971—from a dead-broke, middle-aged writer into a prince of Hollywood and the envy of the literary world. *Daniel Kramer*

The Puzo family having lunch in their new home in Bay Shore, New York, for a July 10, 1970, *Life* photo spread—Erika, his wife, standing at the left, and Mario at the head of the table.
Robert Peterson

Puzo rolling the dice at the Fabulous Flamingo in Las Vegas in 1970, shortly after his arrival in Hollywood.
Robert Peterson

Puzo, Coppola, Evans, and Al Ruddy at the press conference in Los Angeles to announce Coppola as director of *The Godfather*, September 29, 1970.
Judd Gunderson/ Los Angeles Times

Puzo in front of the fabled gates of Paramount Pictures. *David F. Smith/AP/Shutterstock*

Puzo and Coppola, author and director, fellow Italian Americans and immediate friends. *Steve Schapiro*

"I believe in America." Salvatore Corsitto as the undertaker Bonasera, whispering his appeal for justice to Don Corleone, shortly after stating the opening line of the film. *Steve Schapiro*

Three Italian American actors, one with a sign reading "Italians for Italian Roles," picketing at the Paramount gates in Los Angeles, 1971. *Los Angeles Times Photographic Archive, UCLA Library*

ABOVE: Joseph Colombo Sr., powerful founder of the Italian American Civil Rights League, handcuffed after his arrest, March 5, 1971. *New York Daily News Archive/Getty Images*

LEFT: Colombo picketing in front of FBI headquarters, with Rabbi Meir Kahane of the Jewish Defense League, June 8, 1971. *Bettmann/Getty Images*

'Godfather' Film Won't Mention Mafia

By GRACE LICHTENSTEIN

At the request of the Italian-American Civil Rights League, the producer of the film "The Godfather" has eliminated all references to the Mafia and Cosa Nostra from the screenplay, which is based on the best-selling novel about a Mafia family.

Al Ruddy, the producer, also confirmed in an interview that proceeds from the premiere of the film would go to the league. The film begins shooting in 10 days and is expected to be released around Christmas.

Mr. Ruddy announced the changes at a news conference yesterday in the office of the league, at 635 Madison Avenue. He said the changes had come out of several meetings with league representatives, including Anthony Colombo, whose father, Joseph Colombo Sr., is a reputed leader of organized crime in Brooklyn.

"They wanted to sit down with us and see if the movie was going to be an anti-Italian film," Mr. Ruddy said. "We looked at the script together." All that was removed, he added, were three mentions of the crime syndicate.

The screenplay was written by Mario Puzo, author of the book, with the help of Francis Ford Coppola, who will direct the film for Paramount Pictures. Mr. Puzo did not participate

Continued on Page 34, Column 2

Al Ruddy, center, producer of "The Godfather," telling of changes. With him are Anthony Colombo, front, and Nat Marcone of the Italian-American Civil Rights League.

The New York Times

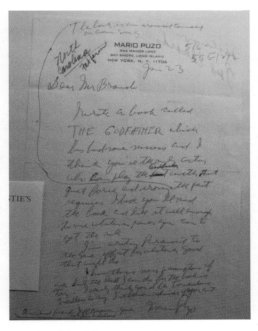

LEFT: Anthony Colombo, Ruddy, and League president Nat Marcone at the press conference, March 19, 1971. *New York Times news clip*

RIGHT: "I wrote a book called The Godfather": Puzo's letter to Marlon Brando, January 23, 1970. *Barry King/WireImage/Getty Images*

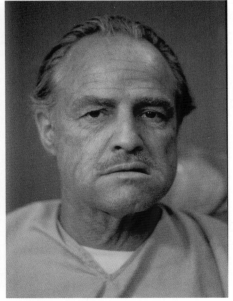

Brando: before, as a forty-seven-year-old actor; after, as Don Corleone. *Steve Schapiro*

"Hurricane Charlie": Yvette Bluhdorn, associate producer Gray Frederickson, Charlie Bluhdorn, and Coppola on the set. *Paramount Pictures*

A King and His Three Sons: Al Pacino (Michael), Marlon Brando (Don Corleone), James Caan (Sonny), and John Cazale (Fredo). *Steve Schapiro*

Coppola rehearsing Brando in Don Corleone's study. *mptvimages.com*

Al Pacino and Diane Keaton (as Michael's fiancée, Kay Adams) in bed at the St. Regis hotel, where Coppola had set up the shot and then "left them alone." *Paramount Pictures/Photofest*

Keaton and Pacino at the wedding of Connie Corleone (Talia Shire) and Carlo Rizzi (Gianni Russo), where Pacino would begin his "transformation," from military officer into Mafia don. *Steve Schapiro*

The Family Corleone: Robert Duvall, Tere Livrano, John Cazale, Gianni Russo, Talia Shire, Morgana King, Marlon Brando, James Caan, Julie Gregg, Al Pacino, Diane Keaton, and Jeannie Linero. *Steve Schapiro*

Al Martino as Johnny Fontane singing "I Hav[e] But One Heart" to the bride, Talia Shire. *Steve Schapiro*

"If the audience doesn't jump out of their seats on this one, you have failed," wrote Coppola, here showing John Marley (as movie mogul Jack Woltz) how to lay in a bloody bed with a horse's head. *mptvimages.com*

The Corleones meet with the drug dealing Virgil "The Turk" Sollozzo, played by Al Lettieri. *Paramount Pictures/Photofest*

"He looked like he could eat raw meat." Richard Castellano and the fierce former wrestler Lenny Montana. *Mondadori Portfolio/Zuma Press*

LEFT: Montana in the strangulation scene he felt might win him an Academy Award nomination. *Steve Schapiro*
RIGHT: Brando bowing to the Little Italy crowds on Mott Street before getting shot. *Steve Schapiro*

LEFT: Brando as Don Corleone, going down in a blaze of glory. *Steve Schapiro*

BELOW: Brando and the brilliant John Cazale as Fredo at the assassination attempt. *Paramount Pictures*

"I'll kill 'em both": Pacino being coached by Castellano on how to handle a pistol. *Paramount Pictures/ United Archives Gmbh/ Alamy*

Sterling Hayden as Captain Mark McCluskey, Lettieri as Virgil Sollozzo, and Al Pacino being instructed on gunning them down. *Paramount Pictures*

ABOVE: Cinematographer Gordon Willis about to film the double-murder scene in Louis Italian American Restaurant in the Bronx. *Paramount Pictures*

RIGHT: Clothing the Corleones: Costume designer Anna Hill Johnstone, who would be nominated for the 1973 Academy Award for Best Costume Design, with Coppola in Louis Italian American Restaurant before the killing scene. *Paramount Pictures*

Filming in Sicily: Angelo Infanti as Fabrizio, Simonetta Stefanelli as Apollonia, Franco Citto as Calo, Pacino, and Coppola.
mptvimages.com

Stefanelli and Pacino in the doomed car she's learning to drive.
mptvimages.com

Russo and Shire as the warring newlyweds Connie Corleone and Carlo Rizzi.
Steve Schapiro

Caan being wired for the bloody tollbooth assassination scene. *Steve Schapiro*

Caan as Sonny raging against Russo as Carlo. *Paramount Pictures/ Photofest*

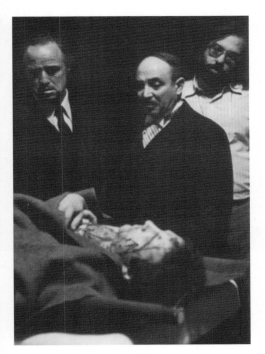

ABOVE: The corpse of Sonny as the undertaker Bonasera prepares to repay his Godfather by burying his eldest son. *Steve Schapiro*

RIGHT: Life imitating art: "Before we started working on the film, we kept saying, 'But these Mafia guys don't go around shooting each other anymore,'" said Coppola. *New York Daily News Archive/Getty Images*

FINAL

DAILY NEWS
NEW YORK'S PICTURE NEWSPAPER ®

10¢

Vol. 53. No. 3   New York, N.Y. 10017. Tuesday, June 29, 1971   WEATHER: Partly cloudy, breezy and warm.

COLOMBO SHOT, FIGHTS FOR LIFE
Assailant Slain by Bodyguard

Bleeding profusely from head wounds, Joseph Colombo is placed inside ambulance after Unity Day shooting.
Five Pages of Stories Begin on Page 3; Other Pictures Centerfold

Top Court Nixes Parochial School Aid
Stories on Page 2

Brando being prepped by makeup artist Dick Smith, with cue cards nearby. *mptvimages.com*

The Succession Scene: the old Don Corleone and the new Don Corleone, the torch being passed. *Paramount Pictures/Photofest*

"The Godmother of *The Godfather*": Paramount's publicity and promotion mastermind Marilyn Stewart (right), whose campaign began before a single frame of the film was shot. *Steve Schapiro*

ABOVE: Henry Kissinger, Robert Evans, and Ali MacGraw at the premiere of *The Godfather*, March 14, 1972, New York.
Hulton Archive/Getty Images

LEFT: MacGraw and Kissinger at the Italian American–style dinner in the St. Regis hotel after the premiere screening.
Everett Collection

Brando and Jim Thomas, his Native American friend, whom he enlisted to attend *The Godfather* premiere on his behalf in Native American regalia (over his tuxedo).
Courtesy of Jim Thomas

Al Ruddy with his Best Picture Oscar at the 1973 Academy Awards, alongside Liza Minelli (Best Actress, *Cabaret*) and Joel Gray (Best Supporting Actor, *Cabaret*).
Bettmann/Getty Images

Mario Puzo, triumphant. *New York*, August 21, 1972.
Dan Kramer

The Godfather Sweeps the Underworld: "Godfather Movie Marquee" by Paul Peter Porges, *The Saturday Review*, April 22, 1972.
Claudia Porges Beyer and Vivette Porges Collection

10

TABLEAU: EACH FRAME A PAINTING

He wanted it to be operatic," production designer Dean Tavoularis said of Francis Ford Coppola's vision for *The Godfather*, a vision he imparted to his creative team during a six-hour meeting on January 25, 1971.

"From the beginning Francis said, 'I want to have a meeting.' And in that meeting we went through the script, and it was there that the style of *The Godfather* came from."

Four creative powerhouses—director, cinematographer, production designer, and costume designer—gathered in Paramount's New York City offices in the Gulf+Western Building to debate and dissect every aspect of the film, which Coppola saw as "the contrast between good and evil, light and dark . . ."

To paint this mysterious world, they would "really use darkness . . . ," he said. "We'd start out with a blank sheet of paper and paint in the light, and the camera would never move."

Later, some members of the various factions would war against the young, untested director, most notably the cinematographer Gordon Willis. But for this meeting they were one, all focused on the same goal: cinematic excellence.

Gordon Willis, a pug-nosed, wiry-haired son of Broadway dancers from Astoria, Queens, was the perfect cinematographer to achieve

Coppola's goal of painting with darkness. Willis, then age forty, was known as the "prince of darkness," for his mastery of sparse lighting and accentuation of shadows had made him famous in an era that leaned toward bright light and primary colors. He was, by his own admission, difficult to work with, but he became one of the most sought-after cinematographers of his time. "If there were a Mount Rushmore for cinematographers," wrote Stephen Pizzello, editor in chief and publisher of *American Cinematographer*, "Gordon's features would surely be chiseled into the rock face."

Tavoularis, then thirty-nine, already had a reputation for turning the ordinary into the sublime. A Greek American from Lowell, Massachusetts, he had just returned from a season of traveling around Europe and working with the Italian director Michelangelo Antonioni. Having learned his craft at Disney Studios, he was coming off a couple of acclaimed films with the director Arthur Penn, including *Bonnie and Clyde*—whose bloody violence had impressed Coppola. "It's one thing to see someone shoot someone," he would tell Tavoularis in the production meeting. "But if there's a detail—the way the blood turns into mist. . . . I saw that in *Bonnie and Clyde*. I thought it was just absolutely wonderfully done."

At fifty-eight, costume designer Anna Hill "Johnnie" Johnstone was the veteran of the group. She had spent her career digging through friends' closets and rummaging through thrift stores, getting her start in costuming on Broadway in 1937 before switching to film. She had cemented her reputation by designing the costumes for Elia Kazan's classics *On the Waterfront* and *East of Eden*.

Then there was Coppola, the youngest member of the team and—for the moment at least—its undisputed leader. He had hired a court stenographer from the International Reporting Service to record every word uttered in the production meeting. In case he needed to review or revise anything afterward, or perhaps to leave a record for posterity, the resulting eighty-four single-spaced pages offer an extraordinary window into the behind-the-scenes process of Francis Ford Coppola and the artistic team he assembled to create *The Godfather*.

Coppola began the meeting by laying out his intentions. "He didn't want to make a traditional gangster film," said Tavoularis. "He wanted to show them as humans and see the human side of their lives, the family side of their lives: loving their children and then turning around and committing terrible crimes and brutal murders."

Coppola had a word for it: "operatic," said Tavoularis. "This dark operatic image, where the camera is fixed and things come into the frame and things leave the frame, but the camera doesn't cut that much, it doesn't pan that much."

The fixed-camera technique would create cinematic tableaus, which Gordon Willis already favored. "As I mentioned to you, I tend to lean toward the tableau," he told the group. Willis wanted to make each frame in the movie like a painting, filled with characters who pass in and out of the picture. The style, he observed, was in keeping with films from the postwar period: "If you looked over films that are so-called contemporary films, you'd find there are no zooms. But tableau is a very strong form of statement."

From the beginning, Coppola set a tone of intense, freewheeling collaboration. "I figured the best way to start," he said, "was literally take the script . . . and go through the script from the first scene to the last, and everyone have the opportunity to—no matter what area you have thought about, or disturbed you, be it the script changes, just [discuss] the part you didn't like."

Everything, at this point, was on the table, and dissent was not only permitted but encouraged.

"It's sort of a classic in my mind," Coppola continued. "It would be a very respectful, well-mounted film, with nothing in it that would detract from the period. As we have talked about it—to forego the use of stylish 1970s film phenomenon and try, in some way, to get the essence of the period without being an old-fashioned movie."

Coppola had ordered numerous films from the 1940s for inspiration about the time and place. But Coppola didn't want to make another 1940s film. His goal was to draw on the old to create something entirely new: a movie *informed* by the visuals of the 1940s, but using modern, if subdued, filmmaking techniques. "It would be a mistake ... to rebuild a 1945 or a 1940 movie," Willis agreed. "I think we are talking more of an impression of one than constructing a film in the way they would have."

The movie, Coppola said, would open with an extremely stark and dramatic tableau: beginning with one man shrouded in darkness: Amerigo Bonasera, the undertaker, giving his speech to Don Corleone. "I like the idea of starting the movie this very way, with Bonasera," he said. "Just starting with, 'I believe in America,' because it's what the whole movie is about. It's saying that our country should be our family; in a way, that it should afford us the protection and the honor that, in a strange way, this Mafia family does; but that we should look to our country in this way.

"I see this ... one little, unimpressive man telling you what amounts to a very touching story," he continued. "If it's very good, the showing, somehow, at the end of his big speech—earth-moving—with him as he goes to the Don, but to reveal the Don in the most impressive way possible."

From the very first frame, Coppola sought to convey the main theme of the film: how Americans as a whole must rely on their family for what America fails to provide them, and in the case of the movie that family is Don Corleone.

After the opening scene, the movie would shift to the wedding of Connie Corleone, an extravaganza of Italian American food, music, dancing, and family values, undercut with the business required of Don Corleone on this special day. "I am going to change the wedding quite a bit," said Coppola. "I am going to try and make the wedding more of an experience and much less of a scene. In other words, I am going to, literally, take all the dialogue out of it and I am going to immerse the audience in the wedding and kind of make it a real experience, with hundreds and hundreds of details."

When he first read the wedding scene in Puzo's book, Coppola said, his head was "full of lots of speeches."

For the film, he envisioned a boisterous celebration, with as many as five hundred extras as wedding guests, everyone "talking full-voice. That might be a nice tone right there; because everyone is talking at the top of their lungs to everyone else, and no one is listening."

Coppola wanted to capture it all: the children running amok, the drunken guests swilling wine, the vintage cars, the conversation going back and forth a mile a minute. But no caterers—everything at an Italian wedding would be homemade. He vetted his team's suggestions, responding unenthusiastically when a game of bocce ball was proposed. "Bocce ball is one of those things people put in a movie about Italian Americans," he said.

"The Italian family," Coppola continued, "is like the three fat cousins who are sitting at the tables with these tremendous heaps of food [and] the little kid whose father is trying to get him to sing. A hundred things, like a carnival, because there are a lot of people and things to immerse the audience right into. . . . And lots of food, much of which people have brought themselves. And the dancing and the music. Can we build like a dance floor?"

Coppola was rolling now, launching into one of his high-powered, extremely persuasive, all-enveloping presentations, which his colleague Walter Murch would call "a Jedi mind trick."

"People just sit there and let it wash over them," said Murch.

"Would there be one band or different bands?" Coppola asked.

"The wedding, in a way, has as its prime theme to show the enormous power and deference that people show to the Don," Coppola continued. "So, we might make it very clear that people are fostering their gifts, sending their bands and sending their wedding cakes and—*I love the confusion of it!*"

They settled on one band but included a lineup of informal acts of entertainment—all vying for opportunities to impress their powerful host Don Corleone: an accordion solo, dancing, singers of all ages, everyone sporadically queued up, happy and drunk, eager to get up and pay homage with their talents.

"It wouldn't be formal; it would be sort of put on by the people," said Coppola.

"How many people could you visualize in this area?" Johnstone asked.

"You could get four or five hundred people," Tavoularis said.

"That's what we are talking about!" Coppola exclaimed. "It's got to be *big*."

The studio executives, he warned, "are going to shave us down."

But he was determined to implement his plans for a big and expensive wedding, because it would be "the first statement that's made."

The lively, sunlit outdoor celebration would be juxtaposed with Don Corleone indoors in his dark office, quietly and calmly conducting the family business, the two worlds occasionally brushing up against each other. "We present in this wedding scene a fusion of family and business," Coppola said. "You should never see the wedding without some evidence of the business being conducted. And you should never see the business conducted without some evidence of the wedding. . . . Anything that makes it very clear that very big business is going on at the same time that a family ritual is going on."

Willis suggested a tracking shot between Vito Corleone's office and the wedding, while Johnstone pointed out that no one had airconditioning in 1945. Doors and windows would naturally be wide open on the hot summer's day, further blurring the line between business and family.

The office could be an addition to the main house, perhaps a glassed-in porch that opened onto the wedding scene, Coppola mused. Then he hit on a more elegant solution: instead of viewing the entire wedding from the office, only a single detail would be seen, a detail meant to be hidden from the wedding guests, further reinforcing his theme of darkness juxtaposed with light. "A place where they bring the dirty dishes," as he put it. In the final cut of the film, this concept would be realized in a noisy dining room—glimpsed only as the don's office door opened and closed—filled with platters of food and half a dozen "mamas." Coppola was adamant that all of the wedding's catering be managed by an informal brigade of female guests.

"Do you think ten waiters are enough?" Johnstone asked.

"They wouldn't have waiters," Coppola said.

"They wouldn't?"

"Not waiters. Anything you associate with a wedding, in terms of waiters and servants and such, they didn't have. The women would do it. The food would be sandwiches ordered from Manganaro's, which is still there on Ninth Avenue, or food that the different women brought. . . . They had a tremendous amount of booze because it all would have been given. There might even be some barrels of wine."

"And also those big bottles that are woven with straw—big ones," said Tavoularis.

"A lot of the wine would have been made by the old men that came," Coppola said. "So there should be lots of varieties of them. Some of them would just have brought in gallon bottles with paper labels. Except for, probably, a couple of things, the booze would be there by the case, because of someone who owned a nightclub."

The brainstorming session moved on to what the guests would be wearing.

"Would the women be in black, some of the older women?" Tavoularis asked.

"First of all," Coppola said, "no one would come in any kind of really formal dress at all. The only one in the formal attire would be the wedding party. . . . The kids would come in confirmation clothes, and most of the people would come in their Sunday clothes. But there would be no one who is really sharp and chic."

The one exception would be Michael Corleone's girlfriend, Kay, one of the few non-Italians at the wedding. "She should dress definitely stylishly," Coppola said. "I want a feeling of jealousy."

The director also had a vision for the wedding guests. "My idea is that there would be a lot of young women," he said.

"Would they wear hats?" Johnstone asked. "Every picture of this era, everywhere, women always had hats."

"Let's have a rule in this movie that women *always* have hats," Coppola said. "That really brings the period—but it's a little bit like a picnic, in a way, the feeling of the wedding, more than even a formal wedding. The women wore funny clothes. Even now you can go to an Italian wedding, with the flowers, and the things, and the colors."

"Yes, with the flowers," Johnstone said.

"And a lot of girls," added Coppola.

"Young girls, teenage, that haven't married," said Johnstone.

"Because that's a big thing," Coppola said. "You always have all these female cousins, and during the war, there would be very few young men. There would be a lot of fellows in uniform."

Including Michael Corleone.

"Is Michael in the Marines or the army?" Tavoularis asked.

"I think he is in the army," Coppola said. "Whatever it says in the book. I'd like to be faithful to the book."

Costume designer Johnstone voted for Michael being a Marine, as he had been in Puzo's book. "They had that big, fancy uniform, which, depending on the size of the actor, whether it's a long jacket or what—" she said.

"The dress uniform," Coppola said. "I don't like that. . . . I like a uniform that really looks period. The Marine uniform had leather strapping and stuff, and you really know it looks like something."

"I would hate to see somebody as short as Al in a long jacket," Johnstone said.

The rest of the male members of the Corleone family, in contrast to the guests, would wear formal tuxedos, preferably black jackets instead of white. "There is one question that I just want to make sure of," Johnstone said. "You talked about the Don and an ill-fitting dinner jacket. Are we playing the Don this way? I mean, they are very wealthy, but they do not dwell on their wealth, express their wealth?"

"In the book, it said that the Don, on first look, was not an impressive man," said Coppola. "He was a man you might pass over under any other circumstances. In fact, the doctor in the hospital, it seems, does pass him over, until he sees the way other people relate to him. The idea is of a king when you are playing a king in a play. If you play the king with tremendous this-or-that, all the other people do [pay] homage to him. But a real king could come down in slacks and you would know he is the king by the way everyone else reacts to him.

"I think it is so with the Don," he continued. "You know that he is the Don, not because of any class that he has—he is so powerful and classy that you don't have to do that. He can be comfortable and go about his own business, and he feels comfortable about the way that everybody would relate to him. And the idea of a Don as a casual, unimpressive man.... I don't think that the Don was comfortable in a tuxedo. I don't think that the Don owns a tuxedo, and he didn't even want to go down for the fitting."

Johnstone ran down a list of the extras they had for the wedding, a mix of actors and real-life Italian Americans. "For now," she said, "we're leaving it that Michael is in uniform, Kay is dressed in a formal dress. A lot of children all in—some of them in the short pants and others in confirmation clothes. Seventy-five or one hundred fifty children, seventy-five to one hundred fifty women. Eight bridesmaids, and the men—fifty to one hundred. I have about five in the orchestra, and fifty in suits and twenty-five in uniform, in the whole group."

"Somebody has to have the accordion," Willis insisted.

"That was a big thing," Coppola agreed, "accordion lessons."

"It's going to be a lot of work if we go [into] the detail," Willis said.

"*Getting hundreds of details!*" Coppola exclaimed. "If we get the people right, and if they're really starting to do it and enjoy it, there will be hundreds of details that are really happening—with the beer keg getting stuck and the beer flooding."

NOW THAT THE wedding party was mapped out, conversation turned to the look of the film, which of course would be in color, which meant something entirely different to Willis.

"We are doing a color movie, right?" Willis asked. "I, generally, feel that I work ... to get the color in a movie down to where it's a minimum, so to speak.... I don't care for blue and I don't care for too many primaries, because there is so much color built into the structure of motion pictures. . . . I don't know how anyone else feels, I sort of like that earth tone—blacks and browns and things like that, generally speaking."

"All three of us have agreed to that," Tavoularis said. "Also, the nature of this film being a masculine film with gangsters, and it's like—not a colorful film. And, besides that, I just have a personal preference for staying away from bright colors."

"I have always," Coppola said, "even for other films, always believed in a muted color."

Willis wanted the film to look like an old rotogravure newspaper magazine, old and dark and impossible to look away. "I want to shoot all the New York material," Willis said. "It's a chocolate color . . . brownish, chocolate. When you put it across, it doesn't really destroy the color; but what happens is, in things like blues and browns and things, it tends to make it dirty . . . So when you go to Sicily, they increase it [the light, the color] a little bit . . . it becomes a little thicker for effect. But when we bounce out of New York and go to the Coast—I am still kicking around in my mind—"

"I hate to be a wet blanket," Coppola interrupted. "I'd like to explore things like the nature of the lipstick women wore . . . They really wore red lipstick, and what will happen if we pull everything down and they got this red lipstick sticking out?"

"They always had kind of a purplish lipstick," Tavoularis said.

"I'd like to go into all of the makeup of the times," Coppola said.

"It wouldn't mean anything," Willis said. "What I'm talking about wouldn't interfere with the basic structure."

"I was talking about the general muting of color," Coppola said. "If we start sticking primary lipstick and stuff in and treat makeup the way those women actually did, would that be a glaring or distracting detail?"

"You have very little opportunity for much makeup on women," Johnstone pointed out. "How many times do you see women? At the wedding is the first time, but it's not as much as you think."

Coppola and his team momentarily seemed to be on different wavelengths.

"I am talking even more conceptually," he explained. "I am saying, What are the facts, colorwise, of that period, and how can we make use of it?"

He suggested the team watch 1945 color movies "to see what we can learn from them."

"I think you will waste time," said Johnstone.

The issue touched on a deeper concern Coppola must have had. "You know what I am trying for is having a very great and real movie, that the picture should be very—kind of sensible and very well mounted," Coppola said. "I have eliminated a number of areas where directors usually go for a style, to give it its own style. . . . I have already given away certain things: use of tableau, use of the cameras in an eccentric kind of way, use of dialogue. . . . Where are we going to get the style?"

"It's going to happen," Willis assured him.

"One thing related to another, or one piece related to another," Tavoularis explained. "It's *structurally* the style that you are looking for. As long as, by the time we shoot this movie, everybody has the same idea. Movies have a way of taking off and taking on their own personalities once you are into it for a week, and it's hard to turn them around."

The gap in experience between the director and his team was beginning to become clear. But Coppola trudged confidently forward.

"Right," Coppola said. "Stylistically, the one thing I like, in a way, is the camera very often being on the wrong thing."

Instead of placing the camera on the central action or character, Coppola wanted the audience to "get the inference," instead of communicating everything directly. Willis jumped in about the scene where the turncoat driver, Paulie Gatto, is shot dead in the driver's seat of a car while Clemenza is relieving himself by the side of the road. "You have one thing in your notes, which I think you abandoned, but it was very good: When what's-his-name stopped the car and got out to take a leak in the bushes, to be on him, and you *hear* the shooting."

"I want to do a lot of that," Coppola said, meaning the camera is on one thing while the action is somewhere else. He cited a scene where Don Corleone is "looking out the window, and the scene is really happening off camera."

Or, Coppola went on, take an even more familiar scene: people talking around a table. "Rather than cutting back and forth on who-ever is talking," he said, the camera would move from person to person, without regard to the dialogue. "Let's say I was talking, and [the camera would] just be on you. I am talking and maybe you have a word or two and go to [someone else]. And almost go through the table, irrespective of what's happening, in a way. That's sort of an eccentric choice and we can do a lot of that type of stuff."

Coppola also suggested utilizing nonlinear storytelling, just as Puzo had so effectively done in his novel. "The way the book works, he is constantly fooling you. . . . And my new idea, or one I was going to play, was that instead of doing the full backup, you actually overlap the action. Maybe what I would do would be, kind of, say that the Don has been killed, and get the shock and cut right to the murder. So that you are getting the results first and then the cause. But you are doing it without liberty to back the entire audience up. They say, 'My God, your father is dead!' The next thing you see is the Don coming out to get shot."

For now, Tavoularis didn't like the idea and neither did Johnstone.

THEY NOW DELVED deeper into the cinematography.

"Again, just stylistically," Coppola continued, "in terms of moving a camera. Generally, we would consider this film usual from a rela-tively static camera. And the camera, generally, would only move if it had to move to keep someone it wanted. And to use the dollies, to use a dolly to move where we might be tempted to use a zoom."

Willis agreed. "I think we should cut the zoom lenses right off," he said, only half joking.

Willis had another concern: the cars. "There are quite a few interiors of automobiles," he said, "where they are talking and riding to places. That ought to be done here on a stage or in a garage."

"Not moving?" Coppola asked.

"Not moving," Willis confirmed. "To me, night is one thing. It's dark out and you see lights."

That, he said, "you can get away with on a stage—it's dark out, so you make lights pass by."

But it's not worth shooting night scenes in a moving car "for what we are going to get out of it on the screen."

"What about actually using the city?" Tavoularis asked, pushing as always for authenticity. He suggested using old "process footage," real footage of New York streets from time gone by. "If we found some good process? Like driving from the [Don's house] into the city, it's all black with a few lights going by; but when they pick up Michael in town and they're driving there, they're going right down Broadway."

"I don't like to do it," Willis said. "I have done a lot of map work. First of all, I don't like what it introduces structurally into the plane. But besides that, it can get into technical masturbation, of doing something when all is said and done."

"Is it easier?" Coppola asked.

"If we had some good process footage of Broadway," Tavoularis said.

"You mean, process plates they made in those days?" Coppola asked.

"Well, they're available," Willis said. "What I'm asking for is to think the scenes out and see if they can't be played properly in the car, without getting hung up on bridges, or lighted areas like Broadway and things like this. You are going to be able to have 1945, as long as the buildings are of that period. But I, frankly, would stay away from any type of process. It's going to be a pain. The only thing I'm saying is that night interior in the automobile can be done on a stage and intercut with whatever highway material we do."

"How do you vibrate the car?" Coppola asked.

"You shake the car and grips," Willis said.

"What do we use?" Coppola asked. "Our cars? Or do we have to make—"

"I think we can use the real thing," Tavoularis said. "Take the door off. They have mock-up cars. You make them, then you get into problems."

"Dean is right," Willis said. "We can get the real car."

"I think that's fine for a lot of things," Tavoularis said, "but what about something like [the drive to Louis Italian American Restaurant with] Michael and Sollozzo?"

"There are problem areas," Willis responded to Tavoularis.

"I think something that is really specific, we can pin down to a point," Coppola said. "Either we do it that way or this way. But generally, there is a lot of hopping in and out of automobiles going from Long Island to the city."

"What about sound?" Tavoularis asked.

"In an automobile," Willis said, "you can get away with murder because you have something around you anyway."

Coppola had other concerns. Among the most pressing was financing: the film's budget, originally set at $2 million, was now quickly heading toward $6 million.

"Another factor I would like to take into consideration," he said, "we have [only] so much money to spend, I would rather spend it on those scenes which we want to spend it on, instead of some little scene that is five lines. I think that's a big part of it, selecting where we want to spend the bread."

"Shooting the cars on the stage would save us money," Tavoularis conceded.

So would cutting a short sequence aboard a cross-country flight from New York to Los Angeles, it had often been suggested. But Coppola argued that the flight scene was crucial to the development of Tom Hagen, consigliere to the don. "Essentially, I wanted to get across that Hagen was not yet the consigliere, or counselor, that if he did get promoted it was a very unusual thing, since he wasn't Sicilian."

Besides establishing Hagen's character, Coppola imagined the scene serving as the linchpin of several other emerging story lines, foreshadowing "trouble" from Paul Gatto and the newlyweds Connie and Carlo.

"There are fifteen different points and expositions happening in [the] . . . three pages," he said. "The thing I tried to do was to take a hub and build satellite things in the hub. . . . The hub is high on the plane and every scene revolves around it. . . . I put him on the plane and based around that scene, I conducted little, tiny things, which were all to relate back to Hagen and come out again."

Coppola's storytelling instincts were sound, but there was another problem: they needed the actual airplane, a glamorous 1946 Lockheed Constellation, once the ultimate cross-country airliner, commissioned by the reclusive billionaire Howard Hughes.

"As for the Constellation," Coppola continued, "we wanted to get a period plane and have very few people in it. Everyone says it's no different; I know it would be different. I don't care what anyone would say, I can't believe if you flew up in the air and put the camera in the aisle, that it would look exactly the same. For one thing, it would be vibrating."

"It should vibrate," Tavoularis said, "and the noise."

"I have flown Connies," Willis said, referring to the Constellation. "God, the noise was devastating!"

"They wanted to cut this scene," Coppola said of the cost-conscious executives at Paramount. "I don't know what it would save them. It's not going to be a two-hour shot."

"Why?" Willis asked. "Because they don't want to get the plane?"

"Tony [Dingman] found three planes in California," Coppola said.

"You'd have to go if we do it in LA," Tavoularis said to Coppola. "We would have to do it in Lancaster, which is thirty miles away."

"Unless we can do the second unit," Coppola said.

"Our problem is," Willis said, "if we fire everything off the second unit, it's going to have a patchwork look to it, because we are never going to get the right idea.

"Maybe we can find a chassis, an old Connie," he went on. "Things might be able to be brought in. We might be able to strip the wings off."

Willis still wasn't sold on the scene. He had another suggestion: "If you get pressed for time, say the hell with the Constellation."

Coppola wouldn't budge an inch on that. "I did the Constellation for a number of reasons," he said. "I like the idea of the difference of flying in those days. The fact that I really cut back was to show that it was eleven hours of flying and to use that reflective moment for Hagen to say, Who is Tom Hagen? What is his position?"

"I am just saying," Willis replied, "*if* you are in trouble."

The Constellation wouldn't make it into the picture at all. Hagen's landing in Los Angeles would be achieved through old footage of a plane landing. But Coppola's devotion to the scene cost him in authenticity: Tom Hagen's flight aboard the aircraft is set in 1945, but the Constellation didn't enter commercial service until the following year.

NEXT, COPPOLA STEERED the conversation to the explosive scene where Tom Hagen first meets Jack Woltz, the iron-fisted movie producer determined to never give Johnny Fontane the part that would make him a star.

"I thought about rewriting the first scene with Woltz and Hagen," Coppola said. "Instead of having it at Woltz's office, have them brought into a place on the lot or on a stage. And there is a bunch of chairs, a whole row of chairs with fifty young men and women, very handsome and obviously all the studio stars, maybe outside in the studio, linking arms with everybody. I just thought of Hagen being brought to this man.

"In other words, he is not really getting a real interview. He is being *allowed* to talk to him and do it in a moving, stopping way. Tom is, literally, being put in the position of having to talk while he is walking . . . I like the idea of Tom with a big shot, where you can't even sit down with him. You have to catch him between his other things; 'talk-to-me-while-I-am-taking-a-walk' kind of thing. That really puts Tom in second place."

"I know that everybody would be against this," Tavoularis said, "but I think Warner's [lot] is so much better."

"It fits better as a location," Coppola agreed.

"Here is an idea," Willis said, spotting another opportunity to put the camera on the unexpected thing. "The last cut you have written here. Remember, 'A lawyer with a briefcase can steal more than a hundred men with guns'?"

He was quoting one of Puzo's favorite lines in his novel, which spoke to the inequities of the business world, which Puzo felt was filled with as many criminals as the Mob, as his son Anthony would later elaborate upon: "He called himself a romantic writer with sympathy for the devil. He felt businessmen were far more criminal than the Mafia, especially the Hollywood moguls . . . [who] would cheat you blind if you let them."

Willis liked that image. "Cut to the painted backdrop, or something similar, so that you don't see them at all," Willis continued. "You are in limbo, and you *hear*." Then Jack Woltz says to the seemingly lowly Tom Hagen, *I'm listening.* "Maybe at that point we will pull back and pick up the shot."

"Sort of beginning the scene over Woltz's world," Coppola said.

"So you don't know where you are on the first zoom," Willis said. "It gets away from another device of having to set up where he is and all that kind of thing. The idea that I had in shooting was—'A lawyer can steal more with a briefcase . . .' and the next thing you see is this really impressive building, or something to say power; and there is Hagen, unarmed, only with a little case. It's like David going off to slay Goliath."

"I think the real idea that we have to get across is the odds," Coppola said. "Anyone who has ever had to go to a Hollywood studio—it seems like the most difficult thing: how are you going to get in the place, with all the gates and walls around it?"

"That's what I'm getting at," Willis said. "The power thing."

In the next scene, Woltz refuses the request to put Johnny Fontane in his movie, and the don somehow—some way!—arranges for the infamous bloody horse's head to end up in the movie producer's bed. Coppola wanted the scene to be big and grand, with an impressive stable for Khartoum, the prized stallion that would be slaughtered to send Woltz a message. "Do we have any estates with real stables?" he asked.

"We are working on it," Tavoularis said.

"It would be a pity if we had to build anything," Coppola fretted.

"I don't think we would have to," Tavoularis assured him. "It's a matter of how far we would have to go out. The stables are outlawed in Bel Air."

"The idea I want, is that I don't want to make Woltz look like a fool," Coppola said. "I want the audience to think, [*What*] *the hell are they ever going to* [*do to*] *get that guy to give him the part?* I am also interested in values on the other side of the kingdom. They are roughly the same age, and both come from humble streets, the Don from the New York Italian section and Woltz is a West Coast Jew. Again, a powerful man, and a phenomenon and a real street fighter.

"Just as the Don doesn't have servants, Woltz has," Coppola continued. "We all judge people by their face values, which is the point of this. Woltz should really seem to be the favorite. You should really think he is the most powerful man. He has just as much or more; from the way he lives, it looks like he even has more money. He should be. That way, they're never going to be able to get him, because it brings out the idea that the truly powerful men in the country are that way. You don't hear about them too much; you don't see their photographs.

"And the whole sexual thing about Woltz, that he hangs on, with such desperation, to his sexual identity, where the Don has long ago worked that out."

Who truly possessed the most power would be settled in the horse's head scene, which posed another challenge. The bedroom needed to be extremely impressive, Coppola noted, with lots of lights. But more importantly, he wanted to use a *real* horse's head, fresh from a slaughterhouse.

"I guarantee that if you didn't say it," Coppola said of the studio bean counters, "they would have given me some phony horse's head."

Coppola was adamant about the blood, which of course had to look real. He had emphasized this in a long "Special Effects" memo he had sent to his team, which detailed eleven of the bloodiest scenes in the movie. He was determined to present the most striking and original special effect: "a shattered eyeglass or a bullet hole through a hand can be much more unsettling and moving, than a ton of innards and blood," he wrote.

"In general, blood has never looked right to me in a film," he added, and Coppola was determined to get the blood exactly right in *The Godfather*.

"In all the photographs we have, it seems much thinner, much more watery than in those shots where the guy's pants are soaked," he said in the production meeting. "And in the movies, it always seems thick and syrupy. Why not use real blood, twenty gallons of animal blood? Any butcher will give you blood."

"It coagulates," Tavoularis pointed out.

The blood was critical, because this scene "will be the first time that people would really react," Coppola said. "We should have blood that coagulates."

"We made up a mixture," Willis said. "When you put it on, it soaks your shirt like water. But it still had the consistency of blood that would congeal. The makeup man did a very good job, and he made it out of a Karo [corn syrup] base. The whole point was that it would congeal after a while. But it was thin enough so that when you put it on something, it would soak it, it wouldn't roll off."

"What about the color?" Tavoularis asked.

"Blood is much more believable when it has the brown-black kind of color," Willis said.

Everyone agreed.

They discussed a sequence that would eventually be cut from the film entirely, in which Paulie Gatto and a couple of Corleone soldiers deliver Bonasera's long-awaited justice: tracking down and brutally beating the two college boys who had assaulted the undertaker's daughter.

"We had an idea, Gordon," Tavoularis said, meaning he and Coppola, "of playing it in Brooklyn, by the El . . . and with the sound of the train. The whole idea of the sequence would make this particularly frightening—the slowness of it and the deliberateness and the professional aspect of it. Instead of it being with two guys beating each other up, each blow is placed and selected to see if he has broken the arm in quite the right place. There is a very frightening professional thing about it."

"What kind of neighborhood is it?" Willis asked.

"It's an Italian neighborhood," Tavoularis said.

"Because there are sections of Brooklyn that are really rough to work in," said Willis.

"I don't think it's that rough," said Tavoularis.

"Do you think we are going to need some kind of stunt device on this thing, to make it look real?" Coppola asked. "Somehow, we want to show the teenagers of that period—not teenagers, but young guys, without getting into those clichés."

"What they were concerned about in 1945," Tavoularis said. "The girls' number one concern was their figure, and the boys were concerned about their build. From a college survey, the number one problem facing the young then was acne."

"It might be good for the boys to have some medication on their faces," Coppola said. "The only thing that I want to avoid is where you get into the young people of 1945, to avoid any Archie comic clichés."

Coppola was also concerned about clichés involving the overriding theme of family—especially in Don Corleone's home. He suggested drawing up "a list of movie clichés that are big danger points."

"One thing I was going for was a scene with him and his family," Coppola continued. "The idea is of another conversation happening in the kitchen, a woman's conversation. Finally, they ask them to close the door because you [can] hear—and remember this is a family—I thought of a kid practicing violin or the accordion."

"I like the violin," Tavoularis said. "They're not all going to be gangsters when they get older. He might be a concert pianist."

"You really have got to be careful," Coppola said, "because in every movie ever made the old grandfather is playing with the kid. Without exception. And not that that isn't true; but they are clichés because they are true and, therefore, used a lot. So I may not go hog-wild with the children as I would normally do."

Deciding to avoid clichés in the house was one thing, but first they needed to find the house—one that aligned with the don's lifestyle and influence. In Puzo's novel, the Corleones lived in what they called "the mall," a complex of eight houses all owned by the don. What appeared to be an unassuming cul-de-sac was, in reality, "an impregnable fortress."

"The outsides were not too impressive, but the insides were," Coppola said, referring to how mobsters hid their wealth.

"I don't think that will work," Tavoularis objected. "I think the size and even grandeur [should] come across correctly."

"That's a big contradiction," Coppola said, "because it makes sense that they wouldn't show their wealth. You can't help but not think the guy's a powerful man."

"We should forget the idea of having them hide their wealth and just get a big house," Tavoularis said. "At one time, we were talking about $20,000 or $25,000 [for] 1945 homes, which is pretty meager."

"Vito Genovese lived in a $20,000 . . ." Coppola said of the Mob boss who once lived in a meager home.

"He had an enormous house," Johnstone pointed out. "And when he was brought up on some kind of income charge, he moved into a small, little house."

"That's what I like about that Forest Hills mall," Coppola said of one large, walled home under consideration in Forest Hills, New York. "It wasn't enormous."

Coppola was open to the idea of using separate locations for interior and exterior shots of Don Corleone's home, even though it would make everything more difficult. "So really," he said, "one of our biggest problems is that we are not satisfied with the malls that we have."

"Some people have been looking for so long, it seems like they have looked everywhere," said Tavoularis. "You can almost say it doesn't exist exactly like that."

"I am convinced it doesn't exist like that," Coppola said. "The heartbreak was that we found one that the exterior looked good and it had some lady in it who was dying; and if you moved her, she would die."

Willis touted the benefits of building the interior of the don's home on a soundstage.

Coppola turned to Tavoularis: "Dean, do you want to paint the interior and redress it, or do you want to start from scratch and build it from a stage?"

Tavoularis preferred to use a real interior.

"So would I," Willis said. "I'm just bringing it up to—"

"Bringing it up because we don't have one?" Coppola said. "I thought the nice part [of the Forest Hills mall] was the exterior wall and the nature of the gatehouse. You know important people live there."

Coppola also liked the wall because of the way he saw the house evolving throughout the film. "It goes from a residence with a wedding to a fortress," he said. "But also to give it a feudal feeling that you see in a castle."

"It's kind of meaningful," Willis said.

"You can do so much with a wall and a gate," Coppola said, "and the feeling that something important lies beyond, that we can get away with almost anything."

In the end they would use a Staten Island compound, which they would surround with Styrofoam walls and a gate to create the look of a fortress befitting the Godfather.

ANOTHER ONE OF the don's strongholds, the offices of his olive oil company, would be the site of a pivotal sequence: a meeting with Virgil "the Turk" Sollozzo, the gangster determined to entice the Corleone family to get into the heroin business—or else. It was set to take place at a Little Italy warehouse standing in for the Genco Pura Olive Oil Company in Mario Puzo's novel.

"I have chosen to treat Sollozzo as a sort of mysterious, Satanic figure," Coppola said. "We have talked about him a lot, and now you actually see him revealed in some kind of mysterious way."

Sollozzo would enter the factory by a staircase, and Coppola wanted to hear him coming up before revealing him to the audience. The meeting would be very formal. Everyone shaking hands. A real business meeting, rife with the cutthroat competition of capitalism without any indication of the chaotic violence of the Mob.

"Once, I was in Italy, and all the relatives took folding chairs and put them around in a big circle," Coppola said. "I just thought of that when I did this scene. Obviously, the scene is between two men: the don and Sollozzo. All the other people that are there are attendants to it, but it's like those two men are having a confrontation."

"You want to keep them formal-looking, all done up for this occasion?" Johnstone asked. "They didn't have summer suits. In other words, they have gotten into their Sunday best."

"Yes, very formal," Coppola said. "This is a big meeting. You ought to have the feeling that things that are going to affect us for years to come are going to go on in this room. When it's all over, I had the idea, again, of all the handshakes, and just the time for all this crisscrossing and politeness."

Coppola envisioned the olive oil factory as a collection of offices with big glass windows. It was another device to hide more than it revealed—in this case, to let the audience see things happening, but not hear them.

"I might have someone, during the big meeting, [have the camera] leave with them, and part of the meeting without any sound at all." After the meeting, Don Corleone would call his mammoth enforcer, Luca Brasi, into the office, "and they obviously are talking about something important, which you can't hear, so the glass would serve the point."

Ultimately, clarity would win out over style—the audience would hear it all.

The scene ends with Don Corleone rejecting Sollozzo, which establishes his power—followed immediately by a huge delivery of flowers from Johnny Fontane, in gratitude for landing him the supposedly unattainable part in Woltz's movie. Coppola imagined leaving the don at this high point, but he had two subtle devices for foreshadowing the evil to follow. First, he explained, "I did a little thing where the Don looks out the window and there is a down-shot of Sollozzo's car. I did that purposely; because later in the film, there is a similar shot when the Don crosses the car, and I want it to be evocative. I do that several times in the script, some more deliberate than others. I like the use of repeated moments, even if it's off a little bit."

Now they would cut from summer to the New York winter, the streets covered in snow. "We have passed three months and we don't have to say it," Coppola said. "I want it to focus into the lovers and almost mislead the audience. . . . The best way is to have a very great Christmas."

Coppola meant Kay Adams and Michael Corleone at the department store, shopping for the holidays. His main concern was the cost overruns for so many extras to fill a busy New York City avenue during what is supposed to be the busiest shopping season of the year. They decided to shoot the shots tight, with the camera turned toward Macy's display windows, moving from window to window, each filled with little tableaus to reinforce the period—without the crowds.

"It would keep us from having to dress that whole area," Johnstone said. "We'll dress Macy's, definitely, with Christmas decorations."

Tavoularis circled back to the factory where Sollozzo presents his drug deal. "They said they were going to cooperate," he reported of the owners of the desired olive oil company location, "get their warehouse to get whatever they can from that period. What they don't come up with, we will have to do ourselves."

"It saves us a little bread and it seems right," Coppola said, pleased with the juxtaposition of the jolly holiday and the darkness always lurking around the corner. "Macy's *was* Christmas, and if we dress that whole thing, we might as well use it. . . . I want the breath coming out of their mouths when they talk. I want to fool the audience. I want them to think that it has become a musical. I am going to rewrite the scenes so that you are really touched with Kay, and I want everyone to get onto the wavelength."

The deception was meant to heighten the emotional reaction to the major turning point ahead: the shooting of Don Corleone in the street. But Coppola wanted to ratchet up the tension even higher. "I like the irony," he said, "to use the tone—a sinister theme with Sollozzo, with the happy season with Michael and Kay—to play those scenes opposite each other to get better effect."

"We should always remember that this is the holiday," Coppola said, "and to make use of holidays in the film, because holidays are sort of ritualistic."

(Best & Co. would be substituted for Macy's.)

Then they would cut to Sollozzo's abduction of Tom Hagen, which would take place on a street crowded with holiday shoppers. The brief scene would further contrast cheerful, ordinary life with the menace of the Mob, as well as provide Coppola with another chance to put the camera on "the wrong thing."

"I had the idea that whatever happens with Sollozzo sort of ends up so they go up and hear the door close and you are still at the windows . . . action off camera," said Coppola.

The camera would then return to Michael and Kay coming out of Radio City Music Hall, filming in the direction of the theater to avoid hiring extras. But they would need a newsstand to reveal the headlines about his father's shooting to Michael—and a device to show the growing distance between him and Kay. "She can see all the pain he is going through, but she can't really be a part of it," Coppola said.

"It could be a little café," Tavoularis said, "where the guy is doing something with the steamer—fixing hot dogs or something, and the glass keeps getting frosty."

"I love the idea of the old phone booth," Coppola said, "and her outside in the cold seeing him on the phone and the window getting frost—a separation between man and woman in a time of need."

The phone booth, would, of course, be a big moment in the movie, symbolic of the growing distance between Michael and Kay.

Cut back to the olive oil company, a Christmas tree in the frame. The office manager cleaning up, and Don Corleone leaving for the evening.

"I think that is where I use the high angle," Coppola said. "The shooting of the Don is the worst confusion. If two guys came into this room right now and started shooting us, they would be confused and we would be confused. It would just be a very unusual thing; and I feel that as I read this thing. Where the fruit rolls and [Fredo] drops his gun—and, in a way, we are taking, maybe, ten seconds and examining ten seconds more carefully through the use of detail."

"We should, for the Don's shooting, maybe, look at the Kennedy— both of the Kennedy shootings," Tavoularis suggested.

"Just the sense of confusion," Coppola said.

"The confusion there," Tavoularis continued, "and also the fact that everybody in the auditorium knew him and liked him. . . . The people would be crying. People would be panicked."

"There is a touch of confusion in the Kennedy murder, or any public murder," Willis said. "It's marvelous."

"It's not a horror or shock," Coppola said. "It's a 'what happens' kind of thing. And I think if we could catch that, it would be beautiful."

"They could expect it with the Don," Tavoularis said.

"That's a more complex idea," Coppola said, "but that's very true. And it happened before, according to the story; before, in the olive oil war. You want to have the feeling with the Don, when he's shot—it's the end of the day; he's going home from work; he is tired. He's an older man, and he is going to pick some fruit up and go home and see his wife and his children."

The scene should be shot just before dusk, and Coppola wanted to keep witnesses out of full view, looking on from almost out of frame, accompanied by the sound of people crying.

Back at the Corleone residence, the family would plot their next move.

"I had an idea that Sonny never really takes his father's desk until a certain point. "That even while he operates [within] sight of it, he doesn't really sit down," said Coppola. "So the desk should represent the old man."

Sonny would take charge of family operations for now, but the desk—like the unconscious Vito Corleone—would remain in limbo.

Then the action would shift to Sollozzo in a Quonset hut holding Tom Hagen hostage.

"I got that idea because in those days they had lots and lots of Quonset huts," Coppola said. "I also wanted to avoid the typical scene where four gangsters are sitting around the card table in an old apartment . . . where they got the hostage. I was just about to say there would be stacks and stacks of boxes, which is also a cliché. That's why I picked a Quonset hut."

"Maybe the scene is stronger playing the whole damn thing in one long shot," Willis said, "in one tableau."

"Would [Hagen] have anything with him that was too big to wrap?" Tavoularis asked.

"The presents he had with him," Coppola said.

"I mean being kidnapped with it," Tavoularis said. "I am sure he would have a number of packages and he would have them all intact. And this is the irony: When he goes back to the house, when he has finally gotten out at two in the morning, he has all the stuff."

"You really are always reminded of the hour," Coppola said, "the pressure."

Coppola turned to the description of Luca Brasi, then yet to be cast. He wanted to mislead the audience once again. "Luca Brasi should be a main character," Coppola said. "Everybody is waiting for him to do some incredible thing. And at this point, I will, somehow, do another flashback, whether it will be this way or some better way. And we go back to when they couldn't hear through the glass. The Don had turned Luca on to sort of being a spy, and we get into Luca's room. He is such a bizarre character; I would like the whole thing to be eccentric. It's all so exotic. He lives in a strange way. He is really a fascinating kind of character."

"What kind of place would he live in?" Tavoularis asked.

"In the book, he had a railroad apartment where he lived in the end, with another family," said Coppola. "I don't think we have the time to get into that. I think we are going to say just a room and, in some way, just pretend, when you are talking of how Luca dresses and lives, make believe that he is really a main character. It's like Hitchcock and *Psycho*. If we can make the audience believe that Don Corleone is the main character of this piece, the way Mario did, and when we shoot him and incapacitate him, they are thrown. . . . Then Sonny is the main character. It's sort of the way the book told its story. I sort of like it.

"Going on," Coppola continued, "we now get into the beginning of the Clemenza–Paulie Gatto murder. I will have to, probably, shorten this. I sort of like the red herring aspect of this. My idea was that, first of all, Clemenza's house would have some suburban Long Island look."

"Does he have kids?" Tavoularis asked of big, burly Clemenza, whose wife reminds him, "Don't forget the cannoli!"

"No," Coppola said. "But to link him to the kind of neighborhood where these homes, although they're nice, are all in a row. And he says hello to his neighbors every morning when he works in the garage. He's got one of the few postwar cars, which he obviously paid under the table to get. It means a lot to him; he is the American Valachi, the American successful man who has a nice house and money and everything and is a 'good guy.'" Coppola turned to "Johnnie" Johnstone. "My concept for him, Johnnie, is a veteran."

Johnstone nodded approvingly.

Coppola's initial concept for Clemenza was that of "a *Popular Mechanics* man" who had returned from the war "and was unemployed for seven, eight months. He is not a hood. He is the American man, the American blue-collar man. He is going to do his job here after serving his country; they reward him with nothing but unemployment."

Which led him to work for Don Corleone. The shooting of Paulie Gatto scene was to take place in the car, and Coppola insisted that once the character who would kill Paulie got in the back seat he wouldn't be seen on camera.

"The audience knows that he is going to blow Paulie Gatto's head off," Coppola said, "though throughout the whole scene you are really uncomfortable."

"Now, is this still winter, as far as I am concerned?" asked Johnstone.

"Yes," Coppola said, turning to Tavoularis. "Dean, this is our catch-all. And the whole idea is that you are waiting for his head to be blown off and it never does.... After he says, 'Pull over,' we do our trick. The question we have to decide is, if it's late in the day when it happens, if we want to go for dusk or just day. We might get into night. I think crimes and murders, even beatings—violence is better in the daytime, because people always play it at night.... It's a wild concept to bring it out in the daylight because it makes it more real and horrible."

Willis and Johnstone agreed.

"This shot," Coppola asked, "could it be done in one shot? Could you, literally, go away with Clemenza, move with him over the car while he goes—all with sound; and when you come back, the window is blown out and the guy is dead? It's possible if we had another car and move it in. Is it worth it?"

"Well, the shots are certainly enough to do," Willis said. "The hang-up is, of course, the automobile."

"I mentioned it to the special effects guy," Coppola said, "so he has it in mind, trying to do it in one shot."

"It's a good idea," Willis said.

"Just get the guy into the other car," Coppola said, "and rolling the other car into the weeds or something."

"Because they have another car stashed there," Willis said.

"They had it preplanned," said Coppola. "They knew exactly where it was going to be. High weeds."

They moved on to Michael Corleone returning to his fallen father's house, "a stranger in his own home," said Coppola. Clemenza would be at the stove, cooking for the soldiers with Michael at his side, "and the idea of Michael being on the phone with Kay and her wanting (him) to say he loves her with these guys eating. Use that again to remind you that they are real people, and, although these are world-shaking events, they are in the kitchen."

And when Clemenza instructs Michael on how to fire a pistol, Coppola said he wanted "the feeling to it that you were down in the cellar with your favorite uncle, with stacks of *Popular Mechanics*, and he was giving you pointers on how to work. Except telling you how to kill a man."

Even the arrival of the dead fish in the bulletproof vest—signaling the death of Luca Brasi—would reinforce the mantra of home, of evil invading a living room, envisioned by Coppola as "nothing special, except to feel that it looks homey."

"NOW, THE FAMOUS hospital sequence, a desolate place," Coppola said of the scene where Don Corleone is hospitalized after being shot. "There should be very little activity. There's no one there, and I think it would be nice if there still were Christmas lights in the hospital. This is a Hitchcock suspense scene. It's a scene of revelation. At each step, you learn more and more how dangerous the situation is. An empty hospital, if you note in the script, left little evidence that people had just been there. You might think about that and come up with better ones."

"Sandwiches and things," Tavoularis said.

"And cigarettes still burning," Coppola said.

Coppola had an idea to introduce a character visiting the don, to ratchet up the suspense and highlight the theme of reciprocity running through the film. The audience would think it was an assassin, come to finish off the don, but it would turn out to be "a good-natured Italian kid" carrying a bouquet of flowers—Enzo, the baker, come to pay his respects.

Johnstone worried that the audience might not remember the character. "You have to identify him with the wedding," she said. "You have to establish it and this, to me, is the biggest job that I have, to keep track of all these people in the audience's mind."

"Well," Coppola said, "that's the problem."

He noted that he might cut an earlier scene with Enzo, to save time. "I have a three-and-a-half-hour movie here. Essentially what I am saying is that this may be another sequence that we might predesign for real suspense, like every little ounce of suspense."

Next, Coppola said, Enzo and Michael Corleone stand in front of the hospital, to safeguard the don. "We might spend a lot of time with that," he said. "Let him stand there a little while, let nothing happen."

Then McCluskey, the corrupt Irish police captain, arrives and punches Michael in the face. "I have the sinister nature with that punch, which implies almost a Michael point of view," Coppola said. The only question, he said, was whether it would confuse the audience if the scene ended there. "Mario felt that you might be uncertain as to whether the Don was all right," he reported. "Did they then go into the hospital and kill the Don? What do you feel?"

"My personal feeling is that I sort of hate to draw pictures for people," said Willis.

"I couldn't go on after he hit him," Coppola said, meaning he wanted to end the scene after the punch.

"You don't need it," Johnstone said.

"I would like to use Bellevue again," Tavoularis said, turning to the subject of using the famous New York hospital as a location" for the cataclysmic punch. Coppola wanted the cop, played by Sterling Hayden, dressed like a general, "a lot of brass" to show his seeming invicibility.

"Is there a French hospital?" Coppola asked. "Are there old buildings or something?"

"Well, they're old buildings," Tavoularis said. "The French hospital and the others really don't look like hospitals. It would [look like] a hotel. It's a kind of ordinary building in the middle of the block, and Michael would have to stand on the curb and the cars would go by."

"So you like Bellevue best," Coppola said. "We'll go look at that."

*   *   *

COPPOLA MOVED ON to Michael being picked up in Times Square, which would be filmed in front of the flashing neon of Jack Dempsey's Broadway Restaurant. From there he is taken to Louis Italian American Restaurant, in the Bronx, where he kills Sollozzo and McCluskey. It was a long sequence, nearly three pages of script in the car alone, and Coppola thought it might be worth doing live instead of on a soundstage. Willis agreed, but there were issues that needed to be resolved.

"This is probably where they go over the bridge and make a U-turn and come back again," Willis said. "That's going to be a hard trick to do."

"We can do that someplace else," Tavoularis said.

"Any bridge you want," Coppola said, "as long as we can get a great shot of a car leaping off the ground and zipping the other way."

"Bridges are a pain in the ass," Willis said. "The people who run them are a pain in the ass."

"So we should get at that right away," Coppola said.

"The George Washington Bridge," Willis said, "unless there is a genius with a better idea. Some employees in the company tend to not want to even let you near the place or anything like it."

Or maybe the Tappan Zee Bridge, he added—the since-replaced cantilevered span across the Hudson River. "They have cooperated in the past, I remember. But it's a small bridge with a long causeway. We'd better feel out every major bridge.

"One good thing about the George Washington Bridge is that there is a divider to stop head-on collisions," he continued. "Once you reach the tollbooth on the Jersey side, I think that the divider stops. There is a lot of light on that bridge, you can get to a highway, and there are several places that you can get a very good shot there."

Still, he warned, it was going to be tough to pull off the dramatic U-turn. "The chances of our getting the bridge for a turnaround are almost nil."

"Any bridge?" Coppola asked.

"Just about any bridge," Willis said. "Maybe the Tappan Zee."

"Really?" Tavoularis said.

"Yeah, it's rough," Willis said. "As I said, maybe there is somebody. But the other problem is that obviously it's not a stunt that we can say, 'All right, when you get there, turn around and we'll be rolling,' because there are cars all over the place and so we can't clear the bridge."

"What about doing it in the middle of the night?" Coppola asked.

"Well, it's still a bridge," Willis said. "They won't do it, I don't think; but, at any rate, it's possible. My alternative thing is—I am just thinking of sources to get over the bridge and through a tollgate and get over the bridge and do the swing around to the other side of the bridge and back through the tollgate."

"That's no way near as good," Coppola said. "But I would really like to shoot for the effect. There are so few good stunts and stuff to really make it good. Frank, who is in there doing all the car work, is the guy who did *Bullitt*, and maybe we could if we scheduled it. . . . We can get him to do that one stunt, and with a second unit—"

Willis cut him off.

"If we schedule it for four or five o'clock in the morning maybe," he said. "But the George Washington Bridge would be ideal."

"This is one of the things we should get a real priority on," Coppola said.

Once Michael arrived at the restaurant for the film's most violent killing, Coppola wanted to ratchet the action to the hilt. It would follow Mario Puzo's description of the killing, with so much blood that it turns into "a fine mist of sprayed blood," with the velocity of bullets fired at close-range. "This is another scene that I am going to predesign, or try to," he said. "It goes into the ratio of how we are going to blow the guy's head off and the pink mist in the air. That will all be done in tremendous detail."

"Shouldn't the pink mist come from Sollozzo's head?" Willis asked.

"It's going to be Sollozzo's head," Coppola said. "There is going to be a pink mist. It's wholly unrealistic. I think it's great—the operation from that point on in that pink mist in the air."

Willis pondered the scene's framing, given that Michael gets up to retrieve a gun from the bathroom in the middle of the dinner. "The killing, the tableau thing again," he said. "It's a reprise in style, but I think it will work in the killing. But if, for instance, if you do one whole master tableau in the restaurant—maybe the master goes for ten minutes. Because he comes back from the can, right?"

"You won't be able to get the effects in the long shot," Coppola said. "But you can go right up into the killing and the excitement."

It would be done in "the middle of a well-lighted restaurant," he said. "Again, an old idea of taking the violence into the lights. The killings are always in the dark corner."

And when Michael leaves the restaurant and gets into the getaway car, he "vanishes from the story altogether."

All of it, Coppola stressed—from the wedding that opens the film to Michael's ascension as godfather—should defy audiences' expectations of a crime film. It would be more painterly than pulpy: stylish, "sensible," and stripped of clichés. "Again, I am trying the tableau," he said. If he could pull it off, his entire movie could be like that, one long series of tableaus, of fantastic, beautiful pictures in a world of ugliness and evil, which, taken as a whole, would tell his story, and turn that story into art. "You will see, I will even . . . even do it in the script," Coppola said.

Willis and Tavoularis and Johnstone did see. For the moment, they were all in harmony with their director, striving to bring their collective talents and experience to bear on every detail in the film, no matter how minute. But it was getting late. Coppola called for a break. They had gotten only halfway through the script, but the director promised they would regroup in a week and finish designing the movie, scene by scene. If they met again, however, it wasn't recorded by a court stenographer. So the rest of their ideas, and the plans they made, would have to be told by those who survived the torment of what came next:

The filming.

11

LOOKING FOR PLACES TO KILL PEOPLE

Okay, let's begin," said Francis Ford Coppola.

It was a windy Wednesday afternoon, March 17, 1971—Saint Patrick's Day—and the Corleone family was sitting down to dinner. Less than two weeks before cameras were slated to roll, Coppola was already running behind on finalizing the script, locations, budget, casting, and myriad other details. But now his actors were in New York. He had to welcome them and lead them. "But where?" he asked himself on a to-do list, on which he had written: "eat together, Italian Family style."

Early on the morning of Friday, March 19, the cast awoke to find call sheets under their doors:

"3:30 p.m. at Patsy's," it read, "First Avenue & 117th St."

"Most of the actors were staying at the Park Lane Hotel, and the call sheet advised them that a car would pick them up at a certain time for the rehearsal," said Gianni Russo, who had landed the coveted role of the unscrupulous, wife-beating son-in-law Carlo Rizzi.

Patsy's was perfect. It was one of the best Italian restaurants in East Harlem, the favorite of not only movie stars but also members of the Mob. Since 1933, the who's who of Italian America had dined at its tables: Dean Martin, Joe DiMaggio, Frank Sinatra, and even Mario Puzo. It was often described as a restaurant where gangsters gathered on one side of the restaurant while New York City cops sat on the other.

"What better joint to rehearse an epic gangster movie?" said Russo.

Patsy's was authentic down to its restrooms, which must have inspired Puzo to include the restaurant's glorious old-fashioned commode in his novel, "with a space between the water container and the wall," where Michael Corleone's gun would be planted. Coppola had taken Al Pacino to Patsy's to show him that toilet for the pivotal shooting scene. But Patsy's proprietor didn't allow the scene to be filmed in his restaurant, out of respect for the Mob. "The real bad guys don't shoot cops," he said.

Gianni Russo arrived at Patsy's around 3:30 p.m., dressed in his customary Brioni suit, a twenty-five-year-old would-be wiseguy and neophyte actor arriving for his first rehearsal.

"And there at the bar was Angelo 'Cheesecake' Ruggiero [longtime friend of John Gotti's and future Gambino capo] and Anthony 'Fat Tony' Salerno [future Genovese underboss]," Russo explained. "People ask me, 'Were there any Mob guys there?' and I always say, 'There was a hundred years of good behavior at the bar.'"

"Hey, Gianni, what are you doing here so early?" one of the made men asked Russo.

"I'm here for the rehearsal," he replied.

"What?" asked the stunned mobsters. "What are *you* going to do in the movie?"

"I got the part of Carlo," he said, which drew blanks. "Because they hadn't read the book."

He strode into the back room, where the actors who would bring the Corleone family to life sat around a long, food-laden table. "In one room we had the real guys and in the other room we had the make-believe guys," said Russo.

"At the head of the table was Brando," remembered James Caan. "I was on his left, Pacino was on his right, and Bobby Duvall was next to Pacino."

Brando's first rehearsal had been earlier in the afternoon, the star arriving in a black velvet jacket over an orange cashmere turtleneck sweater, with a *Godfather* script under his arm. "It was like Christ had come down from the cross," remembered Al Ruddy. The cast immediately fell silent with reverence and awe, until the world's greatest living actor cracked a joke, which no one seems to remember, but that everyone agreed set the tone for the evening. From this dinner forward, the cast didn't merely respect Brando, they loved him.

There was copious food and wine, the table heaving under the weight of antipasto, pizza, pasta, and everything imaginable, all arranged by Coppola, who "does everything very grand," said James Caan. "My job was to set the table, that's what a nice Italian girl does," said Talia Shire. "Francis put us all together, and my job was to serve the meal . . . to Marlon Brando! Holy shit! This is Marlon Brando! And the dinner was telling you the story of this family, which is American and Italian, and how the meal is very important."

Most of the cast members were "new to each other," said John Cazale, who would immortalize the role of the middle son, Fredo. "We stood there not knowing what to do."

Finally, Brando opened a bottle of wine and "broke the ice," he added, "and started the festivities."

That's when they *knew*. "He was acting with us the way the Don would have acted with his own family," said Cazale. And that's when everyone also knew to follow Brando's lead. "Everyone was doing what their roles were," said Pacino. It was "crazy," he added, but it was also brilliant. "I remember [Brando] got up early on and introduced himself and walked over to Diane [Keaton]. He said, 'Hi, Diane, I'm Marlon Brando.' And she looked up, shook his hand, and said, 'Yeah, right, okay, good, fine, that's okay.'"

As the Corleone family came to life, Coppola sat at the far end of the table, beside Sterling Hayden, the veteran actor who would play the corrupt police captain, watching as the family he had fought so hard to cast finally came together. "It was the first time they had all met, and all I did was have them improvise for two or three hours, over a meal, that they were family," Coppola said. "They'd never met before really, and it was like playing at a family, a kind of sensual opportunity for them to relate to each other. It was very, very valuable.

"After that, the characters existed."

BY THE TIME he sat down at the dinner table with the cast, Brando had already figured out how he would bring the character of Don Corleone to life. A week before the cast dinner, he had descended upon New York, checking into the Hotel Elysée on Fifty-Fourth and Madison and leaving a Do Not Disturb order on his phone until noon.

When the Teamster driver arrived for the 9:00 a.m. pickup, he was informed that he'd have to wait for the star to awaken. After rising, Brando began the transformation, from a forty-seven-year-old has-been into Don Corleone for one final makeup and costume test before his real scenes—and career resurrection—began. He had rehearsed his character for months, once receiving Coppola and casting direc-tor Fred Roos in a house he was renting while filming in London. Ever the actor, Brando was in the bathtub when they arrived, and they could hear him practicing his lines in Don Corleone's guttural rasp.

Now, with the character embedded in his mind, Brando was ready for it to take over his body. He sat before a mirror in his dressing room on the second floor of the old Filmways Studio, where the film's makeup wizard Dick Smith, and Brando's personal makeup man, Philip Rhodes, worked their magic: applying layers of a liquid latex compound to his face that, when stretched and dried, would create the appearance of wrinkled skin. Age spots and yellowed teeth added to the aging process, which took an hour and a half—and would require even more time as Corleone grew older. "Marlon was willing to sit in the chair as long as needed—but no longer," Smith would later explain. "We created makeup that wouldn't require three hours of his time."

Once the makeup was done, Brando inserted the mouthpiece, which made his jaw sag and his cheeks jut forward. His ponytail long gone, his hair was dyed black and sprinkled with gray at the temples. On each foot, he wore a ten-pound weight to slow his movements, and padding was added around his waist for a belly grown fat from a lifetime of spaghetti and veal Milanese. "My god, we had to pad him up and make him look older and fat," said Gray Frederickson. "He had a washboard stomach and was in great shape."

Added to this was the voice, which he has spent so long perfecting, a gravelly growl, to "be like a bulldog," Brando would say.

When the transformation was complete, he walked onto the soundstage on that March midafternoon, and everyone present did a double take. "The change in his appearance is astonishing," Ira Zuckerman reported in *The Godfather Journal.* "Even at close range, the makeup cannot be detected."

He walked over to the props that Coppola had laid out, while the Italian folk music Coppola had selected played. Brando fiddled with the food and wine bottles, and then prepared to face the camera, which Gordon Willis was ready to wield like a weapon, capturing the powerful visage that would make or break the film. "How much of me are you going to film?" mumbled Brando as Don Corleone. He needed to know *all* the details, to ensure he was acting in a way that the camera could pick up perfectly.

"He works with impressive intensity and concentration; he mumbles to himself as he goes through the actions of drinking wine, singing, peeling and eating oranges," wrote Zuckerman.

The camera was soon switched off, but Brando remained in character, deep within himself in his flesh-colored earplugs, which he always wore on set, to "help him to concentrate by shutting out the extraneous noise and making him listen more carefully to the actors he's playing with," said his assistant, Alice Marchak.

He was no longer sluggish, problematic, midcareer-in-the-dumps Marlon Brando.

He was now Don Vito Corleone, the crooked king of both his family and his underworld, and he was bound for a level of glory that even Brando could not have imagined.

*   *   *

IT WAS EARLY evening, when the rehearsal dinner at Patsy's was done, and the actors climbed into their cars to return home or to the hotel. Caan and Duvall, old friends from working together on Coppola's *The Rain People*, rode together, Duvall driving. And when their car turned onto Second Avenue, they came up alongside the car carrying Brando.

For Duvall, it was like riding beside God. "The godfather of actors," he called him, the star who Duvall and his friend Dustin Hoffman idolized. "If we mentioned his name once, we mentioned it twenty-five times in a day," said Duvall.

For all the stories of Brando's on-set tirades and difficulties, there was also another side to the legendary actor: the prankster, a lover of practical jokes who had been known to drop water balloons from the rooftop of his apartment building on West Fifty-Second Street onto random passersby. His pranks would continue on the set of *The God-father*. While shooting the scene of him being carried up the stairs of his home on a stretcher after being shot, Brando secretly had three hundred pounds of sandbags inserted into the stretcher, and as the procession of extras, crew members, and Teamsters attempted to carry him, the laughs grew louder by those in on the joke.

His reputation for practical jokes was almost as famous as his legendary intensity. And the other actors knew it. If Duvall revered the actor, then he also saw this as a chance for some fun.

"Come on," Duvall said to Caan, "moon him!"

"Are you crazy?" said Caan. "I don't do that. You're the king of that."

But Duvall persisted, and Caan rolled down his window, lowered his pants, and stuck his butt out the window, showing the legend, well, *everything*.

Brando was "falling down" laughing, Caan remembered. "And we went away crying, laughing. That was the first moon of my life, to Brando, and it was on the first day we met."

It was the ultimate icebreaker—and the first hopeful sign, for the actors at least, that after all the drama that had led up to their casting, maybe filming this movie was going to be fun. The next day, the actors made a bet as to who'd be named the "Mighty Moon Champion" by the end of the shoot, which Brando won by a landslide after dropping his pants and bending over before the entire cast and crew—including hundreds of extras—during the massive wedding scene.

That camaraderie would prove to be essential for the actors—save for Al Pacino. "Marlon, Bobby Duvall, Jimmy Caan, they got along really well with each other, and they were funny, so there were funny things happening on the set, which eased strains," he said. "But I stayed a little bit out of it because I felt Michael was a private person. And I kept that with me all the time. Michael was always a little outside. He was the youngest so he really had to observe, to look, and he was prepared when he finally took over because he'd learned a lot of things just by observing."

The hijinks the other actors continued to pull on each other made their work fun and the camaraderie showed. Coppola, however, would get no part of it.

Instead of mooning, his lot would be misery.

"It was," Coppola later said of filming *The Godfather*, "the most miserable time of my life."

He said it even surpassed the ordeals he faced on the typhoon-wracked set of *Apocalypse Now*, shot in the Philippines in the spring and summer of 1976, which pushed the cast, crew, and director to the brink of madness.

"They were both nightmarish productions," he said. "But perhaps *Godfather* more so, as in truth I was really powerless, whereas on *Apocalypse Now* I had made three successful award-winning films."

ON THE SURFACE, Coppola played the confident leader, all set to start shooting his biggest movie to date. He had won his casting battles, as evidenced by the actors gathered around the table at Patsy's; he was in New York, the location where he had always wanted to shoot the movie; he was finally ready to commit his vision of *The Godfather* to film.

Secretly, though, he was still terrified.

"Making the first *Godfather* film was like nonstop anxiety, and wondering when I was going to get fired," Coppola said.

The location that he had fought so hard for—the real New York, not some Paramount soundstage or run-down section of St. Louis or Kansas City—only made his job harder. "You can't shoot in New York at our pace and not feel the pressure," said Al Ruddy. "There's an old adage in the business: 'Unhappy sets make great movies.'"

So the motley cast and crew that converged upon New York in March 1971 shared both excitement and uncertainty. "It was all like a joke," said Robert Duvall. "Because no one knew what it was going to be."

At Coppola's back, however, stood the future of film. "When we walked on the set the first day, there were the department heads, who were the best," said James Caan. "Like Walter Murch, the best sound guy in the world for the past twenty years. Gordy Willis, the best cinematographer. Dean Tavoularis, design; Dick Smith, makeup. Every one of them were geniuses. All of them would make it to the top of their fields. That was not an accident."

Coppola was a whirlwind: finalizing locations, meeting with his creative team, handling last-minute script revisions and coordinating tests and costumes and makeup. The film would eventually be shot in 120 New York area locations over 67 days, a tight schedule and a very long script, which caused some grousing. "Paramount was all over Francis [saying], 'We're not gonna start with a 173-page script,'" assistant producer Steve Kesten later told *Premiere* magazine.

And Robert Evans was watching everything like a hawk:

March 5, 1971, GODFATHER—Notes on script . . . Francis Coppola from Robert Evans:
    "Feel that the character of Sonny is not nearly as Flamboyant and exciting as in the book. The sexuality that everyone remembers

*is totally missing in the script. I think the size of his cock and the
horse's head are the two most remembered scenes from the book and
the former is so lacking that I think we would be criticized for not
doing more with Sonny."*

On and on the memo went: "Who is going to play Mama
Corleone? . . . Fredo's casting—I'm not sure I'm satisfied . . . Are you
sure the picture can be cut with a straight-forward story if you decide
not to go with flash forwards? . . ."

For Coppola, the war began anew each morning when "five guys
in a station wagon" picked him up around five thirty. And he would
depart the apartment, which reeked of paint fumes and was filled with
the cacophony of his family, for location shots in the city or interiors
in the old two-story Filmways Studio building in Harlem.

At 5:30 a.m. on March 23, 1971, the filming commenced. The
mammoth production began lurching about the city like some loud and
ungainly army: one filming unit, both for live locations and studio-built
sets, a battalion of cars, trucks, buses, and as many as seventy-five to one
hundred personnel—camera crews, lighting crews, grips, prop crews, set
dressers, makeup, hair, wardrobe, production, Teamsters, security, chefs,
and food servers—all led by the bearded young stalwart director dressed
in battle regalia with crowds trailing their every move. "Godfather fever
was gripping the city in a big way," wrote Gianni Russo.

It began with Christmas in springtime, 1945. Best & Co., the
department store at Fifty-First and Fifth, which had conveniently shut-
tered the year before, had been restored to its 1940s glory, bedecked
with giant wreaths and candy canes. Vintage taxis, police squad cars,
and other rescued relics filled the street where the sixty-member crew
was engulfed by crowds of observers on all sides. One hundred and
forty-three extras, dressed in period attire, stepped out of two buses.
"Soldiers and sailors, WACs, Christmas shoppers, nuns, taxi drivers,
etc.," wrote Zuckerman.

Most authentic of all were the principal actors. Their pockets had
been filled with what Coppola called "rehearsal props" to inform their

characters—old lighters, rosary beads, key rings, toothpicks, pocket-knives, hip flasks, pistols, perfume bottles, and, for some, packets of fake heroin and more—as if the old items would rise up and transform them into the Corleones. They were dressed in period attire provided by the costume wizard who would be nominated for a 1973 Oscar for her work: Anna Hill Johnstone. Coppola had first discussed costumes with Theadora Van Runkle, who was red-hot, fresh off designing the sexy Texas outlaw attire for *Bonnie and Clyde*. But Van Runkle had read Puzo's book, and she couldn't get the bloody horse's head scene out of her head.

"I asked Francis, 'Is the horse part going to be in there?'" Van Runkle later told film historian Jennifer Peterson. "And he said, 'Yes.' So I said I wouldn't do it.

"I turned it down because of the horse," she continued. "Do you believe that? And everybody said, 'You are such an ass. What is the matter with you?' But I just couldn't do it."

Coppola turned to Johnstone, then in her late fifties, a veteran costume designer of stage and screen and a favorite of directors Sidney Lumet and Elia Kazan. She was "the nicest woman," said Van Runkle. "She always smiled at me and was enthusiastic and full of energy. She had a certain masculine presence; she was like a Nordic guy . . . like a sailor boy or something. She had so much vitality . . ."

No bloody horse's head could stop Anna Hill Johnstone.

"While preparing for the filming of *The Group* in 1965, [she] divulged some tricks of her craft," noted the *New York Times*. "She combed through the closets and attics of friends in Riverdale and scrounged through thrift shops on the East Side of Manhattan looking for just the right clothes for the story's era."

Johnstone had assembled the vintage clothing that would turn contemporary actors into 1940s gangster royalty. "She was wonderful and gave me wisdom that served me throughout my entire career," said Coppola.

And now the actors and extras stood on the sidelines, awaiting their first miracle:

Snow on command.

While the wizards of the movies could turn back time, they couldn't make it snow. The flurries that had dusted the streets that dawn had dissipated with the arrival of the moviemakers, leaving it to the producer who had tamed the Mob to make it snow. Al Ruddy, who had ordered snowmaking machines, was confounded when the temperature rose above the machines' ability to operate and was forced to haul out plastic snowflakes and wind machines to re-create that snowy day in 1945.

At 8:00 a.m., the cameras rolled—Diane Keaton and Al Pacino exiting Best & Co. amid the swirl of fake snow—along with immediate criticism. Keaton was a head taller than Pacino, and she "moves like a colt learning to walk," Zuckerman quoted someone on the set as saying. But any thought that Coppola might replace her—and Gordon Willis said he'd better do it quick if he was going to do it at all—turned out to be only rumors.

From there, the production moved to Polk's Model Craft Hobbies on Fifth Avenue and Thirty-First Street, for the quick scene where Sollozzo abducts Hagen emerging from the toy store, his arms filled with Christmas gifts. Then it was back to Michael and Kay, exiting Radio City Music Hall. The marquee read *The Bells of St. Mary's*, just as it had in December 1945, while real ushers from the theater had to advise paying customers that the Elaine May movie *A New Leaf* was actually playing. As college-boy-turned-soldier Michael Corleone steps out of the music hall into what would soon be his new life, Kay Adams asks him, "Would you like me better if I were Ingrid Bergman?"—the star of *The Bells of St. Mary's*—just as she spotted the headlines at a newsstand:

Vito Corleone Feared Murdered
Assassins Gun Down Underworld Chief

Michael rushes into a phone booth, leaving Kay outside its windows, a subtle signal of their coming estrangement.

At 2:00 a.m., Coppola wrapped for the day, not completely satis-fied. He had shot what he had envisioned in the production meet-ing: three disjointed scenes that would meld together in a time warp, a montage that would turn time upon itself: the Christmas couple, the abduction of Tom Hagen, the headlines, and, finally, shot nearly a month later, the don exiting his olive oil company and into the attempt on his life.

All of this was on the page and apparently in the mind of Francis Ford Coppola, although no one else seems to have seen its majesty.

They only saw Coppola's shortcomings.

THE DIRECTOR COULDN'T sleep. His apartment was cramped, with his two sons, his pregnant wife, his father, and his sense of impending doom. "I was in a cold sweat," he would later say. When sleep finally came, it was filled with horrible dreams: of being fired, replaced, discarded. The studio felt he was "great on character relation-ships and too timid with the violence," he said. Then, the director Elia Kazan, who had directed Brando in *Viva Zapata!* and *On the Water-front*, would arise in his dreams, which would turn into nightmares. "I kept dreaming that Kazan would arrive on the set and would say to me, 'Uh, Francis, I've been asked to . . .'"

Coppola's wife, Eleanor, was equally miserable, seven months pregnant, and caught in what she called "a total nightmare," living in a borrowed apartment, "to save money because we had all these debts."

The pressure intensified, with whispers around the set that the studio had dispatched a "spy" to keep a tight watch over Coppola and the seemingly plagued film. "Be careful what you say in front of any-one who isn't a regular on the production staff or the tech crew," one member of the crew warned.

The "spy" was an extremely fit, middle-aged, tightly coiled man with a shaved head, whose name alone struck fear in film crews: Jack Ballard. He was dressed casually, in attire that seemed more suitable to golfing. But every film to Jack Ballard was tantamount to fiscal combat. His mission: "to keep an eye on the day-to-day production planning, scheduling and shooting," wrote Zuckerman, and immediately advise Paramount of any overruns.

"He will report back to the studio every day."

Meaning he would report directly to Robert Evans.

"He was Bob Evans's Luca Brasi," said the film's sound effects supervisor Walter Murch. "He was an enforcer. If Evans wanted something done, and he didn't want to be the bad guy, Ballard would do it."

Ballard would stalk the set and production offices from that day forward, always in the background, but always watching, recording, and calculating the bottom line. For him, art was secondary to "the final dollar, the final penny, the final number of days you're going to shoot," said one of the film's coordinators. "For Jack, the dollar, the schedule and the number of days and hours shooting were all important rather than what's the movie about or was the script or the performances any good. Jack only had one thing, and that was the hammer, the bottom line, the dollar, and there was nothing you could pull over his eyes." (Stanley Jaffe, Paramount's former president, added, "Jack Ballard was a really good below-the-line executive, and constructive, not destructive.")

Coppola vs. Ballard was now added to the director's growing list of conflicts. "Everything I did he was there, countermanding my orders," said Coppola. "They were convinced this was the worst picture ever made, that I'm the worst director ever."

The arrival of Jack Ballard was "the nail in my coffin," he added. "A persistent production man with a shaved head who was there to terrorize me into submission."

MEANWHILE, PRODUCTION DESIGNER Dean Tavoularis was spending his days and nights "looking for places to kill people," he said.

The search for the perfect restaurant for the pivotal scene where Michael Corleone guns down Virgil Sollozzo and Captain McCluskey had dragged on for months. First, the owner of Patsy's in Harlem, whose old-fashioned toilet was the perfect place to stash a murder weapon, declined. Then, the owner of Mario's on Arthur Avenue in the Bronx said no, too, saying he preferred his restaurant to be famous for its menu instead of murder.

"You're always looking," said Tavoularis of those long-ago days in late 1970 and early 1971 when mom-and-pop Italian restaurants dotted the landscape of New York and its environs. Finally, he drove past Louis Italian American Restaurant beside the elevated train trestle at 3531 White Plains Road near Gun Hill Road in the Bronx, and he immediately *knew*.

"It was like a dream," he said.

He walked inside and scanned the small single room: "the back bar, the ceiling, the walls, more perfect than the exterior," he said. When he noticed that the drab linoleum floor covered a fantastic old mosaic, he lobbied to strip off the linoleum and restore the original mosaic floor, at a cost of $8,000, which Jack Ballard must have hotly disputed.

Now, the cast and crew were walking across that fabulous floor and back in time to shoot a scene that would become as familiar to its audience as a personal memory. But on the day the scene was shot, it turned into a calamity.

By this point, Pacino, having only been in low-key scenes with Keaton, was extremely unsure of himself. Every morning at 5:00 a.m., he would bolt awake in bed in the tiny apartment he shared with the actress Jill Clayburgh in a sweat as cold as Coppola's. "Playing Michael was a hellish experience," Pacino said of those bleary dawns he spent thinking "about where I was in the film, what the transition was. That's why I have to block out a part, to figure out the transition from one block to another. I had to be sure I was building up to the point where Michael takes over from the Don."

Now he felt his job was on the line.

"They accepted me because Jerry Schatzberg, my great friend and director, gave them eight minutes from *The Panic in Needle Park*," said Pacino in a 2019 *GQ* interview. "And when they saw the footage they hired me. . . . They were going to fire me about two weeks into it. They didn't care for what they were seeing."

"I believe in you, but you've gotta take a look at the footage," he remembered Coppola telling him.

"So I went to the Paramount building and looked at the footage," said Pacino. "Because I knew this was it. My job was over now."

He watched himself in the film. He didn't think it was good, but neither did he think it was bad. It was part of his plan, which he had spent countless hours contemplating. "I thought the power of the role was in the transition," he explained. "From this kid who you don't know quite who he is, where he's going. And then before you know it, he becomes this leader."

In the scenes so far, which Paramount hated, Michael was still the quiet college-boy-turned-Marine-captain. But he was about to become a man through a double murder, which would mark the beginning of Michael Corleone's ascent as his father's successor. At that point, low-key Michael would explode on-screen with a velocity that would surprise the audience, just as it surprised the two dead men in the restaurant. "You would say, 'Where did *he* come from?'" Pacino explained.

He had to start slow and subdued, so that his transition would be thunderous.

But nobody knew this but Pacino.

"Hit Hard and Bloody!!" Coppola wrote on the page of the restaurant scene in his *Godfather Notebook*. "Mist of Blood" and "Hitchcock" and "Get this for the audience!"

And in his typed outline in the notebook, he further mapped it out. "Incredible suspense and tension. Image of the car jumping the divider; the empty restaurant with the three men almost in the middle of the room around the small round table, exposed. . . . Sollozzo and McCluskey sympathetic and reasonable. The blood on the waiter's jacket. The mist of blood hanging in and coloring the air."

Then, with the gunshots, "Time standing still with the reactions . . . McCluskey's fork frozen midair as he watched Sollozzo's brains fly through the air."

Coppola wanted the scene to be as bloody on the screen as it had been in Puzo's pages, particularly the way in which Sollozzo's brain explodes in "a huge gout of blood and skull fragments," and the air becomes "full of pink mist."

But achieving these effects would not be easy, and it fell in part to Dick Smith, the makeup artist who helped transform Marlon Brando into Don Corleone.

"We decided to use red powder—simple red face powder that was packed in an air tube," Smith said. "We filled a tube with the powder, ran it up behind Lettieri's head, and blasted the powder out as the shot was fired."

For the shooting of the corrupt police captain McCluskey, Smith had rigged a special effect for the gunshot wound to Sterling Hayden's head—a miniature explosive device called a sqib, which would show one bullet piercing the police captain's throat and another through his forehead. Filming the scene required more than an hour to reset after each man was shot.

At least Pacino knew how to handle the pistol. He had been instructed by his scene partner Al Lettieri, who was playing Sollozzo. Lettieri's brother-in-law was the organized-crime figure Patsy Eboli, and Lettieri would not only help Pacino with the pistol but also the pivotal scene in which his character would be so shockingly gunned down. Speaking fluent Italian, Lettieri coached Pacino on his Italian. But now, in the restaurant with the cameras rolling, Pacino was struggling, tripping over his Italian dialogue, which required doing the scene again and again, in the presence of actors he regarded as gods. "I remember it was a long day . . . like fifteen hours in a storefront without a camper," he said. "I was there with the great Sterling Hayden and Al Lettieri, two of my favorite people. Here I was, basically an unknown, with Sterling, who had made a hundred films. He was a legend and they treated him just as lousy as a newcomer. I was shocked."

"If I have to eat any more of this spaghetti, I'm going to explode," Sterling Hayden complained.

Finally, Pacino reworked the scene at the restaurant table on the fly, ad-libbing a switch from Italian to English. He looks over at McCluskey—busy with his dinner and obviously not paying attention—then turns to Sollozzo and says in English, "What I want, what's most important to me, is that I have a guarantee: no more attempts on my father's life."

Shortly after that, Pacino says, "I have to go to the bathroom."

Instead of coming out of the toilet blazing, Pacino returns to his seat. The crew waited until the train that consistently and loudly rumbled by had cleared out. Then, the cameras rolled and Coppola called "Action." The dialogue was clear, but the sound of a train's screeching brakes was added in later. So in the film, the sound of the train rushes through Michael Corleone's head just before he stands, points his pistol, pulls the trigger and leaves two men dead at the overturned table.

It was magic.

It was pink mist. It was chaos. An overturned table. And two men left dead.

Then, they shot it again—and again—and as the one scheduled day of production bled into the next, the crowds began to expand, apace with the cost overruns. The light was fading and overtime was about to kick in.

"Once we do it once, we do it twice, and Francis wants another one," said assistant director Fred Gallo.

"And Pacino's saying to Francis, 'What's my motivation?'"

"And I couldn't help it. I said, 'Your motivation is you've been working for sixteen hours and the sun is coming up and everybody wants to get the hell out of here!'"

Outside the restaurant, the Bronx neighborhood streets had become filled with fans, hundreds of them, "gathered under the elevated on White Plains Road," Zuckerman wrote. They could hear the action, but they couldn't see it, because the windows of the restaurant had been covered in gel to control the light.

There was one more shot to film, the production finally moving out of the restaurant and onto the street: Pacino, having committed the double murder, fleeing the scene by climbing into a getaway car.

Dawn was about to break. Under the stress of the late shoot, without the proper rehearsal, and with Pacino still desperate to prove himself, the actor stood outside the restaurant, waiting for the getaway car. The driver, apparently, had not been told to stop. And so Pacino made a dangerous choice:

He *leapt*.

As the car slowed down, he jumped onto the running board, trying to make a smooth getaway. But with no time to rehearse the scene, the driver didn't know about Pacino's maneuver and started to speed away. Then, calamity: Pacino misjudged his leap—he landed in the street, wincing in pain. His ankle was hurt, really hurt. Pacino was rushed to an emergency room, bringing a halt to the day's work. "I thought it was a sign from God; that now that I was injured they would have to release me," Pacino would later say.

His feelings of remorse were captured by Zuckerman in *The Godfather Journal*: "If this foot is really bad maybe Francis can rewrite the script to have Michael on crutches or using a cane," Pacino said on the way to the hospital. "Maybe a recurrent war injury. I just hope he's not angry. What a dumb thing to do. But nobody told me what was supposed to happen after I ran out of the restaurant!"

The news from the hospital was not good—Pacino had sprained his ligament—and his doctor ordered him to stay off his feet, sidelining Pacino, along with the schedule. "Pacino is given repeated pain-killing injections and gets around the set on crutches, in a wheelchair or with a cane," wrote Zuckerman. Coppola was equally paralyzed, and surely felt the hot breath of Jack Ballard at his back. "They really were pushing to get rid of me," Coppola said.

Next on the schedule: 7:00 a.m., Monday, April 12, New York Eye and Ear Infirmary. It would be the first scene with Marlon Brando as Don Corleone, in a hospital bed after being shot in the street. The executives were anxious to see if the faded superstar could deliver. If Brando bombed, Coppola's ass would be even further on the line.

Brando left New York for LA every weekend to spend time with his young son Christian, then thirteen, returning on the Sunday red-eye to report for work Monday morning.

At 6:00 a.m., his plane landed.

Brando was not on it.

He had missed his flight, delaying his first day on the set.

Coppola was boiling. Insanity on the set, insanity at home, pressure closing in. One night, after another hellish day of filming, he returned to his borrowed apartment, passing his pregnant wife, two young sons, and other family members and headed into the bedroom. He stripped the blanket off the bed and started furiously tearing. *Rip, rip, rip,* until the blanket was in shreds and he collapsed on the naked bed. "If you want to tear a blanket, you have to cut into it," said Eleanor Coppola. "He was in such a fury, he just tore it up."

AT 6:00 A.M. on Tuesday, April 13, Brando finally returned to New York, and filming continued.

His first scene was easy. All he had to do was lie in bed with feeding tubes in his arms in the hospital, where assassins had been dispatched to kill him. Excitement about the legendary actor's presence on-set—especially after the disappointment of the no-show the day before—spread through the cast and crew, as well as the hospital staff. "It's great for everyone's morale—patients and staff," a doctor told Zuckerman.

Two days later, the production descended on Little Italy—at 128 Mott Street—for the scene of Don Corleone and his family hearing the deal offered by Sollozzo in the olive oil factory.

"I must say no to you," mumbles Marlon Brando as Don Corleone. "It's true, I have a lot of friends in politics. But they wouldn't be friendly very long if they knew my business was drugs, instead of gambling."

Coppola wasn't satisfied with Brando or Caan in that first take in the olive oil factory, and he decided to reshoot the scene. But on the day of the reshoot, the problems with the filming were becoming apparent to the cast.

"Don't tell anyone, but the kids in that last scene were wearing winter clothes and it's supposed to be the middle of summer," Al Lettieri, the actor playing the dark, evil, drug-dealing Sollozzo, said while awaiting his turn before the camera.

An associate responded, "At this point, with all the problems on this film, it doesn't really make any difference."

On April 19, the production moved into broad daylight to film the scene of Don Corleone being shot in the street. Three days later, Zuckerman reported that Coppola was exhausted and in "a bad mood and says he hasn't slept for the past three nights. Several times he shouts, 'For once in my life I want complete silence on the set!'"

Along with the turmoil on the set, and the violence playing out on the streets, the real-life Mob was still looking for ways to play a bigger part in the picture.

THEY WERE THE "Vampires," as Francis Ford Coppola called them, the mobsters that Mario Puzo had warned him against. Be careful, Puzo said. "Don't let them in."

So Coppola shut them out, just as he would a vampire. "The vampire can't come into your house unless you invite them over the door," he said. "But, once you invite them over the door, then you're theirs."

Unable to come through the front door, the Mob entered through the back: through the good graces of actors. One day, preparing for a day's filming in Little Italy, Marlon Brando heard a knock on his trailer door. Russell Bufalino, the boss of northeastern Pennsylvania, whose tentacles were spreading across the Eastern seaboard, had sent two envoys "to say he wanted to meet me," Brando would later write.

Bufalino was no minor mobster. He was rumored to have been involved in some of the defining crimes of the twentieth century, from the Bay of Pigs invasion to the Kennedy assassination to the disappearance of Jimmy Hoffa. In 1964, a Senate subcommittee called Bufalino "one of the most ruthless and powerful leaders of the Mafia in the United States."

His influence stretched from interstate trucking and coal-mining unions, from Buffalo to Havana, with casinos, loansharking businesses, and powerful unions all under his control. Of course, singer Al Martino had claimed that Bufalino had stepped in to help him land the role of Johnny Fontane. And nearly fifty years after the release of *The Godfather*, Joe Pesci would be nominated for a Best Supporting Actor Oscar for playing Bufalino in Martin Scorsese's 2019 film, *The Irishman*, alongside Al Pacino, who scored a nomination in the same category for his portrayal of Jimmy Hoffa.

The door to Brando's trailer opened and in they came: "One was a rat-faced man with impeccably groomed hair and a camel's-hair coat, the other a less elegantly dressed man who was the size of an elephant and nearly tipped over the trailer when he stepped in," Brando would write. The overweight mobster, not even knowing how to pronounce Brando's first name, said, 'Hi, Marlo, you're a great actor.'"

Then Bufalino entered the trailer, as regally as a king, "complaining about how badly the US government was treating him."

Brando was at a loss for words, but it didn't matter. Bufalino "changed the subject, and in a raspy whisper said, 'The word's out you like calamari.'"

Their intel was good: spicy calamari lunches from Vincent's restaurant in Little Italy had become Brando's lunch routine.

By the time Brando stepped out onto Mott Street as Don Corleone, soon to be entrapped by his would-be assassins, wiseguys dotted the crowd, which was hanging out of tenement windows, staring through storefronts and restaurants and bars.

They crowded around to watch a street opera of bullets and blood. Again and again, Brando dutifully performed the scene, rushing across Mott Street from the fruit stand toward his hapless son Fredo to flee his pursuers, then collapsing in the street with the blasts of the gunfire. Each movement was followed by a round of thunderous applause, despite the assistant director's urgings to the crowd to wait until Coppola called "*Cut!*"

Brando played to the crowd, rising from the street and bowing and grandly sweeping his hand across the streetscape. "I think when he heard all those people applauding, it must have reminded him of when he was in the theater," said Nicholas Pileggi, the only reporter authorized to visit *The Godfather* set on that April day in 1971, for a *New York Times Magazine* story. Pileggi, who knew the area well, having covered Little Italy and its crimes and controversies since 1956, recognized two wiseguys watching the filming. They were dressed in sporty style, with open-collar shirts and man jewelry, and were reduced to "giddy little teenagers" by the action and excitement and the stars. Critiquing Brando's performance as a Mafia don, however, they judged it as inferior, saying they would have preferred Ernest Borgnine or Anthony Quinn in the title role and that Brando's old-fashioned clothing didn't reflect the flash of the dons of their day.

"A man of that stature would never wear a hat like that," one of the wiseguys said of Brando. "He makes the old man look like an iceman . . . He should have a diamond belt buckle . . . and a diamond ring and tie clasp."

They felt his two assassins were equally weak.

"They hold pieces like flowers," one of them complained.

Above it all, in a nearby Little Italy café, sat a bona fide Mob boss, Carlo Gambino, the sixty-eight-year-old smiling, low-key king of the New York Mob, the gangster on which Mario Puzo had, in part, based Don Corleone. He was a shrewd businessman and an undisputed leader who, like Don Corleone, detested drug dealing, both for moral concerns and for how easily the Feds could coerce testimony from lower-level gangsters picked up on drug charges. The almighty Gambino had risen up from teenage hit man in his hometown of Palermo, Sicily, to reign, unofficially, over the ruling council of Mafia dons that governed the Italian Mafia across America. He was smart and careful, despite numerous attempts by the authorities to nail him over his long career, he had served only twenty-two months in prison (in 1937).

He had arrived that day in Little Italy, the seventeenth day of *Godfather* filming, with five bodyguards and his brother Paul, dutifully holding court in a Grand Street café. There he sat, just like the godfather Brando was playing down the street, to listen to the needs of his constituency, "racketeers, dishonored fathers and deportable husbands . . . ushered before him, one at a time, from a waiting area in a restaurant across the street," Pileggi wrote in the *New York Times Magazine,* a coffee-shop court before "the final judge to people still willing to accept his decisions as law."

Pileggi knew where Gambino held court, and he knew that once his business was done, Gambino, tiny in size but gigantic in stature, couldn't resist walking around the corner to watch the filming along with everyone else.

"The real godfather watched *The Godfather*," said Pileggi.

The wiseguys Pileggi quoted who had been critiquing Brando's performance scattered with the news that Carlo Gambino was heading their way.

"Kee-risst! Shoo!" one said.

Yet Gambino's power was matched only by the benevolence of the man whose power was felt in every day of the filming: Every time a location appeared, every time a Teamster complied, every no that had turned to yes, that was the supreme power of Joe Colombo. When the father of a crew member was rushed to a hospital after suffering a heart attack, he languished alone and unrecognized—until a basket of flowers and fruit arrived with a card signed "Mr. and Mrs. Joseph Colombo, Sr."

"The patient had never met Colombo, had never seen him, but the presence of that basket changed his hospital life," reported Pileggi. Doctors and nurses began taking extra care of the patient.

Dieticians arranged for special foods, visiting hours were extended.

The patient, like the movie production, had been blessed. That welcome extended to shopkeepers, homeowners, restaurateurs, and neighbors on the streets of Little Italy. *The Godfather* had become "a home movie," Pileggi wrote.

By noon, the sun was high in the sky, and Coppola called "Cut" for the day because the overly sunny footage wouldn't match the earlier darker film. Thus ended the peculiar gathering of two of the most ferocious forces on Earth—the moviemakers and the Mob. They had been joined for a few hours, despite Puzo's warnings to keep the mobsters out.

They were in now. Yet it would be the actors who would get the drop on the gangsters, vampiring their essence and committing it forever to film, leaving them naked and exposed in what a vampire cannot abide: the sun.

In 1972, Michele "The Shark" Sindona, the shadowy Sicilian Mafia moneyman who had helped finance the purchase of part of the Paramount lot, would vent his frustrations over a dinner with Charlie Bluhdorn and the director Dino De Laurentiis.

"It's all your fault, with that stupid damned movie!" he bellowed, according to Nick Tosches's biography of Sindona, *Power on Earth*.

"Blame your friend here," Bluhdorn said, referring to Dino De Laurentiis. "He makes the damn things; I just own a company."

"Never mind him," Sindona said. "I know Dino a long time. He's bad enough. But you! *The Godfather* is yours, Charlie."

"I meant it," he later reflected. "Every Italian who is sent to jail in this country is going to get an extra five years on account of that stupid fairy tale."

LESS THAN A month into filming, Coppola was running further and further behind schedule. He couldn't even take the time to attend the Academy Awards—he had been nominated for cowriting the screenplay for *Patton*, which Coppola indeed won.

"Tense. Very tense," said Robert Duvall from on the set. "They're not all like this. It must come from the top. Pressure, money, bigness does it. Very tense atmosphere. This film should have been made with an all-unknown New York cast, low budget, and no big-studio pressures."

Coppola was under siege. Jack Ballard was "consumed with getting Francis out of there and saving the picture," remembered Gray Frederickson. In increasingly frequent, and increasingly negative, phone calls to Paramount's West Coast headquarters, Ballard would insist that the movie was unsavable, and, indeed, the studio was said to be interviewing other directors to take over. "Every time he sent in the dailies, he would send a list of where Francis had screwed up," Frederickson said of one of Coppola's supposed replacements, Aram Avakian, who was the film's editor.

The dailies from the early footage of Brando were particularly damning. It was the first chance for the executives to see whether their gamble on Brando would pay off. They settled into their seats in Paramount's screening rooms on both coasts. The lights dimmed and the footage flashed across the screen. It wasn't good: Brando mumbled; James Caan stumbled over a critical line.

In Los Angeles, Bob Evans and Peter Bart looked at each other. *Were they wearing sunglasses?* They weren't. Darkness was, of course, exactly what the Prince of Darkness, cinematographer Gordon Willis, was seeking—a film that he wanted to look "like a newspaper photograph in bad color."

But to the executives, it just looked bad. Adding to it all, Brando was petting a stray cat that had wandered onto the set and into the movie. The cat was purring—*loudly*—into the radio microphone attached to Brando's shirt. "I can't understand Brando, and I can't see the actors," Evans told Bart.

"Brando had the implant in his mouth and was mumbling, and you couldn't see the set," said Frederickson. "So they said, 'This is a disaster, this picture.'"

With Brando's mumbling, the lighting dim to the point of darkness, the footage was "judged unacceptable," wrote Ira Zuckerman. "The new rushes are also disappointing. Dramatic points are made sloppily, if at all. Brando underplays to excess; his mannerisms work against the character and he looks grotesque in close-ups. . . . The question on everyone's mind is whether the scene can be saved by editing."

All this bad news was being funneled through Ballard back to

Evans and Paramount. "They hated us," said Frederickson. They hated the $100,000 spent on Don Corleone's office set. They hated the $10,000 spent on the desk alone. "They were used to Rock Hudson and Doris Day Technicolor movies, but this was dark, gloomy, and they couldn't even see the set that they spent so much money on, or the ten-thousand-dollar desk."

Coppola felt lost. "They were convinced that this was the worst picture ever made, that I'm the worst director ever," he said. Add to this the exhaustion and the inability to sleep. After one screening, a physician arrived to examine the worn-out director—and prescribed the sleeping pills he had requested.

"If you wanted to go for that exaggerated dark look, why didn't you prepare us for it?" Peter Bart asked him. "I'm on your side. I would have prepared my colleagues."

"I'm fixing it," Coppola told Bart, adding, "Willis is an asshole."

"But he's your asshole," said Bart. "You hired him. Talk to people, Francis. This is not the time to brood; it's the time to lead."

"Things are getting better," Coppola pleaded with Bart.

Instead, they were getting worse.

"Coppola works listlessly and mechanically, requesting numerous takes of each shot for no apparent reason, as each one seems not different from the one preceding," wrote Zuckerman.

"He's very insecure," said one crew member. "He doesn't know what he wants or how to get it. What a lousy picture this is going to be!"

"I've worked on lots of features, but this one's a real bitch," said soundman Chris Newman. He compared *The Godfather* set to the professionalism of other films he'd worked on, films produced on schedule and under budget, with the crew getting a "nice bonus from the producer."

But on *The Godfather*, Newman said ominously, "I think there's some big trouble up ahead."

Duvall assumed that another director was already somewhere on the set, biding his time before Coppola got the ax, wrote Harlan Lebo in *The Godfather Legacy*. "In case Francis was fired," Duvall said, "he goes right in."

And Pacino was convinced he was going to be fired any day.

"Francis Ford Coppola . . . was the only one who wanted me in *The Godfather*," he said. "Nobody else wanted me. They simply wanted to fire me."

Then, at long last, a good omen arrived, in the form of a falling leaf. It happened during the wedding scene, in which Pacino and Keaton are first seen together. Pacino noticed that Marlon Brando was watching them.

Just then, a single leaf fell from a tree, landing on Pacino's shoulder.

"And I just took the leaf and I did something with it," he said. "Then Marlon came over to me at the end of the [scene], and he just leaned in and said, 'I like what you did with the leaf.'"

The glory was short-lived. "Where do we go from here?" Pacino and Keaton asked each other one evening after filming. They couldn't remember who asked who the question, because they were both very drunk after shooting a particularly difficult scene. "I mean, we got so loaded after that wedding scene, I can't tell you, we were on the floor," said Pacino. They told each other, "We're gone. It's over. This is the worst film ever made."

During one tense day, at Filmways Studio, Coppola took a bathroom break. While he was on the toilet, two crew members entered the men's room and started blasting the film, which Coppola overheard from the stall. He raised his feet off the floor so they would not recognize his shoes. "Where did they find this asshole director?" the crew member asked, adding that "the film was a load of shit and the asshole director didn't know what he's doing."

That sentiment was spreading among the cast and crew. "Marlon Brando was a has-been, Al Pacino was a nobody, Talia Shire was his sister," said a leading member of the production team. "You put it all together and you thought, *What the hell is Francis doing?*"

By then, Coppola was accustomed to the idea of being fired. "I was getting 'fired' every other week," he said. However, he kept right on directing, until those who wanted him gone became too many to count and could no longer be ignored.

"THE STUDIO WAS covered in rats," said Al Ruddy.

He was referring to the old Filmways Studio, which was actually covered in rats, which were eaten by the cat in Marlon Brando's arms in the opening scene of the movie.

But people were out to get Coppola.

Soon the insubordination had infested even those Coppola felt were his allies, including his editor, Aram Avakian, whom he believed to be among his closest advisors and friends.

Avakian was eminently qualified: thirteen years older than Coppola, educated at Horace Mann prep school, Yale University, and the Sorbonne in Paris. He had served Coppola well as editor on *You're a Big Boy Now* and had just finished directing *End of the Road*. Coppola admired and respected Avakian and "looked up to him almost as an older brother," he would later say. And when Avakian asked Coppola to put some of his friends on *The Godfather*, Coppola agreed, which was how he came to know and choose Gordon Willis as his cinematographer. "I made his producer [Steve Kesten] my assistant director, and put a number of members of his team in various jobs. Little did I know that they were angling to have me fired and have Aram step in."

The first signs of dissatisfaction from Avakian, however, came not to Francis, but to his wife, Eleanor. One night Francis and Eleanor went to dinner with Avakian. When Francis left the table to go to the restroom, Avakian told Eleanor, "You know this picture just won't come together." Avakian wore a worried expression, and Eleanor, considering Avakian someone with experience and authority, felt that he was giving her "words of wisdom," she would later say. "Like I should tell Francis to quit or something. He was very discouraging, and I kind of believed him."

But she believed in Francis Coppola more. "He was certainly very frustrated and discouraged at times, but he had a vision of how to make the film and a determination that didn't waver," she said.

Avakian was struggling to cut the scene of Michael killing Sollozzo and McCluskey in the restaurant, which would turn out to be brilliant, like some Cubist painting, but was wreaking havoc on Avakian. "To my astonishment, Ballard announced on a conference call that Coppola 'wasn't up to the job,' that he wanted to designate Aram Avakian, the editor, as the new director," wrote Peter Bart in *Infamous Players,* adding that Ruddy had warned Bart that Avakian "had been hovering around Ballard in a conspiratorial manner."

Then, in the middle of the night in mid-April 1971, one of the thirty-two home telephones rang in Woodland, the home of Robert Evans. It was the red phone, the phone reserved for crises. Evans was, as always, juggling everything at once: his wife, Ali MacGraw; their three-month-old son, Joshua; a dozen other Paramount movies in various stages of production—each with its own set of problems and emergencies. He had been in New York for the first week of filming, and now he was finally back home and was hoping to get some rest.

Then came word from New York: "Evans, we've got a problem . . . It doesn't cut together," he said he was told.

Meaning the scenes of *The Godfather* shot by Francis Coppola couldn't be edited into a cohesive whole.

"Put Aram on the phone," Evans demanded.

"Bob, shot by shot it looks great," Evans wrote that Avakian told him. "Kubrick couldn't get better performances, but it cuts together like a Chinese jigsaw puzzle. We spent two days in the restaurant with Pacino, Sterling Hayden, and Al Lettieri. Each take was great, but nothing matches. The fucker doesn't know what continuity means."

"Indigestion turned to heartburn," Evans added.

"Every day the fucker shoots, it's burning money," Avakian added, according to Evans.

"Put Jack Ballard on the phone," Evans said. And the studio

watchdog let it rip. "Ballard's critique of Coppola's incompetence was even more severe than Avakian's."

Gossip spreads quickly on a movie set. Having been told that there was a plot by members of his own production team to replace him as director, and install their own affiliates as their subordinates, Coppola had to act fast. He knew that studios rarely fire directors on weekdays, because they would lose at least two days in the transition from one director to another. "They'll always wait till the weekend," he said. Firing a director on a Friday gives the replacement director the weekend to take over.

"So I took a real chance," said Coppola.

He counted the conspirators: six of them, including Avakian.

"I fired them all on Wednesday," Coppola said. "They were like, 'What do you mean we're fired?' I said, 'I'm the director. Fired. You're out.'"

Later, Coppola would say, "I am convinced that Aram Avakian himself did not participate in the planned coup."

It was instead his first assistant director, Steve Kesten, and a few of his direct hires, who "planned to replace me with Aram. I admired Aram Avakian greatly and feel now that he was innocently affiliated with Kesten, who had been his producer on the film *End of the Road*."

As always, there is another side to the story, which Peter Bart would relate years later:

He was in Paramount's LA offices when he learned of what he called "the Jack Ballard-Steve Kesten plot." Their hopes of replacing Coppola had gone so far that "offers had actually been made by the dissidents [i.e., Kesten] to other directors, such as [Elia] Kazan, to replace Coppola."

Bart marched into Evans's office, interrupting a meeting.

"Do you know about the offers?" he asked.

Evans didn't, but when he was told, his pretty face turned red.

"He was furious, as was I," said Bart. "Both of us believed Francis' work was very strong, reflecting his growing confidence."

"Francis needs to hear from you," Bart told Evans. "Call him now, while we're together," which Evans did.

With the coup quelled, Coppola continued shooting.

He sent the dailies to the West Coast studio. Evans spent the weekend in the editing room watching every frame. He watched Brando's stunning metamorphosis into Don Corleone and he could actually understand some of the mumbling. He saw Al Pacino's transformation from the angel-faced college boy into a cold-blooded killer in Louis Italian American Restaurant.

It wasn't just good.

It was fucking great.

It was a level of genius that Robert Evans couldn't deny. He didn't love Francis Coppola, but he loved movies, and here was proof that there might be a great one in *The Godfather*. The footage of Michael Corleone killing Sollozzo and McCluskey in the restaurant saved Coppola's job—along with Al Pacino's—and, ultimately, the movie. "They kept me after that scene," Pacino said of the killing that was his rebirth. "They wanted me to assert myself, so [in killing two men] there's a kind of assertion."

Even Hurricane Charlie Bluhdorn was blown away.

"I saw the movie scenes, and it's terrific," Coppola remembered him saying. "I want you to come to dinner with me tonight."

Coppola brought along his father, Carmine, and Bluhdorn took them to his favorite New York restaurant, The Palm, for steak and lobster. And here the raging bull of a business magnate threw his arm around his beleaguered director, who had just become his golden boy, and said, "Ah, you're great."

"And from that moment on, he figures we're stuck with this loser," said Coppola. "Let's at least build him up a little. They knew what they had been doing to me. They had been punishing me. We had this big dinner at The Palm steakhouse and suddenly, Charlie Bluhdorn is my best friend."

At that dinner and other meetings to follow, Charlie Bluhdorn confided in Coppola about Michele Sindona, the Vatican bank scandal, and other dark forces. "Little by little, I learned these things from Charlie's lips," said Coppola. Of course, Bluhdorn never intended these conversations to be included in a movie. "However, more than a decade after his untimely death, when Paramount Pictures approached me to do what they deemed a part three, everything that Charlie had said presented itself in my mind."

When *The Godfather: Part III* premiered, on Christmas Day in 1990, audiences watched the result of those conversations, as the movie included Michael Corleone's dealings with a company owned in part by the Vatican whose name, International Immobiliare, was strikingly similar to the company in which Sindona was a major shareholder.

"I don't know why he told me this stuff," said Coppola. "I'm sure he didn't think (or want) I was going to put it in a *Godfather* movie!"

NOT LONG AFTER Coppola's dinner with Charlie Bluhdorn came another killing.

This time the victim would be Paulie Gatto, in retribution for selling out the don for death. Peter Clemenza was given the order to kill him. "Paulie had been his protégé," Puzo wrote in *The Godfather*. "He had helped Paulie 'make his bones'... Paulie had not only betrayed the Family, he had betrayed his *padrone,* Peter Clemenza. This lack of respect had to be repaid."

Clemenza instructed Gatto to pick him up at his home in his own car, "nothing hot," and they would run some errands, all the while planning his execution. "You had to be careful with Paulie, the man was like a rat, he could smell danger," read Puzo's description of him in his novel. "And now of course despite being so tough he must be shitting in his pants because the old man was still alive. He'd be as skittish as a donkey with ants up his ass."

"It's nice outside Clemenza's house," Coppola wrote in his notebook. "Then we get the neighborhood: I guess somewhere like in Long Island: kids playing on the street. Totally suburban. Clemenza, a good neighbor. Maybe he chides Paulie for not being extra careful when they back out the car because kids are playing there. Again: Family and Business."

First comes family, always family.

"Don't forget the cannoli," Clemenza's wife, played by Ardell Sheridan, soon to be Castellano's wife in real life, calls out from the stoop to her husband, after blowing him an affectionate kiss.

"Yeah, yeah, yeah, yeah," Clemenza says dismissively.

The actors took a limo out to a desolate stretch of Route 4 in New Jersey, where Coppola was waiting with the film crew and a dark 1940s Packard. Far in the distance, but unmistakably *there,* was the Statue of Liberty, its lamp lifted high beside the golden door to America. But its back was turned to the little gaggle of tempest-tossed Mob rats about to assassinate one of their own and leave his body on that weed-choked dead-end road.

"Johnny, you're going to hear three shots—*bang, bang, bang*—and you land on the steering wheel," Coppola told Johnny Martino, who played Paulie, as he sat in the driver's seat of the car.

Coppola put a hat on Martino's head and told him that when he called "Action," to pull the string attached to the hat, which would flip it off his head and ignite a squib full of blood that would run down the side of his face.

"Drink some of the red stuff, and let it ooze out of your mouth," Coppola added.

Then, someone slid into the back seat. "An older gentleman with a twenty-two-caliber rifle," said Martino.

"What are you doing?" Martino asked the stranger.

"I'm going to put three bullet holes past your head through the windshield," the man told him.

"What?"

The man told him not to worry: he was a marksman, most recently handling the ballistics on *Bonnie and Clyde.* The bullets would miss his head by at least four or five inches.

Martino called for Coppola.

"Johnny, what's going on?" Coppola asked.

"The guy with the rifle," said Martino.

"Don't worry," Coppola assured him. "He's really good."

"Action!"

It all went like clockwork. Castellano as Clemenza stepping out of the car to take a leak. The prop pistol held by Rocco, the hit man, pointed at Gatto's skull from the back seat. The three shots from the marksman resounding loud and blasting through the windshield. Clemenza momentarily looking up from his business to turn his head slightly. Gatto slumped over the wheel, dead.

Clemenza zips up his pants and returns to the car. And then Richard Castellano, with a decade of stage and screen experience under his big belt, says the line that Coppola had written for him in the script:

"Leave the gun."

The gun, along with the corpse of Gatto, would be left behind as a warning sign to those who had double-crossed the Corleones—or might try to cross them in the future. "The Don's justice is inevitable and complete," wrote Coppola in his notebook. The two murderers prepare to leave the scene of the crime.

Then, without prompting from Puzo's novel or Coppola's script, Castellano remembers the command his wife had given him at home, and utters the ad-lib that would soon become famous:

"Take the cannoli."

From the back seat of the car, Rocco, Clemenza's "trouble-shooter," retrieves a pristine little white bakery box, which Clemenza grabs by the strings in his fat hands.

There was no applause, not even a word of recognition on the set.

Perhaps nobody realized what had occurred until later: that Richard Castellano had just ad-libbed what would become one of the most quoted movie lines of all time:

"Leave the gun. Take the cannoli."

It was the essence of everything: the wife, the kids, the fathers, the mothers, the kitchens, the families, and the food, always the food, and the extremes to which men had to go to put that food on the table. It was about the gun, yes, but it was more about the cannoli. It was about the statue in the distance with its back to the murder scene. It was about the country that had turned its back on these men and their community, for whom only the Godfather could offer justice and jobs and dignity.

Above all, it was about the family.

"There is one reason that movie is successful and one reason only," Al Ruddy observed decades later. "It may be the greatest family movie ever made."

To that point, Mario Puzo's son Anthony wrote of his father, "He believed that nobody had more family values than Italians. That's why they were so good at being in the Mafia. What is *The Godfather*, he often said, but a heartwarming story about a family with great, solid family values?"

12

BADA BING!

It was an unlikely place to find the cast of a major motion picture: a four-bedroom redbrick suburban home in Fort Lee, New Jersey. But here, the cast of *The Godfather* would immerse itself in the life of a family that could have sprung straight from Mario Puzo's pages for an evening of inspiration. Only this wasn't fiction. It was the home of a reputed Genovese crime family capo, Pasquale "Patsy Ryan" Eboli, and he had invited the cast of *The Godfather* to his home for a home-cooked meal.

Producer Al Ruddy, who had become the conduit between the moviemakers and the Mob, had visited the Eboli home before. And Al Pacino had come to the Eboli house one night in a cab—so broke that the family had to pay his cab fare—for a dinner of linguine with clam sauce and lessons on how to handle a pistol.

Tonight's dinner had been arranged by Al Lettieri, the actor who had landed the part of Virgil "the Turk" Sollozzo. He was the brother of Patsy Eboli's wife, Jean.

"How about if I bring some of the cast over for a nice dinner?" Lettieri asked.

Eboli said sure; after all, his brother, Thomas "Tommy Ryan" Eboli, who rose from overseeing the West Side Manhattan docks to become the acting head of the Genovese family after Vito Genovese was imprisoned, had granted permission for Lettieri to get involved with the film in the first place. Perhaps Patsy Eboli thought it best not to be at home that night—as always, the Feds were watching the house around the clock in a car parked down the street. His wife had prepared some of her famous Italian specialties, set the table, stocked the bar, and awaited the arrival of the movie stars.

The doorbell rang at 7:00 p.m., and there they were: Marlon Brando, James Caan, Morgana King (the jazz singer suggested by Lettieri to play Don Corleone's wife), Gianni Russo, Al Lettieri, and Al Ruddy. They all went downstairs into the family room, where the table was set beside the pool table and the bar. Music played, drinks were served, and the party began.

The dinner that Jean Eboli prepared was magnificent. Her daughter Gio shuttled between the kitchen and the family room, serving food and wine as the cast became acquainted with the Eboli family. Brando dug into the eggplant parmigiana with such relish that olive oil was soon dripping down his chin. "Jean, this is the best eggplant I've ever eaten!" he exclaimed to his host. James Caan danced with Gio, while everyone reveled in the real-life world of the fantasy they were portraying on-screen.

For that evening, the Ebolis' home was all light and laughter, but soon it would turn dark and bloody. A year after the dinner, at 1:00 a.m. on July 16, 1972, Tommy Eboli would be found dead on a Brooklyn street, having been struck by five bullets to the head and neck. His brother Patsy's career would come to an even more mysterious end in 1976, when he disappeared, leaving behind a bill for long-term parking at Kennedy Airport, where his Cadillac was found abandoned with the keys in the glove compartment.

Now, as the evening was coming to a close, Brando was sitting on the family-room steps when James Caan came to sit beside him. By now, what Caan would call a "warm feeling" had washed over them from the wine, the food, and the Eboli family's hospitality.

"Jimmy, if you could have one wish, one thing that you really want in life, what would that be?" Brando asked in his signature rasp.

"Jesus, let me think," said Caan, who at that moment, sitting in Patsy Eboli's home with a leading role in a Paramount film, seemed to have everything—and nothing.

"I guess, to be in love," he said.

Brando stared at his costar and smiled.

"Yeah, me too," he said, and then added, "Just don't tell my wife."

THEY WERE IN love, all right, with the Mob.

They were in love with their actions, their backgrounds, their crimes, their families and, most of all, their *moves*. And no one loved them more than the Jewish American actor who would embody an Italian American mobster arguably most authentically of them all.

James Caan as the strutting, bullheaded firecracker of a son Sonny Corleone.

"*What* fucking transformation?" he would later ask of the role for which he would be paid $35,000 and forever be identified. "Obviously, I grew up in the neighborhood."

The neighborhood was Sunnyside, Queens, and he was a rarity: the son of a meat merchant who became a famous actor. "Not too many dancers, singers, and actors come from my neighborhood," said Caan. "But a lot of bartenders and mailmen and thieves."

From here, he would adopt the strut and the bravado, studying—and copying—the way he'd seen gangsters always touching themselves as if they were gods touching gold. "They've got incredible moves," Caan told the *New York Times*. "I watched them with each other and with their girls and wives. It's incredible how affectionate they are to each other. There's tremendous interplay. They toast each other—'cent'anni,' 'salute a nostra'—all this marvelous old world stuff from guys who were born here and don't even speak Italian."

After landing the part of Sonny, Caan went deeper into character development, hanging out with the boys ("Pistol Petes," he called them) at the Copacabana—the legendary New York nightclub where Joe Gallo would spend his last hours celebrating his birthday before he was gunned down outside Umbertos Clam House—or wherever else wiseguys could be found. Caan built the character of Sonny from the ground up. He bought a pair of two-toned ten-dollar shoes off the rack in a used-clothing store, so tight that they hurt, which gave Sonny his strutting, cocky, lady-killer gait, as he hauled around, as Puzo wrote, a heart that "was admitted to be as big as his organ."

He returned to the old neighborhood in Queens, and hung out with those he had long known, some connected, others not. Caan reveled in embedding himself in his source material. "Jimmy Caan," marveled Robert Duvall, "he hangs out with the mafioso guys on the East Coast and the rodeo cowboys on the West."

"I had some friends," Caan would admit. "I don't condone crime, and I don't know of any dishonorable things that they did. But I know they weren't shoemakers or bankers or whatever."

He was soon in the presence of Mob royalty, including Carmine "the Snake" Persico, the Colombo family capo who earned his nickname (which he apparently hated) for double-crossing the Gallos. Persico famously represented himself in the trial that saw him sent away for 139 years, for conspiracy to commit murder, racketeering, and running a criminal enterprise—though authorities alleged that he still managed to wield tremendous power even from inside federal prison.

"I knew a couple of guys, not as well as I came to know them during the making of *The Godfather*," said Caan.

"I didn't learn from Carmine," Caan would say before Persico's death, in 2019. "I mean, he'd be a great character to learn from, but he's away. If he comes back as a frog, he has to go back in again."

He had someone else to rely upon, "one of my dearest friends," he said. "A guy named Andrew Russo."

He was referring to Andrew "Mush" Russo, the first cousin of Carmine Persico who went on to serve as street boss of the Colombo family, with whom Caan was as close as family.

"Just really just loving, loving people that would do anything for me and I for them," Caan said. "And I went to his daughter's wedding. And, oh, my God, that picture's in the paper like I was Sonny Corleone. I said, what the hell. I don't know what Andrew did or didn't do. But the *Times* declared him as like 'the big boss.' I don't know. All I know is that if I'm hurt or I'm sick, they're the first to call and vice-versa. And we've been close for all these years. I've never been asked to do anything."

Soon, Caan was hanging around real gangsters so often that some undercover agents who didn't recognize Caan as an actor thought "he was just another rising young button in the Mob," Nicholas Pileggi wrote in the *New York Times*.

He had their language and mannerisms all down cold. "One guy always talked to everybody like you were across the room from him—even when he was sitting beside you," he recalled in Peter Cowie's *The Godfather Book*. "I used him as a model."

Used him so convincingly, and totally, that Caan sometimes lost himself in the role. When he went home for dinner with his parents, he would say, "Hey, Ma, pass the fucking salt," he said. After which he would apologize. "Holy Jesus, what did I say? I'm *sorry!*"

The voice and the movements came easy. "You can watch and fake that," he told Pileggi. "But their language, that's something else.... They have a street language all their own. It's not Italian, certainly, and it's not English. One guy, to indicate to another that someone they both knew had been killed, raised his hands in front of him, fixed his fingers like guns and pointed them to the ground. 'Baba da BOOM!' he said, and they all laughed."

Into the memory bank went "Baba da BOOM," to be withdrawn later, big-time.

In the beginning, though, the great James Caan, rising star, was stuck.

It was the pivotal scene in the Genco Olive Oil Company. "Location at 128 Mott Street, in the heart of Little Italy," wrote Ira Zuckerman. "With its dark mahogany walls and office partitions, it's marvelously authentic looking." But behind the physical authenticity, the production was in disarray, "falling behind at an average of two days a week. It is the general opinion of the crew that Coppola is overcovering scenes by shooting many more takes than is necessary," Zuckerman noted.

One line came to represent at least some of the problems.

Caan was stuck on the scene where Sonny interrupts the don during the meeting about going into the drug business with Sollozzo, the line that would launch all to follow—the shooting of the don, the killing of Sollozzo and McCluskey, the exile of Michael to Sicily—and he had played it so flat that reshoots were required. "Caan's only line, a very important one, lacks definition and fails in the intended effect in each of the several takes that are shown," Zuckerman wrote.

The line came after Don Corleone declines Sollozzo's offer to join him and the other families in the drug business, which the don says quietly and kindly, only to have his hotheaded son blurt out, "Oh, are you tellin' me that the Tattaglias guarantee our investment?"

The line, the spark that would light the fuse for all that followed, required an explosive outburst.

"I was just kind of lost," Caan said. "I just really didn't have anything to grab onto."

Day after day, he tried to come up with a solution. One night, staring at himself in a mirror, it hit him. "I was shaving to go to dinner or something, and for some reason I started thinking of Don Rickles [the comedian famous for rapid-fire "insult comedy"]. Because I knew Rickles. Somebody was watching over me and gave me this thing: being Rickles, kind of say-anything, do-anything."

The next morning he had Sonny's personality down cold. "Aw, are you telling me that the Tattaglias guarantee our investment?" he cracked, with a rapid-fire, Don-Rickles-meets-the-Mob bravado that elevated his character to a whole new level.

"I busted everybody's balls from there on in," Caan said. "Ruddy, I told him, 'You got enough money. Get that fuckin' suit cleaned. You've been in the same sweater for the last week!'"

Not long after that, in a scene after his movie father had been gunned down in a hit organized by Sollozzo, a phrase arrived from Caan's subconscious. He was on the set that had been built for Don

Corleone's dark-wood, masculine study, which Dean Tavoularis had designed to be a near-holy sanctum. With the don near death, his heir apparent, Sonny, stalks the room like a caged tiger as he and those around him debate their first steps in retribution.

"They want to have a meeting with me, right?" says Michael, who then outlines a plan: set the meeting with Sollozzo and McCluskey. "Now we insist it's a public place—a bar, a restaurant—someplace where there's people, so I'll feel safe."

They'd find a way to plant a weapon at the meeting place, knowing that he'd be searched when he arrived . . .

"Then I'll kill them both," says Michael.

To which Sonny struts over to his little brother, with the cane Pacino had been using after tearing his ligament, and says, as a joke that showed his mocking disbelief upon hearing his kid brother say he not only intended to get involved in the family business but to gun down two men in cold blood:

"What do you think this is, the army, where you shoot 'em a mile away? You gotta get up close, like this—*bada-bing!* You blow their brains all over your nice Ivy League suit."

Bada-bing.

It was an ad-lib sent straight from improv heaven and would quickly become a mantra for mobsters and aspiring mobsters, so much that Coppola would say, "Jimmy should have royalty on that 'bada-bing,' whether or not he picked it up from the guys he was hanging out with."

Later, it would serve as the name of Tony Soprano's strip club in *The Sopranos.* "'*Bada-bing? Bada-boom?*' I said that, didn't I? Or did I just say '*bada-bing*'?" Caan said. "It just came out of my mouth—I don't know from where."

As for subsequent scenes, well, after his breakthrough, Caan felt free. To improvise. To explode. To have Sonny come strutting out of his sister Connie's wedding and confront the actors playing FBI or other agents. To rip the camera from an interloping photographer and throw it smashing on the ground. "None of that was scripted," he said. "When I grabbed that poor extra as he took the picture—the guy must have had a heart attack. Then I remembered my neighborhood, where guys could do anything, as long as they paid for it afterwards, like they apologized. I broke some expensive big, old camera, threw that on the ground. I had this guy choked. Luckily, Richie [Castellano, as Clemenza] grabbed me. And then I took out a twenty and threw it on the ground and walked off. Francis just loved it. I'd just sprung a leak, you know?"

ALL WAS MERE prelude to the bloody scene where Caan as Sonny would beat up Gianni Russo as Carlo, as retribution for Carlo's brutal belt whipping of Connie.

Russo was the wild card in the cast: an overnight actor who had won a leading role, which he would have to fight to keep, from his first day at rehearsal in Patsy's restaurant.

As the newcomer amid professionals, Russo says he was told not to approach or have eye contact with Brando. So he did his best to keep his distance throughout the rehearsal. Then came the break. Russo was still sitting at the table in Patsy's restaurant and the great Marlon Brando approached *him*.

"You gotta big movie coming out?" Brando asked.

"No," Russo replied.

"Well, you're a TV actor?"

Russo said no.

"Well, you're not on Broadway, I know everybody on Broadway."

"I said 'You're right again. What's this, a quiz show?'"

"He said, 'Who'd you study with?'"

"I said, 'Study what? What are you talking about? This is my first movie.'"

"And with this, he calls Coppola over and he says, 'Francis, this guy's playing my son-in-law, Carlo.' And Francis rather reluctantly says, 'Yeah.' *Like, I know.* But he had nothing to do with casting me. He was told I would play Carlo. Brando says, 'Francis, he marries my daughter, he undermines my family, he gets my son, Sonny, killed . . .'"

Alarm bells sounded in Gianni Russo's brain.

"I'm listening to Brando and I'm thinking, *Wait a minute. This guy's trying to get me fired.*

"Not knowing protocol, I didn't know I couldn't dismiss the director," said Russo.

"I said, 'Francis, can you go over there a minute?' And he walked away. Now the whole room went quiet. You could hear a pin drop. And I put my arm around Brando and I walked him in the back room. I didn't want to embarrass him. And I'm face-to-face with him; our noses were almost touching, and I said, 'Mr. Brando, all due respect. I know who you are. Don't fuck this up for me, do you hear me?'"

Russo was rolling now, his anger boiling up from his shoes.

"If you screw this up for me, and I get fired, and I lose this part, I will suck on your heart, and you will bleed out right here."

"He stepped back for minute, looked at me, and said, 'That was beautiful. You could do this part.'"

"He thought I was acting," said Russo. "But I meant it."

Now, he prepared to be beaten to a pulp by James Caan's ferocious Sonny Corleone.

A few nights before the scene was to be filmed, the two actors collided in a New York City nightclub called Jilly's, at least as it was told by Russo, who claimed connections to the Mob that went even deeper than Caan's. "I was at the packed bar with wiseguys Tommy Bilotti and Boozy DeCicco, having a few drinks," Russo would write in his 2019 memoir, *Hollywood Godfather*, referring to two soldiers in the Gambino crime family. "Unbeknownst to me, Caan was in the back room with Carmine Persico, underboss of the Colombo crime family."

According to Russo, a conflict arose involving the two *Godfather* actors and the mobsters that night. It ended with Russo convinced that Caan had it out for him, which Caan would deny.

Shortly after that, the two men were scheduled to square off in the famously brutal street beating.

"Sonny's car pulls up; and Sonny beats the hell out of Carlo in front of everyone," Coppola wrote in his *Godfather Notebook*. "And says he'll kill him if he ever touches his sister again. A Tattaglia bagman makes a call, informing that Sonny is in town and can be hit. . . . The sheer violence of Sonny's beating; and helplessness of Carlo, clinging to the iron railing. Merciless. Like witnessing a slaughter."

It was to be filmed on Pleasant Avenue in East Harlem, a six-block historic Italian enclave that "was so protected by the Mob that residents did not lock their doors . . . merchandise would regularly fall off the backs of trucks . . . ," according to the *New York Times*. "There were the late-night poker games in Charlie Ding-Ding's candy store, on 118th Street and Pleasant . . . And there was Eddie the Butcher, whose shop on 119th Street and Pleasant Avenue was rumored to be a front for illicit activity. Locals still joke that he did not sell a pork chop in 40 years, and that the blood stains on his apron never changed."

Caan had rehearsed the scene with the film's veteran stunt coordinator Paul Baxley. Russo believed it would be a staged Hollywood beating. Just fists and feet and beating and kicking. All of which could be easily faked. After all, Coppola was pushing for violence that at least *looked* real. "PITFALLS," he wrote in his scene notes. "If the characters are too Guys and Dollsy . . . If Sonny's appearance doesn't surprise and frighten us."

If the audience didn't believe "that he's going to kill Carlo."

Caan needed to draw fake blood, wreck fake havoc, and Carlo had to seem to cling to life by the thinnest of threads, because he would, after the beating, set up his tormentor, the powerful Sonny Corleone. For death.

If any of this fell flat, or seemed fake, the scene would be a failure.

At which point Sonny took over, and James Caan faded into the background. He and the stunt coordinator drove over to Pleasant Avenue on a Saturday and mapped out the scene.

"You got a broom handle?" Caan asked the prop master.

What?

"You know those big, industrial brooms?" Caan asked. "Can you saw off the end of that handle? It's called an attitude adjuster."

"Where's that in the script?" the prop master asked.

"Nowhere," said Caan.

"How are you going to use it?"

"I said, 'I don't know. Just put it in my car.'"

"Francis never knew it was coming," said Caan. "And I didn't plan it. We rehearsed the scene once or twice, and there was that bat. And I came out. And I threw it at him. Poor Gianni. Francis said, 'That's great. But you missed him by a mile.' I said, 'Francis, I'll knock him out if I hit him.'"

On cue, Caan came raging out of the car with the broom handle, which Russo was seeing for the first time. Russo took off running and Caan chucked the club at him, which Russo would later write landed a blow squarely to the back of his head.

"Cut!" Coppola shouted.

"I was cut, but not badly," wrote Russo.

"Hey, Jimmy," Russo said, "what the fuck?"

"I decided to improvise," Caan said. "Sorry I hit you."

"I smelled a rat," wrote Russo.

The crew reset and filming commenced again. Take after take, Caan threw the sawed-off broom handle at Russo, but on these subsequent times he missed. He threw Russo over the railing, just as they rehearsed. ("I was padded just in case I took a bad fall," wrote Russo.) Then Caan picked up a heavy garbage can lid and slammed it down on Russo, hitting him in his "right elbow, with everything he had, chipping a bone," Russo wrote. He then crawled to the gutter, where he was drenched by an open fire hydrant. The script called for him to be fake-kicked in the chest. "He was supposed to kick me with the top of his foot; he used his toe," wrote Russo.

"He put enough power behind it to break two of my ribs," he continued.

"You touch my sister again, I'll kill you," Sonny pants, before delivering one final kick and striding away.

Caan's take was different: "I went to work with the garbage can . . . I kicked him up to the fire hydrant," he said. "They had to come up with a few close-ups. I said, 'I'm not going to touch you, just react.' He was a little nervous. He said, 'You can't hit me in the stomach as hard as you want, I know karate.' I hit him in the belly. He didn't get hurt.

"I was in pretty good shape. I was really locked in and so focused."

Then "the spell broke," and he looked skyward.

"And when I looked up, guys were hanging off or sitting on the roofs of these three-, four-story buildings," Caan said. "A lot of my friends—Andrew Russo, Junior Persico—they were all there. And when I looked up, they did this make-believe applause, banging their forefingers against their palms. Wonderful, wonderful."

Russo said he went home a wreck.

"It took me a few days to recover from the thrashing," he wrote.

13

"HE LOOKED LIKE HE COULD EAT RAW MEAT"

Now came the wedding scene, which would show at the very beginning of the movie that the Mob was more than brute force, more than bloody fights that left men near death or dead.

"I always wanted to use the Mafia as a metaphor for America," Francis Ford Coppola told Stephen Farber in a 1972 interview for the British monthly *Sight & Sound*. "If you look at the film, you see that it's focused that way."

He would show this dramatically in the wedding scene. He would assemble the stage for those in need of Don Corleone's boundless benevolence. It would come immediately after Bonasera opens the movie with the line "I believe in America," on the only day when the Godfather could not refuse any request from his needy constituency: the day of his daughter's wedding.

From that point forward, Coppola would show how the Mafia and America were intertwined. "Both the Mafia and America have roots in Europe," he said. "Both the Mafia and America feel they are benevolent organizations. Both the Mafia and America have their hands stained with blood from what it is necessary to do to protect their power and interests. Both are totally capitalistic phenomena and basically have a profit motive."

But there was one main difference, Coppola said. "I feel that

America does not take care of its people. America misuses and short-changes its people; we look to our country as our protector, and it's fooling us, it's lying to us."

In the early 1970s, with Nixon in the White House and the Vietnam War and the growing distrust in the government, Mario Puzo's novel had struck a deep chord, and Coppola felt he knew why. "People love to read about an organization that's really going to take care of us. When the courts fail you and the whole American system fails you, you can go to the Old Man, Don Corleone, and say, 'Look what they did to me,' and you get justice."

The wedding would show the don's immense power, introduce the film's main characters, and define Italian American traditions for the audience. "The first thing that interested me when I read it was the many levels going on at once," Coppola wrote in his extremely detailed wedding-scene outline, this one running nine single-spaced pages, in his *Godfather Notebook*. "Michael and Kay, the son who is more of an outsider on the edge of the party with his American Girlfriend. . . . At the same time Sonny is having a hot, unspoken thing going on with the Maid-of-Honor, Lucy, and knowing where his wife and children are at all times is important.

"There are many, many guests—perhaps three or even four hundred, the bigger the better for this first scene . . . They have brought their children with them . . . one fourth of the number should be children of all ages, even infants. Italian people do not leave their children at home . . . Even the children drink wine."

Lucy's dress, while she makes love to Sonny against a bedroom door, should be "practically over her head" . . . Johnny Fontane's grand entrance and the "fuss they all make over him" should make clear "that Johnny is a 'big celebrity'" . . . And throughout it all, with the wedding party raging, Don Corleone listens to the needs of his constituency and grants the favors required of him on this special day.

"The scene with Bonasera is good and very important," Coppola wrote. "It further defines the Don's power, and puts forth the essence of what it is the Don refers to as 'friendship' i.e. a pledge of loyalty . . . It is very important that after Bonasera gives his pledge, that we understand he feels he is now under a grave and frightening obligation to the Godfather."

He listed "TEXTURES" for the wedding scene: "Fat older man dancing with a ten year old girl in a confirmation dress. Her little shoes on his big ones," was only one of these. He defined what he called "THE CORE" ("Introduce the Don, and gradually reveal the breadth of his power, make clear his relationship to Michael . . . Establish the fusion of family and business. Introduce the main characters and subplots of the film").

He noted potential "PITFALLS" ("Clichés, Italians who-a, talka lika-dis; failure to make a convincing setting. People must feel that they are seeing a real thing, with hundreds and hundreds of interesting specifics").

"I am going to immerse the audience in the wedding and kind of make it a real experience," as Coppola had told his artistic team, and the experience would be populated by many members of the very community that served the real Don Corleones.

Even the photographer for the wedding, whose camera would be confiscated by a fellow don, was Joe LaBella, the photographer for Joe Colombo's Italian American Civil Rights League. "He's not a Mob guy; he's my photographer," Joe Colombo told New York casting director Lou DiGiaimo after calling to request that LaBella be cast in the film. And in front of the movie cameras, the actors who had fought so hard against thousands of competitors to win their roles, now assembled for the mammoth wedding at the end of a cul-de-sac on Longfellow Avenue, whose massive fake walls gave the appearance of a fortified compound for the Corleone family.

Securing the estate had not been easy. The location they had chosen required the use of several different houses to create the illusion of the compound that the script called for.

Now, at long last, they had the all-important Staten Island compound. Well, almost had it. Some of the homeowners wanted a little more than a leaky roof repair. "There was one holdout, one guy out of six who wouldn't give us the place," remembered Al Ruddy. Again, like a scene from the movie, Ruddy went to Joe Colombo who had told him, "Anything you need, you come to me. Free of charge."

"Give me his number, I'll call him now," said Colombo, who arranged a meeting with the reluctant homeowner in a local diner. Ruddy and Gray Frederickson walked in to find Colombo with his bodyguard stationed nearby, sitting in a booth with the homeowner. Ruddy was "desperate," he said, because the single holdout could force them to find another location. He promised the homeowner not to damage a blade of grass, and then, when that wasn't enough, he added, "I will give you an additional $25,000 for your son's education."

"Look, Mr. Ruddy," the homeowner responded. "I worked and saved my whole life to buy this house. And I don't like what you are going to do with it. It is not the home of a gangster."

Ruddy looked over at Colombo, who snapped, "Give me the pen."

"Sign the thing," Colombo told the homeowner according to Ruddy, adding, "It's good for our people."

"The guy started shaking," Ruddy remembered. "I felt guilty, like a heavy. The pen almost went through the paper, he pressed so hard."

Now, the wedding is in full swing: hundreds of extras bussed in from Manhattan, and others from across America, the winners of charity events that had auctioned off *Godfather* wedding invitations from Paramount. Authentic food and real wine are served. Dance instructors teach Italian dances. The bridesmaids wear puffy pink dresses and floppy sunhats, all sitting under a massive striped tent. Guests take turns singing traditional Italian songs on a makeshift stage, as the raucous crowds cheer them on. Even Don Corleone's wife—Morgana King in her film debut as Carmela Corleone—is called up on the bandstand, where she sings the comical Neapolitan tarantella "C'è la Luna Mezzo Mare" ("There Is a Moon in the Middle of the Sea"). She turns the stage over to an old man in a double-breasted suit who continues the song, this time in a sexually animated fashion, bringing down the house at the wedding and in the movie theater.

Everyone is dancing, even the big and drunken Clemenza who,

with his tie undone, dances until he is panting and slaking his thirst with homemade wine, which he guzzles straight from a big pitcher, "blowing like a whale as he gulped down the wine," as Puzo wrote.

At one point, Coppola hovered over the scene in a helicopter for a copter shot, only to have the aerial create "a wind 'vortex' within the 'prop' walls so that everything that wasn't nailed down began to lift skyward," Ardell Sheridan-Castellano, who played Mrs. Clemenza, later wrote in her 2002 book, *Divine Intervention and a Dash of Magic*. "Very soon it became a frightening scene out of *The Wizard of Oz*."

Coppola made "a few more passes by helicopter," Sheridan-Castellano added. "Soon those people who were at this point 'drunk as skunks' started waving at the helicopter and began shouting, 'Hi, Francis!'"

Behind the scenes, Gianni Russo, whose character, Carlo, is about to be married to Connie Corleone, found a way to capitalize on, well, everything: the cake, the wine, the soda pop. "I don't know if Paramount knows this," Russo said years later. "I think they paid like $7 a case for the soda and we were buying it for $1.17 a case."

He and others pocketed the difference. He had an off-the-books arrangement with a local baker, who agreed to provide several enormous cakes for free in exchange for publicity—leaving Russo and others to "chop up" the $1,500 that Paramount paid for wedding cakes, he said.

All of this would be dwarfed by the shadow of the "'mysterious' well-dressed gentleman" who showed up on the set of the wedding.

When Don Corleone, his business done, finally steps out to dance with his daughter, his guests were soon in the presence of a future Mob boss: "One could easily take him for a Paramount executive," wrote Sheridan-Castellano, which would turn out to be the biggest surprise of all.

"He's here for me," Richard Castellano said of the stranger at the wedding, perhaps still sweaty and breathless from his wedding dance, when an assistant director moved in to ask the man who he was and what he was doing there.

Castellano and the mysterious man spoke in whispers, after which Castellano told his future wife, Ardell, to forget about the man on the set. "He's no one you should know," he said. "Got it?"

She got it, because she claimed to already know something that most likely no one else on the set that day knew:

That Castellano's stellar performance of Clemenza was not merely due to his experience as an actor; it was his birthright.

His father, Philip Castellano, was a Sicilian, born in the old country, arriving in New York to marry an Italian American and live the American Dream. He was a delegate to the paving and road building union of New York. "We grew up in the Bronx," said Castellano's sister Diann Zecca. All was good until the Depression, when "things went bad for my father, and we ended up in Hell's Kitchen, which was a shock. You had to fend for yourself and learn life. Richard was exposed to that, but Richard was never an aggressive person."

He was thin and fit until he went to a doctor's office for what was supposed to be a routine shot when he was in his twenties, and was injected with an infected needle, which left him with hepatitis. "He started gaining weight," said his sister, weight that he couldn't lose. "After that he was never the same. He kept getting one thing [illnesses] after the other . . . When he told me he wanted to be an actor, I thought, *He's gotta be kidding.*"

He wasn't. He went from stage to screen, and in 1971, was nominated for an Academy Award for Best Supporting Actor for *Lovers and Other Strangers*, so entrancing audiences that his sister would say that when she saw him on stage or screen, "I forgot he was my brother."

In real life, according to his wife, he had a dark secret, which he confided to very few.

"When Richard told me that he too was being considered to play a role in *The Godfather*, I was somewhat concerned," Sheridan-Castellano would later write. "You see, I knew something about

Richard S. Castellano that no one else knew, not even his immediate family. You see, Richard had been 'Blood Born' into the 'real' Mafia."

He hadn't actually joined "the Family" to engage in the "Family Business," she added, but he nonetheless "carried the profound loyalty and ethical code that was the original Mafia."

Castellano had been given permission "to walk away from the Family."

But that permission came with a caveat: "that he would never again have any contact (in any way) with 'Family Members.' Why? As Richard explained it, if he had contact he might hear or see something that he shouldn't. It was quite possible that as a result of such exposure he might be forced into a position of having to give 'testimony' at someone's trial."

Now, he had a leading role in the movie that would come to define the Mob.

"I couldn't resist asking, 'Will the Family object to your being in *The Godfather*?'" asked Sheridan-Castellano, to which Castellano smiled.

"If they want me, they know where to find me," he said.

They had found him, and were checking on him. On the set of the movie. In the wedding scene where Castellano as the capo Clemenza played a pivotal part.

Who was the strange man that Richard Castellano told his future wife to forget about?

"It wasn't until December of 1985 when the news came across the television that Paul Castellano had been murdered outside of Sparks Steak House that I was able to turn and ask Richard the question I had posed many years earlier," wrote Sheridan-Castellano, who knew what she called "the rules," forbidding talking about "family members" while they were still alive. "He was the man who came to visit on the set of *The Godfather*, wasn't he?"

"Yes," Castellano finally admitted. "He was my uncle."

Which would mean that the actor playing Clemenza was a blood relative to the future head of the Gambino crime family, a man known as the "Howard Hughes of the Mob."

In 1981, five years after succeeding Gambino as boss of the family, Paul Castellano would build a giant compound for himself out on Staten Island. Rarely venturing back into Manhattan, on one rare occasion that he did—for a steak at Sparks—he was gunned down by four assassins in an unauthorized hit commissioned by a Gambino capo, John Gotti.

Art was imitating life . . . and life imitating art.

But again, what is true and what is false isn't certain.

"Richard had absolutely no connection to the Mob," insisted Diann Zecca. What her late sister-in-law, Sheridan-Castellano, wrote in her book was "total exaggeration," she added, possibly invented for publicity. "To bring drama to it." *What could be better than a real mobster with a leading role in* The Godfather? "Because our name is Castellano. We're no relation [to the Mob Castellano]. Richard was a very mild-mannered person, as was my father. If he were connected, we would have lived a much better life."

Before Sheridan-Castellano died, in 2014, Castellano's sister tried to set her straight.

"Ardell said to me, 'You just don't know,'" said Zecca, as if the omertà of the Mob extended to Richard Castellano's family.

"It made me laugh," said Zecca. "She had that way of exaggerating things and taking over . . ."

Other central characters would also be introduced at the wedding: first and foremost, Michael Corleone, embodied by Al Pacino, now no longer the scruffy Broadway actor, but a clean-cut soldier with a killer haircut that almost cost a barber his life. "When the studio felt Al Pacino was too scruffy, we brought him to a real barber and told him to give him a haircut like a college student," said Coppola. "When the barber heard it was for the guy who might play Michael in *The Godfather*, he literally had a heart attack and they had to carry him to the hospital."

While Michael sits at an outdoor wedding table with Kay, the luminous John Cazale appears as Fredo, drunken to theatrical perfection and being introduced to Michael's girlfriend. And Robert Duvall as Tom Hagen, who, Michael explains, his brother Sonny found as an orphan in the street "and so my father took him in."

Then, there is an enormous mountain of a man sitting alone and talking to himself in a mumble, rehearsing what he will say to his boss on this auspicious day of his daughter's wedding.

"Michael . . . that man over there's talking to himself," Kay says upon noticing the big man. "See that scary guy over there?"

"He's a very scary guy," says Michael.

"Well, who is he? What's his name?"

"His name is Luca Brasi—he helps my father out sometimes."

He is practicing his lines, grateful to have been invited to the wedding of the don's daughter, desperate to show the Mob boss the respect he deserves, and terrified that he is going to screw it up.

Suddenly, the action is interrupted by the euphoric arrival of Johnny Fontane, accompanied by delirious screams of the young women at the wedding, a shriek from the bride, and a command by Mama Corleone, "Johnny! Johnny! *Canta na canzone!* Sing a song!"

As he sings "I Have But One Heart" to the delight of all, Kay presses Michael to tell her how his father knows Fontane. And Michael reluctantly, but firmly, tells her of the bandleader who, for $10,000, wouldn't let Johnny Fontane out of his contract. "So the next day, my father went to see him, only this time with Luca Brasi. Within an hour, he signed a release for a certified check of one thousand dollars."

"How'd he do that?" asks the innocent Kay.

"My father made him an offer he couldn't refuse," says Michael.

"What was that?"

"Luca Brasi held a gun to his head, and my father assured him that either his brains or his signature would be on the contract."

The character of Luca Brasi had to be as fierce on the screen as it had been in the novel. The don's enforcer was "a man to frighten the devil in hell," wrote Puzo. "Short, squat, massive-skulled, his presence sent out alarm bells of danger."

The role of Luca required an actor of immense size, someone whose mere presence could project menace and evil. Forty potential Lucas scrolled down Fred Roos's casting list, the front-runner being Timothy Carey, the actor with the face of a death mask, known for playing doomed, psychotic, homicidal roles, from a fearsome gunman in Stanley Kubrick's *The Killing* to the gangster Flo in John Cassavetes's *The Killing of a Chinese Bookie*. But while Carey would be remembered mostly as a character actor, he carried himself like a star—with a star's demands. "He wanted his own trailer in New York," remembered Al Ruddy. "I told Timothy, '*Marlon Brando* isn't getting a trailer.'" And so Tim Carey passed—or was passed on—which left it up to Lou DiGiaimo, who "was casting the extras," said Roos, to find a respectable Luca. "And when you do extras, you have to meet hundreds and hundreds of people."

From morning until midnight, DiGiaimo saw potential extras: "You say, 'I'm involved in *The Godfather*,' and they all kissed my ass," he said. "People would wait for me in my office. They'd roll up with a meal."

Sometimes, he went into the field, camera in hand, taking "Polaroids of a hundred guys in Brooklyn with bent noses."

Some potential actors threatened, others cajoled, all wanted in. Even Joe Colombo called him, firmly but politely, with casting suggestions, said DiGiaimo.

Yet far into the filming, the part of Luca Brasi remained uncast. Then *he* found them.

THE BIG MAN was "on a treadmill to oblivion," syndicated Universal Press columnist Philip Nobile once observed. It had been nearly a decade since he was a championship wrestler, dazzling bloodthirsty crowds and punch-drunk opponents for twenty-five years as the Masked Marvel and Chief Chewacki. Now, at forty-eight, Lenny

Montana was punching a clock as a public relations man for a Long Island storm-fence company, moonlighting as a bouncer at Manhattan clubs like the Copacabana, and working as a bodyguard, some say, for the Mob, lugging around his 6-foot-6-inch, 320-pound heft like a beastly burden. "He was a collector for the Colombos," said Gianni Russo. "If you were late, they would send Lenny Montana to collect the vig [interest] on loan-sharking money and threaten deadbeat bookmakers. He'd walk in and they'd run to get the money."

"I live the part of a heavy," Montana told Nobile.

And a heavy he had been, embroiled in a botched attempted murder plot in 1967, which saw the target escape unscathed and Montana, born Leonardo Passafaro, and others indicted for attempted murder and other charges. The charges against Montana were dismissed, except for one: he pleaded guilty to misdemeanor conspiracy. "Your past record as far as any criminal convictions is clean," the judge noted in a March 9, 1971, hearing, giving the former wrestler a suspended sentence and placing him on probation. So by the spring of 1971, he was a free man, and luck shown on him one fortuitous day.

As Montana told it, he was visiting his mother in Brooklyn when he noticed police barriers had been erected around the neighborhood.

The police weren't looking for him, but the filmmakers surely were.

"They're shooting a scene for *The Godfather*," he was told.

Montana lumbered over to the barricades, where he stood head and shoulders above the crowd, and soon caught the eye of producer Al Ruddy, into whose vision the big man arose like something out of a good bad dream.

"He looked like he could eat raw meat," a former opponent once said of Lenny Montana. "Two cauliflower ears, kind of a square face, and always looked like he needed a shave. He just looked like he could eat people up."

The Godfather's casting directors had long been searching for the actor to play the don's fearsome henchman Luca Brasi with little success. Now, here was someone who looked even more ferocious than the menace in Puzo's fiction, standing anonymously in a crowd.

"Hey, fella, can I see you for a minute?" Ruddy asked the man.

"I turned around because I'm thinking he is talking to somebody behind me," Montana later said. "But he meant me."

"Ever do any acting?" asked Ruddy.

"I wrestled for twenty-five years on television," Montana replied, according to the writer Dan Lewis in a 1972 newspaper story. "I guess you can call that acting if you want."

Ruddy escorted the big man through the barricades and into Francis Ford Coppola's trailer, where Coppola did a double take.

"That's Luca Brasi," said Coppola.

"I'm Lenny Montana, not this guy Brasi or whoever you're talking about," said the big man.

"Then he says, 'Would you like to be in the picture?'" Montana later said. "I said, 'Yeah, I don't mind.'"

He would claim he was paid $1,000 a week for eighteen weeks.

"I didn't know who the character was. I took no screen test. Coppola gave me a script and I went on location and shot it."

Soon he was on his way to the studio for the indoor wedding-day scene: May 3, twenty-seventh day of shooting. He was standing next to "this old-looking guy," he said.

"Is Brando here?" asked Montana.

"Brando is expected," said the "old guy," who turned out to be Brando.

"Just be natural," Marlon Brando told Montana. Don't go by the script, he added, and forget about acting school.

Standing before the great Brando in full evening dress and a white tie, he stumbled over his lines, delivering them in a deep staccato that sounded like a joke.

"*Don Corleone, I am honored and grateful that you have invited me to your daughter's wedding . . . on the day of your daughter's wedding—*"

"Jimmy," Coppola said to James Caan, "do something."

"Do what?"

"Loosen him up or something."

"Well, Fran—"

"Just go ahead, do it."

Caan took Montana off to the side.

"Len," he began, "you've got to do me a favor."

"What?" Montana said, apparently unaware his rehearsals were being critiqued.

"When you say, 'Don Corleone' stick your tongue out, and I'm going to put a piece of tape on your tongue that says 'Fuck you' on it, right?"

"No, Jimmy, stop," Montana pleaded. "Don't make me do this."

"Everybody's gonna laugh," Caan assured him. "Lenny, you've got to trust me. We need to get laughs in here. Everybody's going to sleep. Laughs are great. Brando will cry laughing. Please just do it, right? Trust me. I beg you."

Montana finally relented and stuck out his tongue, which Caan said "was as big as a shoebox." Caan wrote "Fuck you" on a piece of surgical tape and affixed it to Montana's tongue as the crew was readying the shot.

"Remember," Caan said, "when you say 'Don Corleone,' stick your tongue out, right?"

"Okay, let's roll," said Coppola.

"Don Corleone," Montana began and then stuck out his tongue.

Fuck you.

"Brando's eyes almost pop out of his head and he doubles up with laughter," wrote Ira Zuckerman. "Montana deftly turns in a half-circle so the other actors and the crew can see. Even Coppola cannot resist the joke."

The next day, Brando approached Montana.

"Luca," he said.

As Montana turned, Brando stuck out his tongue. Written on surgical tape was *Fuck you, too.*

A year after the film's release, Montana was interviewed by Nobile. Had Montana struggled much with the role? "No, I didn't have no problem, because I had such a great director who coached me through there."

There were some things Coppola's new star didn't need to be coached on.

"Let me put it this way," Coppola said, referring to a scene requiring Montana to load a pistol. "I said, 'Okay, take out the gun and flip it open and put bullets in and spin it. Can you do that?' And he looked at me and said, 'Are you kiddin'?'"

Offstage, Montana entertained the filmmakers with stories of "the life."

"He used to tell us all these things, like, he was an arsonist," remembered Gray Frederickson. "He'd tie tampons on the tail of a mouse, dip it in kerosene, light it, and let the mouse run through a building. Or he'd put a candle in front of a cuckoo clock, and when the cuckoo would pop out, the candle would fall over and start a fire."

When Al Ruddy's assistant Bettye McCartt broke her watch, a cheap red one, Montana noticed. "He said, 'What kind of watch would you like?' and I said, 'I'd like an antique watch with diamonds on it, but I'll get another fifteen-dollar one.' A week passes, and Lenny comes and he's got a Kleenex in his hand wadded up, and he's looking over his shoulder every step of the way."

He placed the wad of Kleenex on her desk. She opened it, and there was an antique diamond watch inside. "And he says, 'The boys sent you this. But don't wear it in Florida.'"

Whether or not he was a Mob enforcer, he certainly had the size and the look. "I mean, he used to collect some money," Caan said of the wrestler-turned-actor. "I don't know what he did. I know he didn't show pearls for the Queen of England."

Soon, Caan and Montana were out together with friends in New York, watching Benny Goodman at the Rainbow Room in Rockefeller Center. Montana was notoriously frugal and never carried more than twenty dollars in cash, said Caan. Usually, when the bill came, someone else paid. But on this night, the check was outrageously large, and Lenny Montana reached for it.

"I'll take care of it," he said.

With the check in one hand, Montana picked up a glass of ice in the other and tossed it over his shoulder onto the large party behind.

"What are you doing, you son of a bitch!" one gentleman from the table shouted.

Montana slowly rose. "It took him like a half hour to get up, he was so big," said Caan. Montana grabbed the man, which quickly attracted the manager's attention, who pleaded with the big man to stop.

"You want to see this every night?" Montana asked the manager.

"No!" the manager replied, at which Montana shoved the bill in the manager's hand, turned to Caan and the others, and said, "Let's go. I took care of it."

Meanwhile, back on set, Coppola had an idea. Montana had been struggling so badly with his lines—why not keep one of the flubbed takes, and introduce a short scene of Kay overhearing him practicing? And so the actor's stumbles and misspoken words, rather than bringing down a scene with Marlon Brando, became the stuff of legend:

"Don Corleone, I am honored and grateful that you have invited me to your daughter's wedding," but Luca pauses, horrified to have screwed up the speech he practiced so hard. "On the day of your daughter's wedding. And I hope that their first child be a masculine child. I pledge my ever-ending loyalty."

It was sensational, perfect, yet another of the memorable scenes in the film.

Still, Luca Brasi has to die. And he would have to die violently, in one of the most chilling scenes of the film. "It means Luca Brasi sleeps with the fishes," Richard Castellano, as Clemenza, says when the late enforcer's bulletproof vest is delivered to Sonny Corleone. Inside the vest are two large fish, a message from the killers, who ambushed the seemingly unkillable Luca Brasi after the don sent him to see what intel he could glean from Bruno Tattaglia.

"FIND OUT ABOUT THE GARROTE," wrote Coppola of the scene in which Luca Brasi would be stabbed and strangled by Sollozzo, Bruno Tattaglia, and an assassin who sneaks up on the big man from behind. "How it's used, its tradition, how long it takes. EVERY-THING."

Montana didn't have to worry about dialogue with a garrote around his throat. And while his inexperience as an actor may have hampered earlier dialogue-heavy scenes, his experience as a professional wrestler would enable him to turn Luca Brasi's violent death into an all-time film classic. Even so, "the strangler scene," as Montana called it, would push him to his limits. "A man put his life on the line."

Meaning, *him.*

"It had to be real effective."

A prop knife was welded to a thin brace and fitted to Montana's hand, then covered with makeup and a stream of fake blood. "The makeup man covered everything in skin embalming," said Montana. Al Lettieri and the actor playing Bruno Tattaglia, Tony Giorgio, keep their own hands pressed over Montana's as a third man—the assassin with the wire—appears behind Luca Brasi to garrote him.

"What made that scene so effective was the editing," said the makeup artist Dick Smith, in Harlan Lebo's *The Godfather Legacy.* "I've talked to many people who swear they saw the knife go into the hand."

For nineteen hours, Montana was strangled, again and again. While the director and his crew struggled to get it down right, the actors who were trying to restrain the mountainous Montana kept getting tossed off by his towering strength.

"The lighting wasn't right," he said. "I fainted about five or six times. My ears and nose started bleeding. I got hemorrhages because I was holding my breath and blowing out. This was no trick photography."

"So that's why your eyes seem to pop on the screen?" he was later asked by Philip Nobile, whose story was titled "Who Was That Bug-Eyed Man?"

"The man actually strangled me," said Montana. "He put the pressure on with a rope. He pulled real tight, and I helped by holding my breath. Sometimes I would black out and lay off about four or five hours. But being that Francis Coppola wasn't getting strangled, he didn't care how long we took."

"What if your strangler went too far?" he was asked.

"Well, from all my years in wrestling, when guys put the sleeper hold on me, I knew exactly when it was time to stop," Montana explained, without clarifying if he was referring to the wrestling ring or the movie. "I would bang on the bar when I had enough, and there was a doctor standing by with oxygen."

LENNY MONTANA WASN'T the only one who had trouble when it came time to shoot with the mighty Brando. Al Martino was perfect as the fading crooner, so comfortable with the fame and the fall. But when it came time to shoot his biggest scene, in which he breaks down before the Godfather while relating the pitiful story of the producer who wouldn't give him the role in his new, big studio picture, Al Martino *froze*.

It came soon after he sang the Vic Damone hit "I Have But One Heart" for the wedding party, after which he was warmly welcomed by the don and ushered into his study. Martino would later complain that his role had been minimized by Coppola, perhaps under pressure from Sinatra, to which the director would respond, "Johnny Fontane's role was only minimized by his [Martino's] own inexperience as an actor." To which Martino would fire back, "I was completely ostracized on the set because of Coppola. Brando was the only one who didn't ignore me."

By then, bigger problems had begun.

"He's doing a Vegas act when he is talking to me," Al Ruddy remembered Brando telling Coppola of Al Martino's performance in the study. "What am I going to do?"

Without time for further delays in the schedule, Coppola asked Brando to do his best and he would loop in dialogue and add footage later. The cameras roll. Johnny Fontane sits atop the Godfather's desk in his study, grieving over the Hollywood big shot who won't give him the part and—horror!—breaking down in tears before the mighty Mafia chieftain, now embodied by Marlon Brando.

"Oh, Godfather, I don't know what to do, I don't know what to do," Martino whimpers as Johnny Fontane.

At which point Brando, unscripted and at the end of his rope, leaps from his chair, grabs Johnny Fontane's hands, and slaps his god-son *hard* across the face.

"*You can act like a man!*" he roars. "What's the matter with you? Is this how you turned out? A Hollywood *finocchio* who cries like a woman?"

"Martino didn't know whether to laugh or cry," said Caan, who was present on the set that day.

Multiple expressions flash across Martino's reddened face in the finished film—from jest to embarrassment to humiliation—but the scene was on film and it *worked*.

"**I WANT YOU** to rest well, and a month from now this Hollywood big shot's going to give you what you want," Brando tells Johnny Fontane after the famous ad-libbed slap across the face.

"That's too late," replies Fontane. "They start shooting in a week."

"I'm gonna make him an offer he can't refuse," says Corleone, beside which Francis Ford Coppola wrote in his notebook "WHAT POWER!"

As with everything, Coppola envisioned the famous horse's head scene from Puzo's novel to be even more terrifying on-screen than it had been on the page, in which the Hollywood producer Woltz awakens in his "huge bedroom as misty as a foggy meadowland" to find "severed from its body, the black silky head of the great horse Khartoum . . . stuck fast in a thick cake of blood."

He wanted to go further than Woltz's bloodcurdling scream, deeper than the terror of what might befall Woltz next, beyond what Puzo described as Woltz's "maniacal raving" that ended with a call telling Johnny Fontane "to report for work the following Monday."

He wanted to put the horse's head not at the end of the bed, as Puzo had, but beneath the sheets with the actor John Marley as Woltz, "to reveal, in a horrifying way, what the Don has decided to do to convince Woltz of the seriousness of his intentions," he wrote in his scene outline.

He needed the perfect horse's head, a head that would resemble the head of Khartoum, the racehorse that Woltz would so proudly show off to Tom Hagen—a regal head to symbolize the last request to be granted by Don Corleone on the day of his daughter's wedding. With this head, the don would exhibit his awesome power. He would accomplish for Johnny what the singer couldn't do for himself, he assured him after the slap in his study.

Tom Hagen was dispatched to meet with the studio big shot, and the sunny, evocative chords of "Manhattan Serenade" swelled, selected by Robert Evans as the essence of California. Sunshine, palm trees, Hollywood. The lone figure of Tom Hagen in a fedora, carrying a heavy briefcase, walking through the immense lot of Woltz International Pictures, was actually a body double on the Paramount backlot, to save money.

Hagen finds Woltz on a soundstage, where the powerful studio chief dismisses the don's emissary with violent slurs, only to later receive him for dinner at his grand estate and a tour of his stables, where he shows off his prize possession, his $600,000 racehorse, Khartoum. Then, over dinner comes the second refusal, even more violent than the first, in which Woltz explodes in anger and kicks Tom Hagen off his estate. "Now you get the hell outta here! And if that goombah tries any rough stuff, you tell him I ain't no bandleader! Yeah. I heard that story."

"The Core: sets up the Don's first real opponent: Woltz makes us feel the promise he (Don Corleone) gave Johnny is almost impossible to keep," wrote Coppola of the brilliantly bloody showdown to come.

It was new, and it was ancient, and it was perfect. In the silence of the night, the don's tentacles reach across America and seize the seemingly all-powerful Jack Woltz, slaughtering what he loves most. "That horse's head thing was strictly from Sicilian folklore, only they nailed the head of your favorite dog to your door as the first warning if you didn't pay the money," Puzo would later say.

"He never asks a second favor when he has been refused the first," Tom Hagen tells Jack Woltz as a warning when he said he couldn't grant Don Corleone's request to give Johnny Fontane the movie part and adds, "Just tell him he should ask me anything else."

"Scene Eight: Woltz's Bedroom," Coppola wrote. The camera would pan across Woltz's quiet estate, now devoid of uniformed maids and manservants, and slip into his bedroom, "almost like some unwelcome intruder's point of view." In contrast to earlier imagery of "Woltz the guarded man," Coppola wanted to evoke a sense of anxiety and vulnerability. "Woltz wakes up very early. . . . Then feel[s] the wetness, and seeing that it is blood, and he (and we) thinking it is his, then he quickly sits up, already in a level of terror from the blood on his hand, and sees the severed gory head of Khartoum."

"The Core: to reveal, in a horrifying way, what the Don has decided to do to convince Woltz of the seriousness of his intentions . . ."

"Pitfall: that it's not horrifying enough. If the audience does not jump out of their seats on this one, you have failed. Too much in the Corman Horror film tradition would also be a mistake. One must find the perfect balance of horror without losing the thread of the overall film. Deliver it and get out."

On May 20, the fortieth day of shooting, Coppola prepared to shoot a scene that he would later say he would "loathe: I hated the whole Hollywood section," Coppola told Stephen Farber in 1972. "But I had to do it because of that stupid horse's head. I had to do this, I had to do that, and by the time I did what I had to do I never had time to make some of the points I wanted to make."

First, he had to source a dead horse. A horse whose bloody head would immediately convince Jack Woltz to give Johnny Fontane the part in the movie. Silver-haired, suave, and able to project the fierceness at the core of the outwardly stylish studio chief, John Marley, as the producer Woltz, was a Hollywood veteran, whose last role as Ali MacGraw's father in *Love Story* earned him an Oscar nomination.

Now, Marley was in a massive bedroom inside the palatial home called Falaise on the Gould-Guggenheim Estate, Sands Point, Long Island, "a castle surrounded by acres of woods, formal gardens, hot houses, stables, a pool and private beach on the sound," wrote Ira Zuckerman.

The elegant actor, then sixty-three, was dressed in silk pajamas beside a rented bed. The weather was wet and cold. In the estate's stables, six real horses were being brought in at 3:00 a.m., one of them to stand in as Jack Woltz's prized stallion, Khartoum. As for the dead horse's head, Paramount, whose executives might have been pressured by animal-rights activists, was against using a freshly killed horse's head. So a taxidermy head arrived from Hollywood, "probably a horse that died in a John Wayne movie, with gray hair and split leather," said Al Ruddy. "It was dry and dusty and stuffed with hay . . ." said production designer Dean Tavoularis. "And it only weighted two or three pounds. The actor would be kicking it and bouncing it . . . It wuld be a total moronic disaster."

Of course, it was soundly rejected by Coppola.

"Francis is a stickler for everything being right-on accurate," said Ruddy's assistant, Bettye McCartt, who was called in on horse's head duty. "Francis comes in and sees the head and says, 'I can't use that. It's not a racehorse. They have a different kind of head than a regular horse's head. I *have* to have a racehorse's head.'"

"Find a racehorse's head," Ruddy told McCartt.

She called a local taxidermist shop. No luck. The head of a racehorse was difficult, if not impossible, to find.

"Someone said, 'Call this place in New Jersey, where they make dog food out of horses,'" said McCartt.

She called the dog-food processing plant. "They said, 'As luck would have it, a racehorse had been put down the day before.' And they said if I came out, I could get the horse's head."

"The head had to be dissected from the body with a hatchet, not a saw, so there is a jagged end to the horse's head," instructed Tavoularis. A pickup date was set, but some say the Teamster drivers, upon hearing the nature of the cargo, revolted and refused to pick it up.

Later, a reporter asked Tavoularis, "How could you dare kill a horse for a movie?"

"Excuse me?" he responded, exasperated. "Do you have a dog?"

Yes, she did.

"Well, that horse was killed for your dog. Not for this movie."

"I took one of the limousines . . . and I had him stop at the market and we brought big green garbage sacks and we went out to New Jersey and got this head, which smelled worse than anything you could ever imagine," said McCartt. "The driver is hysterical, because it smelled beyond . . ."

Tavoularis had a steel box constructed with a pan in the bottom for dry ice to keep the head cold and delivered it to the makeup artist Dick Smith. "I'm going to bring the horse's head around and you can put the makeup on," Tavoularis forewarned Smith, adding, "It's gruesome. It's going to be terrible."

Early one morning, four "big guys arrived, carrying the horse's head in this big steel cabinet with four latches on it," said Al Ruddy. "They open it up and there it is, this horse's head hacked off at the neck, its tongue hanging out and all the entrails and all the blood. John Marley almost jumped twenty feet."

They placed the head, still partially frozen from the dry ice, on the bed and doused it with fake blood.

As instructed, John Marley slid under the yellow satin sheets, doing his best to keep his legs away from the bloody mess at the foot of the bed.

"Not enough blood," commanded Coppola, at which point two gallons of prop blood, made from Karo syrup and powdered red food coloring, were doused on the horse's head, the bed, and the actor.

Some crew members remained outside the room where Marley would pull back the blood-soaked covers and so convincingly scream again and again, take after take. By the time it came to break for lunch, Marley had been in the bloody bed for "eight, nine hours easy, covered in blood with a horse's head," said assistant director Fred Gallo. Adding to his misery, the windows had to be kept closed for sound purposes. So there was no breeze, just a stifling hot and surely smelly room, where a veteran actor was now trapped in a bed filled with blood and gore.

"Francis, if we get him out of this bed, we are never going to get him in it again," said Gallo.

So they shot right through lunch, with meal penalties for the crew until the bed was "literally a pool of blood and bedclothes and pajamas had to be changed many times," wrote Zuckerman.

"Okay now, John," Ruddy remembered Coppola telling Marley, "straighten out your legs."

Marley straightened out his legs, and as his bare skin touched the frozen horse head, or possibly merely performing as rehearsed, he erupted in a bloodcurdling scream.

"'Ahhh, ahhh, ahhh!'" remembered Ruddy. "He couldn't stop screaming. He was going mad. It was, to be fair, gruesome, and even if you're not faint at heart, it would scare the shit out of you."

"He was a trooper," said Tavoularis.

"When Coppola finally yelled 'cut,' Marley jumped from the bed.

"It was disgusting," said Ruddy, "but, boy, it worked."

The scene would be a classic, but, again, few realized it at the time. Instead, Jack Ballard, Paramount's watchdog over the production, still second-guessing Coppola at every turn, bore down even harder on the director. Before the last shot of the day was filmed, Coppola yelled out, "I'll call Charlie Bluhdorn and tell him I want Jack Ballard taken off the picture. I'm tired of having him on my back all the time."

There was yet another scene to be shot: Marley in the stables showing Tom Hagen his prized racehorse, Khartoum.

The blood-drenched actor headed off to take a shower. "I asked Marley if he wanted to keep the bloody pajamas as a keepsake," said Gallo.

"I'll tell you where to put those pajamas," he replied.

14

DANCING ON A STRING

The old Filmways Studio, on 126th Street in the middle of East Harlem, where so many famous films had been shot over the years, was a nice studio in a rough neighborhood.

On many mornings Brando and his assistant, Alice Marchak, would report to work at Filmways for makeup and wardrobe, the star's expectations low but demands on him high. "Marlon still thought that *The Godfather* would only be a B picture," Marchak remembered.

One day, after they were dropped off at Filmways by their driver, Brando and Marchak noticed a new car parked at the curb.

They both stopped to stare.

The car was sitting on the asphalt on its chassis. Someone had stolen the wheels.

"Suddenly Marlon grabbed me by the wrist and pulled me with him as he started running," said Marchak.

"This is a dangerous neighborhood!" shrieked Brando. "If those two men see the Godfather, they'll shoot!" There wasn't a soul in sight, as far as Marchak could tell, but she didn't stop to argue.

They ran up the studio's stairs to Brando's second-floor dressing room, where Marchak collapsed on the couch "huffing and puffing and Marlon fell to the floor laughing and out of breath, too."

"What two men?" she asked after catching her breath.

If Brando had seen them, they were now long gone.

Brando and Marchak were safe for now. Whatever imagined threats existed outside the building were nothing compared to the battle about to begin inside the studio. Even with the crew insurrection quelled, Coppola still wasn't completely in control of his movie. Jack Ballard was still on the set, on the phone, and breathing down his neck, watching every penny and every move. And cinematographer Gordon Willis was going from cantankerous to combative—especially over the issue of actors hitting their marks.

ACTORS THINK MARKS ARE GERMAN CURRENCY, read the sign on Willis's camera, on sets he lit so tightly "so if an actor would just move a foot slightly one way or the other, he'd go into darkness," said Gray Frederickson.

Willis wanted the actors' marks "adhered to [to] the nth degree," Coppola would tell *Premiere* magazine, while he strove for spontaneity from his actors and scenes to "give life."

Willis felt that Coppola's experience lay in "on-the-road, running-around filmmaking . . . You can't shoot a classic movie like video theater," he said, adding that one day the director would want to do "cinéma vérité"—the loose, documentary style of shooting that Coppola had utilized in most of his previous work—and the next day "a thousand-millimeter lens"—a giant telephoto lens that required careful setup and planning.

"Francis would drive Gordon nuts," said the makeup artist Dick Smith.

He'd prepare a scene one way and change it, even after Willis was already set up. He'd "veer between one thing and another," said Willis. He'd rewrite scenes in the morning or on the spot. "Francis's scripts are like a newspaper," Dean Tavoularis would say of Coppola's quest for perfection. "There's a new one every day."

Neither man seemed willing to give an inch, both believing their approach was essential to getting the best movie possible.

"Francis would lock himself in his office, and Gordon wouldn't come out of his trailer," producer Al Ruddy told the author Harlan Lebo.

The battle between director and cinematographer came to a head in the old studio on the set built as the Corleone family dining room. The cast was rehearsing the dinner scene that would follow the shooting of Don Corleone, everyone around the table, with Sonny at the head.

It wasn't going well. Coppola's incessant rewriting of scenes and rehearsals with his cast were proceeding too slowly for Willis. He was ready to shoot and fed up with the constant—and *slow*—drive for perfection.

Coppola wanted to change the shot; Willis said he needed to relight it.

"I want to shoot *now*," said Coppola.

"I'm not ready," replied Willis, already at the end of his rope. Now that rope would snap.

"You don't know how to do anything right!" Willis exploded at Coppola, in full view and earshot of everyone, leaving the soundstage.

Coppola continued the rehearsal "as if nothing has happened," as Ruddy and Frederickson rushed onto the stage to quell any further conflict.

"Let's shoot it now," Coppola commanded of the family-dinner scene, then shouted, "Get me Chappie, get me Chappie!" referring to cameraman Michael Chapman.

Chapman ran off the set and into the restroom, where he lowered his pants, sat on a commode, and locked the stall door, unwilling to come between the warring director and the cinematographer.

It had now been thirty days and nights of intense shooting. Constant conflict and criticism. A quelled insurrection among his crew. And now, his director of photography had walked off the set, jumped in his car, and was driving home to Nyack, New York.

"Fuck this picture!" Coppola screamed. "I've directed five fucking movies without anyone telling me how to do it. I want to make the fucking shot now and we will, even if the fucking director of photography has to be thrown off the picture!"

Alarmed, Frederickson tried to calm Coppola, who bolted from the set and ran through the old studio, up the stairs and toward his second-floor office, which was near Marlon Brando's dressing room.

"I heard thundering steps on the stairway and in a flash a wild man appeared at the top of the stairs and crossed the hall," said Marchak, who had just stepped out of Brando's dressing room and was standing in the hall when the wild man came thundering by.

"He was trying to get through his office door, which wouldn't open by knob," said Marchak. "So . . . *Crash! Bang!*"

A fist went through the door. It crumbled and hung by its hinges.

"My God! Maybe he's shot himself!" Ira Zuckerman quoted someone he kept anonymous saying on the set down below.

"I was stunned by it all and then realized the wild man was Coppola," said Marchak. "Finally, Marlon came into the dressing room."

"Francis lost it," she told him.

Brando, well-accustomed to director tirades on his sets, was immediately asked by his assistant, "Were you the cause?"

For once, Brando could honestly say no.

"He may be let go," Brando said of the constant rumors of Coppola being replaced. "But I told Francis, if he was fired, I would walk."

Ten minutes after smashing his door, Coppola returned to the set, "red as a beet," said a witness on the set, but ready to resume work.

Carpenters were called to put a new door on Coppola's office, and Frederickson drove to upstate New York to retrieve Willis.

And by the next day, the filming sprang to life anew.

FIVE DAYS LATER, Coppola was back on the soundstage, filming the lusty, panting quickie between Sonny and maid-of-honor Lucy Mancini on the day of Connie Corleone's wedding.

Sex—so crucial to the success of Puzo's novel—would be less central to the film. But the sex scene between Sonny and Lucy at the wedding was important; it would establish Sonny's volcanic temper and temperament early on in the film. The scene would be filmed separately from the wedding itself, with the small bedroom set, upon whose door Sonny and Lucy would have their thunderous tryst, crowded with crew members hoping for a peek. "People always come around for the killings and the sex scenes," Willis told Zuckerman at the time. But the crowd was out of luck: Coppola asked everyone but the camera crew to leave, in order to give the on-screen couple some privacy. They had to content themselves with listening to Caan and Jeannie Linero—a comedian whom producer Norman Lear discovered in Las Vegas and would later cast in his sitcoms—moan their way through the eight takes required to get the scene.

The pressure to keep on schedule was unabating, but Coppola still insisted on getting all the details right, taking the time to show James Caan how to enact the love scene.

Across town, in the Coppola family's cramped New York City West Side apartment, his wife, Eleanor, was about to go into labor with the couple's third child. The night before, the director George Lucas and his wife, Marcia, had come to dinner, passing through New York on their on their way to Europe for a backpacking trip. "They came to supper and hung out at our apartment because their plane was like at eleven that night," said Eleanor.

It was obvious to all that Eleanor was nearing the end of her nine-month term.

"You could have it on my birthday, you know. It's tomorrow," said George Lucas. After the Lucases left for the airport, the labor pains began.

She called her husband on set and told him to come home.

Coppola grabbed a camera to film the birth and then rushed off to the apartment to pick up his wife and rush her to the hospital.

Early the next morning, a baby girl was born. They named her Sofia.

Born on George Lucas's birthday, in the middle of the making of *The Godfather*, she would of course become a director. But first, she would be an actress. Three weeks after she was born, Sofia Coppola appeared in the baptism scene in St. Patrick's Old Cathedral, on Mott Street, playing a boy—the son of Connie and Carlo Rizzi—a precocious talent practically from birth.

IN THE FIRST days of June 1971, the phone rang high in the hills above Los Angeles in the Hutton Drive home of Robert Towne, then thirty-six. At that moment, the future Oscar-winning screenwriter's experience was limited to television, some uncredited work on *Bonnie and Clyde,* and a couple of Roger Corman films. He knew Coppola through Corman, and now, Coppola was asking for a favor that Towne, well, couldn't refuse.

Coppola felt it important to show the transfer of power between not only Don Corleone and his son Michael but the old generation and the new. However, the passage had not been fully written. Brando was three hours late for his call on June 2, partly due to dissatisfaction over the pivotal scene, which would occur after Michael returned from his exile in Sicily to assume the mantle of godfather.

Brando condensed his feelings in a few terse words.

"I don't want to be inarticulate," he told Coppola.

When Brando finally emerged to shoot the scene, it would be done in a long shot with plans to dub in dialogue later. Brando made the most of it, telling dirty jokes to Pacino throughout the scene, since he had no dialogue to read from the cue cards he used throughout the filming.

A poker game was being played. Brando would receive $40,000 a week for every day he worked over his contracted schedule for delays he didn't cause, having agreed to penalties if he were personally the cause of the delay, as Paramount had demanded in his deal. Now Coppola needed to create a scene between the dying don and the dawning don. Where to turn? He had littered the margins of his notebook with notes to "Ask Mario," which he surely often did. But Mario Puzo hadn't written a succession scene in his novel, which Coppola now imagined to be a centerpiece of the last act of his movie.

Puzo was by now somewhat estranged from the production, having left shortly after Ruddy cut the deal with Joe Colombo. "At about this time I quit the picture as consultant, not because of any of this, but simply because I felt I was in the way," Puzo wrote. "Also, in most of the arguments I had lately been siding with management, rather than the creative end. Which made me very nervous."

So Coppola went to a screenwriter for help.

Robert Towne was in his kitchen when he got the call, an SOS from his longtime friend in New York. "He needed help," Towne remembered. "There was never a scene between father and son," Towne said Coppola told him. "And he needed one. And I said, 'Well okay.'"

Towne had heard the rumors: that *The Godfather* was in trouble, that "it was a mess," he said. And now Coppola was evidence of that, calling *him* to help him out with a single scene in exchange for, well, what? It certainly wasn't for the money. "Francis and I were old friends, and I don't remember . . . they paid me a few thousand dollars, I think," said Towne. "I was pretty unknown, you know?"

He packed light: maybe a shirt, an extra pair of jeans, his toothbrush, and, most importantly, his grayish-brown IBM Selectric typewriter. He also had a copy of Mario Puzo's novel.

"I don't want [it] to be inarticulate," Coppola added, echoing what Brando had told him.

"So you want to talk?" asked Towne.

"Yes," said Coppola.

"That was the extent of my instructions," said Towne.

Landing in New York, the screenwriter went directly to the Gulf+Western Building, where Coppola showed him the footage from his troubled production. His old friend Francis, usually a Roman candle of boundless energy and excitement, now looked haggard. "It was the end of shooting, and he looked like shit," said Towne.

But the footage that he screened for Towne looked like solid gold. "It was *so* good," said Towne. "I actually thought it was the best footage I'd ever seen, and I told Francis. He looked stricken when I told him, because he thought I was crazy. Because he had basically been brainwashed by everyone. And I thought it was absolutely brilliant."

Had Coppola made a mistake in even calling him? Towne imagined Coppola thinking. *Is he just trying to kiss my ass?*

Then he met with Brando, briefly, and Brando told Towne the same thing that he had told Coppola: "I don't want to be inarticulate."

He wanted to talk. And talking on paper is what Robert Towne did best.

He lugged his heavy typewriter into the Manhattan apartment that the actor Buck Henry had loaned him for the occasion. It was already early evening when he set up his typewriter, alongside a copy of the shooting script, on Henry's desk in the living room. He ate a sandwich he'd bought from a delicatessen and went to work. Towne knew where his scene would come in the script and what Coppola hoped it would achieve: the passing of the torch from one generation to the next, from Vito to Michael, Brando to Pacino.

He looked at the cover of Mario Puzo's novel with cover designer S. Neil Fujita's rendering of the puppeteer's hands and the strings dangling down. Fujita had painted a somewhat similar hand in a 1955 painting, spurred by the lynching of Emmett Till, a fourteen-year-old African American brutally murdered in Mississippi that year. Fujita knew Mario Puzo, and "was in contact with him," said his son Kenji. And his inspiration for the stark and striking image of the puppeteer's cross surely came from Puzo's novel, with its recurring mentions of strings being pulled and men refusing to be "puppets dancing on a string pulled by the men on high," as Don Corleone says in the book. For Towne, the cross was "a clue," he said, a place to begin. It was close to midnight when the words came. The light. The breakthrough. The language. It flowed from book cover into Towne and soon poured out through the typewriter onto the page.

"I didn't struggle," he said.

These two men, somehow both gentle and tough, voice words

that could have been said by every father to every son, as they sit in Don Corleone's garden. "THE DON, older and frailer, and MICHAEL ... talking and eating," read the scene that Towne wrote.

"What's the matter? What's bothering you? I'll handle it. I told you, I can handle it. I'll handle it," Michael says to his aging father, who replies, "I knew that Santino was gonna have to go through all this. And Fredo ... well, Fredo was ... I never wanted this for you. I work my whole life, I don't apologize, to take care of my family, and I refused to be a fool, dancing on a string held by all those ... big shots."

Those strings. Which were the key to everything. "It's a great tragedy of a man and the son he worships, the son who embodied all the hopes he had for his future," Al Ruddy would later say of the pivotal scene.

He recited the lines by heart: "I thought that when it was your time, that you would be the one to hold the strings. Senator Corleone. Governor Corleone ..."

Ruddy sighed. "That's his dream," he said. "But what happened? The kid is put into the fucking line to save his father's life, and he becomes a gangster, too. It's heartbreaking."

"We'll get there, Pop," Michael assures the aging don. "We'll get there."

Around four that morning, Towne called his best friend, Edward Taylor, a Rhodes-scholar-turned-college-professor who had been Towne's roommate at Pomona College. From that point forward they were inseparable, Taylor helping Towne on every script, becoming his collaborator and muse—even helping him, in an uncredited assist, with the script for *Chinatown* that would win Towne the Oscar for Best Original Screenplay in 1975.

"It was in the middle of the night, and I'm sure I woke him up," said Towne.

He read Taylor the scene.

"He thought it was pretty good."

Which was good enough for Towne.

Two sleepless hours later, at 6:30 a.m., Coppola picked him up at

Buck Henry's apartment. Towne climbed into the back seat with the director as the driver drove them out to the Staten Island compound where Brando and Pacino would film the scene. The stakes were high. Brando was leaving the next day, and there was another last scene to shoot—the don's death in his garden. So today was the only day they had to nail what would become known as the succession scene. "If they didn't get it that day, he [Coppola] was never going to have him [Brando] again," said Towne.

Coppola sat in silence for the first forty-five minutes of the ride. "Any luck?" he finally asked.

"Well, I think so," said Towne, and he passed him the clipboard with the two-page scene.

Coppola read it and liked it.

By the time they arrived at the compound, the "*Let's* show it" had turned into "*You* show it to Marlon Brando," according to Towne.

He found Brando sitting in his high makeup chair, "having his cheeks put in," he would later say. After a few moments of pleasantries, Brando said to Towne, "Read the scene."

Towne was "instantly furious that he [Coppola] would put me in this position."

Read a scene to Marlon Brando? Towne was perplexed. *I'm fucked if I don't read this well*, he remembered thinking. But he would be even more fucked if he attempted to act it out for the master. So he read it "flatly," without emotion. When he was finished, Brando turned to him and said, "Read it again."

Which Towne did, after which Brando "proceeded to take the scene almost line-by-line, asking me what I meant at every moment."

For Towne, it was probably "the most detailed 'taking apart' of a scene" he had ever experienced.

"Would you mind staying here for the shooting of it?" Brando asked. So they all went into the garden, where the scene was quickly written on giant cue cards for Brando to work from. Shooting the single scene took all day, from early morning until early evening.

When it was done to the satisfaction of all, Brando turned to Towne.

"Who are you?" he asked.

"I'm nobody really," replied the screenwriter. "I'm just a guy."

"Well," Brando replied, "I don't know where you came from, but I'm glad you're here."

Afterward, Coppola asked Towne if he wanted a screen credit, to which he said no. "It's a fucking scene, man!" he said, then added, "Thank me if you win the Oscar."

So when, in 1973, Coppola stood on the stage at the Academy Awards, accepting the Oscar for Best Adapted Screenplay, "Son of a bitch, he did," said Towne.

The next day, June 4, the sun was shining for Brando's last day, in which the don would fall dead of a heart attack in his garden while playing with his grandson. Most of the cast and crew had gathered on the set to bid farewell to Brando, who by then had become beloved by all.

Attempting to calm and befriend Anthony Gounaris, the three-year-old playing his grandson, Brando put an orange peel in his mouth and growled like a monster, which scared the child actor, who broke down in tears. All of which Jack Ballard felt unnecessary, said Coppola. "He tried to stop me shooting the scene with Marlon and his grandchild in the tomato patch, and almost did—but I bootlegged it."

FRANCIS FORD COPPOLA was exhausted.

It was 10:00 p.m., June 9, 1971, and the director had spent fifty-three days shooting *The Godfather*. The on-set doctor had prescribed him sleeping pills to help him through anxiety-racked nights and shots of energy-boosting vitamin B$_{12}$ to get the director through the marathon schedule.

With filming finally wrapping for the day, Coppola looked to a young assistant and asked, "Do you still want to direct films?"

After the chaos of the shoot, the assistant could have been forgiven for saying no—indeed, it wasn't clear that Coppola himself would still answer yes if the same question was put to him at this moment. But the director continued on.

"Always remember three things: Have the definitive script ready before you begin to shoot. There'll always be some changes, but they should be small ones. Second, work with people you trust and feel secure with. Remember good crew people you've worked with on other films and get them for your film. Third, make your actors feel very secure so they can do their job well."

As he left the set for the station wagon to return to his borrowed apartment, Coppola added one more thought: "I've managed to do none of these things on this film."

The frustrations and uncertainty that had dogged Coppola throughout filming only grew more intense as shooting dragged into the summer. A week after the don's death scene, Coppola was at Calvary Cemetery in Queens, one of the largest and oldest cemeteries in the country, the final resting place of cops, politicians, and mobsters alike. It was the day to shoot Don Corleone's funeral, complete with 150 extras, twenty hearses and limousines, and, everywhere, a fortune in flowers. By sunset, Coppola hadn't gotten the shots he felt he needed, and the anger bubbled up and exploded—at no one in particular, just the film in general.

"Fuck, fuck, fuck ..." he said, pounding his fist into his hand, walking toward Gray Frederickson. "This picture is a waste of my time with this impossible schedule."

In the middle of the cemetery, he was desperate to break something, anything. But he was trapped in a landscape of dirt and stone. Finally, he spotted something breakable: Gianni Russo's gallon of Almaden white wine, which the actor had sipped steadily throughout the filming.

He moved to smash the bottle over a gravestone, but "thinks better of it," wrote Ira Zuckerman in *The Godfather Journal*.

Instead, he hurled the bottle down the hill and into the street, onto which it loudly smashed.

Coppola grabbed his saddlebag and scurried into a space between two towering mausoleums, where he sat with his head in his hands.

Nothing seemed to be going right for the director. And the stakes were only getting higher, with a scene that would cost the studio dearly in special effects yet to be filmed: the killing of Sonny Corleone.

The scene was shot on an abandoned strip of Long Island, where Dean Tavoularis had erected an entire toll plaza from nothing, to stand in for the Jones Beach Causeway.

"Sonofabitch!" James Caan, as Sonny, explodes, after taking the phone from his mother and hearing Connie sobbing on the other end, which could only mean that his sister's louse of a husband had beaten her again. This time, Sonny wouldn't beat Carlo to a pulp; this time he would kill him. But Carlo had struck first, ratting out Sonny to the Barzinis, so that Sonny was marked for death, his temper lit by the cries of his own sister.

It was magnificent in its mutinous sense of evil, and Coppola, as had Puzo, would kill off Sonny in the most violent fashion, in an "incredible overkill, as in ZAPATA," Coppola wrote in his notebook, referring to the 1952 movie *Viva Zapata!*, directed by Elia Kazan and starring none other than Marlon Brando. "They just riddle him, they can't afford that he survive. YOU MUST GET THIS FROM THE EXTREME KILLING. The kick after he's already dead ... That shows how they hate him."

Most of all, he added, the audience had to realize the nature of the "ambush, AT THE MOMENT THAT SONNY DOES."

"Open the goddamn gate. Get off your ass!" Sonny exclaims as he sprints to his 1941 Lincoln Continental coupé, before the gates of the Corleone compound open and he races out to what is supposed to be the Jones Beach Causeway. Here, the ultimate ballet of bullets and blood by a hit squad of tommy-gun-toting gangsters would commence. Beneath the bravado, however, James Caan was, like Coppola before him, terrified. "I wouldn't be honest if I said it didn't make me a little nervous," he later admitted.

The assassination of Sonny was a technical marvel, rivaling the bloodbath Arthur Penn created for the death-car massacre of *Bonnie and Clyde*, in 1967. Two hundred bullet holes were drilled into the car and filled with squibs—tiny explosive rounds that could be remotely detonated—and another hundred were attached to the tollbooth. Most importantly, Caan was also wired to explode. His suit was packed with 110 brass casings, filled with gunpowder and fake blood—more casings than had ever been used in a movie before. His face was covered with specially designed blisters packed with more fake blood and attached to fine fishing line, which would be pulled by crew members from afar once the gunfire began. One of the men working on special effects confessed to Caan that he had never put that many squibs on anyone before in his life.

If that wasn't enough to alarm any actor, producer Al Ruddy whispered in Caan's ear an hour before the cameras rolled. "I'm really nervous," he said. "We need you for another two weeks, and you could really get hurt in this scene. It would ruin our shooting schedule for the rest of the picture. So be careful."

"They'd blow a hole in you if you put your hand in front of them," Caan said of the squibs and explosives that encased him. "They sewed them into my shoes! The same squibs they had in the car [that blew the car apart]? Those were the exact same squibs that were on my body."

It all had to be carefully "choreographed like a dance," said Caan, and one small misstep might have meant disaster. The only thing that kept Caan pushing forward? The women on the set, naturally.

"If there were no girls, I probably wouldn't have done it," Caan said. "I was afraid to get my head blown off. But there were girls. You've got to do it when there's girls there, right?"

Beyond the actor's physical safety, the financial stakes for the scene were also high. The special effects for the assassination brought the cost of the two-minute scene to $100,000—money well spent if it all went off as planned and without injuries.

Coppola called action. The toll taker fumbles with Sonny's change as rehearsed, a surefire signal to Sonny that he had fucked up, big-time, confirmed when the toll taker dives down suddenly to retrieve the fallen coins. The car in the lane ahead stops, blocking Sonny's Lincoln, and the four gunmen emerge, machine guns blazing.

"Sonny actually opens the door and steps out of the car, under fire," read the script. "He lets out an enormous ROAR, like a bull, and falls to the ground."

It all went off perfectly. The machine guns, the special effects, the exploding squibs and blisters, the breakaway safety glass on the car and tollbooth, all done without a hitch on the first take—which was fortunate, as another take might have cost another $100,000. Best of all, Caan emerged unscathed, although a bit dazed, checking his hair and scalp for injuries after the director called "Cut!" His suit was tattered, but he walked away without a scratch.

"We blew the hell out of that car," Ruddy later marveled.

15

"I MET HIM, I MARRIED HIM, AND I DIED"

June 28, 1971, a hot summer day, a perfect day for gunfire.

Not in the movie, but in the streets of New York.

In the movie, Coppola was preparing to direct a love scene.

In the streets, plans were afoot to commit a murder.

The Godfather had been filming in New York for sixty-six days. On this morning, with Al Pacino and Diane Keaton in bed together in the St. Regis hotel for a scene that wouldn't make it into the movie, a Unity Day rally for the Italian American Civil Rights League was scheduled to begin at noon a few blocks away in Columbus Circle. Despite the musical acts cued up to entertain—including Sammy Davis Jr., Frankie Valli and the Four Seasons, and B.B. King—the star of the event would undoubtedly be Joe Colombo. The increasingly powerful founder of the League, Colombo had paved the way for the making of *The Godfather* in New York City, and now tens of thousands of people were expected to crowd into Columbus Circle to hear the mobster-turned-civil-rights-activist speak.

Al Ruddy had been preparing that morning to attend the rally and stand alongside Colombo, a show of respect for all of Colombo's help on the movie. But the night before, Ruddy received a call from the shadowy FBI agent who had been communicating with him throughout production. "He never told me his name, but he was the real McCoy, because he told me three or four times things I had to be careful of," said Ruddy.

"Under no circumstance are you to be standing next to Joe Colombo tomorrow at Columbus Circle," said the agent. "Do you understand?"

"I understand," Ruddy replied.

And that was the last time he heard from the mysterious federal agent.

Around the same time, Gianni Russo received a call in his room at the Park Lane Hotel from Tommy Bilotti, a Gambino family associate who would be assassinated in 1985, along with Paul Castellano, outside Sparks Steakhouse, in Manhattan.

"Are you going to that rally?" Bilotti asked.

"What are you talking about? I'm on the dais," said Russo.

"I don't care if you're sitting on Joe Colombo's lap, you're not going," said Bilotti.

Russo says he called Colombo's attorney. "I got a stomach virus," he lied. "I can't sit anywhere other than the toilet for the next couple of hours."

Columbus Circle was jammed with League members, supporters, and spectators to see and hear the crusader Joe Colombo and the musical acts that would follow. Seven years after he had become the boss of one of the five New York families, and a little over a year after he founded the Italian American Civil Rights League, Colombo had banished the word *Mafia* from *The Godfather*, the television series *The FBI*, and the US Department of Justice, as well as put the kibosh on what he felt were unfair portrayals of Italian Americans in such commercials as those for Alka-Seltzer ("Mama Mia, that's a spicy meatball").

Now, Colombo began making his way through the teeming crowd to the stage, covered in streamers the color of the Italian flag, that had been erected beneath the statue of Christopher Columbus and across the street from the Gulf+Western Building. He was at the height of his powers: a self-avowed family man, the father of four sons and a daughter, but to the Feds, as the *New York Times* would remind its readers, he was another kind of family man—"the head of a Mafia family with about 200 members and associates."

Either way, he was the most public Mob boss who ever lived—way too public and outspoken for many.

At 11:45 a.m., just before the rally was set to get underway, Colombo was approached by a man who appeared to be a press photographer. He was carrying a camera and wore an official Unity Day press pass around his neck. Suddenly, he struck a crouching pose— and he wasn't pointing a camera anymore. Instead, he held a pistol, aimed squarely at Joe Colombo. He pulled the trigger three times, blasting three bullets at close range into the back of Colombo's head, neck, and jaw.

For a brief moment, there was confused silence.

Then, bedlam.

Colombo fell to the ground as a police officer tackled the gunman, Jerome Addison Johnson, twenty-five, of New Brunswick, New Jersey. Other officers piled on, attempting to handcuff him. But before he could be apprehended, two more shots rang out—by who, no one would ever know. Now the gunman also lay dead, unable to reveal who had sent him to kill Joe Colombo.

"Would you believe it?" Coppola asked as he watched the news that night in the St. Regis hotel suite where he had spent the day filming Pacino and Keaton in bed. "Before we started working on the film, we kept saying, 'But these Mafia guys don't go around shooting each other anymore.' We thought one of our problems was to make the film relevant."

Suddenly, Coppola watched the television screen segue from Colombo to documentary footage of *The Godfather* from the first day of filming, on Fifth Avenue in New York.

In that instant, the Mob and the moviemakers had again become one.

Colombo was rushed to Roosevelt Hospital, where the scene, once again, mirrored the movie: Joe Colombo, like Don Corleone, lying in a coma in a New York City hospital bed. "Two cops at every entrance," wrote Howard Blum in the *Village Voice*. "No one says it, but many must suspect another attempt on Colombo's life: an attack on the hospital to finish him off. Just like in *The Godfather*."

Colombo would languish in a coma for nearly seven years, ultimately dying of cardiac arrest in 1978, his crusade for civil rights coming to an inglorious end.

The cops and Colombo's associates immediately suspected the Gallo brothers, Joey and Albert, who had long criticized Colombo, "even to the FBI and police officers," wrote Don Capria and Anthony Colombo in *Colombo: The Unsolved Murder*. Joey Gallo, notorious for his erratic temper, openly blamed Colombo for what he saw as the diminishment of the Gallo faction after the 1960s New York City Mob wars.

As the news of the shooting spread across the city, the Gallos swung into action, knowing that they could be the chief suspects for both the authorities and Colombo soldiers intent on vengeance. Joey and Albert Gallo were brought in by the NYPD for questioning. After they were released without charges, Joey walked into a café in Red Hook, Brooklyn. "What a bum rap they're laying on us over here," he said, according to the author Peter Diapoulos in *The Sixth Family*. "We clipped Colombo. Wish the fuck we did. But that J. Edgar Hoover must be creaming his fucking pants. He's going to have his own *banchetto* [banquet] tonight."

Less than a year later, Joey Gallo would be famously gunned down in Umbertos Clam House, in Little Italy, while celebrating his forty-third birthday. The four gunmen were alleged associates of the Colombo family—exacting vengeance for their boss, still lying in a coma.

From there, it was more carnage, in both the streets and the film.

A suite in the Americana of New York, on Sixth Avenue, served as a substitute for Las Vegas. Here, John Cazale as Fredo—dressed like a sunglasses-clad peacock, having been dispatched to Vegas to learn the casino business and stay out of his family's hair—did the dance that would make him famous: parading his unimpressed brother Michael through the doors of the welcome party he's prepared for him, complete with cocktails, musicians, and most importantly, showgirls.

"Draw chips for everybody in the room so they can play on the house!" exclaims the strutting casino chieftain Moe Greene, the Jewish gangster whom Puzo had based on the real-life Bugsy Siegel. The character was being brought to fiery life by the actor Alex Rocco, who touted his underworld-gang connections. "He spun a whole tale of 'Yeah, I used to be in the Mob,'" said Fred Roos. "Without being specific, he implied that he was the real deal. So many of them said, 'I know about this world.' I'd say, 'How do you know?' And they'd say, 'I can't tell you exactly, but I've been around these people.'" ("I might have told him that I was a bookie, and I did some time, but I never made it to the Mob," Rocco said before his death, in 2015.)

Now that Michael has assumed the throne, he wreaks vengeance on his rivals, one don at a time, until all the heads of the competing families are dead, each in the bloodiest cinematic fashion, created by Puzo, embellished by Coppola, and edited by Peter Zinner into a murderous montage. It shifts between Michael attending the baptism of his sister's baby and the killings: Carmine Cuneo, shot dead after being trapped in a swirling revolving door; Philip Tattaglia, riddled with bullets in bed with a woman; Emilio Barzini, gunned down outside the New York courthouse while attempting to flee up the steps, his bodyguard and chauffeur lying dead behind him; Victor Stracci, in the elevator in the St. Regis hotel, into which a breathless Richard Castellano as Clemenza fires two shotgun blasts. And Moe Greene, the Vegas-casino mobster, shot with a bullet to the eye, mid-massage.

Once again, the Corleone family reigns supreme. But Michael has one last score to settle: the backstabbing Carlo Rizzi, who had set up the hit on Sonny. Coppola did the scene by the book, littering the pages in Puzo's novel with arrows and notes: Carlo admitting to Michael that he set up Sonny on behalf of Barzini ("He admits it," wrote Coppola); Michael telling Carlo that he'll be flown to Vegas to live and that he would never "make my sister a widow" ("Important FAKE OUT"), and Clemenza with the garotte in the back seat to strangle Carlo until he kicks out the windshield and is dead ("Surprise to the audience as well. Clemenza [with] the garrote is a total surprise").

"Power," wrote Coppola of Michael Corleone, "is all his."

BY THEN IT was all almost over, at least the New York scenes. On the last night, July 2, after seventy days of filming in and around the city, the crew was back on Broadway, along with the crowds, for the last scene to be shot in New York. It was a clear, hot Friday night, and the throngs watching obediently from behind the barricades watched as Al Pacino stood in front of Jack Dempsey's Broadway Restaurant, waiting to be picked up for his date to kill Sollozzo and McCluskey.

While it was the middle of summer, the set—and Pacino—were dressed as if it were Christmas.

This last day was not without problems—what should have been a night shoot had a call time of 4:00 p.m., and Coppola was astounded to find that another scene to be shot that night in what was supposed to be a quiet pizza parlor was instead on a major thoroughfare thronged with tourists in for the July Fourth weekend. Extras were spotted wearing light sports shirts, in keeping with the climate, and had to be brought coats to sell the notion that it was winter in the movie. Problems, problems, problems . . . and then, finally, a wrap.

Production had fallen far behind schedule, with the Sicily scenes yet to be filmed. Still, it was cause for celebration. The wrap party had been held the night before, at the old Cornish Arms Hotel, in Chelsea, where Coppola, the first to arrive, serenaded his cast and crew on an electric organ. Now, the production crew had their last drinks together at Jack Dempsey's Broadway Restaurant.

By then their leader was long gone.

*   *   *

THE CAR ROLLED down the ancient roads outside the sprawling city of Palermo and through the hills toward Corleone, the small Sicilian town whose name Mario Puzo had appropriated for his American Mafia family. Francis Ford Coppola sat with production designer Dean Tavoularis and associate producer Gray Frederickson, to scout Corleone as a potential location for the scenes in which Michael Corleone, in exile after the double murder, would love and lose his teenaged bride, Apollonia, whose beauty, like a thunderbolt, had taken his breath away.

"When we got to Corleone, I pulled out my camera and started taking pictures out of the back window of the car, and the driver and others in the town went berserk," said Tavoularis.

"No! NO camera!" he was told. "Someone will see!"

It was late July. Coppola had arrived in Rome on July 17, trailed by a cast and crew that was a fraction of the crew in New York, for a two-week shoot. He had interviewed actors in the conference rooms of the Parco dei Principi hotel, before flying down to Sicily on the twenty-second. Now they were in Corleone, the town where so many Italian Mafia bosses were born, and which "had the highest murder rate of any place in the world," Puzo wrote in *The Godfather*. On this summer's day in 1971, many mobsters still lived here—which caused the furor over Tavoularis's camera. "It really set them off because a judge had been assassinated and the authorities thought the assassin was hiding out in Corleone," he said.

But whether or not they could shoot there was beside the point— the town was too urban, and too crowded, to capture Coppola's vision of the "land of ghosts" that Michael retreated to from New York. "You don't want to shoot in Corleone, it's a dirty little town," said Frederickson, who knew the town and from working and living in Catania, Sicily, in his job in civil engineering.

They moved on until they found the perfectly picturesque towns to stand in for what had become the urban and dangerous town of Corleone: the tiny villages in the hills and a few miles away from the coastal resort town of Taormina.

Coppola had fought hard to secure his two weeks in Sicily. To save money, Paramount's executives pushed him to shoot these scenes in the US. But now that he was in Italy, those months of fighting finally seemed worth it. In Sicily, Coppola found some semblance of peace, at least temporarily. "For Francis, it was paradise," said Al Ruddy. "We came in, we didn't make any noise, and there was no fanfare—no one really knew we were there. The shooting itself was fairly uneventful. Everything went like clockwork. We did our stuff and got out."

Even Gordon Willis seemed to have been seduced by the Sicilian light, the temporary splendor, and happiness. "I maintained that all the scenes in Sicily should be sunny, far off, mythical, a more romantic land," he said. "Softer, more romantic, in contrast to the harder, newspaper look of the New York scenes."

Far from the constant surveillance of Jack Ballard and away from the eagle eyes of Robert Evans, Coppola seemed to be in sync with his cinematographer and at peace. Still, Ballard kept tight reins on the production, arranging a complex choreography of international flights and customs to keep the dailies going back and forth between Los Angeles and Italy:

"TWA Flight 845 leaving Rome at 2:00 p.m. every day and arrives Los Angeles 1:05 a.m. next day," read a memo sent to Ballard outlining the logistics. "This means Monday's dailies would be sent on Tuesday, arrive Hollywood Wednesday, run in Beverly Hills same day and we, in turn, would ship Thursday morning."

But Ballard's attempts to tighten the vise from across an ocean fell short.

"[Ballard] told the Paramount people that we were wasting lots of money and they called in an audit and they called Ruddy while we were in Sicily," said Frederickson. "They made Ruddy come back to New York early, and they went through and did the audit. The auditors came in . . . and said this movie was flawless, not a single thing wrong with any of the production."

In July 1971, *The Godfather* arrived in Sicily. Earlier that year, before Al Pacino had even been cast, Coppola had taken care of what was perhaps his most important task in Italy: finding the girl, the beauty to take Michael's breath away, a woman who would arise from the land "like a fantasy," as Puzo had written. "Pitfalls: If Apollonia doesn't make your heart stop just to look at her," Coppola wrote in his notebook.

Stefania Sandrelli was one of Italy's top young actresses, and a front-runner, along with Ornella Muti—who would make her English-language debut as Princess Aura in *Flash Gordon* nine years later. Another front-runner was the beautiful British actress Olivia Hussey, who, while not an Italian, had dazzled audiences as Juliet in Franco Zeffirelli's *Romeo and Juliet*, in 1968. The list of candidates for the role grew to twenty-two, including the American actress Marisa Berenson. A firm offer was made to the Italian actress Ottavia Piccolo, but she was unavailable on the required dates. Then, Coppola was given a photo of an unknown by a talent agent. Her name was Simonetta Stefanelli. Not quite seventeen, she lived at home in Rome with her parents, having dropped out of school at fourteen, "as Italian children are permitted to do," wrote the Associated Press's film-industry reporter Bob Thomas in one of the few interviews Stefanelli has ever done.

Coppola was immediately struck by Stefanelli's beauty and innocence. "I cast her because after we met, when she turned to walk away, she skipped like a young girl," he said.

Stefanelli would read Puzo's novel for the first time after she landed the part. When she came to the scene of Apollonia and Michael in the bedroom on their wedding night, as "their bodies came together in one line of silken electricity," as Puzo had written, the young actress barely flinched at the nude scene. "I had done one in another film," she said. "I don't really like to do it, but if the role calls for it, I will not refuse."

The production team—a crew now trailed by dozens instead of

the hundreds of locals that had looked on in New York—made its way through the little towns of Sicily. Savoca provided the Bar Vitelli where Michael introduces himself to Apollonia's father, the bar's owner: "My name is Michael Corleone. There are people who'd pay a lot of money for that information. But then your daughter would lose a father instead of gaining a husband."

Savoca also provided the perfect church for the wedding and its perfectly authentic locals for wedding guests. Then on to Forza d'Agrò, the gorgeous village where Michael asks, in Italian, "Where have all the men gone?" only to be told, "They're all dead from vendettas."

Then the commune of Fiumefreddo di Sicilia, whose Castello degli Schiavi was the rustic but grand residence of Don Tommasino, where Apollonia would be tragically blown to smithereens in the car she hoped to learn to drive.

The arrival of the actors—Al Pacino as Michael, the Italian star Angelo Infanti as the bodyguard Fabrizio, Franco Citti as Calo, and Corrado Gaipa as the old Don Tommasino (who would later become famous in Italy for a film by Coppola's protégé George Lucas, performing the Italian dub of Obi-Wan Kenobi)—caused little stir in early 1970s Sicily.

But no one could deny the thunderbolt Apollonia, first seen in the sun-drenched fields. "He would want to speak with me, I could tell," Stefanelli, who spoke no English, would later say of her costar Pacino. Instead, she added, they spoke only with their eyes. With her beautiful character, Apollonia, the production of *The Godfather* was filled with love and light for a fleeting moment, only to be once again torn apart.

For Pacino, too, the Sicilian filming had the feel of an ancestral homecoming. "My parents came from here," he later said, "although I never thought much about it. How strange I should wind up playing a Sicilian."

After a drawn-out casting process, months of fraught filming, and countless hours of sleep lost to self-doubt, Pacino finally felt wanted. "The Sicilian people embraced us . . ." he said. "I loved their honesty, openness and hospitality. I had not yet become well-known so I had the luxury of just being another person."

He had become one of them, "living in a tiny room by the water," and welcomed by the locals who opened their doors to him and invited him to share meals at their tables. "Sure, they knew I was in the film, but they didn't know me, they didn't even know what my name was," he said. "That was a pleasure, and the natural beauty of Sicily made one ecstatic."

In the morning, though, he awoke to the blistering heat and the almost unbearable pressure. "It got very hot, sometimes up to 120 degrees. I remember this one particular day, it was scorching hot and one of the extras asked if he could break for lunch, and the assistant director shot back rather harshly, 'No, not yet.' So the extra, who obviously was from the area, had the full woolen suit on in the blazing heat.

"Well, I want a break, it's the middle of the afternoon and I haven't eaten yet," Pacino remembered the extra saying.

"Again, the assistant director shot back, 'No.'

"Then the guy said very nicely, 'Okay, I go,' and the AD said, 'If you leave, you're fired.'

"The man shrugged his shoulders and said, 'Okay,' and something in Italian like 'Good day' or 'Bon voyage,' and he was gone. He walked up the road and just kept going. I couldn't take my eyes off him and thought, *Wow, that's a free man.* I loved it."

Then it was time to leave the sunny island, and the action—and the production—shifted back to darkness: again, for the director who would soon be back at war, this time in Los Angeles, once again against a familiar opponent, Paramount's production chief, Robert Evans, whose vision for the movie seemed so different from his own.

As for the stunning young teenager who portrayed Apollonia, Simonetta Stefanelli, she would sum up her role in the simplest terms:

"I met him, I married him, I died," she later said.

*　　*　　*

THE GURNEY WAS wheeled in and out of the Paramount editing rooms and the sound-editing facilities of the Samuel Goldwyn Studio, in West Hollywood, a hospital bed on wheels on which Robert Evans lay to run his studio's productions. He "looked like a ghost," his lieutenant, Peter Bart, would say. The ghost was obsessed with the movie that had been delivered, a solid block of Michelangelo marble, which had been cut from 500,000 feet of film, almost ninety hours of footage. For Robert Evans, the film had become all-consuming: "He ran it with an editor (which studio chiefs often do) and made some trims and added some scenes," said Bart. "Or parts of scenes. Francis likely would have made the same changes. But Bob made a true contribution despite all the melodrama about the [hospital] bed." High on prescription drugs, or cocaine—and frequently both—he was, at forty-one, a wild-eyed remnant of his handsome, dashing former self. "What started out as a fuck drug all but ruined my life of fucking," Evans wrote in his memoir, referring to his cocaine consumption.

The gurney, which he lay on during the eighteen-hour days of meetings and postproduction work on the film, was apparently the result of a particularly unglamorous injury: a freak tennis accident.

"He played very good but very unbeautiful tennis," said Ali Mac-Graw.

Woodland's tennis court lay near the pool, with its ring of fountains arching toward the heavens, and the famous screening room, whose seats hosted a who's who of the generation's best, brightest, and most notorious talents. The tennis court, though, was reserved for the sane and the sober, a daytime activity to stay fit for the late and bawdy nights.

On one sunny California day, in his perfect tennis whites with his perfect hair, perfect tan and seemingly perfect life, Robert Evans swung his racket back for the ball and unleashed hell upon his future. "He tripped and torqued his back severely," said MacGraw. "It was just a freak slip on the tennis court. It was at the height of the whole *Godfather* thing when dailies, back in the day, had to be seen every night, and commented on."

With Evans, though, it would be hard to separate fact from fiction, and even the source of his back injuries would be disputed. "As for the 'tennis accident,' I am not sure it ever happened," said Bart. "I have always suspected his bad back stemmed from an absence of exercise and difficult personal habits."

Still another source, the Hollywood columnist Joyce Haber, would write in her August 19, 1971, column, "Evans is still signing deals, but Paramount's active VP broke his wrist playing tennis over the weekend. He was in a foursome . . . fell backward and landed on his wrist. 'I went on confidently playing the set like a dope . . . The set I finished with the broken wrist, I won. There was lots of money at stake.'

"On Sunday, Evans ended up at the hospital," Haber reported. "On Monday, he ended up at the office with his arm in a cast."

Evans's broken wrist was the least of his worries. Overshadowing everything was his obsession over *The Godfather*. Now, with his bad back—he would defiantly trudge forward toward his vision of perfection. "I live to touch magic," he would later say. "I'm a Don Quixote in a way. I dream the impossible dream."

Now he was an injured Quixote, not on his horse, Rocinante, but flat on his back on a gurney, ensnared by sciatica, razor pains shooting up and down his legs and radiating across his entire life, a pain worse than "a thousand toothaches," he wrote. And instead of a Sancho Panza to set him straight, he relied on drugs that allowed him to burrow deeper into his *Godfather* fixation. To ease the pain, his doctors prescribed painkillers, and to harness the energy and focus necessary to do the work, Evans self-prescribed the drug of choice in 1970s Hollywood: cocaine.

Years later, in his memoir, Evans would hail the merits of postproduction as "the most important element in the anatomy of filmmaking . . . an art form unto itself."

During postproduction, all the aspects of the picture—"film, dialogue, sound, music and effects"—come together in either "film magic or film mediocrity."

All of this is achieved, or lost, he added, "by highly talented artists, whose contribution is rarely appreciated or spoken of."

Now, though, those "highly talented artists" were under his control, even though he and his visionary director had become estranged. Having delivered his cut, Coppola had fled the mercurial Robert Evans, returning to San Francisco.

After all, Francis Coppola didn't have the right of final cut.

The suits seemed to have won.

At least that's how Evans saw things. But what was fact, and what was fiction, might have been blurred by a drug-induced haze. And what came next was downright hallucinatory, with as many conflicting flashbacks as a bad acid trip, all of them as inflammatory as a nose full of cocaine: the editing.

NO CHEERFUL, JAZZY soundtrack accompanied Francis Ford Coppola's return to California, as it had heralded the West Coast landing of consigliere Tom Hagen in the movie. Like Evans, Coppola was also a ghost, not from a tennis injury but from torturous months of agonizing filming. The constant conflicts, the conspiracies, the blowups and breakdowns of his all-consuming Mafia movie had left him exhausted and beaten down.

He arrived to a home he had purchased but couldn't yet afford in San Francisco, a big Victorian that his wife, Eleanor, remembered as "a big old twenty-two-room mansion on Broadway Street and Fillmore."

It was a proper, but as-yet unfurnished, residence for the rising-star filmmaker and his family to live in on their return from their long stay in the borrowed apartment in New York. But even at home, Coppola couldn't catch a break: After their first night in the house, whose previous tenants had been hippies with dogs, "we got up and we had been eaten alive by fleas," said Eleanor. "These fleas were ravenous! It was a complete disaster."

Flea-bitten at home, and constantly doubted at work, Coppola went to work cutting the endless reels down to a respectable 175 minutes. It had been part of his deal to edit his film in San Francisco, not Los Angeles, because *The Godfather* "is not, has never been and will never be a Los Angeles–based picture," Coppola adamantly wrote in a letter regarding casting, which surely also expressed his sentiment about the editing. He would edit his film with his editors, Bill Reynolds (whose résumé included hits such as *The Sound of Music*), and Peter Zinner in the editing facilities of Coppola's now dormant dream, American Zoetrope.

They began, however, in Coppola's Victorian home, where they screened the voluminous reels of footage, so much footage that the two editors tossed a coin: Reynolds, the winner, would tackle the first half, Zinner the second. The specter of Robert Evans lay heavy upon them all. "We were told by Bob Evans that if we brought in a film longer than two hours fifteen minutes, Paramount would take the print away from us in San Francisco and edit it down in Los Angeles," Coppola told the author Peter Cowie.

Still, he left it long, and showed the 2:53-minute version to . . . well, who actually saw the first long cut isn't exactly clear. Coppola said he showed it to his American Zoetrope colleagues. "It was pretty much a San Francisco crowd," he said. "San Francisco folks that I don't quite remember all the names, maybe George Lucas. I remember the reaction was 'so-so,' not the approval I was hoping for."

Others remember the San Francisco screening in the summer of 1971 as being nothing short of superb. "I was blown away," said the sound effects supervisor Walter Murch. Still others insist they saw it at Paramount's screening room in New York. "There were ten people at that miserable screening," said Peter Bart of the New York screening. "Charlie Bluhdorn and Martin Davis, me and Evans. Francis wasn't there."

"Too talky, no action, will never play in Europe," snapped the head of foreign distribution, according to Bart.

Others felt it was good and maybe great, including Evans, but it was surely way too long for the executive in the middle, between Evans and Coppola, Paramount's former head of distribution and now president, Frank Yablans, who would later say he "didn't particularly like movies." He had become competitive with Robert Evans, two golden boys vying for the attention of the king, Charlie Bluhdorn. And while Evans sought to "touch magic," Yablans sought to grab gold. His mission was to get the studio's films down to a length that allowed exhibitors to maximize the number of screenings and concession sales: which meant just a little over two hours, tops.

Which also meant releasing *The Godfather* as it had been scheduled, during the prime season for film: Christmas 1971. Now the release would be delayed into 1972, which caused "all hell" to erupt from Bluhdorn and Yablans, according to Bart.

"Frank said, 'I don't care what you morons are doing, cut the movie down!'" remembered Al Ruddy.

Almost forty precious minutes had to go.

Coppola received word in San Francisco to mutilate the masterpiece he didn't even know he had. "Francis didn't have all the muscle that he has now," Bill Reynolds told the *New Yorker* in 1997. "We did some drastic editing," and they took the abbreviated movie, now around two hours and fifteen minutes, back down to Robert Evans, who received the director and his team in Woodland, where they would screen the movie in the estate's pool house, which Evans had turned into his screening room.

The lights went down. The Corleones came on. The lights went up. And Robert Evans groaned.

"The movie is longer at two hours and fifteen than it was at two hours fifty-three," he said.

"The picture stinks," he recalled telling Coppola with typical bravado. "Got it? *The Untouchables* is better. You shot a great film. Where the fuck is it—in the kitchen with your spaghetti? It sure ain't on the screen. Where's the family, the heart, the feeling—left in the kitchen, too?"

Then Evans got on the phone to New York and Yablans.

"I just ran it at 2:15, and it stinks," he said, according to Al Ruddy, who said Evans added a threat: "Do this at 2:15 and I'm walking and you can close the fucking studio. Goodbye."

Now, the real work began, Evans would say, the movie overshadowing everything in his life—especially his marriage. At the same time of the screening in his home, Ali MacGraw was preparing to leave to accept an award from the Hollywood Foreign Press Association. Evans told her to go alone, and he would soon follow. (He arrived late.) The day after that, MacGraw flew to El Paso to film the movie that her husband insisted that she accept, *The Getaway*, and Evans wouldn't visit her once during her three months on location with Steve McQueen. "I wanted her to go," Evans later lamented of the role costarring the actor for whom MacGraw would famously leave him.

Evans's life had become *The Godfather*.

COPPOLA'S WORST NIGHTMARE now came true: he was "required" to go to Los Angeles "and finish doing the editing there," said Eleanor Coppola.

He spent weeks with his editing team at the Samuel Goldwyn Studio, and his nights in James Caan's guestroom, as low on cash as he was on optimism.

Again, the two versions of what happened next diverge: Coppola would say he merely restored what he had been forced to remove; Evans would insist that he worked endlessly on the film in postproduction, reel by reel. "Now Bob feels that he found scenes that Francis had left out, scenes of great nuance by characters, and restored those," said Peter Bart. "I do not know who is right. I suspect that, A, Francis is correct in saying that Evans restored what Francis had been forced to remove and, B, that Bob also had a brilliant take on the picture and let scenes run long that had been cut too abruptly. Bob added some nuances and edits that were really helpful, a fresh point of view, as Francis had been working on it for so long. So, the bottom line, to me, was that Bob was right in devoting himself so intensively to the editing. Had Evans and Francis worked together on that, they would have been in total agreement."

By now, though, the two weren't speaking. "They would talk only through me," said Bart.

"Francis kept his distance, which was a tragedy, and no fun for

Evans," Bart continued. "Not to have a relationship with the most important director on the lot. *Chinatown* was taking up a lot of Bob's time, too, very distracting, and he spent a lot of time with Roman Polanski. He and Polanski formed that bond that I wish he had formed with Francis."

Coppola felt he had already edited his film, and that his edit was perfect.

Fifty years later, he expressed his feelings regarding Evans's contribution as follows in an email response:

"What were Robert Evans's contributions to the final edit of the film?" he was asked.

He left the space where the answer would have gone completely blank, presumably meaning that he felt Evans's contributions to the editing of the film were . . . *nothing*.

Bart remembered Evans, exhausted in his rolling hospital bed, constantly being moved by this butler from the editing room to the sound-mixing studio, sometimes wearing "fine black silk pajamas and black velvet slippers with gold foxes brocaded on the toes," according to Peter Biskind's *Easy Riders, Raging Bulls*.

"We rigged up two hospital beds on the stages at the Goldwyn Studios, where we did the mix," said the editor Peter Zinner.

"I'm done, come sit with me, let's go through it," Bart recalled Evans saying late one night in early 1972.

"And I had a sense of dread. *What are we going to see that he's finally relented and given up?*"

"This is the best that I can do," said Evans.

Alone with Evans in the Paramount screening room, Bart watched the finished film.

"It was just an extraordinary job," he said.

By then, though, the power on the screen had sapped the production chief who had commissioned it. "He was physically a mess, just a shadow," said Bart. "Cocaine really wrecks you."

The release had been delayed from Christmas to March, a slow season in which to release a major studio film. With the delay came "an immediate stink," wrote Evans in *The Kid Stays in the Picture*, "spelling 'suicide' to the world of exhibition. What was now thought of as an anticipated event now had the odor of a potential white elephant . . .

"Through the industry, word spread like leprosy: '*Godfather*—a bomb!'"

Then came the buzzards, smelling blood, including the syndicated Hollywood columnist Joyce Haber, through whom Evans often spoke to the world. "Joyce Haber was always around, looking for information," said Bart.

She asked him about the rumors swirling around *The Godfather*.

"And Bob said, 'Don't worry, I am saving the picture. I am in the editing room every day, on my back,'" said Bart.

In late summer 1971, Haber quoted Evans as saying, "I could wait another 10 years to get a property that could explode like this one. I'm going to devote myself to it. The producer, Al Ruddy, is waiting outside right now. *Godfather* has the opportunity of being maybe the biggest picture ever." To which Haber added, "If Bob indeed devotes himself to it, as he did to each detail of *Love Story*, which stars the beautiful Ali MacGraw, his wife, it may well have that opportunity."

"Francis was *furious* about it," said Bart of Evans's prerelease public statements. "And I was, too."

Who won the battle over editing and postproduction?

The movie.

"It's said that a bad movie is an orphan, but a great movie has twenty-eight fathers," said Ruddy. Whether it was Evans's self-proclaimed heroics or Coppola finally getting what he had envisioned all along, no one can absolutely say for certain—but Ruddy insisted that Evans fought his own studio for the longer version. Coppola was the creator, but Evans the warrior, without whom the movie might have been cut short.

"Bob put it all on the line, and that was the determining factor of the success of the movie," said Ruddy.

*   *   *

"**I'M TIRED OF** listening to your hype, Evans," Coppola said amid the editing combat, in which Evans claimed Coppola was reluctant to restore scenes that Coppola insisted he would have done on his own.

"Fuck you!" Evans shot back. "We got a shot to break fifty million in America alone, if you don't compromise."

"Are you on LSD? Only *Gone with the Wind* and *Sound of Music* hit those numbers."

"Yeah, and we will too, if you don't fuck it up."

"And you'll buy me a Mercedes, too, if it does, huh?"

"You're damn right I will."

The war over editing had subsided only for a new and even bigger battle to arrive. This would be "the big one," Coppola would call it. "Over the music."

Coppola had finished filming in Sicily, far from Hollywood and the studio pressures. And here, he was able to hear the haunting music in his head, the theme he was seeking to become his film score. Evans could hear the music, too, and, like everything else in *The Godfather*, it was the polar opposite of what Coppola heard. Coppola heard something like a symphony; Evans heard an all-American soundtrack that would lift the movie from all of its death and darkness. He and Paramount had commissioned Henry Mancini, who had hit the jackpot with "Moon River" for *Breakfast at Tiffany's*, to create a score.

Coppola felt his film required no less a composer than the one Toscanini once called "the Italian Mozart," Nino Rota, the then sixty-year-old composer of the scores of 158 mostly Italian films.

Nino Rota was as elusive as the sound in Coppola's head. Rota's only child, a daughter, who he financially supported as a child and stayed in touch with as an adult, didn't know he was her father until after his death, in 1979. He lived alone, "a lone man with several adopted families," said his nephew Francesco Lombardi. "If he didn't want to do something, he simply disappeared."

At that moment, riding high with the worldwide success of his score for Franco Zeffirelli's *Romeo and Juliet*, he had vanished into his many enterprises. "There was not any hostility to Coppola's project, but he needed time for the thousands of other things he attended," said his nephew. But Coppola found a connection through the veteran Italian actress and screenwriter Suso Cecchi d'Amico, to whom Rota was as close as family. "Probably, Suso simply explained to him that Mr. Coppola was a young and promising director and that the story was good . . . ," said Lombardi.

Coppola arrived in Rota's fifth-floor apartment in the Piazza delle Coppelle, in the heart of Rome, in August 1971. He had a cassette tape recorder and a five-hour cut of his unfinished film, which he showed to the composer on the portable editing device called a Moviola. There was an immediate connection. "I knew his music well, and could sing many of his themes to him," said Coppola. "I didn't feel as if he needed to be convinced at all. He was a wonderful man, and very kind and friendly to me."

Rota was equally impressed with the young director, for whom he "developed a great admiration," he would say. "He belongs, in fact, to that category of directors who, aside from possessing a true knowledge of music, feels it with profound and rapid intuition. Therefore, I listened to him attentively."

The director left his rough cut with the composer, along with instructions. Coppola felt the main theme should be a waltz "to convey the idea that the generations of the family went on and on—one, two, three, one, two, three—inevitable and continuing," he said. "I mentioned that I wanted the love theme for Apollonia to be somewhat 'Arabic' in feeling, as if she represented that sensibility of Sicily, the Arab or Islamic feeling in its tonality."

Rota sat down at his grand piano and immediately struck gold, composing many of the movie's themes—except one, the all-important "Love Theme," "which he took time trying to achieve, but I didn't feel he had captured what I was looking for," said Coppola.

"[Coppola] told me to adapt myself to the film's various situations and to compose a music which could constantly recall the origins of the protagonists, who come mostly from Southern Italy, and Sicily in particular," Rota said. "Coppola insisted that such music had to be embedded with Mediterranean, almost Arabic, melodies, evoking a feeling of nostalgia for the ancient origins of these people who later immigrated to America."

By the time Coppola returned to Rome for a second visit, that September, he had an edited version of his film, and Rota had a surprise. "He met me at the airport, and sang to me the 'Love Theme,'" said Coppola, "which I was very pleased with, as it had the elusive Arab intervals I was hoping for."

Known for recycling and reinventing his voluminous previous work, Rota utilized a big and brassy twelve-note melody he had written for the score of *Fortunella*, the 1958 Italian movie written by Federico Fellini. Now, he turned his jaunty *Fortunella* creation on its head: he slowed it down, and what emerged was something deep, dark, moody, and romantic.

"In this thematic 'call,' one can hear and feel an atavistic sound coming out of the Maghreb," wrote Franco Sciannameo in his book *Nino Rota's The Godfather Trilogy: A Film Score Guide*. "The effect of this melody on the listener can be compared to that of the North African sirocco wind when it surfs across the Mediterranean before blanketing the Southern Italian regions of Sicily, Calabria and Apulia. [A] unique amalgam of hot wind, sea mist and environmental sounds."

Coppola had found the sound in his head.

It wasn't merely music. It was the movie, with Rota's "Godfather Waltz"—hauntingly slow, almost a reveille—setting the scene from the start.

And Robert Evans hated it.

He still preferred Mancini, which he expressed to Coppola and the *Godfather*'s casting director Fred Roos, from his gurney. "He was wheeled into this mixing studio," said Roos, and Evans listened to the Nino Rota music "that you hear *everywhere* now."

"He told us how much he hated it, and that we should throw it out," said Roos.

"It wasn't the kind of music you would hear in Hollywood movies," he continued. "It seemed *small* to him, not worthy of a big picture, with a big orchestra."

It all came to a head six weeks before *The Godfather*'s March 1972 release. A meeting was called at Woodland, where Evans voiced his displeasure with the Nino Rota soundtrack to Coppola, Walter Murch, and others. "Evans hated the music," said Murch.

It brought the film down, Evans said, and the dark picture needed "some bright American music," by Henry Mancini as a counterpoint to all the blood and the bodies. During a hot dog lunch "served by Ali MacGraw," said Murch, Coppola rose and gave yet another of his epic presentations, one of his emotional debates that levels everything— and everyone—in his path.

And when he was done, Francis Coppola threatened to take his name off the movie. "I bluffed," said Coppola, whom Evans claimed to have fired four times during postproduction. Coppola told Evans that he would have to "fire me and hire another director and tell *that director* to remove the music."

"He threatened to take his name out of the picture and take out ads in *The Hollywood Reporter* about what a terrible studio Paramount was," said Murch.

"Evans said, 'Okay, we'll keep the Nino Rota music,'" Murch continued, but he insisted that it would be done his way: both he and Coppola would cut their own version of the music, and play it for two audiences, which those present knew couldn't happen in the three weeks before the scheduled release.

"Right at that moment, Ali MacGraw came in with another plate of hot dogs, and she heard the last thing Evans said [about both he and Coppola cutting the music], and she said, 'Bob, don't forget we're going to Acapulco!'"

"So we had won," said Murch.

"Actually, the film was handled with great secrecy by Evans in those last months," Coppola continued. "There was a stalemate about this for about two weeks. Finally, I said that if we showed the movie to a small preview audience, and they didn't like the music, I'd take it out."

"Who decides if they like or don't like the music?" Evans asked.

"You can," said Coppola, adding, "The rest, as they say, is history."

The screening was a hit. "The audience liked the movie, the music, the acting, everything," said Coppola.

Ruddy loved the music, too, so much that when he ran the scene for his wife that Robert Towne had written, in which the Godfather speaks to his son Michael about his hopes and dreams, he amplified the Nino Rota theme. "And as I did so, I could see tears streaming down my wife's face," he said. "That's how powerful the music was."

The score would become a classic—and most likely would have won Nino Rota the Best Original Score Oscar, but the Academy determined that part of the "Love Theme" had been used in a different form in *Fortunella*. The score was on the ballot, then off, then up for a special vote to determine its eligibility before finally being disqualified. Still, the music was a hit, and not just with moviegoers—several versions, including a few that added lyrics to Rota's instrumental, made their way onto the American music charts.

They would play the music for Evans one more time before the movie's release.

"Okay, Walter, good luck," said Coppola.

What?

"I have to go back to San Francisco, do something with the music and we'll see what happens," he said.

Murch tried to think like Evans, he said. "I thought, *What is it about the music that he doesn't like?*"

He focused on the horse's head scene. The music over the scene was "a little soft," said Murch. "Francis and Nino Rota had chosen to do a kind of carousel-type thing to play against the horror."

Murch made it a little edgier: the lively carousel-style music outside of the home, then "as soon as you see a little smear of blood on the pillow," the carousel music becomes "dissonant," lacking harmony, and "really dissonant when he pulls the sheet away."

Then the screams begin.

"I called Evans in and said, 'I have something to show you,'" said Murch.

Evans came into the sound studio and lay upon his hospital bed. He watched. He listened.

He leapt off the bed. "It's great! It's great!" he exclaimed. "Get me a telephone!"

He was given a phone with a long cord, and dialed Charlie Bluhdorn in New York.

"Run it back to the beginning of the reel!" he commanded, and once the carousel music began darkening to serenade the horse's head scene, Evans ran up to the screen, triumphantly held up the phone and bellowed, "Charlie, listen to this!"

It was surreal. "We were looking at the head of the studio with a telephone casting a shadow on the screen, and on the screen was the head of Woltz Studios discovering that there was a horse's head in his bed," said Murch.

"It's great," Evans said after hanging up with Bluhdorn. "Keep up the good work."

Jack Ballard's reign over *The Godfather* came to an inglorious end during postproduction in the Paramount screening room. "We were screening the sound effects reel, right after Don Corleone leaves the hospital," said Murch. They were running one track out of many, which meant the finished track was far from complete. Around 8:00 p.m., Jack Ballard walked in and listened to a few minutes of the partial track.

"Then, he stood up and said, 'These are the worst sound effects I've ever heard in my life, and if they're in the final film you're never going to work in this town again,'" said Murch. "Or words to that effect."

The then twenty-eight-year-old Murch spoke up.

"Jack, you don't know what you're talking about. We're just listening to a few supplementary sound effects."

There was a long silence.

"He was swaying slightly, and I said, 'On top of everything else, you're drunk.'"

"He looked at everyone and said, 'You're right, I am drunk, and I don't know what the hell I'm talking about.'"

Then Ballard said the same thing that Evans had: "Keep up the good work."

"And then he turned around and left," said Murch.

ROBERT EVANS HAD yet another fight to go, this one against the ratings board.

"After the picture is finished—all the fights, all the wars, all the controversies—the MPAA voted to give the picture an X or an R," said Evans.

The all-powerful MPAA (Motion Picture Association of America), led by former Lyndon Johnson aide Jack Valenti, was ready to slap a limit on what mattered most: the audience. Upon reviewing a 1970 draft of the screenplay, the ratings board had already flagged the film for an R rating at best, cautioning them against "an overemphasis on blood and gore." They singled out three scenes: the horse's head ("excessive gruesomeness"), the strangling of Luca Brasi ("unduly vivid"), and Sonny's street beating of Carlo ("excessive").

Now that the movie was set for release, Evans girded himself for a fight.

He soon received a call from Bluhdorn's chief lieutenant, Martin Davis.

"Bob, they saw your guinea film," Evans quoted Davis as saying. "And to give it a PG [Parental Guidance under 13], you have to take two scenes out: one is Pacino going to Sicily, the bare-breasted scene on the night of their marriage. And the tollbooth scene of Jimmy Caan."

"You can't take that out!" Evans exploded.

Once he cooled down, he offered a compromise: "I'll take out the bare-breast scene, but the tollbooth scene is indigenous to the whole story."

Both scenes stayed in the movie.

"I insisted on it, and the studio took an R, very resentfully," said Evans. "And that scene [the Sonny assassination at the tollbooth] is possibly the greatest in the whole movie."

THE GODFATHER WAS now ready for release, its final cut, its music, even its promise via producer Al Ruddy to Joe Colombo that the word *Mafia* would never be uttered in the film. One day, at another of the endless test screenings, Ruddy settled into his seat to watch the movie once again.

The lights went down, and the face of the undertaker Bonasera filled the screen.

"I believe in . . . the *Mafia*," came the voice-over. "The *Mafia* has made my fortune."

Ruddy's heart stopped.

"I said, 'What the fuck is *this*?' And then I heard all of them behind me laughing."

The crew had dubbed in the word *Mafia* as a joke.

Still, the fate of *The Godfather*'s success was up in the air.

And most doubtful of all was the director, who confessed: "I was sure people would feel I had taken this exciting, bestseller novel and transformed it into a dark, ponderous, boring movie.

"Masterpiece, hah! I was not even confident it would be a mild success."

16

"A BAPTISM IN BLOOD"

The pieces had long ago been set in place.

The movie that would take the world by storm wouldn't do so by artistic excellence alone, but through the work of the whirlwind who would soon become known as the Godmother of *The Godfather*: Paramount's worldwide head of Publicity & Promotion, Marilyn Stewart.

Having devised and completed *The Godfather*'s campaign, "long before a single frame of the movie was even shot," Stewart said, she was no longer even employed at Paramount when the movie was being readied for release, in early 1972. She had moved out of her office in the Gulf+Western Building to launch her own PR agency. But she had left behind a ticking publicity time bomb that would, like the guns of the Corleones, explode.

A master of timing, she was a Bronx-born publicity pioneer who created carefully calculated advance publicity and marketing campaigns for everything from George McGovern's presidential run to MGM films. But it was her work on *Love Story* that astonished everyone from Charlie Bluhdorn to Robert Evans to those Kleenex-carrying audiences who lined up around the block for an opportunity to cry.

"I changed the way movies were marketed with *Love Story*," she said, her strategy being simple: start early and time everything to erupt upon release.

Her *Godfather* campaign began before Marlon Brando was officially cast. It included an urgent call from Evans: adding to the woes of casting Brando, the star refused to do publicity.

"Why won't Marlon do publicity?" Stewart asked Brando's lawyer, Norman Gary.

It was most likely because of Truman Capote, and his 1957 *New Yorker* story, "The Duke in His Domain," in which the Tiny Terror gutted Brando in a tell-all that the star despised, Brando's lawyer told her.

Which gave Stewart an idea:

"What if he could have approval of his quotes?"

"Nobody gets quote approval," said Gary, who added that if she could get quote approval from a major magazine, Brando would most likely "probably do a select few" interviews.

Stewart fired up the phones. First call: her friend Henry Grunwald, the all-powerful managing editor of *Time*. "Getting the cover of *Time* in those days was as if you got the full newscast of ABC, NBC, CBS, and Fox," said Stewart. "It was as if the whole newscast was devoted to your movie. That's what a *Time* cover meant in those days. And *Newsweek* was pretty close. And *Life* was also pretty powerful."

Grunwald ultimately passed, but *Life* and *Newsweek* agreed to covers. To escalate the magazines' exclusivity even higher, Stewart said that no photos of Brando as the Godfather would appear before their publication. Which was no easy promise to keep. "Before we even started shooting, the word was out on the street: ten thousand dollars for a picture of Marlon Brando as the Godfather," said Stewart, who then launched a new strategy.

"We're going to be shooting on location in Little Italy, how are you going to keep paparazzi from getting a picture?" she remembered Evans asking.

"Nobody knew I knew the Mafia!" she added.

Not only the Mafia but a high-level Brooklyn mobster, whom she had met when she was a young jazz singer in New York nightclubs in a past life.

"I need some help," she said.

"Whatever you need, you got, sweetheart," came the reply.

Extra guards had been hired on the dates when Brando would be filmed in full costume and makeup in Little Italy, but it was the behind-the-scenes protection that worked best. "If anybody sees anybody with a camera, they gotta get that camera and take the film out of it," Stewart told the enforcers.

Flash forward to the Little Italy film set. "And sure enough, some smart reporter had made a deal with some tenant and got into the apartment with a camera, and somebody downstairs on the crew saw it and told the production manager."

There's a guy with a camera up there in that window!

Oh, yeah?

"Two thugs went up to the apartment," said Stewart. "They didn't break his legs, but they took the film out of his camera. Then the word went out to the paparazzi."

Still, two photographers snuck onto the set—or above it. "Paramount Pictures has not allowed the public to see Brando in his makeup during the filming of *The Godfather*, reportedly because a national magazine plans to use a photo of Marlon as Don Vito Corleone on its cover," reported the *New York Daily News* of April 20, 1971. "Paramount tried to keep it that way on Mott St. yesterday—but they didn't reckon with *News* photographers who know more people in Little Italy than the M—— [Mafia] does."

The proof was in the pictures, far from close-ups, but clearly Marlon Brando as Vito Corleone, published in the *Daily News* that April.

The magazine covers would still run, along with simultaneous TV appearances by the stars and the myriad other aspects of Marilyn Stewart's publicity campaign triggered to explode upon the release. Until then, the film was under strict embargo.

And then a reporter snuck in . . .

*   *   *

"WHEN CAN I see the movie?"

Ivor Davis was an LA-based reporter for the *London Daily Express*, a British bloodhound who had heard the talk and read the headlines.

The reporter called Paramount PR, but all they would tell him was that press screenings would be announced soon.

Soon wasn't good enough. Press screenings meant a cattle call, and Ivor Davis wanted a scoop.

One night at Chasen's, the show-business canteen where Mario Puzo had stared down a fuming Frank Sinatra, the reporter told the maître d' about his quest to see the movie that everyone was talking about but nobody had seen.

A few days later, the reporter's phone rang.

"Ivor, they're having a private screening," said the maître d'.

It was a first-look screening for distributors in the private screening room of Bart Lytton's savings and loan. The maître d' said Davis could get into the screening by masquerading as a Chasen's catering waiter. Davis rushed over to the restaurant, where he was given a waiter's uniform and a one-day job.

"Keep your mouth shut," instructed the maître d'.

Davis soon arrived at the savings and loan on Sunset Boulevard for the movie. The bank had been built on hallowed Hollywood ground: the former site of the Garden of Allah Hotel, once the home to silent-movie star Alla Nazimova, and the fabled lodging of everyone from literary lions like Ernest Hemingway and F. Scott Fitzgerald to the stars of the silver screen, including Greta Garbo, Errol Flynn, Frank Sinatra, Humphrey Bogart, and Lauren Bacall. All of that history had been demolished to make way for the modernist S&L and the adjoining Lytton Center of the Visual Arts, with its 150-seat screening room.

Ivor Davis served drinks to the exhibitors for the cocktail hour. Then, when the lights went down, he removed his waiter's jacket, pulled out his notebook, and slipped into a seat in the back row. "The audience gasped," he wrote in his March 3, 1972, *Daily Express* scoop, a review syndicated to the *New York Post* and other papers, as "the camera finally settled on the almost unrecognizable face of one of the world's most famous actors."

But it was more than just Brando's transformation—it was the way he inhabited the role. "It only takes a few minutes to be convinced he is the stooped aging Mafioso chieftain who has survived untold wars but is slowly and inevitably sliding towards old age and senility," Davis wrote.

When the lights came back up, the reporter, along with the audience, was stunned.

The Godfather was a triumph, in Davis's eyes, and it had come in the nick of time. "Paramount Studios desperately needs a winner."

Davis thought they might just have one—with great performances by Brando and Pacino, and "beautifully directed" by Coppola. But the film would be tested with an unproven strategy, a big gamble that Paramount was willing to make that would change the landscape of movie distribution for years to come.

MARCH 14, 1972.

The limousine hired to pick up Mario Puzo and his family in Bay Shore, was a half hour late. Then an hour. Maybe the New York City driver was lost, not knowing his way around the suburbs where the creator of *The Godfather* lived. When the car still hadn't arrived after an hour and a half, Puzo piled his wife and kids into his own car, with his two older sons in the car ahead of them, and raced to the city. "Pissed off," his daughter Dorothy would write in an essay for *Esquire* magazine.

By the time he crossed the bridge into Manhattan, however, Puzo was singing Italian songs: "a very good sign," wrote Dorothy. Because this was the happiest of events, the world premiere of *The Godfather,* which included a dinner at the famed 21 Club and an afterparty for 350 invited guests in the St. Regis Roof Ballroom—both benefiting the Boys' Club of New York.

In their two-bedroom St. Regis suite, the Puzos changed into their formalwear:

Erika in white dress, white shoes, and white fur; Mario in his rented tuxedo with "a blue evening shirt with an awful lot of ruffles," the society columnist Suzy (Aileen Mehle) would write. "But there's a lot of Mario Puzo, isn't there?"

By 6:00 p.m., the Loew's State Theatre at Forty-Fifth and Broadway was overwhelmed: rain, soon turning to snow, along with heavy traffic and streets packed with fans. Charlie Bluhdorn had commanded Robert Evans to create a media "blitz." As promised, Marilyn Stewart had gotten the movie on the covers of both *Life* and *Newsweek* and covered in just about every newspaper and on television, creating a frenzy. "The mobs, the police, the klieg lights, the press, the public relations people were all poised to fall on superstar Brando the minute he emerged from his limousine," wrote Sally Quinn in the *Washington Post*.

The limo that some believed might be carrying Brando pulled up to the theater. The doors swung open, and out stepped—well, certainly *not* Marlon Brando, but an American Indian, as they were still called at the time. He was wearing a flowing, floor-length cape, bloodred and covered in insignia representing Mount Saint Elias, the majestic peak looming over the man's home village of Yakutat, Alaska (population 250), where he was raised as a member of the Tlingit tribe.

His name was Jim Thomas, then thirty-two. Fighting for Native-American rights across America had led Thomas into an enduring, close friendship with Marlon Brando.

Brando had called Thomas from France, where he was at that moment filming *Last Tango in Paris*, but his voice over the phone was gravelly. "He was still in character as Don Corleone," said Thomas.

And as Don Corleone, he had an offer that Thomas couldn't refuse: "I want you to go to the *Godfather* premiere in New York,'" Thomas remembered. "I want you to go in my place, as my friend, in full American Indian regalia."

Which meant full Tlingit regalia, which Thomas would wear over his tuxedo.

It was the latest move in his and Brando's fight to shine a light on the horrific history of injustices against Native Americans. Brando had originally planned to produce and star in a film about the bloody forced displacement of an estimated sixteen thousand Cherokee in the 1830s. It would center around part of the torturous Trail of Tears, which killed thousands, and for Brando, it was clear who the film's villain would be. "Marlon wanted to play President Andrew Jackson for what he was: evil," said Thomas. When that project fell through, they turned their attention instead to the Long Walk of the Navajo and the scorched-earth tactics of frontiersman Kit Carson. Brando would play Carson, not as "the American hero of history books, but as the bad guy, the leader of the march where so many Indians brutally died."

All that had come to naught. So Brando, still determined to bring about awareness, asked Thomas to attend the *Godfather* premiere, and to invite along as many fellow tribesmen and -women as possible, all expenses paid by Paramount. But Thomas could only enlist five others to join him; having never before attended a world premiere, he had told them they were simply going "to a movie," and who wanted to fly across the country for that?

Now, they were stepping out into the maelstrom of klieg lights and deliriously screaming fans, having traversed the clogged and snowy New York streets for an hour in a line of limos a mile long. Thomas was, admittedly, starstruck.

"Three hundred movie stars were there!" he said.

Striking in his red regalia, Thomas was quickly led up to a red velvet–covered platform outside the theater, and soon had a television camera in his face. "I'm Jim Thomas, an American Indian from Alaska," he said, "and I'm here as an invited guest of Marlon Brando, who has been very helpful to me and all American Indians." Brando had asked Thomas to keep his comments politically neutral, and Thomas agreed. His presence at the premiere was statement enough.

With that, Jim Thomas filed into the theater, eventually taking his seat in the same row where Ali MacGraw and Henry Kissinger would sit.

"Mario Puzo, the author, ladies and gentlemen, here he is, the author of this fabulous . . ." exclaimed the outdoor emcee of the movie premiere, the New York City talk-radio pioneer Barry Gray, who stood atop the tiny platform to introduce and interview the luminaries.

"Oh, he doesn't want to talk," said Gray as Puzo and his family entourage passed him by and filed into the theater. "There he goes, ladies and gentlemen."

And here they came: Kennedys and Fords, Raquel Welch ("What will you wear in your next movie, Raquel, baby?" asked Gray), Charles Bronson, Jack Nicholson, Al Pacino "and his beautiful lady," Jill Clayburgh ("Oh, I'm so proud to know you!" exclaimed Gray of Pacino), Francis and Eleanor Coppola (Francis in an orange velvet suit), and so many more.

Then, at last, the regal arrival of Robert Evans, emerging from a long black limousine. Having been unable to produce Brando, Evans enlisted a politically starry replacement, his close friend Dr. Henry Kissinger. "Kissinger? Kissinger? Evans, I love you! *I love you!*" Charlie Bluhdorn had exclaimed when Evans advised him the distinguished US secretary of state would be attending *The Godfather* festivities.

Sandwiching the premiere between snags in the Paris peace talks and a top-secret mission to Moscow the next morning, Kissinger entered the theater with Evans. No longer looking beleaguered or confined to a hospital bed, Evans was now beaming, with Henry Kissinger on one arm and his superstar wife on the other.

Inside the theater, the guests took their seats: the studio brass, the producer, director, author, actors, and invited guests. The lights went down. And went up again nearly three hours later. Some fumed (James Caan, angry that some of his scenes had been cut); some exhaled a sigh of relief (surely the director, happy that at least this part of the event was over).

But most were silent.

"No applause—not a sound—just silence. Scary? No, eerie," Evans would write of the audience reaction.

Then it was back into the rain and snow and on to the raucous, celebrity-studded gala in the St. Regis Roof. Evans had personally arranged *everything*, from taste-testing the food ("No, it's too bland. Get me a new chef. A Sicilian") to the orchestra ("Play *The Godfather* theme over and over until everyone is seated"). "All terribly mama mia," wrote Suzy. "Decorated à la Little Italy with millions of red paper roses hanging from trellises."

Waiters were costumed like Corleone bagmen: striped suits, black shirts, and white ties. A giant ice sculpture was carved in the shape of a submachine gun. It was "exactly like the Italian wedding scene in the film," wrote Sally Quinn. "With people embracing and kissing each other, dancing wildly, laughing, singing, and downing wine."

The Glenn Miller Orchestra played *The Godfather* theme; Andy Williams sang lyrics that had been added to Nino Rota's orchestral composition.

Finally, at 2:00 a.m., Robert Evans took the stage and thanked everyone, bringing them all onstage: the actors; the producer, Al Ruddy; the studio's owner, Charlie Bluhdorn; even the director, Francis Ford Coppola, whose party smile hid his deep despair.

"I had been so conditioned to thinking the film was bad, too dark, too long, too boring—that I didn't think it would have any success," he would later say. He was so sure of the film's failure—and "worried about supporting my family, now three kids"—that he accepted a script assignment for the Paramount production of *The Great Gatsby*, for which he would bang out a script in three weeks.

A week later, at the Hollywood premiere screening, its audience filled with stars, the reaction was strangely the same as in New York.

Silence.

"The silence of concentration was eerie," wrote the columnist Vernon Scott.

THE STUNNED SILENCE of the audiences—what did it mean?

Producer Al Ruddy was determined to find out.

Soon after the New York premiere. A rainy, mid-March New York afternoon. Al Ruddy and Al Pacino stood outside one of the the-aters where *The Godfather* was playing. They'd already seen the movie "a hundred times," said Ruddy, and no one knew the film better than them. So they weren't there to watch it again.

They were there to gauge the audience's reaction.

"Let's go, we'll come back at the end," Ruddy told Pacino.

A few drinks and almost three hours later, they returned, "ten min-utes from the end," said Ruddy. He and Pacino slipped into two seats near the back. They watched the final scene—Michael Corleone's door closing on Kay Adams's mournful face. They watched the credits roll and awaited the reaction.

Instead of applause, *nothing*.

"The lights come on, the eeriest feeling of all time," said Ruddy. "There was not one sound, no applause, the audience sat there, *stunned*."

The movie's star and producer stared at each other, not knowing what to make of the silence.

Jesus Christ, this is a fucking disaster, Ruddy thought. "People didn't know what to say. They got up and they walked out."

It wasn't a disaster; it was a phenomenon: a film that struck so deep into the hearts of its audiences that they were stunned into silence.

The movie opened across America on March 24, 1972, and even its distribution was a revolution. "Movies were always released in New York with one print on the East Side and one print on the West Side," said Ruddy. "We had twenty-six screens playing *The Godfather* in New York. I was heartbroken. I said, 'They'll probably run through it in a week and it'll be gone.'"

On the morning after the premiere, Al Ruddy drove to the Gulf+Western Building in the rain. "And I came down Broadway, passed the Paramount Theatre, and there was a line around the block. I don't mean a line in front. *The line was down the street* and around the block. People would pay to have a guy stand in line for them and get 'em tickets. It broke *Gone with the Wind*'s record in a week and a half. Everyone went berserk. Everyone *had* to see *The Godfather*."

Paramount had carefully planned a blitz. Rather than let the distributors dictate how the movie would be shown, Paramount's new president, Frank Yablans, devised a radical distribution scheme: Instead of releasing the film slowly, gradually, letting its audience build via word of mouth in the traditional method called "snowballing," the studio would take just five days to release the film in 316 theaters across the country. And the theaters were going to show the movie the way Paramount intended—all two hours and fifty-five minutes at once, with no intermission.

"Though some exhibitors wanted to book the movie with an intermission, Yablans held firm, even canceling some bookings over the issue," wrote Peter Bart in *Infamous Players*. Paramount dispatched scouts to bust any theater owner who tried to break the movie at the halfway point—the shooting of Sollozzo and McCluskey in Louis Italian American Restaurant—for concessions.

Those clamoring for tickets also included members of the movie's source material—the Mob—one of whose soldiers Ruddy heard from on the day of the premiere. "Hey, they won't sell us no tickets to this thing," said the voice on the phone.

"To be honest, I don't think they want you there," Ruddy replied.

"That's very unfair, don't you think?"

"What do you mean?"

"When they do a movie about the army, the generals are guests of honor, right? If they do a movie about the navy, who's sitting up front? The admirals. You'd think we'd be guests of honor at this thing."

Without Paramount's knowledge, Ruddy snuck out a print and presented a screening for "the boys."

"There must have been a hundred limousines out front," he said. "The projectionist called me and said, 'Mr. Ruddy, I've been a projectionist my whole life. No one ever gave me a thousand-dollar tip.'

"That's how much the guys loved the movie."

It was the result of an unexpected alchemy: All the fights and conflicts—"all this strife," as Bart called it—somehow coalesced into a masterpiece. "Coppola somehow managed to galvanize the tensions on the set into sort of a creative frenzy," wrote Bart in an afterword for the

2002 edition of *The Godfather*. "Al Pacino's performance had an edge because the young actor thought he might be fired at any moment. Coppola was determined to throw everything into his scenes day by day because he, too, felt that every shooting day might be his last."

At that moment, at the dawning of his movie's success, Francis Ford Coppola remained in the depths of despair. He had fled San Francisco for Paris, where he hoped to find peace and quiet to write his next screenplay. He checked into L'Hôtel, a boutique hotel on the Left Bank. Here, in room 16, named the Oscar Wilde Suite—in the hotel Wilde died in on November 30, 1900, after what he called "a duel to the death" with the hotel's once-tacky wallpaper—Coppola struggled to write the screenplay for *The Great Gatsby*. It was another Paramount production, another assignment from Robert Evans, another job he was doing for the money.

This time, he had no prompt book to work from, no action-packed novel as the source material. Coppola had quickly discovered that F. Scott Fitzgerald's literary masterpiece was more resistant to adaptation than Puzo's cinematic bestseller. "I had just realized that there were only two or three lines of dialogue between Gatsby and Daisy in the book and I panicked," he said. Once again, Coppola was terrified, this time because he felt that he would have "to make it all up," meaning the dialogue between two of the most iconic fictional characters of all time.

In the middle of his terror, the phone in his hotel room rang: Eleanor, calling from New York. She knew that her husband felt sure that the reaction to his film was going to be "a disaster."

Instead, she was calling with incredible news. Still in New York after the premiere, she could see a movie theater with *The Godfather* on its marquee just outside her window, and right there, on the street, day and night, was a miracle: lines snaking around the block. Starting in the morning and continuing throughout the day and deep into the night, sometimes with only a five-minute recess between showings.

"Oh, my God, Francis, this is a phenomenon!" she exclaimed. "You won't believe it."

* * *

ALONG WITH THE crowds came the reviews. "*The Godfather* is a baptism in blood, a ripping, tearing blockbuster of a movie, as charged with excitement as a hoodlum using a machine gun, as shocking as the St. Valentine's Day Massacre," wrote Joyce Haber in the *Los Angeles Times*. That same day, March 16, 1972, the *New York Times* published its rave. "*The Godfather* is a superb Hollywood movie," wrote Vincent Canby. "It's the gangster melodrama come-of-age, truly sorrowful and truly exciting . . . scaring the delighted hell out of us while cautioning that crime doesn't (or at least shouldn't) pay."

The critics loved the writing: "It is probably the best transition of a major novel to the screen since *Gone with the Wind*," read the review in the *Los Angeles Herald-Examiner*, followed by approval from the mountaintop, Pauline Kael, the dean of movie critics, in the *New Yorker*: "Francis Ford Coppola, who directed the film and wrote the script with Puzo, has stayed very close to the book's greased-lightning sensationalism and yet has made a movie with the strength that popular novels such as Dickens' used to have."

The critics hailed the return of Marlon Brando. "After a very long time in too many indifferent or half-realized movies, giving performances that were occasionally becalmed but always more interesting than the material, Marlon Brando has finally connected with a character and a film that need not embarrass America's most complex, most idiosyncratic film actor, nor those critics who have wondered, in bossy print, what ever happened to him," wrote Canby in the *New York Times*.

They loved Al Pacino. "The movies have a new superstar—a guy who was just another actor yesterday—in Al Pacino," wrote syndicated columnist James Bacon. "Pacino steals the movie even from Brando's best performance since 'On the Waterfront.'"

They even, for the most part, loved the long runtime, proving the marketing and distribution departments (which argued for shorter) and the distributors (who demanded an intermission to sell more concessions) wrong: "It is swift and theatrical, probably the fastest three-hour movie in history," wrote Charles Champlin in the *Los Angeles Times*. "Yet, full as it is, 'The Godfather' goes by evenly, so we don't feel rushed, or restless, either; there's classic grandeur to the narrative flow," added Kael.

Not all the reviews were triumphant. After praising the film's production value and cast, *Variety* added, "[I]t is overlong at about 175 minutes (played without intermission), and occasionally confusing." "While never so placid as to be boring, it is never so gripping as to be superior screen drama." And the conservative columnist William F. Buckley called it "positively embarrassing," adding that Mario Puzo's novel "is sucked dry of all the juices that made it such an extraordinary feast."

But most agreed with *Newsweek*, which predicted it would be "the *Gone with the Wind* of gangster movies."

Analyzing its success in *Vogue*, the historian Arthur Schlesinger Jr. wrote that the key to the film was that it "shrewdly touches contemporary nerves. Our society is pervaded by a conviction of powerlessness. *The Godfather* makes it possible for all of us, in the darkness of the movie house, to become powerful."

"Francis Ford Coppola's screen version of Mario Puzo's *The Godfather* [is] the year's first really satisfying, big commercial American film," added Canby in the *New York Times*. Less than a year before, Canby had, along with so many others, questioned whether or not a death knell was ahead for films, writing, "The movie industry is collapsing, everybody knows that."

Now even Canby couldn't deny the movie that had, well, saved the movies. "Your film is a real shot in the arm for anyone who loves our medium," *Lawrence of Arabia* director David Lean wrote Coppola after the release. "In the last few years it has seemed to me that our business has been practically taken over by a bunch of fashionable amateurs and now, out of the gloom, comes your movie which puts all the nonsense into perspective. (Even that mean little bastard on the London 'Times' is forced to call it 'a stunningly professional piece of work.')"

In *The Godfather*, Coppola had created "what [Boris] Pasternak calls 'The presence of art,'" Lean wrote. "Whether you know it or not it's there, very strong—almost the leading character, and because it's so powerful it gives those terrible characters a size which can't have been written in the script and I almost resent you for making me accept them as human beings whom I should tolerate—and I did—very much so until a couple of days after your magic wore off!"

Across America, and the world, audiences were experiencing the same magic, awakening from what seemed to be a three-hour trance.

Then it began minting money.

The Godfather hauled in $465,148 in its first week alone from just the five Manhattan theaters, "the largest one-week total ever for a motion picture," marveled the March 23, 1972, *Hollywood Reporter*. By the following week, the movie had racked up $7,397,164 across 322 theaters in the US and Canada—and the momentum was just beginning. In less than a month after the opening, *The Godfather* was grossing $1 million *a day*, the first film ever to break the magical million-dollar mark. Many theaters were showing it practically around the clock, opening with a 9:00 a.m. screening and closing with a last run at 3:30 *a.m.*—which, for a movie with a nearly three-hour runtime, left a scant two and a half hours each day when *The Godfather* wasn't showing.

"Godfather: Boon to All Pix" read the *Variety* headline just weeks after the release of the movie that was on its way to revitalizing its industry. Encouraged in part by the critics, and the built-in audience from Puzo's novel—which was rereleased alongside the film in a 1.5-million-copy Fawcett paperback edition—*Godfather* mania swept America. The throngs overwhelmed theaters, clamoring for tickets and forming lines around blocks, coast to coast, prompting the *Los Angeles Times* to run an instructional "guide for making Godfather line-waiting not only tolerable, but fun."

Entitled "Lifestyles for Waiting in Line to See 'Godfather,'" the story's advice included: lining up for the 9:30 a.m. Sunday showing instead of the more popular times; walking to the theater instead of driving as surely there will be no place to park; choosing something else to do on a first date (to avoid looking like a loser in light of a likely sell-out). "And keep your eyes open. . . . In one line alone, reportedly, there was one childbirth (and she didn't cry once throughout the film's three hours), two arrests and one divorce (the man remarried). Bringing a musical instrument is enjoyed by all and your Christmas shopping can be done in rotation since you'll be passing every kind of store imaginable on your slow route forward . . .

"Let's not sugarcoat it, the lines are enormous," the article continued. "In fact, on a Saturday night they're so long you could conceivably cross three zip codes. 'The Godfather' is more important than life (and the lines are longer). It will no doubt outgross 'Love Story,' outrun Jim Ryun, outlast 'Gone with the Wind,' and possibly emerge as the candidate at the Democratic Convention. It is permeating every area of our lives about now and rumor has it, in fact, that it is sneaking into the Nielsen's and even threatening 'All in the Family.'"

With the bonanza came the thieves: the ticket scalpers, black-market print bandits, and greedy theater owners. Some theaters tried to defy Paramount's prohibition on intermissions, which enabled them to sell more concessions to frenzied audiences, which the studio snuffed out and stopped whenever possible.

Frank Yablans's release strategy had worked, so well that in May he sent $500 checks to all of the Loew's theater managers in Manhattan, as a thank-you for handling two months of teeming crowds that had descended upon their sidewalks.

By August, the studio bought major advertisements in the trade papers, announcing that *The Godfather* had crossed the $100 million mark in total gross, a staggering number, and with no end in sight. Just a month after the premiere, the market value of Gulf+Western's stock had increased by $97 million—and the world knew why. The conglomerate was quickly becoming known as "*The Godfather* company."

From there, it was on to worldwide domination. In time for the 1972 Summer Olympics, in Munich, Paramount planned to release the movie in seven languages to capitalize on the international audience attending the games. All box-office records were broken in Japan, the first seven weeks alone bringing in one million viewers. Then came the supreme test: the country of *The Godfather*'s source material: Italy, where producer Dino De Laurentiis had predicted to Charlie Bluhdorn, "If Brando plays the don, forget opening the film in Italy. They'll laugh him off the screen."

Instead, it didn't merely open in Italy; like everywhere else, it overwhelmed both theaters and audiences. Even Sicily received the film with open arms. "Marlon Brando is the envy of all the real Godfathers on the island," the editor of Palermo's newspaper told the *Los Angeles Herald-Examiner*. "They wish they were that good looking and suave."

"Dubbed into Sicilian dialect, the dirty words were dirtier and jokes coarser, much to the delight of the audience, which tittered at each bloodbath," noted a UPI reporter covering the film opening in Sicily.

Back in America, Dino De Laurentiis was preparing his movie based on *The Valachi Papers*, in Manhattan, and was supposedly facing the same reputed "pressures" that Al Ruddy had so artfully navigated for Paramount. "When I first heard Dino was coming to New York to make the film, I figured he had already spoken to the 'right people,'" Ruddy told *Variety*. "It's a delicate subject. It's better to take time and be careful."

By the end of 1972, *The Godfather* was a supernova, the likes of which Hollywood had never seen before. At the Gulf+Western annual meeting, Charlie Bluhdorn announced that *The Godfather* would earn $150 million in worldwide rentals. "Our rate of failures is the lowest in the history of the company," regaled the mogul with the short memory. "And we've got the best ratio of hits against flops in the industry." The movie would go on to earn more than $250 million worldwide, a figure that continues to grow today.

Between *Love Story* and *The Godfather*, Paramount was suddenly the most successful movie studio in the world. Robert Evans was once again Charlie Bluhdorn's golden boy, along with Francis Ford Coppola.

In December, Coppola received a letter from Frank Capra, the legendary Italian American director behind such iconic films as *Mr. Smith Goes to Washington* and *It's a Wonderful Life*. Once rumored to be one of the directors in the running to replace Coppola, he was now writing to express a sentiment shared by many in the industry:

> *Dear Francis,*
>
> *On our way to dinner my wife and I saw 'Godfather' on a small theater marquee—and no long line at the B.O. We rushed in to see it. I expected a lot, of course. But Madonna! It's much greater than I expected. In fact, it's the best film I've seen in the last ten years . . .*
>
> *Admiringly,*
>
> *Frank.*

Then came the 1973 Oscars. *The Godfather* was nominated for ten awards: Best Picture; Brando as Best Actor; Coppola for Best Director; Coppola and Puzo for Best Adapted Screenplay; Pacino, Caan, Duvall each for Best Supporting Actor; along with nominations for costumes, editing, and sound.

Bob Fosse's *Cabaret* was the front-runner, and would win eight of its ten nominations: the sound and editing awards both went to *Cabaret*, and Bob Fosse would ultimately edge out Francis Ford Coppola for Best Director. Pacino, Caan, and Duvall were all passed over in favor of Joel Grey, who won Best Supporting Actor for his part as *Cabaret*'s emcee. Then the tide turned. Jack Lemmon opened the envelope for the Best Adapted Screenplay category: "Mario Puzo and Francis Ford Coppola for *The Godfather*!"

In his suburban New York living room, Mario Puzo sat before the TV (and the pizza), speechless. The frog had become a prince. "But he still felt like a frog; he felt sure he would lose," said Lanetta Wahlgren. "The simple answer is he was too nervous to speak if he won," said his son Anthony. His daughter Dorothy accepted on his behalf.

Coppola thanked Peter Bart, who, he said, "was responsible for getting me this job in the first place, which sort of rescued me from my wonderful, romantic financial adventure in San Francisco, which still lives."

He thanked Robert Towne, as promised, for writing "the very beautiful scene between Marlon and Al Pacino in the garden."

He added "that the best award a director could get would be to have three of his best friends and dear associates and actors—Jimmy Caan, Al Pacino, and Bobby Duvall—all get nominated in the same category."

Next, Roger Moore and Liv Ullmann opened the envelope for Best Actor: "Marlon Brando in *The Godfather*."

Then, instead of Brando, a White Mountain Apache and Yanqui woman named Sacheen Littlefeather rose from her seat, in full Apache dress, and solemnly made her way to the stage. She held her hand out to refuse the award that Roger Moore tried to present to her on Brando's behalf. Then she read a brief statement, explaining that the actor "very regretfully cannot accept this very generous award, and the reasons for this being are the treatment of the American Indians today by the film industry . . . ," which brought an interruption of boos and then applause. "On television, in movie reruns, and also with recent happenings at Wounded Knee."

Finally, the nominees for Best Picture. *The Godfather* was up against *Deliverance*, *Sounder*, *The Emigrants*, and of course *Cabaret*. Al Ruddy's longtime friend Clint Eastwood would present the award, and Ruddy had made a suggestion to Eastwood before the ceremony: "Clint, when you get up there and they say the winner is, just tear it up if it's not me and say 'Al Ruddy.'"

Eastwood didn't have to lie. When he opened the envelope it read, Best Picture, *The Godfather*.

"When he said *The Godfather*, we all had a heart attack," said Ruddy.

He sprinted to the stage to accept the award. All the hardships, all the battles seemed to be instantly forgotten, as Ruddy thanked *everyone*.

"Marlon won the Academy Award, Paramount won the Bank of America Award, and every other award as well," wrote Robert Evans, as Bluhdorn reveled in his studio's success and the sequel that was already in the works, with a slated release date of April 1974. When

Coppola initially demurred directing the sequel, Hurricane Charlie erupted, "Francis, you've got the recipe for Coca-Cola, and you don't want to manufacture any more bottles of Coke!" Coppola signed on for *Godfather II* and, after that, *Godfather III*.

Those who had points, meaning a percentage of the film, each point representing 1 percent of the financials, got rich. The movie made millionaires of Al Ruddy, Mario Puzo, and Francis Coppola—but not its star, Marlon Brando. He had signed to do the movie for only $50,000—well below his typical minimum—along with a few percentage points of the profits, compensation that often ends up being worthless as Hollywood accounting keeps the film from ever "officially" turning a profit. But it was difficult to hide profits on a $6 million movie that was racing past the $100 million mark. A month before principal photography began, Brando's attorney called Robert Evans, saying Brando couldn't pay his taxes and needed $100,000, which could be applied against his next movie commitment, fast.

"Bluhdorn's face lit up," wrote Evans.

"Give it to him," said Bluhdorn. "We don't want his next commitment. Get back his points. They're worth nothing anyways."

"Bluhdorn's success didn't happen by mistake," wrote Evans.

Brando returned his points, which wouldn't kick in until the movie had done $10 million in rentals—meaning Paramount's share of the revenue from ticket sales—an amount *The Godfather* quickly earned fifteen times over. "For 100 Gs, Paramount took all of Marlon's gross points—eventually costing Marlon $11 million," wrote Evans. "He fired his lawyer, his agent, and everyone else close to him."

MONEY COULDN'T BUY the glory the movie bestowed: resuscitating the career of Marlon Brando, saving Paramount, revitalizing and revolutionizing the entire film industry, turning its stars into icons and its mobsters into folk heroes.

Charlie Bluhdorn's company Gulf+Western would change its

name to Paramount Communications in 1989, reflecting its main business. Many would find it ironic that this industrialist who struck it rich in so many disparate fields would be remembered in large part for a movie and its two sequels. Coppola would dedicate *Godfather: Part III* to Bluhdorn "who inspired it," referring to Bluhdorn telling Coppola details of his relationship with the shadowy Sicilian financier Michele Sindona, whose dark dealings with the Vatican would soon be legendary. Bluhdorn wouldn't live long enough to see that third *Godfather*, but he was all for making more. "Maybe—who knows?—maybe we can go all the way up to *Godfather VI*?" Bluhdorn wrote, before succumbing to a heart attack in 1983, at the age of fifty-six, while flying from the Dominican Republic on his company plane.

Out on the South Shore of Long Island, Mario Puzo lived in the big house he bought soon after his novel became a hit. Just beyond the bedroom, with its purple carpets, was his office, painted his favorite color—pink. He published six more novels, all bestsellers, and became a multimillionaire screenwriter, not only of *The Godfather* and its sequels but also *Superman*, in 1978, and its sequel two years later. Along the way, he learned that two worlds that he had conquered in his writing—Hollywood and the Mob—are really very similar. "I think the movie business is far more crooked than Vegas, and, I was going to say, than the Mafia," he once said at a symposium. "He also believed there wasn't a producer who didn't think that he could write an Academy Award–winning screenplay if [they] just had the time," said his son Anthony. "And he soon learned about the thievery in Hollywood. When they said a picture cost 70 million, it really cost 20 million, and they would steal the 50 million!"

He died of heart failure on July 2, 1999, at seventy-eight. At his funeral, laminated cards were passed out with a quote from his novel *Fools Die*: "Merlin, Merlin . . . Surely a thousand years have passed and you must be awake in your cave, putting on your star-covered conical hat to walk through a strange new world."

It was a reference to Puzo's favorite mythological character, Merlin, and the magic that transformed a dead-broke, middle-aged writer who once lay in a gutter into a prince of Hollywood and the envy of the literary world.

By 2020, Al Ruddy was the senior surviving member of the team that produced *The Godfather*. At ninety, he had won two Best Picture Oscars—one for producing *The Godfather* and a second in 2005 for *Million Dollar Baby*. But the historic deal he made with the Mob was surely the ultimate example of his prowess as a producer who could talk his way into—and out of—anything. This did him little good, however, one night when the dark forces he had once subdued rose up against him once more.

Midnight in his Coldwater Canyon home above Beverly Hills. Someone at the door, which Ruddy rose to open. Only to find a massive shadow before him, blocking out every inch of light. When his eyes gained focus, he recognized the shadow as not merely a man but a monster, a giant:

It was Lenny Montana.

Perhaps at this moment, the early warnings of Mario Puzo came back to haunt Al Ruddy. He had turned to the author for advice when problems first arrived with Joe Colombo and his family and followers over filming *The Godfather* in New York. *What the fuck do I know about Mob guys?* Ruddy thought before meeting Joe Colombo back then. He called Puzo and said, "Mario, I gotta go meet this guy, Joe Colombo, and I wonder if you would like to come with me."

Puzo was shocked. "Are you insane?" he replied. "Ruddy, you are out of your league. This is not a Hollywood guy. You're dealing with a guy who's very dangerous. . . . Not only will I not go with you, but if you go don't tell him you even know me."

Ruddy had ignored Puzo's advice. Not only had he taken the meeting; he had also made a deal with Joe Colombo and had met others with "connections." Now, on this night, at his door to his home, stood the result of getting too close to the real thing.

Without a word, the 320-pound wrestler-bouncer-bodyguard who played Luca Brasi reared back one of his ham fists and brought it crashing down across the thin producer's face, with a force and ferocity that Al Ruddy had never known.

The punch lifted Ruddy off his feet. He was airborne. He crashed against a wall and scampered to his feet, bleeding. And there he saw, beside Montana, another man: "Tommy Fingers" Ricciardi, considered by police to be a Colombo family solider, who had been standing near Joe Colombo when he was shot. (Ricciardi would die in 1979.)

"What did you do that for!?" Tommy Fingers exclaimed, trying to calm Montana down before he had the chance to slug Ruddy again. It worked. Montana turned to leave, but before he did, he slammed the front door so hard it almost came off its hinges.

Who sent the henchmen? Fifty years later, no one could say for sure. Perhaps it was someone intertwined in both the movie and the Mob, which only served to underscore the warning Ruddy had received from Puzo. "Once you are involved with these guys," the author had told him, "you can never get out."

AS FOR LENNY Montana, he left one life behind for another: a career in Hollywood, where he appeared in twenty-one movies and television series before dying of a heart attack at age sixty-one in 1984. "I ask for $70,000 or $80,000 and a percentage of the picture," he told an interviewer, in the limelight of his newfound fame. "If I don't like the author I refuse it."

He said he'd turned down roles in the Mob movies *The Valachi Papers* and *The Gang that Couldn't Shoot Straight* and the television production of Gay Talese's *Honor Thy Father*. "I just didn't believe in the scripts," he said.

"But the thing I'm looking forward [to] is winning an award [for] this *Godfather*."

"An Academy Award?" asked the reporter Philip Nobile.

"Yes, for Best Supporting Actor," said Montana. "I've been told by many people, in fact thousands and thousands, that I should be up for an Academy Award no matter how big the part was. I was effective and real. I think a man should be given an award for a thing like that.... The least the Academy could do is give me a little recognition." (The Academy didn't include him in the nominations.)

WAIT. **WHAT ABOUT** the women? The beaten Connie, the subservient Mama Corleone, played by the jazz singer Morgana King, who was to singing "what Miles Davis was to the trumpet," said her friend Marilyn Stewart. What about the lustful Lucy Mancini, and all the wives and mothers, blowing kisses and making babies. And what about Kay Adams, the New England schoolteacher who only regains her Michael "after the Sicilian village girl, his sexual and tribal soul mate, has been wed and dispatched by a car bomb meant for him," wrote film critic Molly Haskell in the *New York Times*, in a 1997 story entitled "World of 'The Godfather': No Place for Women."

In the movie's ending, the door of Michael's study closes on Kay, who "having been lied to by her husband, Michael (Al Pacino) about his business (the murder of their brother-in-law), leaves his study, shaky but still smiling, to fix herself a drink," wrote Haskell.

Poor Kay seemed to exist only in relation to her husband. Pages of Puzo's novel featuring Kay without Michael or another man nearby didn't make it into the script, whose original draft contained a brief exchange between Kay and Mama Corleone ("an important relationship," Coppola wrote in his notebook), which didn't make it into the film.

Yet that final shot of Kay standing alone outside of Michael's study would become iconic, her profound sense of betrayal and despair conveyed in a single look. The audience at last sees the depth of her character.

And then the door closes.

"It's the closing of the door that has reverberated through our culture almost as shockingly as that other famous door-shutting, Nora's on Torvald in Ibsen's 'Doll House,'" Haskell continued, referring to one woman who leaves her husband (Nora) and one who stays (Kay).

The door that closed in 1972 was far different from the one that slammed in 1879, the year of the premiere of Ibsen's play, with the 1970s ready to roar with the women's liberation movement.

Yes, *The Godfather* was a movie dominated by its male characters, "on the backs of acquiescent women," according to Haskell, but it was also a triumph for at least two women in starring roles: Diane Keaton and Talia Shire.

Keaton hadn't watched the movie for thirty years. But preparing to appear at the forty-five-year cast reunion in 2017, she watched it on her laptop. "I couldn't get over it . . . ," she said at the reunion. "Everything was just astonishing to me, and I was totally surprised because I didn't expect it. And on the fucking computer! I was so shocked by it because I never really paid much attention to *The Godfather* because I always felt like I was the most outsider, weird person in the movie and 'Why was I cast, again?' and I had no voice . . ."

Keaton's charisma injected unscripted strength into the otherwise anemic character of Kay. But, as Haskell wrote, it was only in the following decade, "the leanest for women in cinematic history," that she "lit up the screen with her maverick personality." She would win the 1978 Best Actress Oscar for *Annie Hall*. As for Talia Shire, she would rise from her role as Connie to Oscar nominations for *Rocky* and *The Godfather, Part II*.

The creation soon outshone its creators, rising to the level of myth, its language and lore becoming part of popular culture, as embedded in the new century as the works of poets and prophets were in the old. The term *godfather* entered the lexicon as both a term of power and endearment. The line "I'm gonna make him an offer he can't refuse" was named by the American Film Institute in 2005 as the number two top American cinema quotation of all time, just behind *Gone with the Wind*'s "Frankly my dear, I don't give a damn."

The key to it all was that the movie felt so familiar, its scenes "like a memory," as the actor Alec Baldwin would say, stunning not only its audience but also the industry. "I was pulverized by the story and the effect the film had on me," said the director Steven Spielberg. "I also felt that I should quit. There was no reason to continue directing because I would never achieve that level of confidence and the ability to tell a story such as the one I'd just experienced. So in a way it shattered my confidence."

Finally and forever, Francis Ford Coppola. Hailed as the genius of *The Godfather*, he became a five-time Oscar winner and the recipient of the Academy's 2010 Irving G. Thalberg Award, along with owning a Napa and Sonoma County winery and five luxury resorts. A legend of American cinema, he continues to strive for majesty in film, as he did with the Mob movie that broke box-office records, flying by the $50 million mark in months. Which meant that Robert Evans needed to make good on his bet and buy the director who had by then become his nemesis a Mercedes.

"The day *The Godfather* passed $50 million, Francis bought a Mercedes 600, the most expensive on the market," Evans wrote. "The bill wasn't sent to Paramount, but personally to Robert Evans."

Coppola would of course have his own version of that bonus: that Evans reneged on buying the car at the promised $50 million box-office mark and didn't pay off the bet until the picture had done twice that. "When the picture had done $100 million, George Lucas and I walked into the Mercedes dealership in San Francisco and I said, 'We want to see the Mercedes 600,'" he told Peter Biskind in his book *Easy Riders, Raging Bulls*. He was referring to the custom-made Mercedes whose owners included the Spanish general Francisco Franco and, yes, the pope. "The salesmen kept passing us along to other salesmen, because we looked like slobs and had driven up in a Honda. They showed us a few sedans, and we kept saying, 'No, no! We want the one with the six doors.' So finally some young salesman who didn't know any better took the order. I said, 'Send the bill to Paramount Pictures,' and they did."

The bill for the car was a minor skirmish compared to the war of words that soon erupted.

Coppola struck in 1975, telling *Playboy* that he blamed Evans for the studio's initial resistance over casting Marlon Brando. "We got in touch with Evans, pitched Brando, and listened to him yell at us for being fools," he said.

Evans struck back in a 1977 tell-all interview with syndicated columnist Marilyn Beck. Upon her arrival at Woodland, Evans had his "servants hold all calls," Beck wrote, and let it rip, blaming his obsession over *The Godfather* for throwing his wife Ali MacGraw "into the arms of Steve McQueen."

"All she wanted to do was stay home and be part of my life, but I was too busy to have any time for anything but my career," Evans said. "I pushed her into making *The Getaway* with McQueen, and—talk about twisted priorities—I never visited her once during the three months she was on location with the picture. I was working night and day, eighteen hours a day, getting the original *Godfather* in shape. It was in such big trouble we had to pull it back from intended Christmas release and hold it until March, while I edited and re-edited it time and again. My compensation? Nothing. . . . And if you think I'm bitter, you're right."

"His bitterness also extends to Francis Ford Coppola," Beck wrote, who, Evans said, he'd rescued from oblivion. "When I hired Coppola for *Godfather* everybody thought I was nuts," he said. "He'd only made three movies, and they'd all been failures, but I had faith in him . . .

"He ended up with a fortune and I ended up with a divorce—and not even a thank you."

Evans called Coppola a "fat fuck" in his 1994 autobiography. ("The fat fuck shot a great film, but it ain't on the screen," he said he told Charlie Bluhdorn amid the debate over the movie's length.)

"Evans claimed he had saved the picture because he asked me to put back the half hour that he had told me to take out," Coppola told *Cigar Aficionado* in 2003.

By then the conflict had reached a fever pitch, evidenced by two scorching telegrams between the dueling duo, more than a decade after the release of *The Godfather*. Coppola couldn't remember what sparked his telegram, but soon there they were, printed in full, such a heated back-and-forth that they would be auctioned for $38,400 in 2020 as part of Evans's estate after his death.

12/13/83

DEAR BOB EVANS,

IVE BEEN A REAL GENTLEMAN REGARDING YOUR CLAIMS OF INVOLVEMENT ON THE GODFATHER. IVE NEVER TALKED ABOUT YOUR THROWING OUT THE NINO ROTA MUSIC, YOUR BARRING THE CASTING OF PACINO AND BRANDO, ETC. BUT CONTINUALLY YOUR STUPID BLABBING ABOUT CUTTING THE GODFA-THER COMES BACK TO ME AND ANGERS ME FOR ITS REDICULOUS [*sic*] POMPOSITY.

YOU DID NOTHING ON THE GODFATHER OTHER THAN ANOY [*sic*] ME AND SLOW IT DOWN THAT IS WHY CHARLIE PUT IN THE GODFATHER II CON-TRACT THAT YOU COULD HAVE NOTHING TO DO WITH THE MOVIE.

YOU WILL NEVER SEE THE COTTON CLUB UNTIL IT IS AN ANSWER PRINT. YOU HAVE DOUBLE CROSSED ME FOR THE LAST TIME.

IF YOU WANT A P R WAR OR ANY KIND OF WAR, NO ONE IS BETTER AT IT THAN ME.

FRANCIS COPPOLA

TOTALLY INDEPENDENT LTD
34-31 35 ST
ASTORIA NY 11106

12/14/83

DEAR FRANCIS

THANK YOU FOR YOUR CHARMING CABLE. I CANNOT
IMAGINE WHAT PROMPTED THIS VENOMOUS DIA-
TRIBE.

I AM BOTH ANNOYED AND EXASPERATED BY YOUR
FALLACIOUS ACCUSATIONS, WHEN ALL I DO IS
PRAISE YOUR EXTRAORDINARY TALENTS AS A FILM-
MAKER.

CONVERSELY, YOUR BEHAVIOR TOWARDS ME GLAR-
INGLY LACKS ANY IOTA OF CONCERN, HONESTY
OR INTEGRITY. I AM AFFRONTED BY YOUR GALL IN
DARING TO SEND THIS MACHIVELLIAN EPISTEL [*sic*].
THE CONTENT OF WHICH IS NOT ONLY LUDICROUS,
BUT TOTALLY MISREPRESENTS THE TRUTH. I CAN
NOT CONCEIVE WHAT MOTIVATED YOUR MALI-
CIOUS THOUGHTS, BUT IF THEY ARE A REFLECTION
OF YOUR HOSTILITY, I BEAR GREAT SYMPATHY AND
CONCERN FOR YOUR APPARENT PARANOID-SCHIZO-
PHRENIC BEHAVIOR. HOWEVER, DEAR FRANCIS, DO
NOT MISTAKE MY KINDNESS FOR WEAKNESS.

ROBERT EVANS

By then, they "just hated each other," said Peter Bart.

FOR COPPOLA, THE movie that made him also left him with a sense
of dread.

"I become nauseous when I think about it," he said often. George
Lucas would insist that his longtime friend and mentor was sick over
"the experience . . . not the movie itself."

Still, the film followed Coppola like a dark shadow, its iconic music sickening him when it was cued up to celebrate him when he entered a restaurant or other public place. He was also haunted by the real-life counterparts of the characters he so vividly brought to life on-screen. Once, he encountered a group of "suspiciously tough Italian men."

Recognizing the director, they "were stealing glances at me and talking among themselves."

"I heard the name Mario Puzo on their lips, and a guy who could have played Luca Brasi pushed his way over to me and said aggressively, 'You didn't make him. He made you!'"

To which Coppola could not disagree, later writing, "It is absolutely true that Mario 'made' me, and his novel *The Godfather* changed my life."

Epilogue

THE MAN WHO TOUCHED MAGIC

In the Beverly Hills home that movies built, known as Woodland, Robert Evans sat up in his bed, still glued to the screen.

"It's my most important legacy," he said of *The Godfather*, holding firm to his conviction that he had saved the movie, the studio, and, in many ways, elevated the glory of American film.

He told me this as I laid in bed beside him on that glorious afternoon back in 2008, as the credits rolled and the bedroom lights went up. "When you walked out of *The Godfather*," he said as we returned to reality, "you were in a different world."

It was a far different world when we met that day, both in time and technology. But when it came to the mastery of the film, it was in many ways the same. For Evans, the American film was the purest American art form, standing "alone as the only product manufactured in the US that is number one in every country in the world," he liked to say, always adding, "Excuse me, except for Coca-Cola. But that's bottled foreign."

From this bed, and from this man and those he appointed, *The Godfather* sprang forth, a miracle on both paper and screen, created and inspired by the sons and daughters of immigrants, its characters portrayed by a band of misfits who based their roles on a gang of miscreants, humanized to the point of being honorable.

The physical frames of the movie are constantly upgraded and improved, version after version, from the original film to old VHS tapes to DVDs to pristine new digital prints and other technological upgrades. Yet the story it tells remains exactly the same. It endures as those who made it recede, leaving behind a testament to the glory of the American family, and the steadfast belief in the American Dream, no matter how tattered, no matter how badly those who believe in it are betrayed. As the grieving undertaker Bonasera tells Don Corleone in the very first line of the film:

"I believe in America."

My visit to Woodland came decades after the movie exploded into theaters, but Evans was still counting both his victories and his losses.

"Francis must have made ten million dollars, I suppose, only from the points," he said. "Al Ruddy did seven or eight or ten million . . .

"*I received a divorce.* And no compensation. But I'm not complaining, because I was fortunate enough to be part of a historic art form, and the elevation of it."

Suddenly, he was back in the Paramount screening room, watching the completed two-hour, fifty-six-minute cut that he had fought so hard to release.

"I called distribution, Bluhdorn," he said.

He stared at the screen, recalling exactly what he told them.

"We have magic here!"

Then, it was on to the premiere and the party, which replayed endlessly in his memories.

"It was the highest time of my life," he continued. "And my brother said something very interesting. He said, 'You'll never have a night like this in your life again.'

"Because there's such a euphoria. Everyone had just seen *something* . . . that had mesmerized the five hundred people that were there."

He called to his butler. "I want to show you a picture," he said, and soon we were gazing upon a photograph of him dancing cheek-to-cheek with Ali MacGraw in 1972, the night of *The Godfather* premiere.

Her arms were rapturously draped around his shoulders, the king of the world.

"I was in heaven," he said. "Would you believe, at this very moment, she was madly in love with another man? And I had no idea. Which brings up one *very* important fact in life. Any man who thinks he can read the mind of a woman is a man who knows *nothing*."

From this night, lit by such blinding glory, such dazzling success, Robert Evans descended into darkness: his misdemeanor cocaine trafficking guilty plea in 1980; his box-office disaster *The Cotton Club*, in 1984, for which he once again teamed up with Coppola; his entanglement in a murder scandal stemming from the film, and the eight torturous years it would take him to clear his name. And his wealth, always the ultimate measurement of success in Hollywood, dropping from $11 million in 1979 to *$37* a decade later, which forced him to sell his home, Woodland, which he was eventually able to buy back with help from his pal Jack Nicholson. "He self-destructed, it's as simple as that," his friend the powerful Viacom chief Sumner Redstone would say, before Evans rose again with the 1994 publication of his bestselling rocketship of a memoir, which later became a hit documentary, *The Kid Stays in the Picture*.

His greatest loss, though, was love, most of all his wife Ali. Like Daisy Buchanan in his 1974 Paramount production of *The Great Gatsby*, she was suddenly far away, unattainable, the intense heat that they once had cooling into friendship, his time with their son, Joshua, confined to weekend visits, "the family he had traded, one night at a time, for *The Godfather*," wrote Sam Wasson in his 2019 book, *The Big Goodbye*. "He knew he had fucked up."

"Do you regret that now?" I asked Evans.

"So long ago, you know?" he replied.

Suddenly, the big bed where so many had sat for their audience before the king seemed small, almost to the point of claustrophobia, and the famous producer seemed alone, with *The Godfather* becoming both his medal to wear and his cross to bear.

"This is the last story I'm going to do on *The Godfather*," he said, his deep baritone breaking.

"Why?" I asked, doubting that would be true.

"People are gone, people are dead," he continued. "Richard Conte is dead. Richard Castellano is dead. John Marley is dead. Abe Vigoda is dead. Sterling Hayden's dead. John Cazale is dead. That's just some of them."

With age came forgiveness, even between Evans and Coppola. They had reconciled, to a degree, at the twenty-fifth anniversary of the film, held in San Francisco instead of on Evans's home turf, Los Angeles. "I was on the aisle seat," Evans said, "and Francis stopped and he put his arms around me, and kissed me, and said, 'You must have done something right.'"

In the fall of 2019, Evans was rushed to Cedars-Sinai Medical Center with pneumonia. However, he was soon able to briefly return to his hallowed home of Woodland. He died on October 26 in his portal to so many other worlds, the place where he watched movies: his bed. At the age of eighty-nine, the great voice and indomitable spirit of Robert Evans fell silent.

But the magic, the miracle, remains, on the screen in *The Godfather*.

Acknowledgments

This book began one early winter's day in the Gallery Books offices of my extraordinary editor Aimee Bell, and her associates Max Meltzer and Ed Schlesinger, who instantly shared my enthusiasm for a movie released fifty years ago. Thank you, Aimee, Max, and Ed, for your guidance and gusto, which kept me going throughout the writing and editing of this book. And thank you Aimee for your excellent editing, along with your and Max's continuously illuminating notes and encouragement. And gratitude to Jonathan Karp, Jennifer Bergstrom, Eric Rayman, and Jonathan Evans, along with the Gallery Books publicity and marketing team—Sally Marvin, Lauren Truskowski, and Mackenzie Hickey—for your time and talents.

Endless thanks to the great Eric Bates, Spencer Gaffney, Erica Commisso, Jon Leckie, Lottie Jackson, Barbara Davis, and fact-checkers extraordinaire Susan Banta and Tess Banta.

Literary agent Jan Miller is a mentor for anyone fortunate enough to have crossed her path, which I was lucky enough to do in the early 1990s in Dallas, Texas. She has been spurring me on ever since, as has her illustrious husband, Jeff Rich, who I am blessed to call my friend.

The book could not have been produced without the help of Francis Ford Coppola, who was so gracious in answering my endless questions, and film producer Anahid Nazarian, longtime keeper of the archives of American Zoetrope and everything pertaining to *The Godfather*.

One of my first calls was to Peter Bart, who went from *New York Times* reporter to vice president of production at Paramount Pictures. He was at the studio from the start of *The Godfather* and fostered the film throughout its tumultuous production. His memories and writings on the movie provided me with a path to follow. Thank you, Peter, for your time and insights.

Thank you to the movie's forever-young and prolific producer, the iconic Al Ruddy, and the wonderful Wanda McDaniel.

Francis Coppola's *Godfather* team kindly shared their experiences: producer and former casting director Fred Roos; production designer Dean Tavoularis; associate producer Gray Frederickson; film editor and sound designer Walter Murch; Coppola's assistant Mona Skager; assistant director Fred Gallo; agent Eddie Goldstone; casting director Andrea Eastman; cinematographer Hiro Narita . . . And thank you to Francis Coppola's publicists, Lois Najarian O'Neill and the late Kathleen Talbert.

Eleanor Coppola also provided her indelible memories of those fraught days when she and her young family lived in a cramped New York City apartment in 1971 while the masterpiece was being made.

Thank you to the authors who wrote about *The Godfather* before me, many of whom were kind enough to speak with me and share their insights: Harlan Lebo, Peter Cowie, M. J. Moore, Peter Biskind, Jenny M. Jones, Nicholas Pileggi, Don Capria, Lawrence Grobel, and the fabled Gay Talese.

I am forever grateful to the stars of *The Godfather*: Al Pacino for answering questions for this book, and James Caan, Talia Shire, Gianni Russo, and Johnny Martino, who spoke with me for the *Vanity Fair* article and this book. And to Robert Duvall, who spoke with me in 2008 for the *Vanity Fair* story.

Anthony Puzo, Mario Puzo's eldest son, was kind enough to answer my questions for this book, as had his sister, Dorothy Puzo, for the 2009 *Vanity Fair* story.

Stanley Jaffe, president of Paramount Pictures during The *God-father* films, gave me his time and insights.

And Ali MacGraw, who shared her memories of Robert Evans and the events she witnessed surrounding his reign over *The Godfather.*

My 2009 *Vanity Fair* story, "The Godfather Wars," was an assignment that first drew me into the furies involved in the making of the movie. For that I am indebted to my incredible *VF* editor, the legendary Wayne Lawson, who cheered me on and edited the *Godfather* story and so many others; Graydon Carter, who assigned the story; Matthew Pressman, Wayne's erstwhile assistant; and the story's fact-checker, Simon Brennan. Forever in my gratitude is *Vanity Fair*'s incomparable legal affairs editor, Robert Walsh, along with my *VF* editors Radhika Jones, Doug Stumpf, Eric Bates, David Friend, and Michael Hogan.

Scout Noffke at the Rauner Special Collections Library at Dartmouth University spent days locating and scanning pertinent documents in the library's Mario Puzo Papers. In Los Angeles, my first stop for all things Hollywood is always the Margaret Herrick Library, Academy of Motion Picture Arts and Sciences, whose Kristine Krueger sent so many files which provided rare insights. Thanks also to the library's Barbara Hall and Brendan Coates.

Invaluable in bringing the magic of Mario Puzo to these pages was his first assistant in Hollywood, Janet Snow, who began working with Mario from his very first days in the city of dreams.

Thank you to Puzo's assistant and longtime friend Lanetta Wahlgren and her brilliant son-in-law Miles Fisher.

Gratitude to the dearly departed, who I was fortunate to interview: Robert Evans, who welcomed me into his home (and his bed) in 2008; Al Martino, who spent hours regaling me with tales of music, the movie, and the Mob at Nate 'n Al's delicatessen in Beverly Hills and afterward in his home; Bettye McCartt, who met me in LA and related stories of the horse's head and all the bullets and the blood; Abe Vigoda, who inhabited the role of Tessio and welcomed me into his New York City apartment; Carmine Caridi, who imparted the heart-wrenching story of how he landed the part of Sonny Corleone only to lose it; New York casting director Lou DiGiaimo; Anthony Colombo, who met me in a New Jersey diner and further boosted my fixation on the film; and Alex Rocco, who breathed fire into the character of Moe Greene . . .

Marilyn Stewart, known as "the Godmother of *The Godfather*," spent hours telling me stories of her incredible life and her pioneering work in promoting this film and so many others.

Charlie Bluhdorn's daughter Dominique and son Paul helped me re-create their illustrious father's insatiable pursuit of excellence, both in business and film.

Ed Walters, for your memories of Mario Puzo in Las Vegas.

Alice Marchak, for your insights into Marlon Brando.

Robert Towne, for telling me about the writing of your incredible succession scene.

Mike and Irena Medavoy, Michael Korda, Dick Snyder, Raymond Martino, Jim Mahoney, Martha Luttrell, Kenji Fujita, Stevie Phillips, Neil Olson, Luisa Towne, Steve Casale, Gelasio Gaetani d'Aragona, Michael Quinn, Tom Luddy, Rob Cohen, Alan Selka, Meryl Gordon, and, as always, Wendy Stark, thank you for your time and help.

John Bowers worked alongside Mario Puzo at Magazine Management, and was kind enough to share his memories of those days, as did Josh Alan Friedman, whose father, Bruce Jay Friedman, hired Puzo at Magazine Management; Robert Deis, author of the collection *Weasels Ripped My Flesh!*, which includes many of the Magazine Management classics, opened his archives, which contain many of Mario Puzo's early adventure stories. And Saul Braun, who brought Mario Puzo to G.P. Putnam's Sons.

Nina Rota, for your insights into your brilliant composer father, along with Francesco Lombardi and Franco Sciannameo; Laura Jacobs, for your memories of Candida Donadio; Roger Corman, for your thoughts on your former assistant Francis Ford Coppola; David Shire, for the story of the apartment you loaned to the Coppola family; Brad Krevoy, for your friendship; George and Sally Wieser, for remembering the literary dynamo who brought Puzo's book to the attention of Paramount; Diann Zecca, for the conversations about your amazing brother, Richard Castellano; Ivor Davis, for your insights into getting into that early showing of the film; writer Greg Oliver for sharing your insights into the former wrestler Lenny Montana; Michael Degani, for the entries in Robert Evans's diaries; Michael Alfred in Robert Evans's office; Thomas Myrdahl, for speaking about Jeannie Linero; thanks also to Rip Beyman and David Karp.

And to the photo researchers, Denise Sfraga and Ann Schneider, for sourcing the photographs in this book.

Thank you to Eugene Wu, Hannah Rich, Ambrose and Chili for your everlasting friendship.

To Bart Pepitone, my consistent *Godfather* advisor, for your insights and encouragement.

And to B.J. and Eddie Seal, who I am fortunate enough to have as my brothers.

Selected Bibliography

These works are referred to throughout this book:

Books

Bart, Peter. *Infamous Players: A Tale of Movies, The Mob (And Sex)*. New York: Weinstein Books, 2011.

Biskind, Peter. *Easy Riders, Raging Bulls: How the Sex-Drugs-and-Rock 'n' Roll Generation Saved Hollywood*. New York: Simon & Schuster, 1998.

———. *The Godfather Companion: Everything You Ever Wanted to Know About All Three Godfather Movies*. New York, HarperPerennial, 1990.

Capria, Don, and Anthony Colombo. *Colombo: The Unsolved Murder*. San Diego: Unity Press, 2015.

Coppola, Eleanor. *Notes on a Life*. New York: Nan A. Talese, 2008.

Coppola, Francis Ford. *Francis Ford Coppola Interviews*. Edited by Gene D. Phillips and Rodney Hill. Jackson, MS: University Press of Mississippi, 2004.

———. *The Godfather Notebook*. New York: Regan Arts, 2016.

Cowie, Peter. *The Godfather Book*. Faber & Faber, 1997.

———. *Coppola*. London: André Deutsch. 2013.

———. *The Godfather: The Official Motion Picture Archives*. Insight Editions, 2012.

Evans, Robert. *The Kid Stays in the Picture: A Notorious Life.* New York: Hyperion Books, 1994.

Jones, Jenny M. *The Annotated Godfather: The Complete Screenplay with Commentary on Every Scene, Interviews, and Little-Known Facts.* New York: Black Dog & Leventhal, 2007.

Lebo, Harlan. *The Godfather Legacy.* New York: Fireside, 1997.

Mann, William J. *The Contender: The Story of Marlon Brando.* New York: HarperCollins, 2019.

Moore, M. J. *Mario Puzo: An American Writer's Quest.* New York: Heliotrope Books, 2019.

Petepiece, Andy. *The Colombo Family: A History of New York's Colombo Mafia Family.* Tellwell Talent, ebook edition, 2020.

Phillips, Gene D. *Godfather: The Intimate Francis Ford Coppola.* Lexington: The University Press of Kentucky, 2004.

Puzo, Mario. *The Godfather* (in all its editions). New York: G.P. Putnam's Sons, 1969.

———. *The Godfather Papers and Other Confessions.* New York: G.P. Putnam's Sons, 1972.

———. *Inside Las Vegas.* New York: Charter Publishing, 1977.

Russo, Gianni, with Patrick Picciarelli. *Hollywood Godfather: My Life in the Movies and the Mob.* New York: St. Martin's Griffin, 2020.

Wasson, Sam. *The Big Goodbye: Chinatown and the Last Years of Hollywood.* New York: Flatiron Books, 2020.

Zuckerman, Ira. *The Godfather Journal.* New York: Manor Books, 1972.

Films

The Godfather: The Coppola Restoration. Directed by Francis Ford Coppola. Paramount Pictures, 2008.

The Godfather: The Masterpiece That Almost Wasn't. Directed by Kim Aubry. ZAP Zoetrope Aubry Productions, 2008.

The Godfather and the Mob. Directed by Simon George. Class Films, 2006.

The Godfather Family: A Look Inside. Directed by Jeff Werner. Paramount Pictures and Zoetrope Studios, 1990.

The Godfather Legacy. Directed by Kevin Burns. History Channel and Prometheus Entertainment, 2012.

Periodicals

Anson, Robert Sam. "Hurricane Charlie." *Vanity Fair*, April 2001.

Bart, Peter. "The Mob, the Movies, and Me." *GQ*, June 1997.

Biskind, Peter. "Making Crime Pay: The Making of 'The Godfather.'" *Premiere*, August 1997.

Pileggi, Nicholas. "The Making of 'The Godfather': Sort of a Home Movie." *New York Times Magazine*, August 15, 1971.

Puzo, Mario. "Choosing a Dream: Italians in Hell's Kitchen." First published in Wheeler, Thomas C., ed. *The Immigrant Experience.* New York: Dial Press, 1971.

Seal, Mark. "The 'Godfather' Wars." *Vanity Fair*, March 2009.

Shanken, Marvin R. Interview with Francis Ford Coppola, "The Godfather Speaks." *Cigar Aficionado*, September/October 2003.

Production Documents

Various documents used throughout the movie's preproduction, production, and aftermath provided by Anahid Nazarian, American Zoetrope, San Francisco.

Prologue: To the Mattresses!

Author Interview

Robert Evans

Books

Evans, Robert, *The Kid Stays in the Picture.*

Periodicals

Tyrnauer, Matt. "Evans Gate." *Vanity Fair*, September 1994.

Chapter 1: "I Just Go Out and Kill for Them"

Books

Griffin, Joe, with Don DeNevi. *Mob Nemesis: How the FBI Crippled Organized Crime.* New York: Prometheus Books, 2002.

Humphreys, Adrian. *The Enforcer: Johnny Pops Papalia, A Life and Death in the Mafia.* Toronto: HarperCollins, 1999.

Mass, Peter. *The Valachi Papers.* New York: G. P. Putnam's Sons, 1968.

Schneider, Stephen. *Iced: The Story of Organized Crime in Canada.* Hoboken, NJ: Wiley, 2009.

Tosches, Nick. *Dino: Living High in the Business of Dreams.* New York: Doubleday, 1999.

Periodicals

Abrams, Norma, and Stephen Brown. "Mafia Chief Organizes a Picket Line at the FBI." *New York Daily News*, May 1, 1970.

"Alberto Agueci, Buffalo Mafia Member, $150 Million Heroin Trafficker, Viciously Tortured to Death." http://bpdthenandnow.com/albert_agueci.html.

"Big Day for Italians Clouded by Rumors." *Daily News*, June 28, 1970.

"Boss Has Life-Death Power, Valachi Says." Associated Press, September 28, 1963.

"Details of Gangland Murder in Western New York Outlined (Vowed 'Vengeance' Was Killed Two Weeks Later)." Gannett News Service, January 10, 1969.

Doherty, Thomas. "Frank Costello's Hands: Film, Television, and the Kefauver Crime Hearings." *Film History* 10, no. 3 (1998): 359–74. http://www.jstor.org/stable/3815229.

Gannett News Service. "Details of Gangland Murder in Western New York Outlined (Vowed 'Vengeance,' Was Killed Two Weeks Later)," January 10, 1969.

Gould, Jack. "Costello TV's First Headless Star." *New York Times*, March 14, 1951.

Hunter, Brad. "Crime Hunter: Buffalo Blues—Last Rites for the Mob in Queen City." *Toronto Sun,* May 5, 2018.

"Italo-Americans Press Unity Day." *New York Times*, June 18, 1970.

Phillips, Alan. "Organized Crime's Grip on Ontario." *Maclean's*, September 21, 1963.

Pileggi, Nicholas. "The Making of 'The Godfather': Sort of a Home Movie."

Shannon, William V. "The Godfather." *New York Times*, August 1, 1972.

"Violent Deaths Overtake Defendants in Dope Case." *The Record* (Hackensack, NJ), November 30, 1961.

Other Media

United States of America, Appellee. v. Vito Agueci, Filippo Cottone, Robert Guippone, Luigi Lo Bue, Matthew Palmieri, Anthony Porcelli, Charles Shiffman, Rocco Scopellitti, Charles Tandler and Joseph Valachi, Defendants-appellants. 310 F.2d 817 (2d Cir. 1962).

U.S. Hearing on Organized Crime and Illicit Traffic in Narcotics, October 16, 1963, p. 611.

Chapter 2: The Man in the Gutter

Author Interviews

Anthony Puzo

Gay Talese

George Wieser

John Bowers

Josh Alan Friedman

Lanetta Wahlgren

Michael Korda

Robert Evans

Sally Wieser

Saul Braun

Books

Bart, Peter. *Infamous Players.*

Cowie, Peter. *The Godfather Book.*

Evans, Robert. *The Kid Stays in the Picture.*

Friedman, Bruce Jay. *Lucky Bruce: A Literary Memoir.* Windsor, Ontario: Biblioasis, 2011.

Gino, Carol. *Me and Mario*: *Love, Power & Writing with Mario Puzo, Author of* The Godfather. Smithfield, TX: Aaha! Books, 2018.

Kennedy, Robert F. *The Enemy Within: The McClellan Committee's Crusade Against Jimmy Hoffa and Corrupt Labor Unions.* New York: Harper & Brothers, 1960.

Lewis, Norman. *The Honoured Society: The Sicilian Mafia Observed.* London: Eland, 1984.

Moore, M. J. *Mario Puzo.*

Puzo, Mario. *The Fortunate Pilgrim.* New York: Ballantine Books, 2004.

———. *The Godfather.*

———. *The Godfather Papers and Other Confessions.* London: Pan Books, 1972.

———. *Inside Las Vegas.*

Periodicals

Cleri, Mario. "The Girls of Pleasure Penthouse." *Male*, May 5, 1968.

Deis, Robert, editor. "Weasels Ripped my Flesh! Two-Fisted Stories From Men's Adventure Magazines, of the 1950s, '60s & '70s." New Texture, 2013.

Goldstein, Norm. "Puzo Was Broke." Associated Press, April 15, 1972.

Gussow, Mel. "Mario Puzo, Author Who Made 'The Godfather' a World Addiction, Is Dead at 78." *New York Times*, July 3, 1999.

Mandel, George. "The Godfather Caper: How Mario Puzo Parlayed His World of Gambling, Local Dons and Moguls into the Biggest Hits of All Time." *True*, August 1971.

"Mario Puzo's Brush with the Law." The Smoking Gun, July 20, 2000.

Mills, James. "Why Should He Have It?" *Life*, March 7, 1969.

Paglia, Camille. "It All Comes Back to Family." *New York Times,* May 8, 1997.

"Paperback Godfather." *Time,* August 28, 1978.

Peretz, Evgenia. "How Nan Talese Blazed Her Pioneering Path Through the Publishing Boys' Club." *Vanity Fair,* March 2017.

Peterson, Bob. "Wealthy Father of 'The Godfather.'" *Life,* July 10, 1970.

Puzo, Anthony. "A Note From Anthony Puzo, Son of Mario Puzo." In *The Godfather* by Mario Puzo, 50th anniversary edition. New York: Berkley, 2019.

Puzo, Mario. "How the Mafia Makes Friends." *Indianapolis Star,* March 15, 1970.

———. "I'm more sentimentally attached to *The Godfather*—the more money I make from it, the better a book I think it is." *P.O.V. Magazine,* April 1997.

———. "Choosing a Dream."

Seal, Mark. "The 'Godfather' Wars."

Seligson, Marcia. "'Godfather': History's Fastest Selling Volume." *Los Angeles Times,* August 16, 1970.

Siegel, Jules. "Saying Goodbye to Mario Puzo." Book@rts. Cafecancun.com.

Tucker, Reed. "How Mario Puzo Penned 'The Godfather' to Get Out of Debt—and Made Bank." *New York Post,* March 2, 2019.

Chapter 3: Hurricane Charlie and The Kid

Author Interviews
Dominique Bluhdorn
Paul Bluhdorn
Richard Snyder

Books
Bart, Peter. *Infamous Players.*
Biskind, Peter. *Easy Riders, Raging Bulls.*
Evans, Robert. *The Kid Stays in the Picture.*

Gladstone, B. James. *The Man Who Seduced Hollywood: The Life and Loves of Greg Bautzer, Tinseltown's Most Powerful Lawyer*. Chicago: Chicago Review Press, 2013.

Korda, Michael. *Another Life: A Memoir of Other People*. New York: Delta, 2000.

Masters, Kim. *The Keys to the Kingdom: The Rise of Michael Eisner and the Fall of Everyone Else*. New York: Harper Business, 2001.

Sobel, Robert. *The Rise and Fall of the Conglomerate Kings*. Washington, DC: Beard Books, 1999.

Tosches, Nick. *Power on Earth: Michele Sindona's Explosive Story*. New York: Arbor House, 1986.

Periodicals

Anson, Robert Sam. "Hurricane Charlie." *Vanity Fair*, April 2001.

Bart, Peter. "I Like It, I Want It, Let's Sew It Up." *New York Times*, August 7, 1966.

———. "How Par Wised Up to Wiseguys on Backlot." *Variety*, January 7, 1991.

———. "The Mob, the Movies and Me," *GQ*, June 1997.

Canby, Vincent. "Bravo, Brando's 'Godfather.'" *New York Times*, March 12, 1972.

———. "Sure, Hollywood Is Collapsing, But ..." *New York Times*, May 2, 1971.

"Company News: Gulf+Western Changes Name." Associated Press, June 6, 1989.

Crowther, Bosley. "The Screen: Is Paris Burning?" *New York Times*, November 11, 1966.

Drucker, Mort. "Is Paris Boring?" *Mad Magazine*, September 1967.

Hersh, Seymour M. "SEC Presses Wide Investigation of Gulf and Western Conglomerate." *New York Times*, July 24, 1977.

Martin, Lee A. "Banking for Good, the Mob and the CIA." *Mother Jones*, July/August 1983.

"Millionaires Under 40." *Time*, December 3, 1965.

Mills, James. "Why Should He Have It?" *Life*, March 7, 1969.

Ross, Lillian. "The Making of 'The Red Badge of Courage.'" *New Yorker,* May 17, 1952.

Welles, Chris. "Charles Bluhdorn: With a Multimillion Reach, Wall Street's 'Mad Austrian' Collects Companies." *Life,* March 10, 1967.

Films

The Godfather and the Mob

Other Media

Charles Bluhdorn collected speeches, courtesy of Paul Bluhdorn

Chapter 4: The Bestselling Writer in the World

Author Interviews

Bob Peterson

Ed Walters

Kenji Fujita

Paul Bluhdorn

Books

Evans, Robert. *The Kid Stays in the Picture.*

Kanfer, Stefan. *Somebody: The Reckless Life and Remarkable Career of Marlon Brando.* New York: Knopf, 2008.

Moore, M. J. *Mario Puzo.*

Puzo, Mario. *The Godfather.*

———. *The Godfather Papers and Other Confessions.*

———. *Inside Las Vegas.*

Schwartz, David. *Tales from the Pit: Casino Table Games Managers in Their Own Words.* Las Vegas: UNLV Gaming Press Books, 2016.

Targ, William. *Indecent Pleasures: The Life and Colorful Times of William Targ.* New York: Macmillan, 1975.

Periodicals

Barra, Allen. "What Puzo Godfathered 40 Years Ago." *Wall Street Journal,* August 13, 2009.

Burton, Hal. "Tapestry of Evil: 'The Godfather,' by Mario Puzo." *Saturday Review*, March 15, 1969.

Goldberg, Jeffrey. "Sammy the Bull Explains How the Mob Got Made." *New York Times Magazine*, January 2, 2000.

Jellinek, Roger. "Just Business, Not Personal." *New York Times*, March 4, 1969.

Mandel, George. "The Godfather Caper."

Mitgang, Herbert. "Behind the Best Sellers: Mario Puzo." *New York Times*, February 18, 1979.

Pileggi, Nicholas. "The Making of 'The Godfather.'"

Sanders, Jacquin. "The First Interview with the Author of 'The Godfather.'" *Newsweek Features Service*, March 20, 1970.

Schaap, Dick. "The Godfather." *New York Times*, April 27, 1969.

Thomas, Bob. "Mario Puzo Denies Mafia Payoff." Associated Press, June 27, 1970.

Wolff, Geoffrey. "Blunt Epic of Crime and Terror in Cosa Nostra's Underworld." *Washington Post*, April 6, 1969.

Other Media

Candida Donadio, Laura Jacobs unpublished *Vanity Fair* profile and associated research.

Transcript of Interview with Ed Walters, Table Games Management Oral History Project.

Chapter 5: The Producer: The Man Who Gets Things Done

Author Interviews

Al Ruddy
Anthony Puzo
Janet Snow
Lanetta Wahlgren
Peter Bart
Gray Frederickson

Books

Lebo, Harlan. *The Godfather Legacy.*

Puzo, Mario. *The Godfather.*

———. *The Godfather Papers and Other Confessions.*

———. *Fools Die.* New York: G.P. Putnam's Sons, 1978.

Periodicals

Broady, Joe. "Three Ideas!" *The Sunday Oklahoman,* April 6, 1969.

Dutton, Walt. "The Real Hogan's Hero." *Los Angeles Times,* January 20, 1966.

"Hollywood 'Daffy' Experiment: Tyros Film Low Budget Drama Under Special Universal Program." *New York Times,* March 22, 1964.

Krim, Seymour. "Mario Puzo and Me." From *Missing a Beat: The Rants and Regrets of Seymour Krim.* Syracuse, NY: Syracuse University Press, 2010.

Sterling, Peace. "Producer of 'The Godfather' Film Has Gone From Obscurity to Renown." *Rocky Mount Telegram,* July 12, 1970.

Talese, Gay. "Professional Laughter Finds Life Is Not as Funny as Jokes He's Paid to Cheer." *New York Times,* September 29, 1958.

Thomas, Bob. "Godfather Author Says No Mafioso Connection." Associated Press, June 22, 1970.

Chapter 6: Coppola: A Celestial Occurrence

Author Interviews

Al Martino
Ali MacGraw
Andrea Eastman
Eleanor Coppola
Francis Ford Coppola
Fred Roos
Jan Lettieri
Lou DiGiaimo

Mona Skager
Peter Bart
Roger Corman
Stanley Jaffe
Talia Shire
Walter Murch

Books

Bart, Peter. *Infamous Players.*
Biskind, Peter. *Easy Riders, Raging Bulls.*
Coppola, Francis Ford. *The Godfather Notebook.*
Cowie, Peter. *Coppola.*
————. *The Godfather Book.*
Evans, Robert. *The Kid Stays in the Picture.*
Gelmis, Joseph. *The Film Director as Superstar.* New York: Doubleday, 1970.
Lebo, Harlan. *The Godfather Legacy.*
MacGraw, Ali. *Moving Pictures: An Autobiography.* Beverly Hills, CA: Renaissance Literary & Talent, 2005. Kindle e-book.
Puzo, Mario. *The Godfather Papers and Other Confessions.*

Periodicals

Bacon, James. "'The Godfather' Casting Game Continues." *Los Angeles Herald-Examiner,* October 6, 1970.
Bart, Peter. "As the Censors Move In . . ." *New York Times,* April 10, 1966.
Biskind, Peter. "Making Crime Pay."
Cameron, Sue. "'Godfather' Biggest Thing Since GWTW, Al Ruddy Says." *Hollywood Reporter,* November 6, 1970.
"Coppola Gets His UCLA Master's Degree." *Variety,* March 17, 1967.
"Coppola's Skill As Film-Maker Goes Back to When He Was Eight." *Calgary Herald,* May 22, 1969.
Ellison, Bob. "8 'Bombs' in a Row; Brando Won't Change." *Chicago Sun-Times* special, March 26, 1967.

Garrett, Stephen. "Francis Ford Coppola: What I've Learned." *Esquire*, August 1, 2009.

"Goldwyn Hosts 'Boy.'" *Hollywood Reporter*, December 7, 1966.

Hodenfield, Chris. "Marlon Brando: The Method of His Madness." *Rolling Stone*, May 20, 1976.

Knapp, Dan. "Coppola 'Godfather' Director." *Los Angeles Times*. October 1, 1970.

Madsen, Axel. "Coppola Breaks the Age Barrier." *Los Angeles Times*, January 2, 1966.

Murray, William. "Francis Ford Coppola: *Playboy* Interview." *Playboy*, July 1975.

Nachman, Gerald. "Coppola of Zoetrope—Older, Wiser, Poorer." *Los Angeles Times*, November 7, 1971.

"No Stars for 'Godfather' Cast—Just Someone Named Brando." *Variety*, January 28, 1971.

Reed, Rex. "Offering the Moon to a Guy in Jeans." *New York Times*, August 7, 1966.

"Ruddy Vows No Big Stars for His 'Godfather' Pic." *Hollywood Reporter*, July 13, 1970.

Setlowe, Rick. "Paramount's Gamble Four Years Ago on Mario Puzo Has Really Paid Off." *Variety*, September 30, 1970.

Shanken, Marvin R. "The Godfather Speaks."

Simons, Dan. "Cinema San Francisco Style." *Entertainment World*, March 27, 1970.

———. "'Rain People' by the Rule Breaker." *Los Angeles Times*, September 7, 1969.

Wayne, Fredd. "'Godfather' Casting: An Italian Uprising." *Los Angeles Times*, February 28, 1971.

Other Media

Coppola, Francis Ford. Letter to Gerald K. Smith, International Photographers Local 659, January 29, 1971.

Roberts Evans datebook.

Films

Filmmaker—A Diary by George Lucas. Directed by George Lucas. 1968.
The New Cinema. Directed by Gary Young. 1968.

Chapter 7: *The Miracle on Mulholland*

Author Interviews

Anthony Puzo
Dean Tavoularis
Francis Ford Coppola
Hiro Narita
Janet Snow
Lanetta Wahlgren

Books

Biskind, Peter. *Easy Riders, Raging Bulls*.
Coppola, Francis Ford. *The Godfather Notebook*.
Lebo, Harlan. *The Godfather Legacy*.
MacGraw, Ali. *Moving Pictures*.
Marchak, Alice. *Me and Marlon: A Memoir*. Ashland, OH: Book-Masters, 2008.
Puzo, Mario. *The Godfather Papers and Other Confessions*.
Russo, Gianni, with Patrick Picciarelli. *Hollywood Godfather*.

Periodicals

Goldstein, Patrick. "His Eye for Spotting Talent is Unmatched." *Los Angeles Times*, January 27, 2004.
"How Gianni Russo Muscled His way into 'The Godfather,'" *Hollywood Reporter*, February 1, 1972.
Murray, William. "Francis Ford Coppola: *Playboy* Interview."
Shanken, Marvin R. "The Godfather Speaks."

Other Media

Bart, Peter. Memo to Mario Puzo, July 13, 1970. Rauner Library Collection, Dartmouth University.

Puzo, Mario. Letter to Marlon Brando. Rauner Library Collection, Dartmouth University.

Films
The Godfather: The Coppola Restoration

Chapter 8: The War over Casting the Family Corleone

Author Interviews
　　Abe Vigoda
　　Andrea Eastman
　　Carmine Caridi
　　Francis Ford Coppola
　　Fred Roos
　　James Caan
　　Robert Duvall
　　Robert Evans
　　Stevie Phillips
　　Talia Shire

Books
Cowie, Peter. *The Godfather Book.*
Evans, Robert. *The Kid Stays in the Picture.*
Grobel, Lawrence. *Al Pacino: In Conversation with Lawrence Grobel.* Simon Spotlight Entertainment, 2008. Kindle e-book.
Puzo, Mario. *The Godfather Papers and Other Confessions.*
Zuckerman, Ira. *The Godfather Journal.*

Periodicals
Biskind, Peter. "Making Crime Pay: The Making of 'The Godfather.'" *Premiere,* August 1997.
"A Brooder Marked for Glory, The Early Sorrows of Al Pacino." *Family Weekly,* March 2, 1975.

Carragher, Bernard. "Is She Kookie, This Diane Keaton?" *Philadelphia Inquirer,* May 14, 1972.

Chase, Chris. "Will the *Godfather*'s Son Live to be a *Godfather*?" *New York Times,* May 7, 1972.

Cuskelly, Richard. "A Talk Show 'Kook' Becomes a Blithe-Spirited Star." *Los Angeles Herald-Examiner,* December 23, 1973.

"Cut Directors Down to Size: Bob Evans: 'We Keep Control.'" *Variety,* February 3, 1971.

"The Godsons." *Time,* April 3, 1972.

"Heir Apparent to The Godfather," Pacino profile. *Life,* March 31, 1972.

Hubbard, Kim, "Diane Keaton Looks Back on Her Epic Romances with Woody Allen, Al Pacino and Warren Beatty." *People,* June 15, 2017.

Kilday, Gregg. "Al Pacino on the Lam From 'Godfather' Fame." *Los Angeles Times,* June 25, 1972.

Shanken, Marvin R. "The Godfather Speaks."

"The Story Behind 'The Godfather' by the Men Who Lived It." *Ladies' Home Journal,* June 1972.

Sufrin, Mark. "The Godfather Al Pacino, Superstar of 1975." *Saga: The Magazine for Men.* Brooklyn, NY: Gambi Publications.

Other Media

Casting lists, courtesy of Francis Ford Coppola, American Zoetrope.

Videos

Al Pacino. *Inside the Actors Studio.* Various interviews.

"Diane Keaton and the Men She's Kissed." *The Ellen DeGeneres Show,* Season 9, Episode 66, December 13, 2011.

"Is He Dreaming . . . Paramount's pretty smart . . ." *USA Today* video.

Chapter 9: The Godfather vs. The Godfather

Author Interviews

Al Ruddy

Ali MacGraw

Bettye McCartt
Dean Tavoularis
Eddie Goldstone
Gray Frederickson
Nicholas Pileggi

Books

Capria, Don, and Anthony Colombo. *Colombo: The Unsolved Murder.*
Evans, Robert. *The Kid Stays in the Picture.*
Lebo, Harlan. *The Godfather Legacy.*
Petepiece, Andy. *The Colombo Family: A History of New York's Colombo Mafia Family.* Victoria, BC: Tellwell Talent, ebook edition, 2020.

Periodicals

Abrams, Norma, and Stephen Brown. "Mafia Chief Organizes a Picket Line at the FBI."
Burton, Anthony. "Colombo Says FBI Bugs Creep Even into Bedroom." *New York Daily News.* April 1, 1971.
"Colombo Acquitted in Conspiracy Case." *New York Times*, February 27, 1971.
Davidson, Sara. "Sinatra MC's Salute to Italo-Americans." *Boston Globe*, October 20, 1967.
"A Day in the Life of a Top Oscar Nominee." *Chicago Tribune*, March 28, 1973.
Federici, William. "Big Day for Italians Clouded by Rumors." *New York Daily News*, June 28, 1970.
———. "Joe Colombo: OK, I'll Be a Mafioso for Good." *New York Daily News*, July 3, 1970.
Ferretti, Fred. "Corporate Rift in 'Godfather' Filming." *New York Times*, March 23, 1971.
———. "Italian-American League's Power Spreads." *New York Times*, April 4, 1971.
Gage, Nicholas. "Colombo: The New Look in the Mafia." *New York Times*, May 3, 1971.

"Italo-Americans Press Unity Day." *New York Times*, June 18, 1970.

Kaplan, Morris. "Rebuttal Witness Barred, Colombo Trial Nears End." *New York Times*, February 26, 1971.

Lichtenstein, Grace. "'Godfather' Film Won't Mention Mafia." *New York Times*, March 20, 1971.

Maeder, Jay. "Stairway to Heaven: Joe Colombo's Great Civil Rights Crusade." *New York Daily News*, October 27, 1998.

Montgomery, Paul L. "Thousands of Italians Here Rally Against Ethnic Slurs." *New York Times*, June 30, 1970.

———. "Italians to Hold Rally Tomorrow." *New York Times*, June 28, 1970.

Oelsner, Lesley. "Reputed Brooklyn Mafia Head Arrested on Perjury Charges." *New York Times*, March 7, 1970.

"Par Burns Over 'Godfather' Deal, But Will Rub Out Mafia." *Variety*, March 23, 1971.

Penn, Stanley. "Colombo's Crusade: Alleged Mafia Chief Runs Aggressive Drive Against Saying 'Mafia.'" *Wall Street Journal*, March 23, 1971.

Pileggi, Nicholas. "Sinatra Wow's 'em at New York, Italian-American League Rally." Associated Press, October 20, 1967.

———. "The Making of 'The Godfather': Sort of a Home Movie."

Puzo, Mario. "The Italians, American Style." *New York Times Magazine*, August 6, 1967.

Rose, Robert. "All Those Stories About Brando? Here's What Filming Was Really Like." *Detroit Free Press*, March 19, 1972.

———. "Secret's Out: Brando Is a Pussycat." *Philadelphia Inquirer*, March 19, 1972.

Scott, Tony. "Ruddy Raps Extras Guild, Won't Shoot in Its Jurisdiction." *Variety*, September 2, 1970.

———. "'Godfather' Director Coppola Unhappy Ruddy Has Nixed NY Locale." *Variety*, October 9, 1970.

Smith, Sandy. "The Crime Cartel." *Life*, September 1, 1967.

Tomasson, Robert E. "Colombo is Guilty in Perjury Case." *New York Times*, December 24, 1970.

SELECTED BIBLIOGRAPHY

413

Whitney, Craig R. "Reputed Mafia Leader Linked to Picketing of FBI." *New York Times*, June 9, 1970.

Wilks, Ed. "A Gangster's Legacy—Violence and Death." *St. Louis Post-Dispatch,* June 4, 1978.

"Yes, Mr. Ruddy, There Is a . . ." *New York Times,* March 23, 1971.

Films
The Godfather and the Mob

Other Media
Colombo, Joe. The Gangsters Incorporated Forum

Landi, P. Vincent. Grand Lodge of the State of New York, Order Sons of Italy in America, letter to Paramount Pictures Corporation. March 20, 1971.

Smerillo, John. Protest letter to Francis Ford Coppola. Undated.

Chapter 10: Tableau: Each Frame a Painting

Author Interviews
Dean Tavoularis
Francis Ford Coppola

Books
Biskind, Peter. *Easy Riders, Raging Bulls.*
Zuckerman, Ira. *The Godfather Journal.*

Periodicals
Biskind, Peter. "Making Crime Pay: The Making of 'The Godfather.'" *Premier*, August 1997.

Yamato, Jen, and Anita Busch. "Gordon Willis in Memoriam: Francis Ford Coppola, Woody Allen, More Remember Oscar-Nominated DP." Yahoo! Entertainment, Deadline. May 19, 2014.

Production Materials

Production meeting notes provided by Francis Ford Coppola's American Zoetrope, International Reporting Service, January 1971.

Chapter 11: Looking for Places to Kill People

Author Inteviews
Al Ruddy
Anthony Puzo
Dean Tavoularis
Dick Smith
Eleanor Coppola
Francis Ford Coppola
Fred Gallo
Gianni Russo
Gray Frederickson
James Caan
Johnny Martino
Nicholas Pileggi
Robert Duvall
Talia Shire
Walter Murch

Books
Bart, Peter. *Infamous Players.*
Brando, Marlon, and Robert Lindsey. *Songs My Mother Taught Me.* New York: Random House, 1994.
Coppola, Francis Ford. *The Godfather Notebook.*
Cowie, Peter. *Coppola.*
———. *The Godfather Book.*
Evans, Robert. *The Kid Stays in the Picture.*
Lebo, Harlan. *The Godfather Legacy.*
MacGraw, Ali. *Moving Pictures.*
Puzo, Mario. *The Godfather* (all editions).
Russo, Gianni. *Hollywood Godfather.*

Schneider, Stephen. *Iced: The Story of Organized Crime in Canada*. Mississauga, Ontario: John Wiley & Sons, 2009.

Tosches, Nick. *Power on Earth: Michele Sindona's Explosive Story*. Westminster, MD: Arbor House, 1986.

Zuckerman, Ira. *The Godfather Journal*.

Periodicals

Biskind, Peter. "Making Crime Pay: The Making of The Godfather."

Chilton, Martin. "I don't believe in God—I believe in Al Pacino': How one of our greatest living actors kicked his boozy, brawling ways." *Independent*, April 25, 2020.

Farrance, Sterling. "Leave the Gun, Take the Cannoli: The Hitman as Family Man." Essay in *Anatomy of a Film*. UC Berkeley, Spring 2018.

Grenler, Cynthia. "You're Hot, You're Difficult, You're Finished—That's Aram." *San Francisco Examiner*, December 17, 1972.

Morin, Tracy. "Hall of Famers: Patsy's Pizzeria." pizzahalloffame.com.

Pileggi, Nicholas. "The Making of 'The Godfather': Sort of a Home Movie."

Seal, Mark. "The 'Godfather' Wars."

Shanken, Marvin R. "The Godfather Speaks."

Films

The Godfather: The Coppola Restoration

Videos

"Diane Keaton American Film Institute Lifetime Achievement Award Event." June 8, 2017. YouTube.

"*The Godfather* 45th Anniversary Reunion." Tribeca Film Festival. April 29, 2017.

"Al Pacino Looks Back at the 'Godfather' Films, 'Scent of a Woman,' and more." Interview by Kevin Polowy. Yahoo Life, October 26, 2017.

Production Materials

Coppola, Francis Ford. "To-do list: Makeup Notes." Undated.

Rehearsal Schedule, Friday, March 19. Courtesy of Francis Ford Coppola.

Robert Evans Memo. Notes on Script, March 5, 1971. Courtesy of Francis Ford Coppola.

Other Media
"An Oral History with Theadora Van Runkle." Academy of Motion Picture Arts and Sciences, Academy Oral Histories.
V., Leo. "Al Pacino and Harold Becker Q&A American Cinematheque." *Film Talk,* March 27, 2019.

Chapter 12: Bada Bing!

Author Interviews
Al Ruddy
Giovannina Bellino
James Caan
Robert Duvall

Books
Coppola, Francis Ford. *The Godfather Notebook.*
Petepiece, Andy. *The Colombo Family.*
Puzo, Mario. *The Godfather.*
Russo, Gianni. *Hollywood Godfather.*
Zuckerman, Ira. *The Godfather Journal.*

Periodicals
Kilgannon, Corey and Vincent M. Mallozzi. "On Pleasant Avenue, A Mobbed-Up History Is Hard to Live Down." *New York Times,* January 5, 2004.
Perlmutter, Emanuel. "A Key Gang Member Slain in Brooklyn." *New York Times,* July 17, 1972.
Pileggi, Nicholas. "The Making of The Godfather: Sort of a Home Movie."
"Reputed Crime Leader Missing." *New York Times,* July 26, 1976.
Seal, Mark. "The 'Godfather' Wars." *Vanity Fair,* February 4, 2009.

———. "'Family Ties': *The Godfather* cast's dinner at home of Pasquale Eboli during the filming." Vanityfair.com, March 2009.

Wilson, Michael. "After 4 Decades, Memory of a Mob Killing Still Draws Gawkers." *New York Times*, September 6, 2013.

Films

The Godfather: The Coppola Restoration

Chapter 13: "He Looked Like He Could Eat Raw Meat"

Author Interviews

    Al Ruddy

    Bettye McCartt

    Dean Tavoularis

    Diann Zecca

    Fred Gallo

    Fred Roos

    Gianni Russo

    Gray Frederickson

    James Caan

Books

Coppola, Francis Ford. *The Godfather Notebook.*

Lebo, Harlan. *The Godfather Legacy.*

Sheridan-Castellano, Ardell. *Divine Intervention and a Dash of Magic: Unraveling the Mystery of the Method.* Bloomington, IN: Trafford Publishing, 2002.

Zuckerman, Ira. *The Godfather Journal.*

Periodicals

"2 Death Plot Suspects Surrender; 5th Hunted." *Newsday,* June 19, 1968.

Ardell S. Sheridan Obituary. dignitymemorial.com.

Farber, Stephen. "Coppola and 'The Godfather.'" *Sight & Sound* (London) BFI, Autumn 1972.

Lewis, Dan. "Wrestling Was the Only Acting School He Needed." *San Antonio Express,* April 20, 1972.

Nesmith, Jeff. "Mafia 'Soldier' The Mole Lives Quietly Here." *Atlanta Constitution,* June 24, 1972.

Nobile, Philip. "Who Was That Bug-Eyed Man?" Universal Press, January 22, 1973.

Oliver, Greg. "Montana Was Wrestler Before He Died So Well in The Godfather." SlamWrestling.net, October 29, 2009.

Other Media

The People of the State of New York v Leonard Passafaro, AKA: Lenny Montana. May 22, 1970.

Chapter 14: Dancing on a String

Author Interviews

Alice Marchak

Eleanor Coppola

Gray Frederickson

James Caan

Kenji Fujita

Robert Towne

Books

Coppola, Francis Ford. *The Godfather Notebook.*

Jones, Jenny M. *The Annotated Godfather.*

Lebo, Harlan. *The Godfather Legacy.*

Wasson, Sam. *The Big Goodbye.*

Zuckerman, Ira. *The Godfather Journal.*

Periodicals

Biskind, Peter. "Making Crime Pay."

Itzkoff, Dave. "How Francis Ford Coppola Got Pulled Back in to Make 'The Godfather, Coda.'" *New York Times,* December 2, 2020.

Steele, Gregg. "On Location with *The Godfather*, A Discussion with Gordon Willis." *American Cinematographer*, February 24, 2020.

Other Media

"Dean Tavoularis." IMDB.com.

"Great Cinematographers: Gordon Willis." *Internet Encyclopedia of Cinematographers*. cinematographers.nl/GreatDoPH/willis.htm.

Chapter 15: "I Met Him, I Married Him, and I Died"

Author Interviews

    Al Ruddy
    Alex Rocco
    Ali MacGraw
    Dean Tavoularis
    Eleanor Coppola
    Francis Ford Coppola
    Franco Sciannameo
    Fred Roos
    Gianni Russo
    Gray Frederickson
    Peter Bart
    Walter Murch

Books

Cowie, Peter. *The Godfather: The Official Motion Picture Archives*.
———. *The Godfather Book*.
Diapoulos, Peter, and Steven Linakis. *The Sixth Family: The True Inside Story of the Execution of a Mafia Chief*. New York: Bantam Books, 1977.
Evans, Robert. *The Kid Stays in the Picture*.
Lebo, Harlan. *The Godfather Legacy*.
Zuckerman, Ira. *The Godfather Journal*.

Periodicals

Beck, Marilyn. "No More Seven Day Weeks for Filmmaker Robert Evans." *Morning News* (Wilmington, Delaware, and other newspapers), May 1977.

Blum, Howard. "At the Hospital: Just Like the Godfather?" *Village Voice*, July 1971.

"Colombo Assailant Was Hired by Mobsters, Police Charge." *Chicago Tribune*, July 3, 1971.

Column including details of Evans tennis accident. *Los Angeles Times*, August 19, 1971.

Cooli, Fred. "Colombo; They Got Joe!—Is the War On?" *New York Times*, July 4, 1971.

"Family Reunion." *People*, March 24, 1997.

Farrell, William E. "Colombo Shot, Gunman Slain at Columbus Circle Rally Site." *New York Times*, June 29, 1971.

Haber, Joyce. "Puzo at Work on Godfather Sequel." *Los Angeles Times*, August 16, 1971.

Sragow, Michael. "Godfatherhood." *New Yorker.* March 16, 1977.

Thomas, Bob. "Simonetta Stefanelli, Untouched by Her Fame." Associated Press, May 11, 1972.

Van Gelder, Lawrence. "Colombo: A Man with Several Roles." *New York Times*, June 29, 1971.

William Reynolds Obituary. *Guardian*, August 15, 1997.

Production Materials

Sicily call sheets, courtesy of American Zoetrope

Films

The Godfather, The Coppola Restoration

Other Media

Coppola, Francis Ford. Letter to Gerald K. Smith, International Photographers Local 659. January 2, 1971.

Flyer for the Italian American Civil Rights League's Second Annual Unity Day in New York. June 28, 1971.

Chapter 16: "A Baptism in Blood"

Author Interviews
Al Ruddy
Francis Ford Coppola
Ivor Davis
Marilyn Stewart

Books

Coppola, Francis Ford. Introduction to *The Godfather* by Mario Puzo, 50th Anniversary edition. New York: Berkley, 2019.

Cowie, Peter. *The Godfather Book.*

Evans, Robert. *The Kid Stays in the Picture.*

Puzo, Mario. *The Godfather* (all editions).

Periodicals

"$1,000,000-a-Day 'Godfather' Pace." *Variety,* May 17, 1972.

Archerd, Army. "Just for Variety." *Variety,* April 4, 1972.

Bacon, James. "Al Pacino: New Superstar with 'Godfather.'" *Los Angeles Herald-Examiner*, March 15, 1972.

Beck, Marilyn. "No More Seven Day Weeks for Filmmaker Robert Evans."

Canby, Vincent. "Bravo Brando's 'Godfather.'" March 12, 1972.

———. "A Moving and Brutal 'Godfather.'" March 16, 1972.

Champlin, Charles. "'Godfather': The Gangster Movie Moves Uptown." *Los Angeles Times*, March 19, 1972.

Cocks, Jay. "Show Business: What Is the Godfather Saying?" *Time,* April 3, 1972.

Coppola, Francis Ford. "Gatsby and Me." *Town & Country*, April 16, 2013.

Dallos, Robert E. "'Godfather's' Take Bigger Than Expected." *Los Angeles Times*, December 13, 1972.

Davis, Ivor. "Smuggled into 'Godfather' Screening." *Los Angeles Herald-Examiner*, London Daily Express Services, March 3, 1972.

"Exhibitors Break 'Godfather' Rule; Sneak in Intermissions." *Variety*, April 18, 1972.

Faso, Frank, and Theo Wilson. "Marlon Makes Mott Street Scene." *New York Daily News*, April 20, 1971.

"Film Review: The Godfather." *Variety*, March 8, 1972.

"*Godfather* Re-Release Draws Well at Castro." *San Francisco Examiner*, March 25, 1997.

"'Godfather' Sets Industry Record." *Hollywood Reporter*, March 23, 1971.

Green, Abel. "'Godfather': Boon to All Pix." *Variety*, April 5, 1972.

Haber, Joyce. "Godfather Debut." Syndicated in various newspapers, March 19, 1972.

Hargrove, Peter. "Marilyn Stewart: Publicity Queen Behind the Scenes." *IBR News*, January 15, 2002.

Haskell, Molly. "World of 'The Godfather': No Place for Women." *New York Times*, March 23, 1997.

Heller, Wendy, and Michele Willens. "Life-styles for Waiting in Line to See 'Godfather.'" *Los Angeles Times*, April 16, 1972.

"It's Everybody's 'Godfather.'" *Variety*, March 22, 1972.

Kael, Pauline. "Alchemy, Francis Ford Coppola's 'The Godfather.'" *New Yorker*, March 18, 1972.

"Kills 'Em in Sicily Premiere." United Press International, October 13, 1972.

"Mafia Insisted on Its Own Preview of 'Godfather,' Producer Reveals." *Box Office*, December 17, 1973.

Puzo, Dorothy. "Daughter of 'Godfather.'" *Esquire*, December 1972.

Quinn, Sally. "It Was a Really Big Scene, But Where Was Brando?" *Washington Post*, March 16, 1972.

Schlesinger Jr., Arthur. "*The Godfather* Plays on Our Secret Admiration for Men Who Get What They Want." *Vogue*, May 1972.

Scott, Vernon. "Even Hollywood's Applauding." United Press International, March 1972.

Suzy. "The Godfather Premiere Was Terribly Mama Mia." Syndicated column, March 21, 1972.

Tusher, Will. "Seven-Language 'Godfather' Bow with Munich Olympics." *Hollywood Reporter*, August 7, 1972.

Zimmerman, Paul D. "Brando as The Godfather." *Newsweek*, March 13, 1972.

Other Media

Capra, Frank. Letter to Francis Ford Coppola. Courtesy of Francis Ford Coppola and American Zoetrope.

Lean, David. Letter to Francis Ford Coppola. Courtesy of Francis Ford Coppola and American Zoetrope.

Francis Ford Coppola and Robert Evans Telegrams. Julien's Auctions online catalog.

Epilogue: The Man Who Touched Magic

Author Interview
Robert Evans

Periodicals

Bernstein, Jacob. "Looking Back on the Making of 'The Godfather' with Francis Ford Coppola." *New York Times*, November 16, 2016.

Feeney, Mark. "The Kid Takes a Bow." *Boston Globe*, August 4, 2002.

"Show Business: The Making of *The Godfather*." *Time*, March 13, 1972.

Wasson, Sam. "The Last Days of Robert Evans." *Los Angeles*, April 2020.

Index